OIL

atrium
international

Author: Arco Editorial Team
Editor: Francisco Asensio Cerver
Publishing Director: Nacho Asensio
Graphic Design & Layout: David Mataró
Translation: Harry Paul

Copyright ©2000 Atrium Internacional de
México,S.A de C.V.

C/ Fresas, 60
03200 Colonia del Valle
México
e-mail: atriumex@laneta.apc.org

Commercial office in Europe
C/ Ganduxer 115, 4º
08022 Barcelona, España
Tel.: 34-93 418 49 10
Fax: 34-93 211 81 39
e-mail: arcoedit@ibernet.com

ISBN: 84-8185-230-9
Dep.Legal:
Printed in Spain

atrium

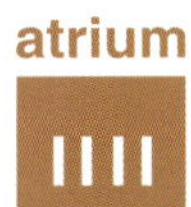

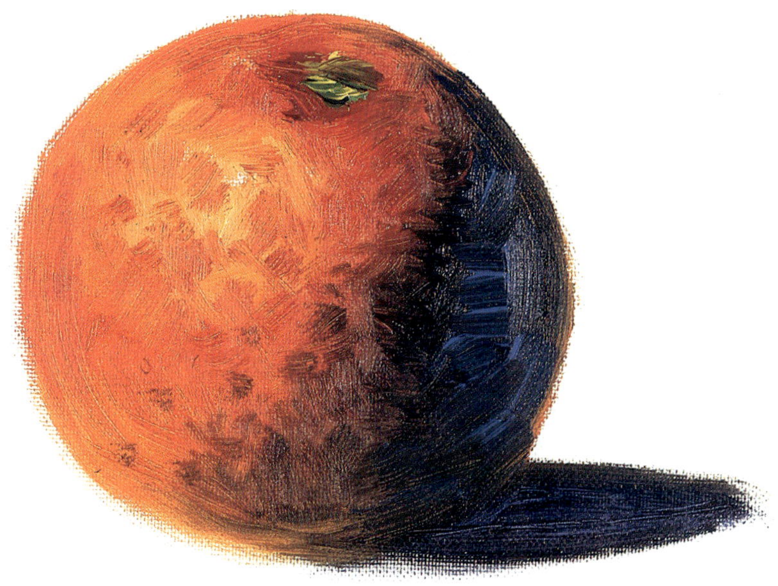

Introduction

We are going to learn how to paint in oil colors. From the next page onwards you can start to get to grips with this medium, the leading technique known to the present day. Preferred by the Baroque painters, the top artists of today still vouch for it.

If drawing is technically vital when beginning in the exciting world of art, it is oil colors, with their tractable nature, which allow us to achieve full artistic expression. In this book we are going to teach you how to get the most out of your creativity, mastering the palette, brush and the oil colors themselves so that you will soon be capable of doing striking pictorial representations.

However, nothing will be possible unless the student is prepared to work in the early stages in a disciplined way. He or she will have to practice, and keep on practicing, never feeling discouraged. Be prepared to start over as many times as necessary, correcting your mistakes until you can express on the canvas what you were aiming at. We, through the pages of this book, will teach you the techniques which will help you realize your aspirations. However, it is you who has to bring forth your artistic inspiration and the self©motivation to enable you to correct the errors you may make. Above all, we would remind you that inspiration alone is not enough to learn how to master a technique as complex as oil painting.

Many years' teaching experience, and many students who can today be proud of their oil painting skills, endorse our affirmation that genius, inspiration, and creative capacity alone come to nothing if they are not accompanied by a thorough mastery of the technique. This is learnt in the early stages: good habits die hard.

Follow the instructions given here and do not be afraid to start again if something does not quite look right. Cast aside your fear of the blank canvas and start to experiment with the materials until you are familiar with them. Mix the colors as a kind of plastic entertainment and then transfer them from the palette to the whiteness of the canvas. Gradually, without rushing, forget about time and you will be transported by the unmatchable sensation of painting in oil colors.

Arco Editorial Team

CONTENTS

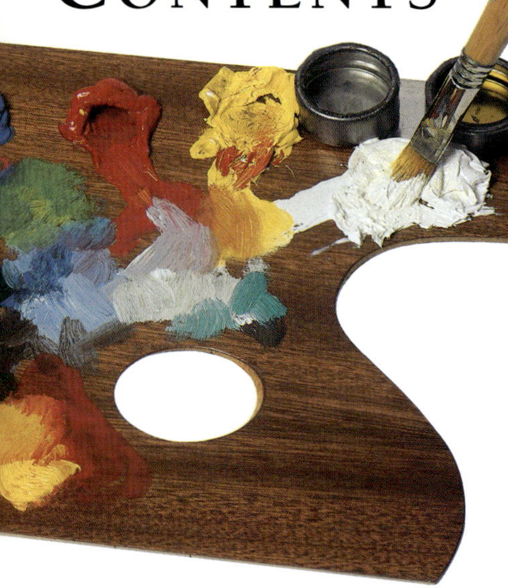

Chapter 1

Oil painting. First steps.

Oil painting is a pictorial method which uses an oily, opaque, dense and quick drying medium. Distinct to watercolor, it can be used on any previously prepared surface.

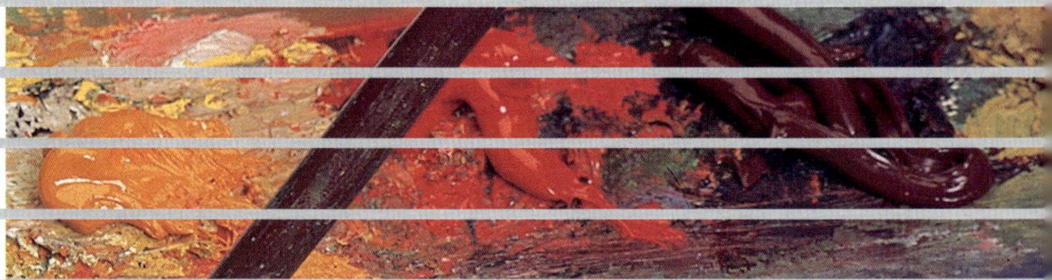

The painter's studio must be an uncramped, luminous and comfortable space where it is possible to work without stress.

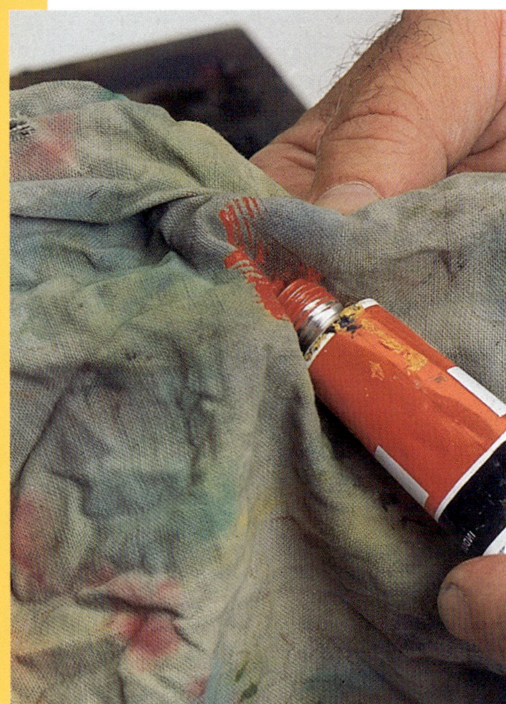

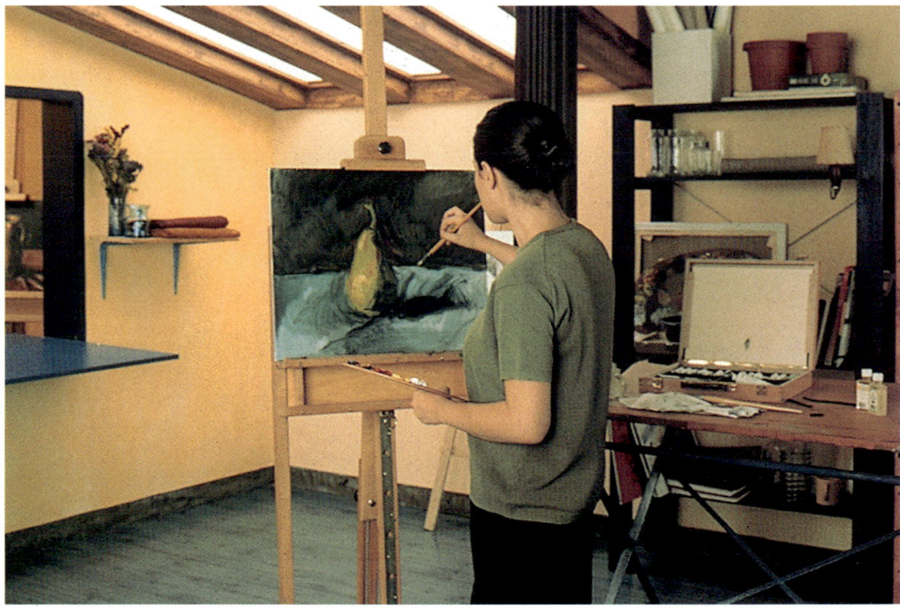

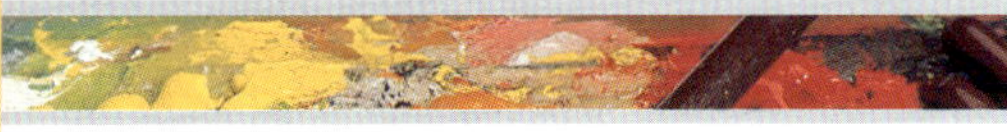

When you have finished with one color, it is wise to wipe the tube mouth with a cloth.

The appearance of oil colors and how they are used today.

Before oil colors came onto the scene artists painted in tempera. It was a technique in which color in pigment form was mixed with glue or with egg yolk. Consequently, the colors obtained were dull and once dry lacked contrast. When oil colors emerged, introduced from Flanders to Italy and Spain to meet the changing requirements of the Renaissance, painting became much more realistic, as can be seen in this illustration of the Immaculate Conception with two young priests by Francisco de Zurbarán (1598-1664). In this piece, kept in the Museum of Art of Catalonia in Barcelona, the luminous colors confer the painting a very realistic feel. Its volume is perfectly defined and it has been preserved until the present day with its strength and the color contrasts undiminished.

In this chapter we will set down the first steps in the oil painting technique, placing special emphasis on the preparation of the colors in the palette and the correct use of the brush to get the stokes desired. We will then move on to describe what the painter's studio should be like. Before going on to anything else, it is important to know that oil colors are not dissolved in water but in turpentine oil or pure turpentine, or its substitute, white spirit.

Oil colors

Oil colors are found in the market in different forms and qualities. If it is the first time you use this medium it is recommendable to buy tubes of the following colors: yellow, green, red and white. Above all do not go for the cheapest because their low quality means that it is difficult to learn how to use the medium.

Opening the tubes

When opening the oil color tubes be very careful not to squeeze too much so that you do not leave grungy paint around the mouth. When you have placed some paint on the palette be sure to quickly put the lid back on, not because it is going to dry up but to avoid losing the lid. The wrong lid on the wrong tube means you may end up using unpure paint.

The lid can be loosened by gently warming it with the flame of a lighter from a safe distance.

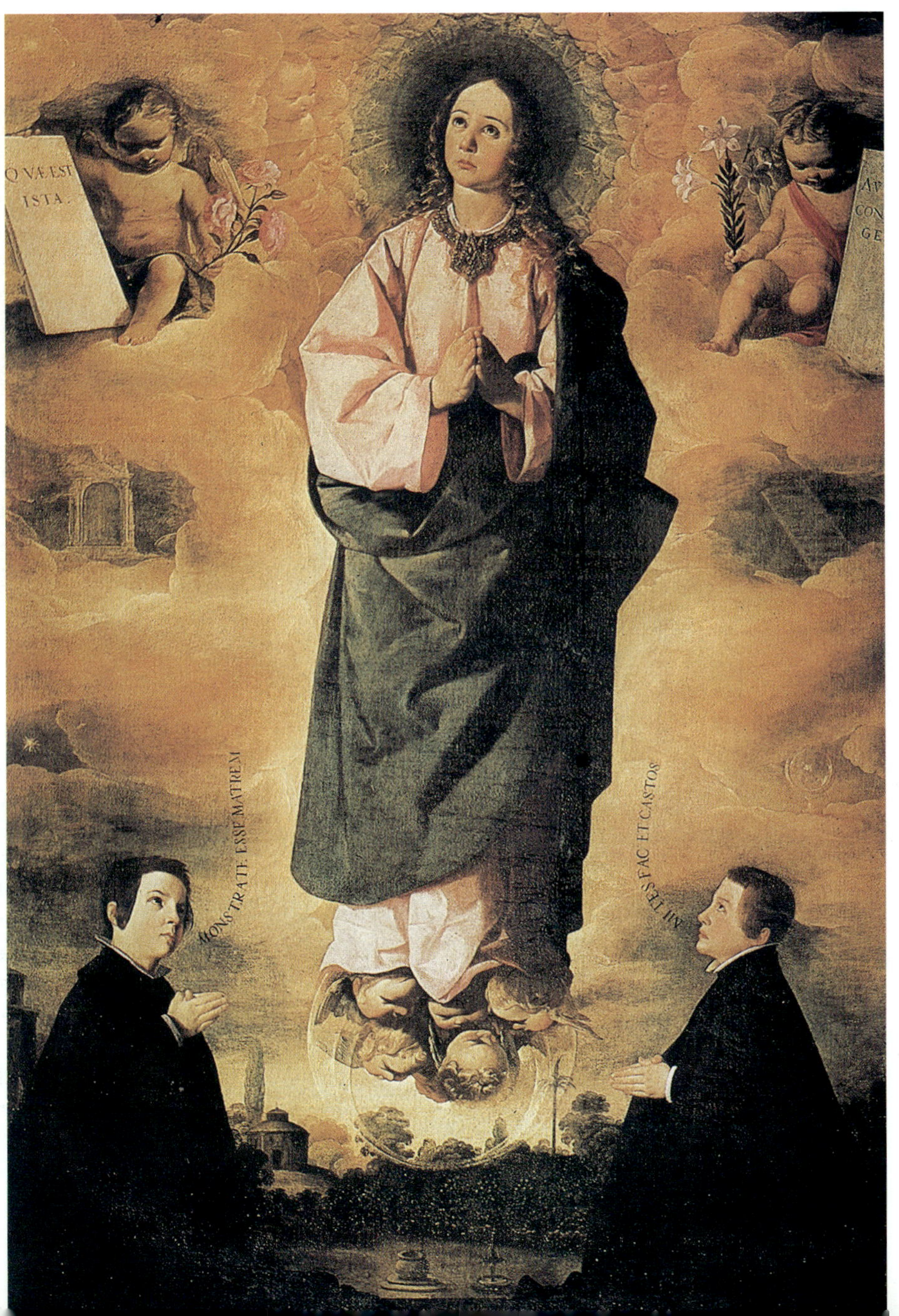

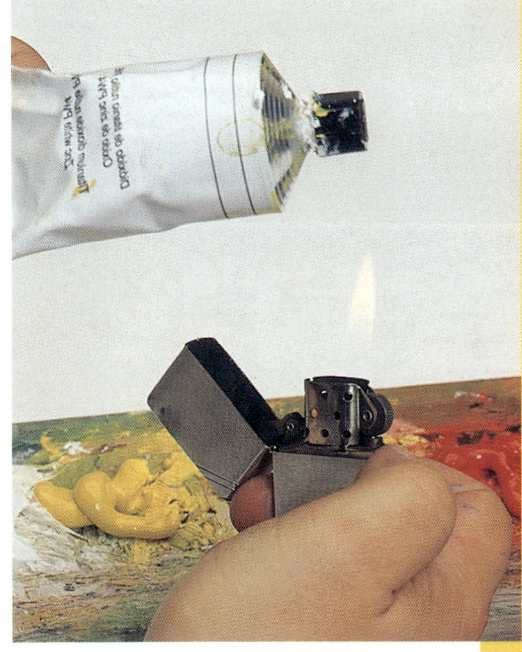

Wipe off the mouth of the tube. Always, after using a color and before putting the lid on, the tip must be cleaned so that the lid does not get stuck. An old cloth does the job just fine.
Sometimes the artist may forget to clean the tip before putting the lid on. If the lid does not twist because the paint has dried out and become sticky, a cigarette lighter has to be used. Gently bring the flame near to the tip, being careful not to overheat or burn the tube.

Be careful not to melt the plastic nor overheat the tube.

Putting the paint on the palette

Once the oil color tube is open squeeze the base as if it were a tube of toothpaste until sufficient paint is on the palette. Never press in the central part because the tube would become deformed. As oil color spreads quite well a little amount is enough to paint quite a large area. Do not place the paint in the center of the palette because this is the space reserved for mixing. Put it to one side.

Picking up the oil color.

When it comes out of the tube, the oil color is ready for painting. A basic rule is not to dirty the brush handle so that you do not spread the paint around the palette. It is enough just to drag part of the color away from the main block and to rub it over several times with the bristles until the color is uniformly impregnated.

Testing out the color

Once the brush is loaded with color you can do the first strokes to test the medium. The best support are small pieces of white paper. These first tests consist of simply doing rapid strokes to see the different results and to start the process of familiarization. If the oil color is too dense, try softening it with a little turpentine oil which can be applied directly to the painting until the texture is suitably diluted. Later on we will go into how to use the brush, but for the beginning we will just note that it is important to clean it thoroughly after every session.

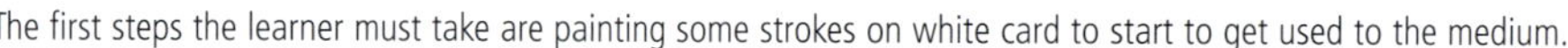

The first steps the learner must take are painting some strokes on white card to start to get used to the medium.

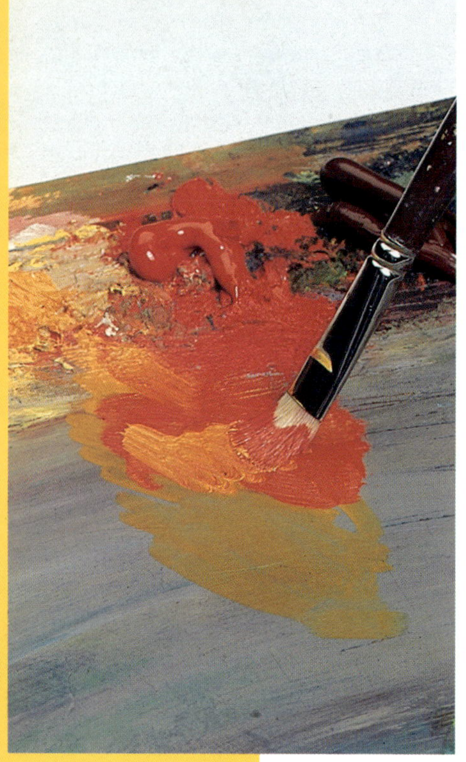

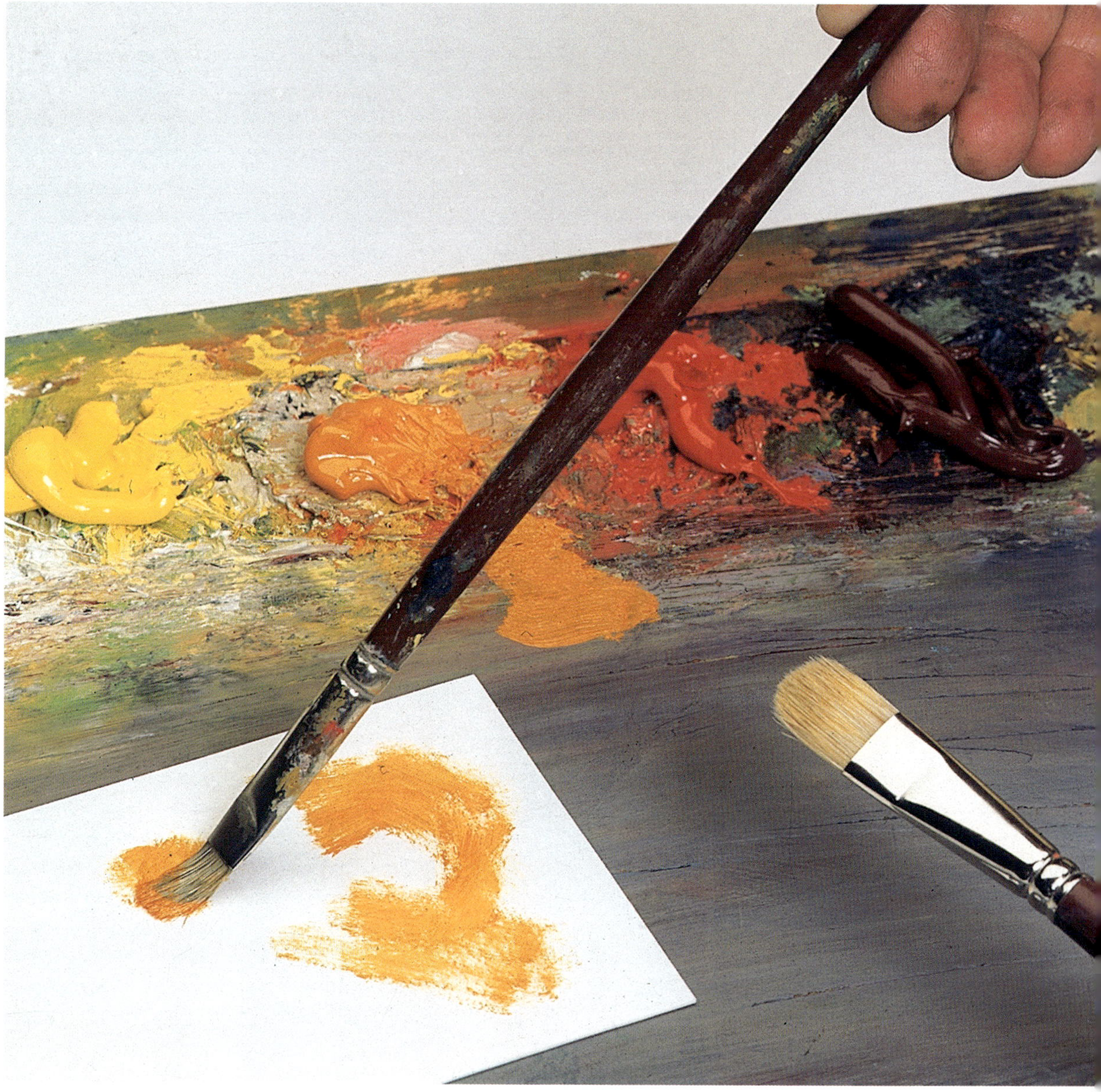

Turpentine oil.

You must never start to paint without turpentine oil or pure turpentine, a product which enables you to clean the brushes, remove any fresh stain and to dilute an excessively dense oil color. Oil colors are composed of dry powder pigments mixed with selected refined linseed oil and therefore they have a buttery feel. So when you want to obtain a more fluid paint than what comes out of the tube, wet the brush in turpentine oil and mix it with the paint on the palette in a zigzag movement. It will become more transparent. Do not overload the brush with turpentine oil.

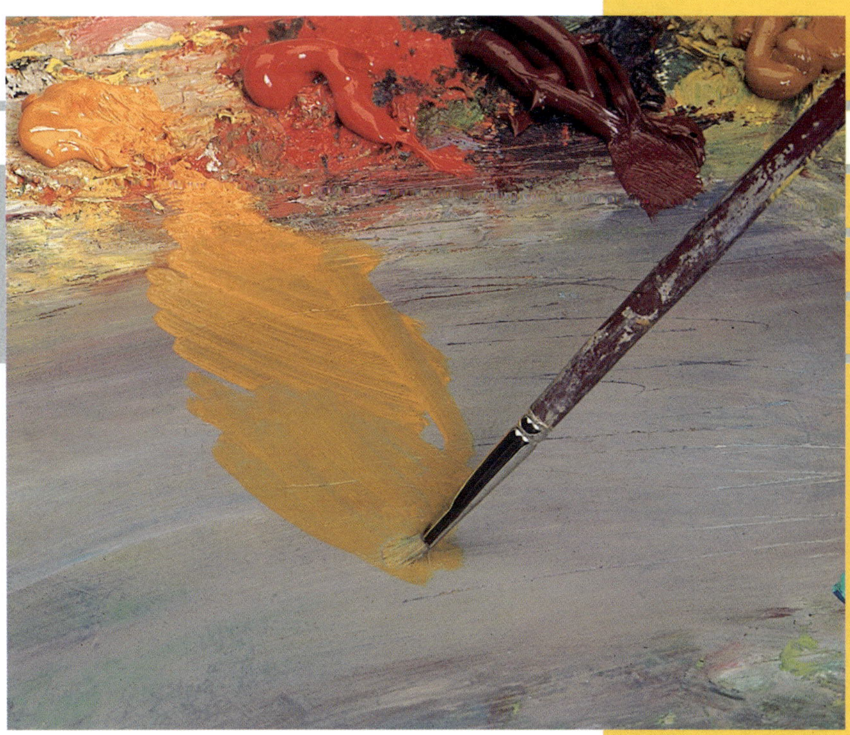

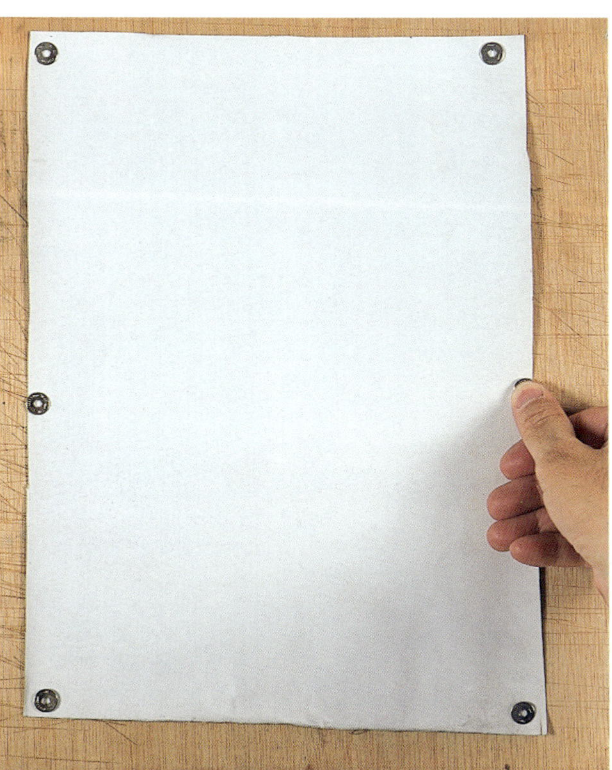

To prepare the support on which you are going to paint, once it is cut to the right size fix it firmly to the board with drawing pins.

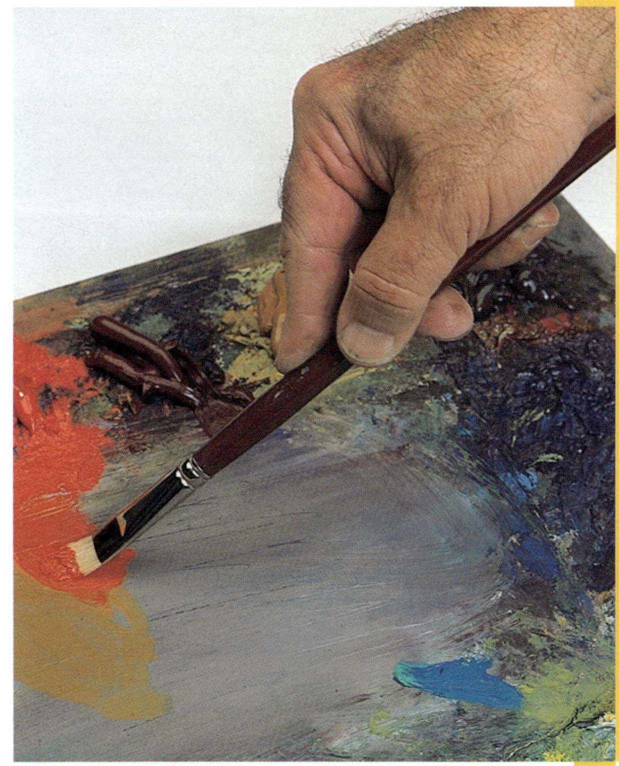

Holding the brush half way up the handle.

The support and the space in which to paint

Any type of surface, provided that it is suitably prepared, can be used to paint in oil color. To start out little rectangular oil canvases can be bought and pinned down to the board. They do not have to be top quality. Card can also be used. Whatever you do, testing is always messy and many supports are going to become dirty so use disposable material. Another consideration is that oil colors are a more complicated medium. It has a longer drying time and can be stained, or spoiled, while still fresh. Therefore a space dedicated exclusively to this artistic activity is necessary, with a table, a lamp and an easel so that you can work comfortably.

Holding the brush

Having seen a few basic ideas about how to use the tubes of paint, now we will learn how to hold and use the brush, and how to clean it after every session.

In the oil technique the brush can be used in different ways, although it must always be held between the index and ring fingers and the thumb. Depending on how you grip the handle it can be lead with the arm, the wrist or the fingers. Correctly holding the brush is fundamental to facilitate the paint application and to perfect the stroke.

Half way up

If the brush is held half way up, the handle rests on the inside of the hand, so do not press too hard. Holding it this way gives quite a lot of mobility and allows the color to be dragged firmly. It is the wrist which controls the stroke.

In the palm of the hand

Another way of holding the brush is to slide the index finger down the handle as seen in the image. The brush becomes an extension of the arm and enables you to do a straight stroke in a movement controlled by the arm.

Like a pencil.

When the brush is held as if it were a pencil, the give and take between the fingers and the wrist allow the stroke to be controlled. This is ideal for short, rapid strokes and small lines for depicting grass, hair, and wood texture on the canvas.

Holding the tip

When the brush is held so high up, there is a great deal of mobility and the movement can be lead by the arm, wrist or fingers.

The brush held in the palm of the hand.

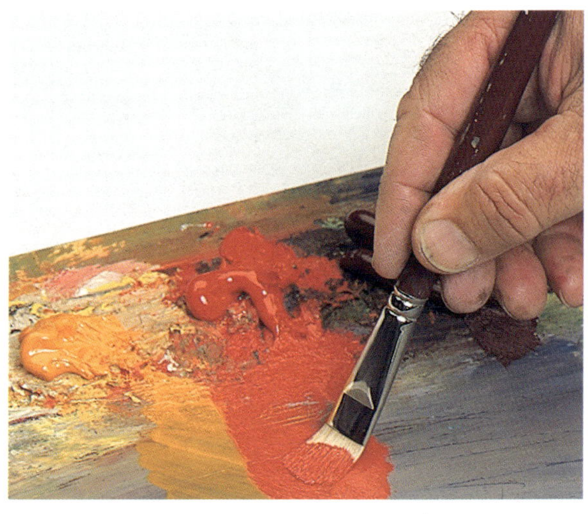
The brush held as if it were a pencil

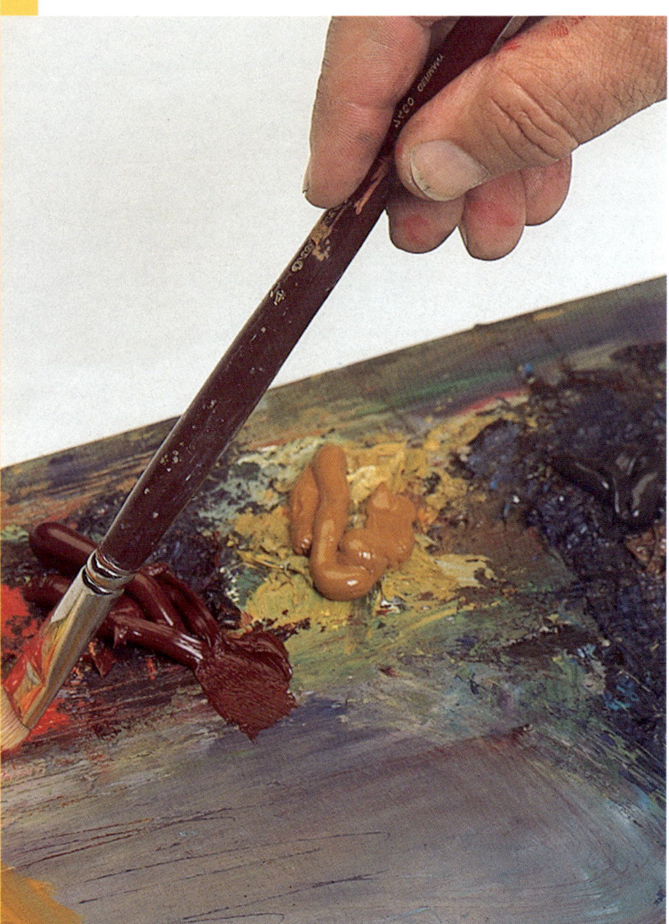

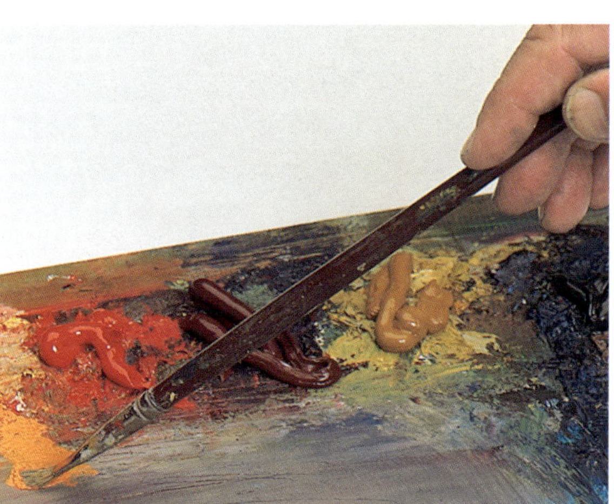
The brush held at the top.

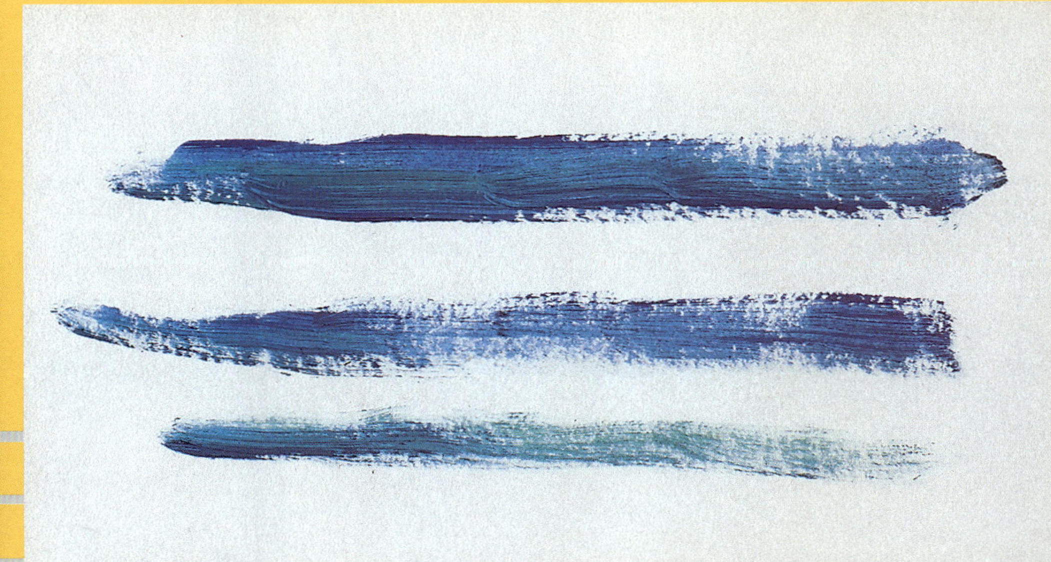

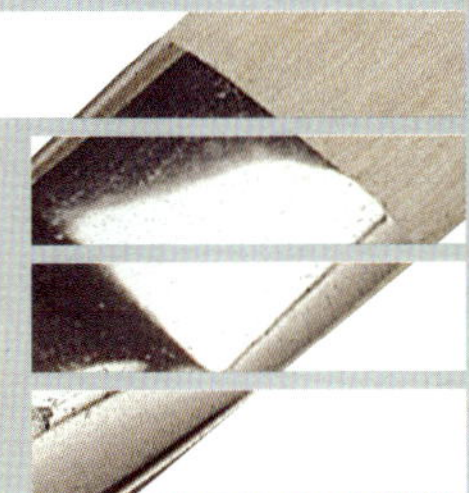

When straight, long strokes are realized the color runs out and the line fades away at the end.

These short strokes have been done with a certain pressure.

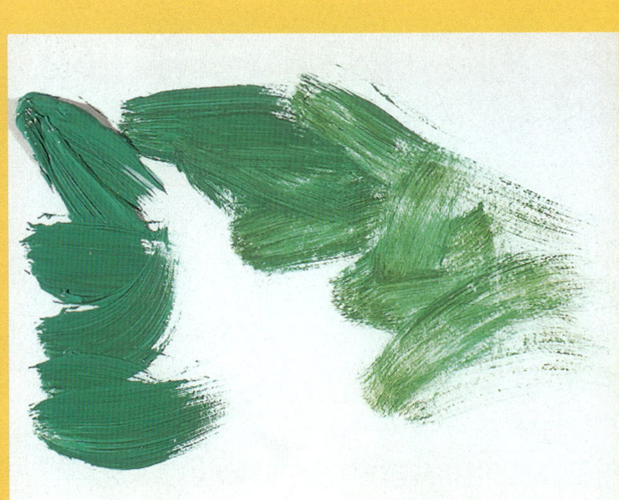

When free strokes are done, the brush direction is controlled by the twisting of the wrist and the bending of the fingers.

This type of stroke is basically used for drawing, but not close up, and is very practical for doing sketches. You have to bear in mind that due to its mobility it is a very wide stroke, difficult to control in detail.

Cleaning the brush.
At the end of each session the brush must be cleaned thoroughly, otherwise the paint would dry up and irreparably clog up the brush. There are some basic steps to be followed to clean the brush. Firstly wipe it off gently with a piece of newspaper. This will eliminate the greater part of the paint.
Afterwards, introduce the brush into a jar of turpentine oil and shake it around until all the color has been removed. Repeat these two operations as many times as necessary.

Thirdly, mix water and soap powder in another jar and swirl the brush around until all the turpentine oil is dissolved. Then put a few drops of soap on the palm of your hand and do a few circular movements until a foam is worked up. Rinse it out with water until all the turpentine oil and oil color are gone. Once it is completely clean dry it off with a cloth.

How to clean the brush.

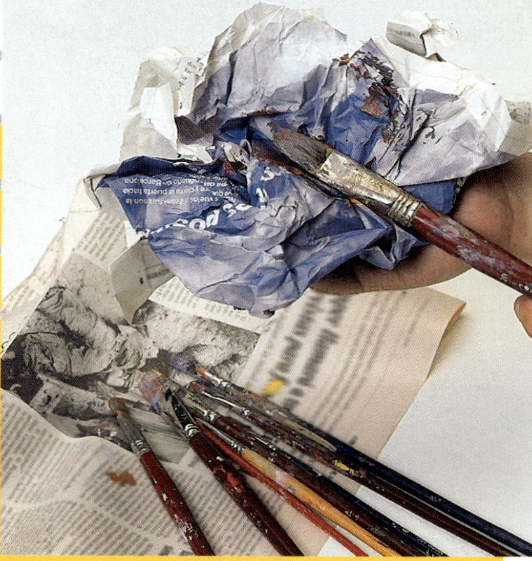
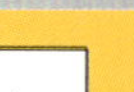

Clean the brush on newspaper.

Wash it in soap powder and water.

Introduce the brush into a jar of turpentine oil.

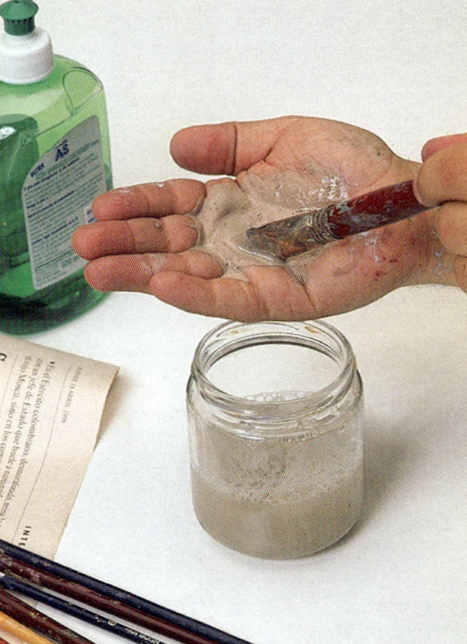

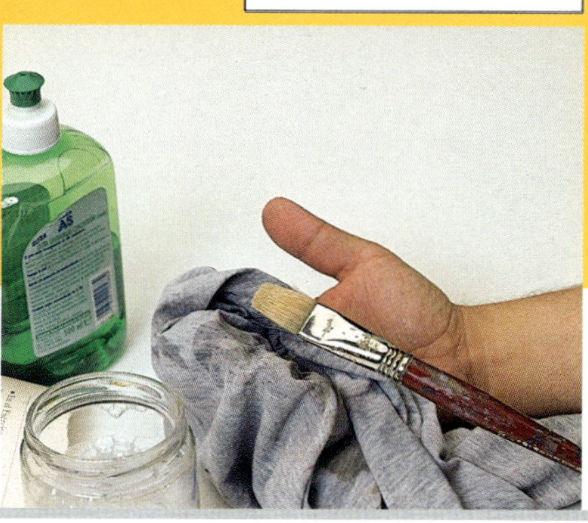

Dry it with a cloth.

Summary

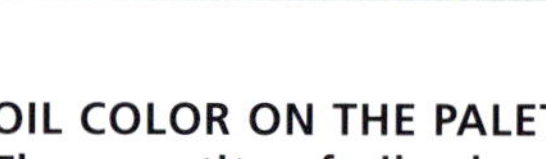

OIL COLOR ON THE PALETTE
The quantity of oil color deposited on the palette must not be greater than a little blob. The color is applied from one side of the palette.

THE TUBE
Once the color has been deposited, the lid must be put back on immediately.

MORE FLUID COLOR
Oil colors are dissolved by adding a little turpentine oil.

HOW MUCH COLOR?
When picking up color, only the brush tip must be impregnated.

HOLDING THE BRUSH
Depending on how the brush is held it will be lead by the wrist, fingers or the entire arm.

CLEANING THE BRUSH
After painting the brush must be cleaned thoroughly.

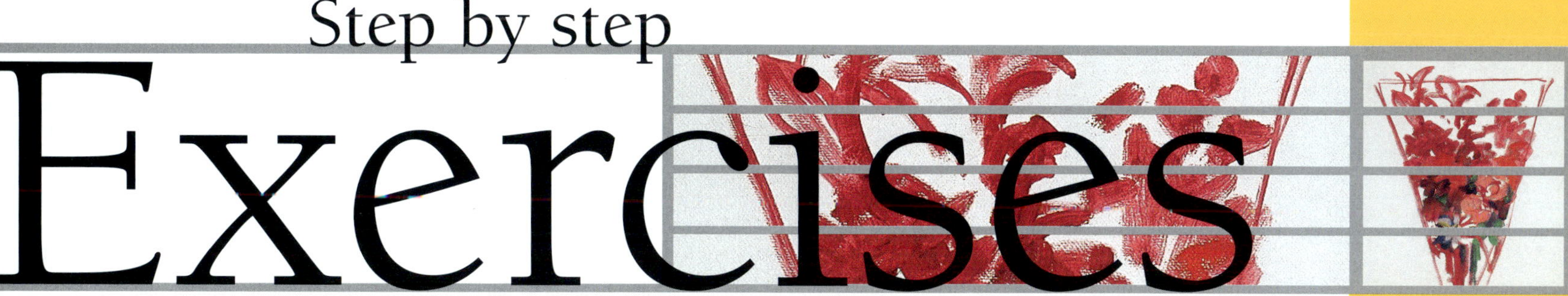

Step by step
Exercises

FLOWERS WITH FREE STROKES

To get familiar with oil colors and to learn how to master them it is necessary to paint.
It is trial and error: at the beginning the results may not be what you are hoping for. It is not
sufficient to just do free strokes and color masses. You have to form them into something
recognizable and structured.

To do this exercise we have chosen some flowers but it is not the top priority that the
resemblance is exact. What is important is that as we go along we will practice different
types of strokes. This is the exercise's principal objective.

Necessary material

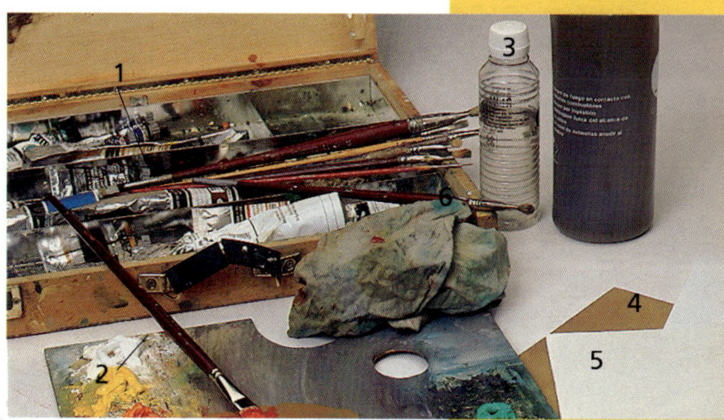

Oil colors (1), a brush
(2), turpentine oil (3), a
board to hold the
canvas (4), canvas or
primed card (5), and a
cloth (6).

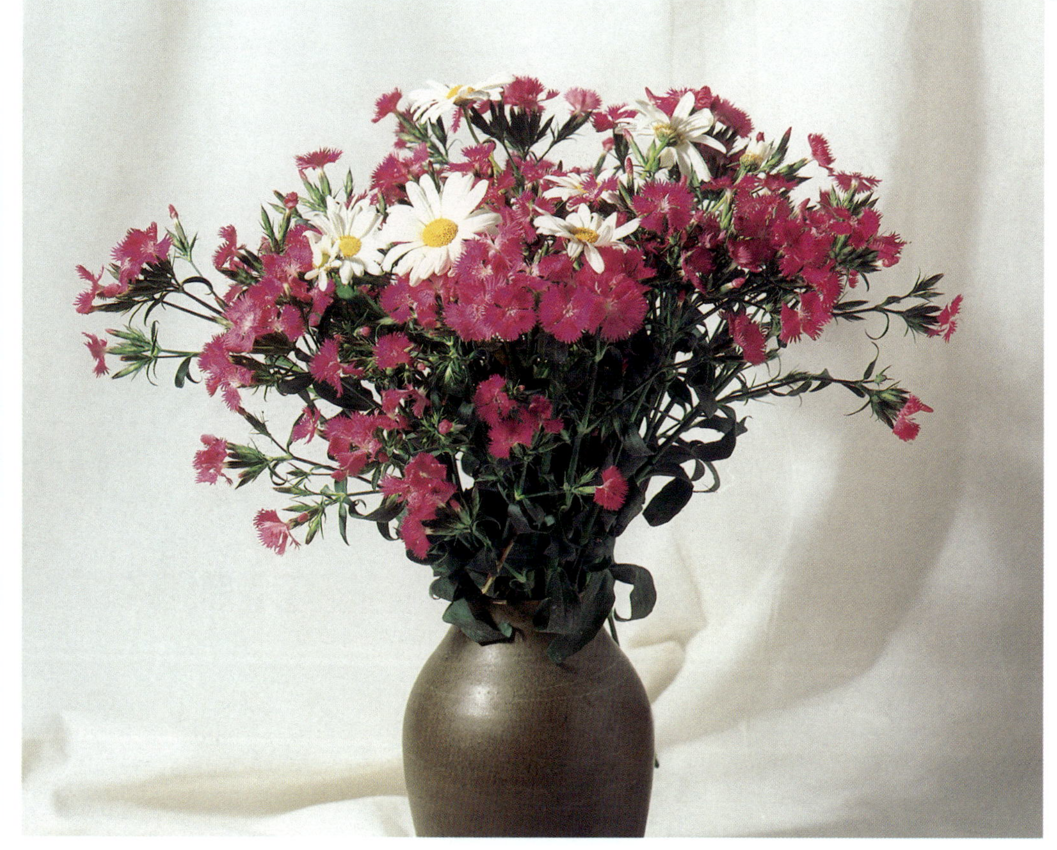

Exercises

1·This exercise is started with the color carmine. Using a long and fine stroke, draw a stretched triangular shape that is going to enclose the flowers.
The brush is held by the top to do some free strokes in the middle of the triangle.

2·When the brush is nearly out of paint, before picking up more oil color, do a few free strokes in the upper part, painting them almost without color.
 Load more paint onto the brush. If the paint is too thick, dip the brush into turpentine oil or its substitute, white mineral spirit. The paint can then be thinned on the palette. If it becomes too liquid, squeeze it out on a cloth so that it does not drip or run on the canvas.

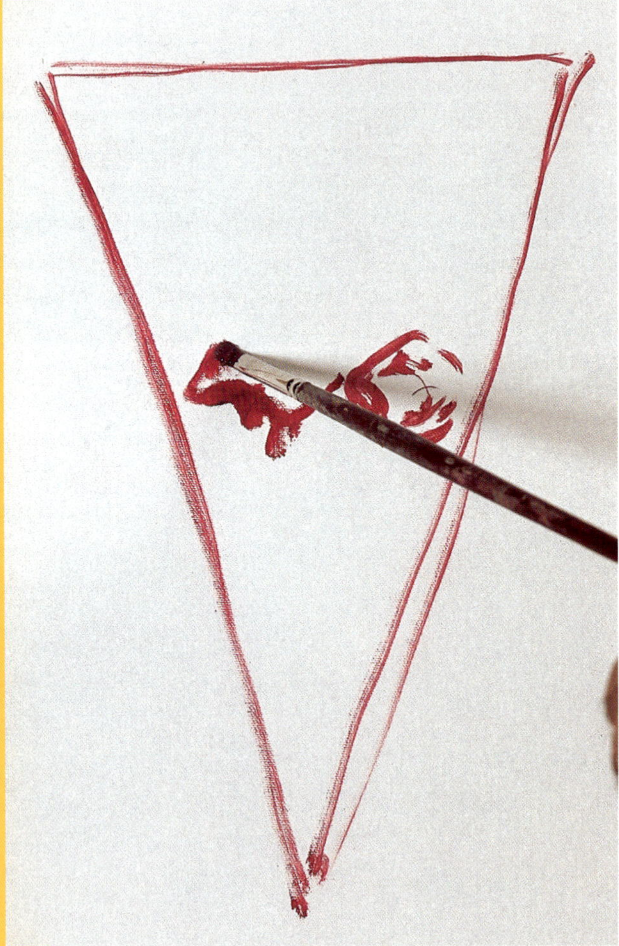

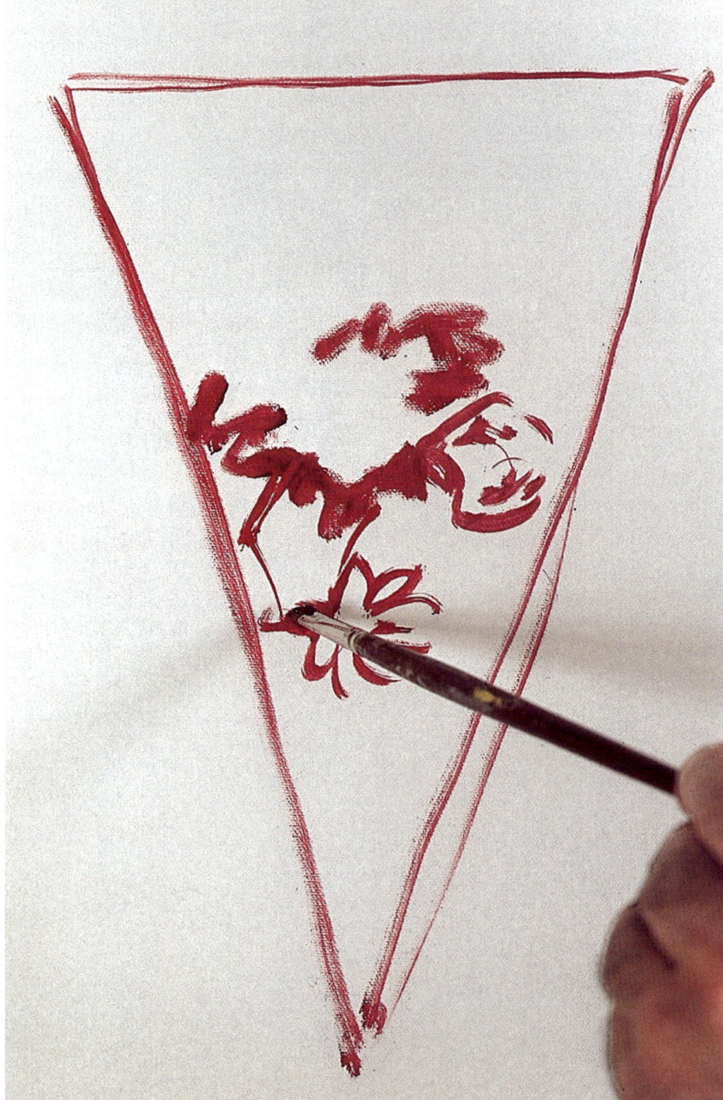

3·As you can see in step three, start to
paint a daisy.
Hold the brush as if it were a pencil and
do a few free strokes in the upper left
part. This time the color is much denser
and the strokes have to be smaller.

4· With the index finger extended along
the handle, do straight strokes in the
lower part of the triangle.

Paint some very free strokes on the right,
just as you did in the first step, holding the
brush from very low down so that you can
guide it by simply moving the fingers.

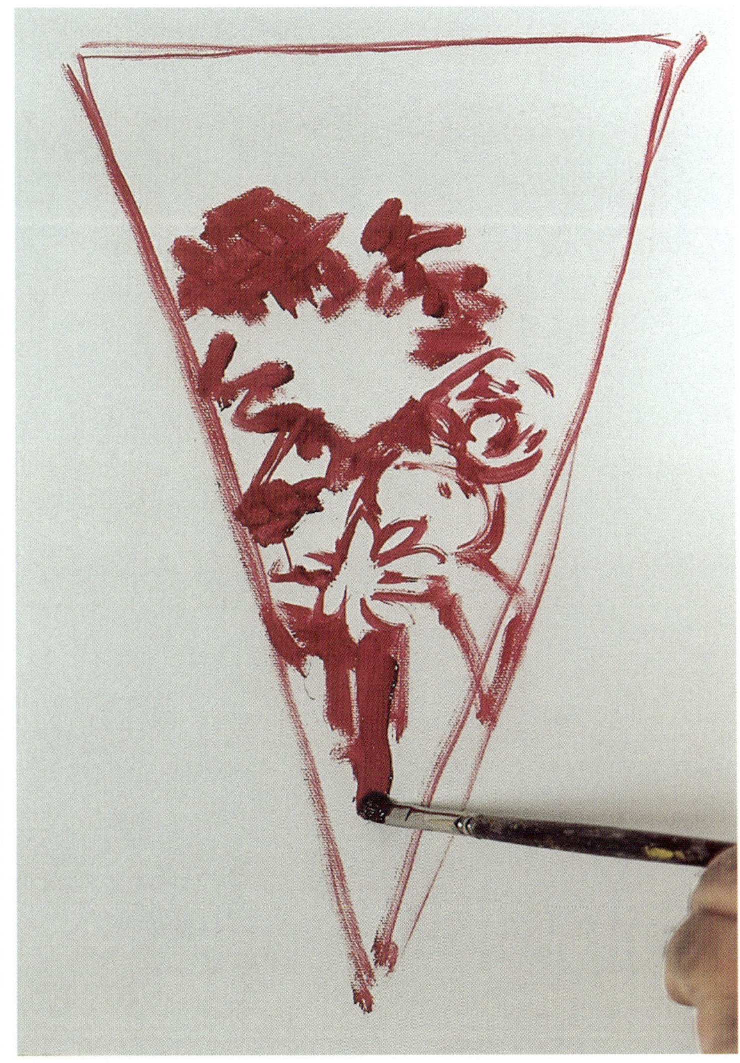

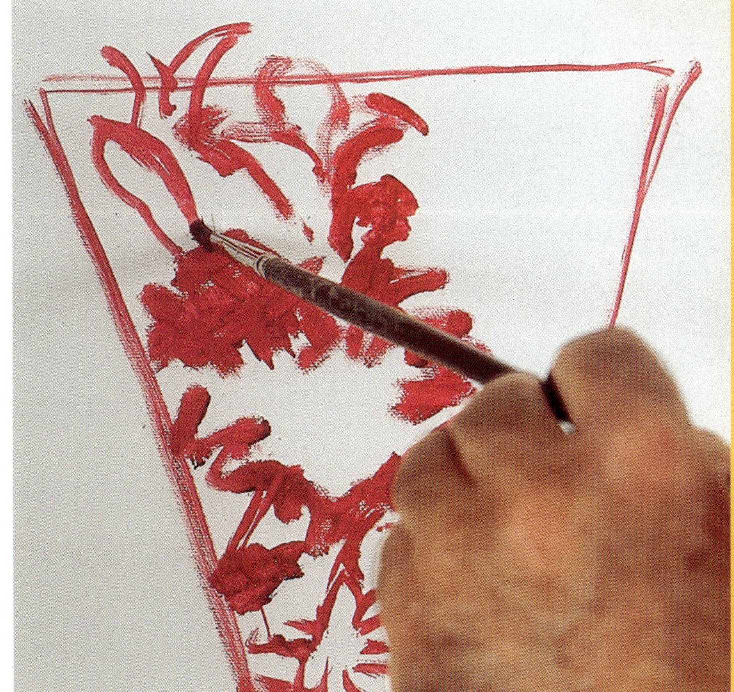

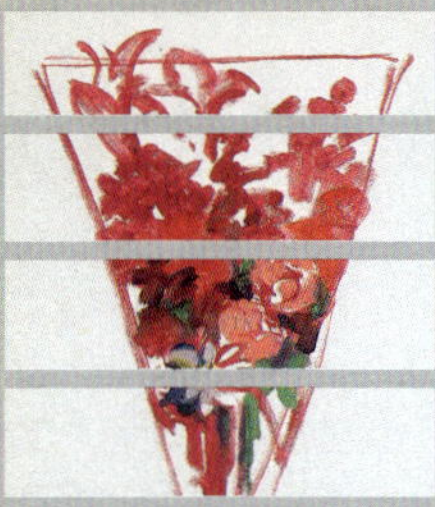

Exercises

5·Once you have practiced all the strokes presented in this chapter, always using the same color so that the true intention of the stroke is not lost, you can add some other colors: white, pink, red, green, dark blue and yellow, as shown in step five. It is not a question of doing mixes but rather of practicing how to handle the brush and to master the stroke.

Draw the form of the lower flower in the bunch with short, red strokes

6·In step six, paint the center of the daisy with very small yellow strokes. Next to it paint in a dark blue stain.

The petals are painted with short, very precise strokes, as we practiced before.

Do strokes with a little green between the flowers.

It does not matter if part of the adjacent color gets dragged too. Do not try to correct this if it happens.

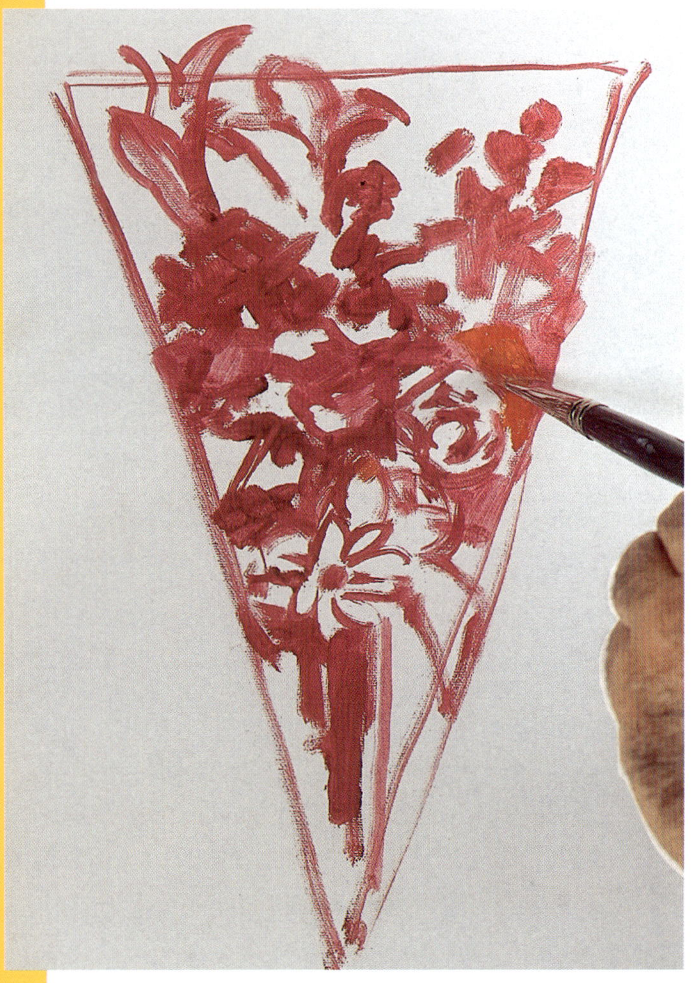

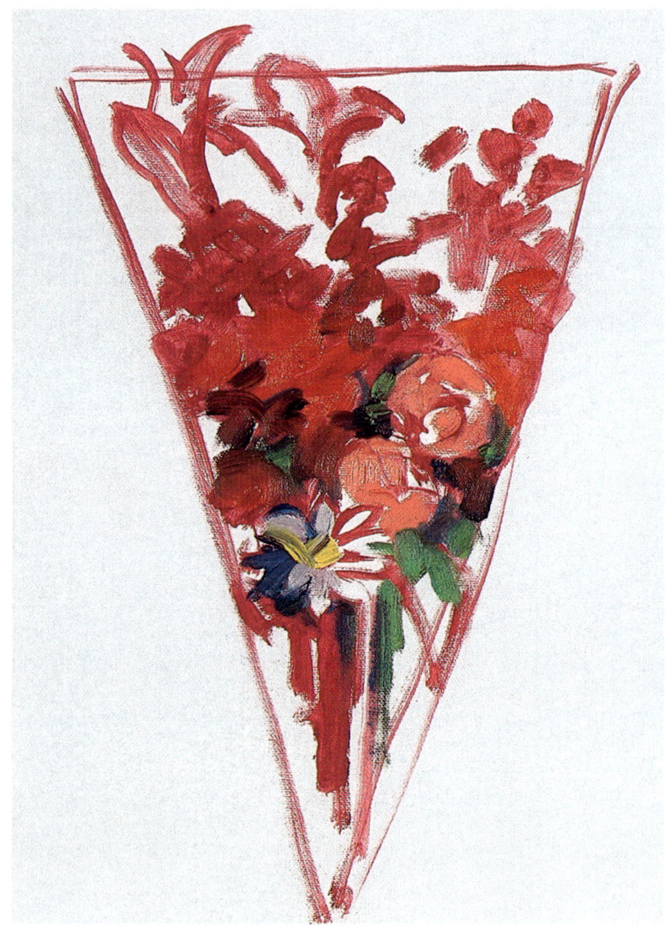

7·Start to paint the background with a little white and blue. The stroke must be long and vertical. Go over it several times as if they were piled up, constantly dragging a bit of the color from the last stroke.

When you come to the zone where the flowers are painted, the stroke must be short and well defined. To do this you will have to hold the brush as if it were a pencil.

Mix the dark colors on the palette until you get a denser color. Use this tone, holding the brush by the top half, to do two curved strokes that define the rim of the vase, and two other lines for the sides.

Without cleaning the brush, wipe the color white on the palette and stain the left side holding the brush by its lower half. Press with your finger to guide the line precisely.

You will now have finished this oil exercise with strokes and color masses. As we said before, it is not important that the resemblance to the model be exact, rather it is a question of practicing the different ways of holding the brush.

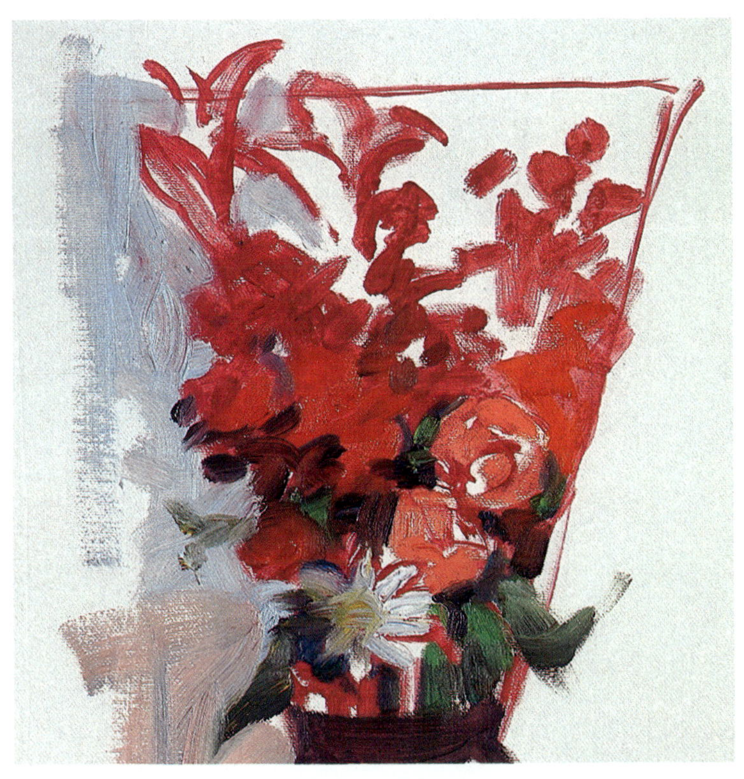

Summary

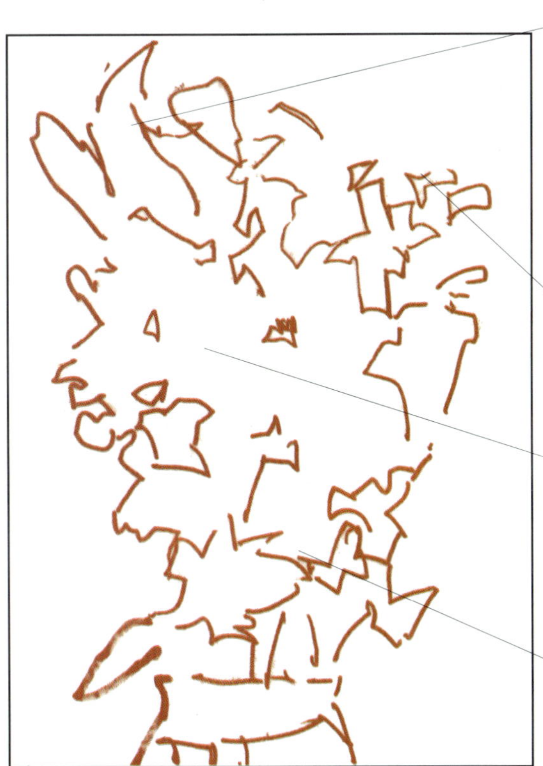

The brush is almost out of paint. Before picking up more, do a few free strokes.

Use the brush as if it were a pencil.

Hold the brush by its highest point

Short, very precise strokes.

Chapter 2

Oil colors. First steps

Oil colors offer enormous chromatic possibilities due to the richness of their nuances and intense luminosity. To master this medium it is necessary to fully understand the theory of color and the chromatic range.

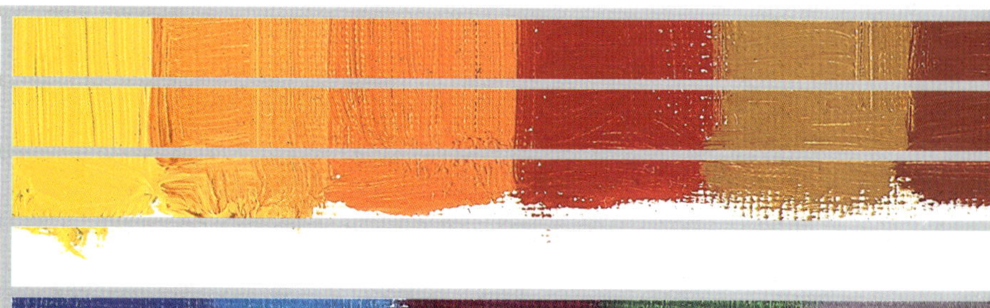

To start to paint you have to use the three basic colors. Mixing them on the palette is easier if it is varnished.

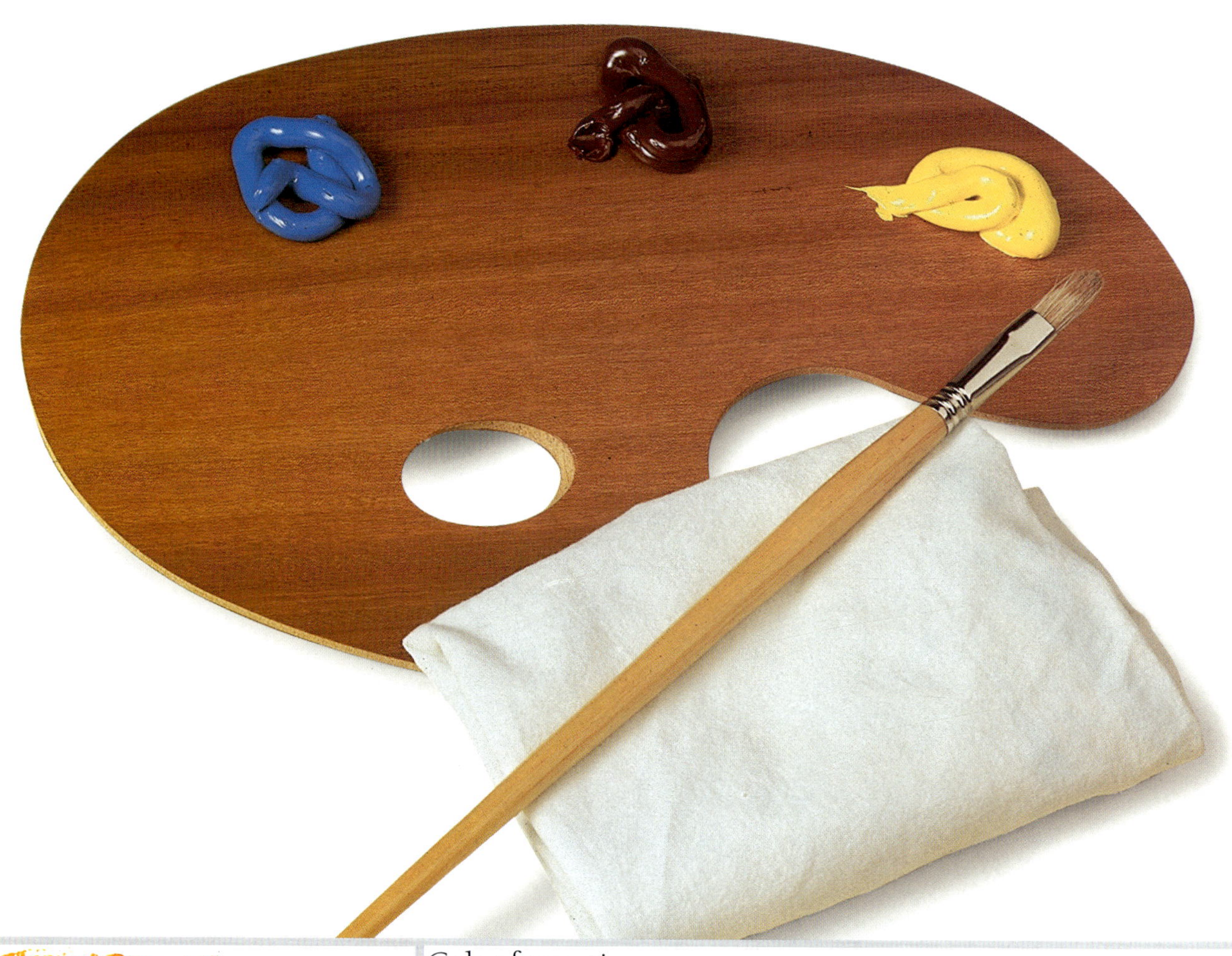

Color formation

This chart shows how the colors are formed from mixing them. In the upper part there are the primary colors; mixing them gives rise to the secondary colors. Mixing two or more secondary colors produces a broken color, also called a tertiary color.

Oil colors are a versatile medium that allow you to work with very opaque colors or with almost transparent tones, depending on the characteristics of the linseed oil and turpentine oil that are added. In this chapter we are going to study the thinning and darkening of the color mixes.

We will then study the theory of color and will take a look at the color ranges, questions which are common to all painting mediums but which can be practiced comfortably with oil colors because they are very controllable and slow drying.

A dense, opaque medium

Oil colors are dense, which means that the paste that forms the color is sufficiently oily so as to create thick layers of paint on the canvas. Moreover, as they are slow drying it is possible to go back to a work session after some time without it having dried completely. This means that you can work tranquilly.
Another characteristic is that it comes out of the tube opaque but can be made lighter by adding a dissolvent (linseed oil or turpentine oil).

Color and the palette

When you are preparing the oil colors you should only put on the palette the amount of color you are going to use; it is a waste of time and space filling up the palette with colors you will later throw away. Start working with the three basic or primary colors: cyan, magenta and yellow. The color cyan is blue, and magenta is a reddish carmine. When you load them on to the palette, separate them so that you can do the mixes comfortably. Use good quality colors and a palette with a varnished surface so that the color does not

Order in which to place the colors on the palette.

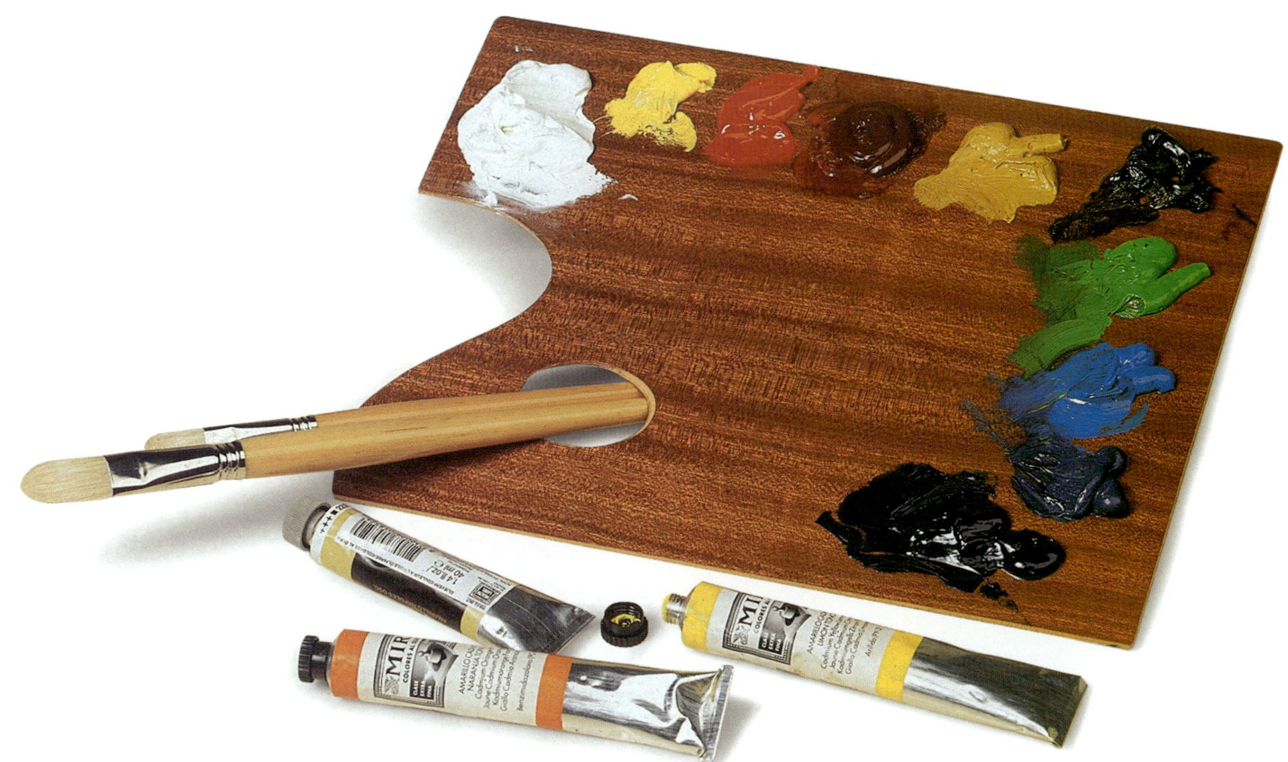

Yellow   Magenta (carmine)   Cyan (blue)

Primary colors

Orange   Green   Violet

Secondary colors

Brown

Broken color

penetrate into the wood.

Distribute the colors on the palette. When you are painting with a wide range of oil colors they must be laid out tidily on the palette so that can handle them easily. They should be placed as follows: firstly, on the left, the color white. You will always need quite a lot of it. Afterwards, going down the tone and chromatic scale, yellow, red and carmine. These colors are followed by the earth colors like ochre and burnt umber. Finally, place green, blue, dark blue and black.

Mixing colors. Start mixing by dragging the first color towards the center of the palette, trying only to pick up the exact quantity you are going to use. Afterwards, on top of this, drag the secondary color until a new homogeneous color is created. If you do not get the tone desired, you can add more of one of the two colors, repeating until the hue is correct.

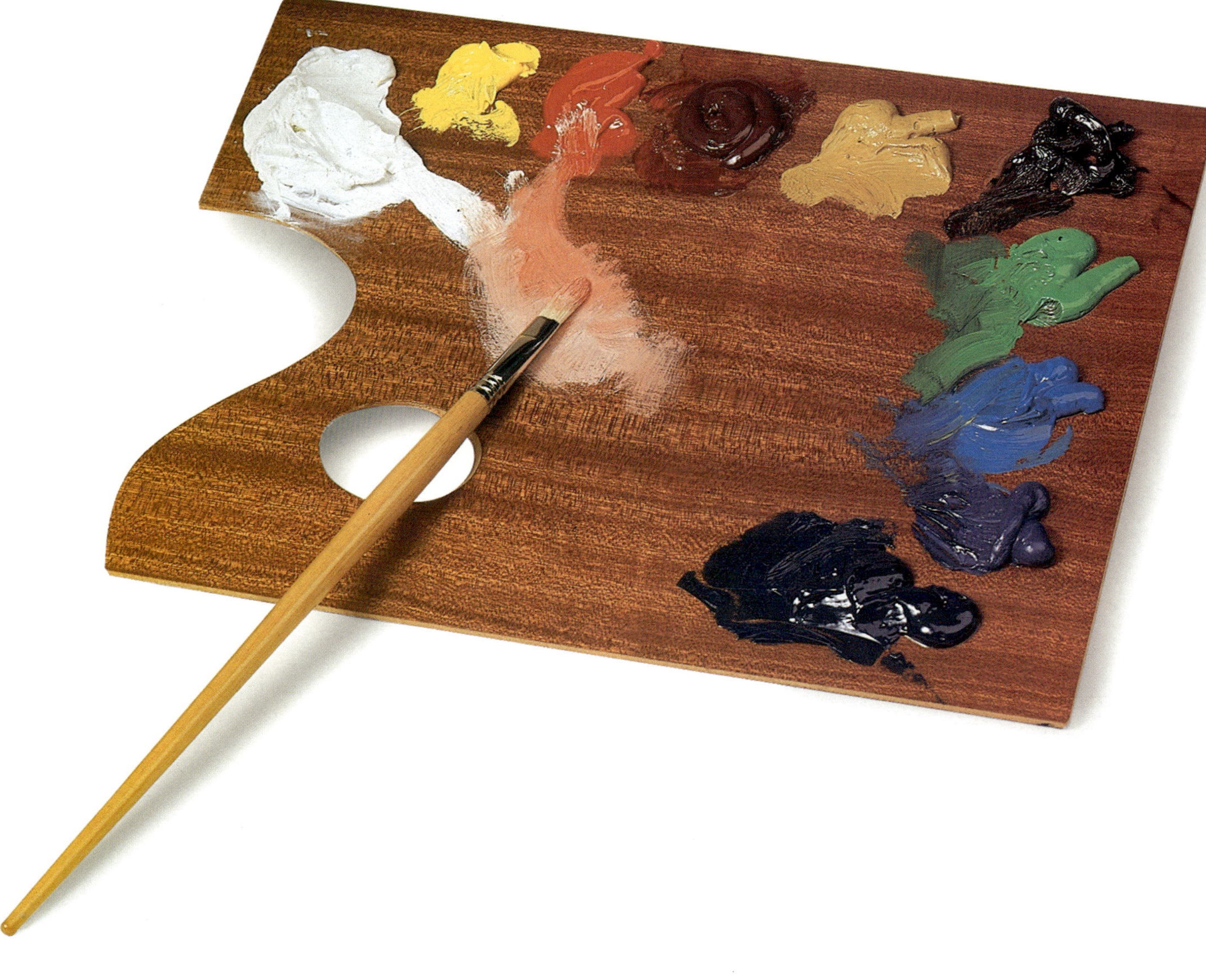

Harmonious and chromatic range

Colors can be classified according to their tone and intensity, forming what are called harmonizing or chromatic ranges which can be warm, cool or broken. Everything starts out from the theory of color, there being three basic or primary colors: yellow, cyan and magenta. When two primary colors are mixed together, they create the secondary colors, which are orange, green and violet. When secondary colors are mixed together they create broken, or tertiary, colors, among which brown stands out.

The warm range

The colors that make up the warm range are a result of mixing together magenta and yellow (reds and oranges) with earth tones. This means that the warm range is formed by, among others, orange, red, carmine, ochre, sienna, and burnt umber.

A landscape painted in warm colors. Observe how the cool colors, like green, have been mixed with red to give them a warm tone.

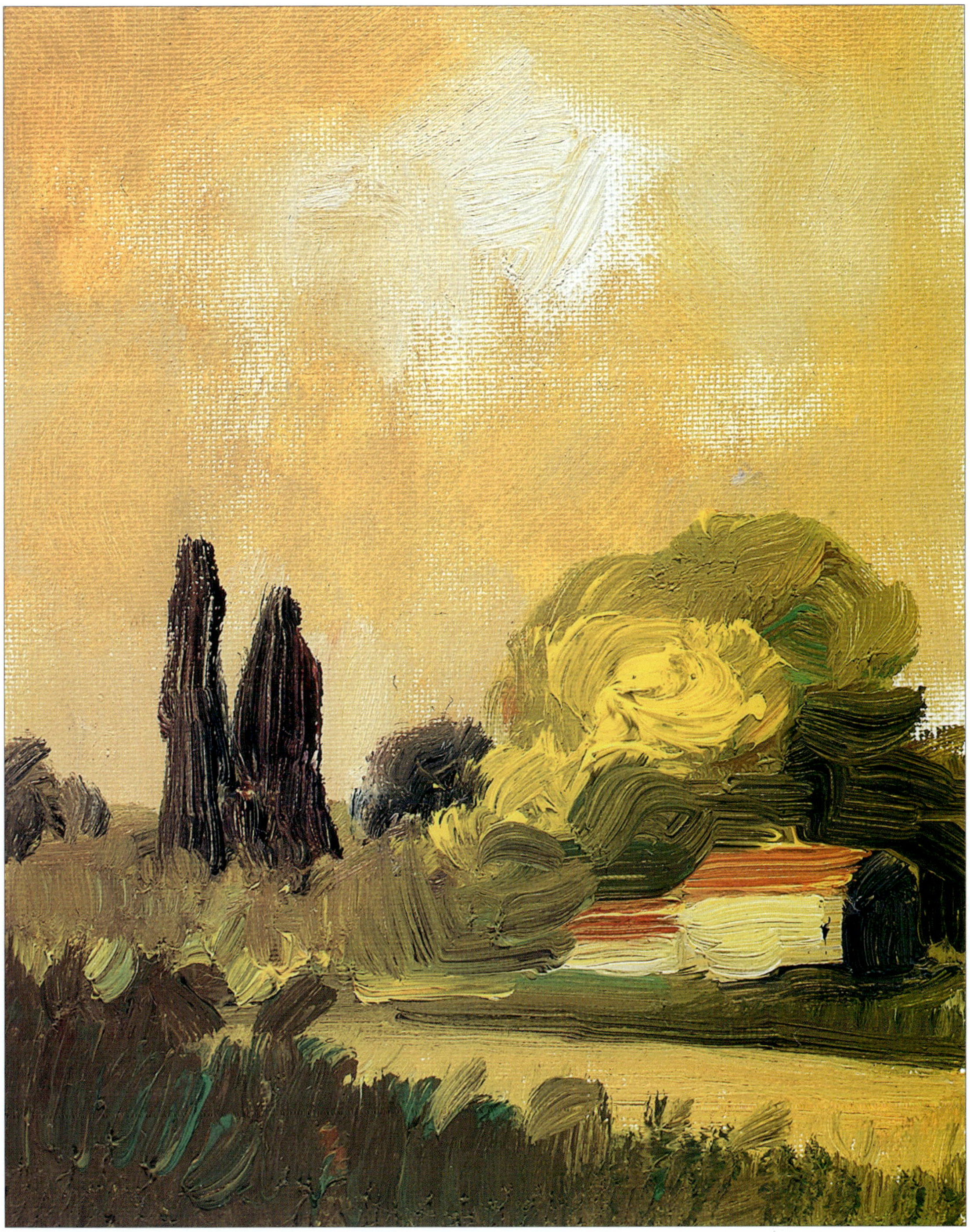

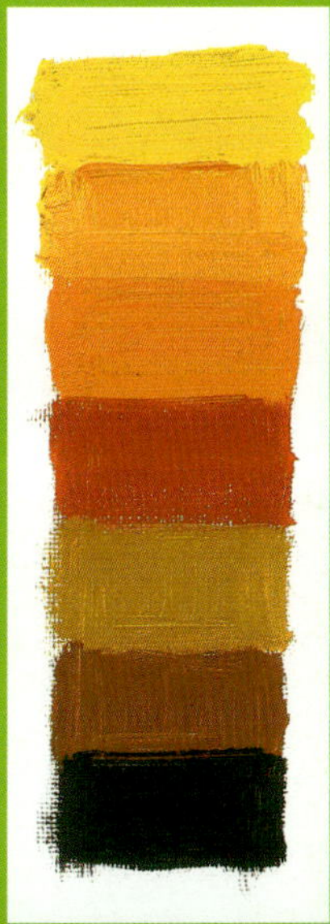

A sample range of warm colors.

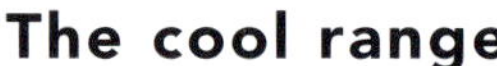

A sample range of cool colors.

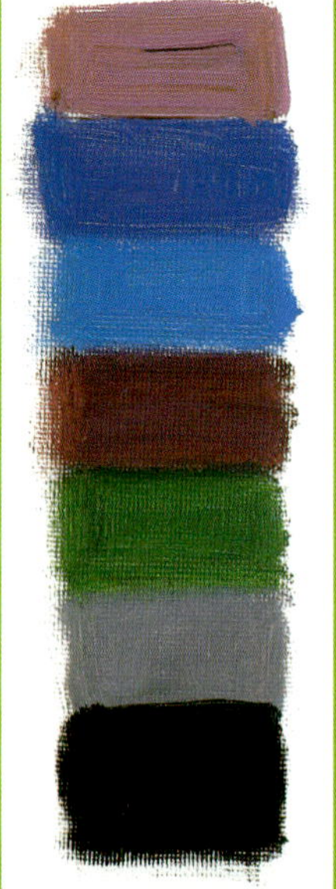

The cool range

The basic cool colors are the blues and those obtained from mixing cyan with yellow and magenta: that is to say the greens and the violets. Therefore, the cool range is composed of the colors blue, green, violet and purple.

The broken range

The broken range is formed by gray and brown tones, which have been created by mixing secondary colors or a primary color with its complementary color. Although these colors are lacking in brightness, when they are used in harmony, without mixing them either with warm or cool colors, they can make a great contribution to creating eye-catching attractive oeuvres. Although many works are painted with colors from the three ranges, if ever you want a picture to have chromatic unity all its colors must belong to one range, be it warm, cool or broken.

A landscape painted in cool colors.

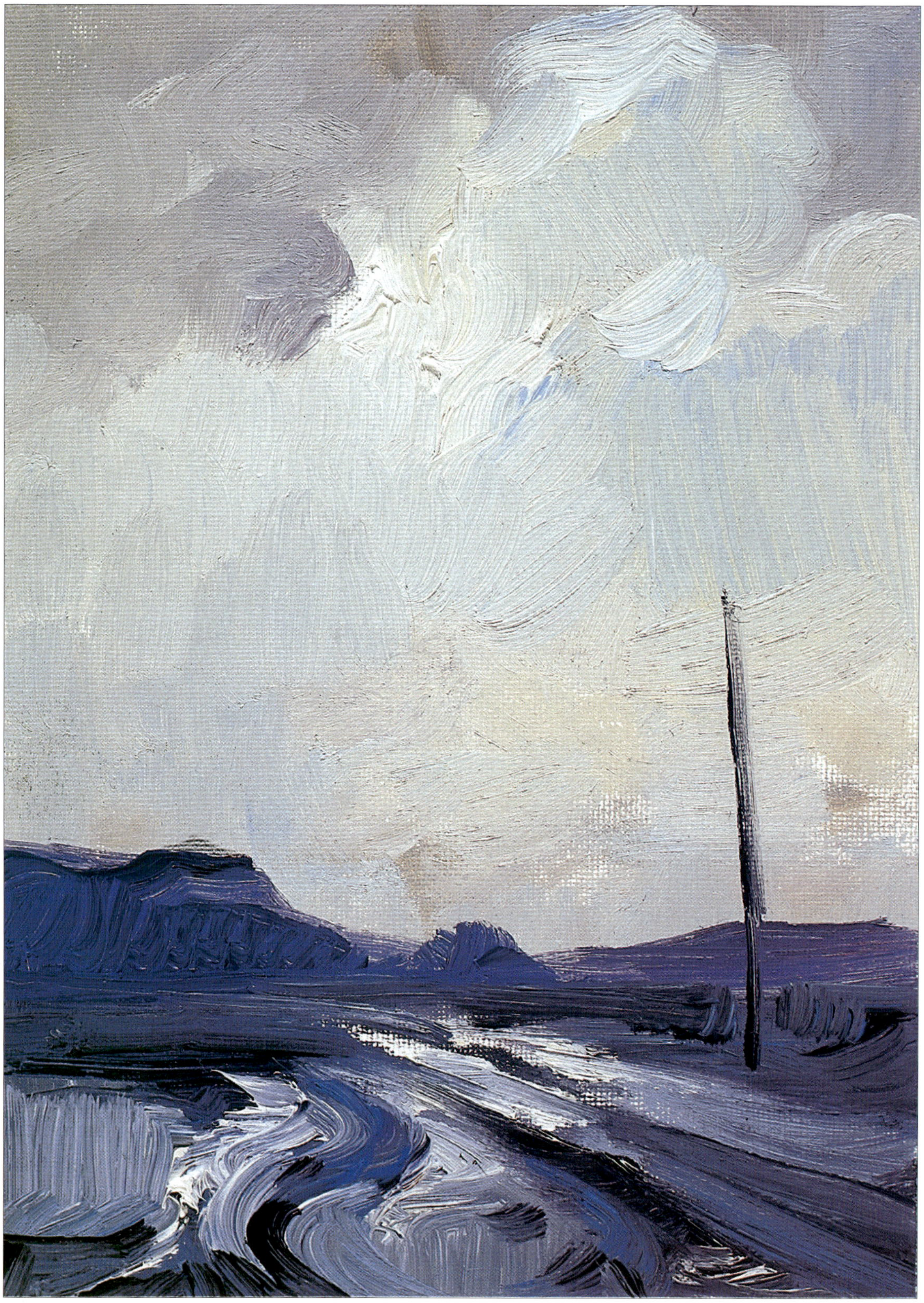

Lightening and darkening

When working with oil colors you must be especially carefully when darkening or lightening a color because depending on how you do it, the color will become stronger and more contrasted, or duller and more lackluster. Losing contrast is particularly significant in oil painting because the medium is known for its richness in this aspect.

Lightening a color.

When you want to lighten a color, although this may seem surprising at first, never mix it with white for you would merely take away the vitality and brightness of the original tone without achieving anything positive. White, which is almost never pure, is principally used to grayen tones or to cover very defined zones.

The lightening of a color must always be done with more luminous colors from the same range. If a landscape is painted and the colors on the left are lightened with clearer tones, while on the right white is used, you will be able to see that the first fragment retains its luminosity and strength. However, on the right a fogginess clouds the image.

In the first strokes you can appreciate the paste like quality of the oil colors, capable of giving volume to the petals of the flower.

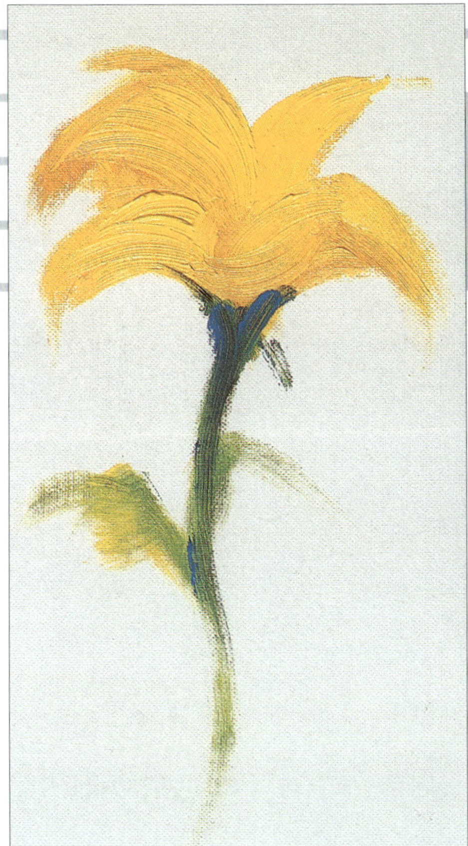

Trying out oil colors

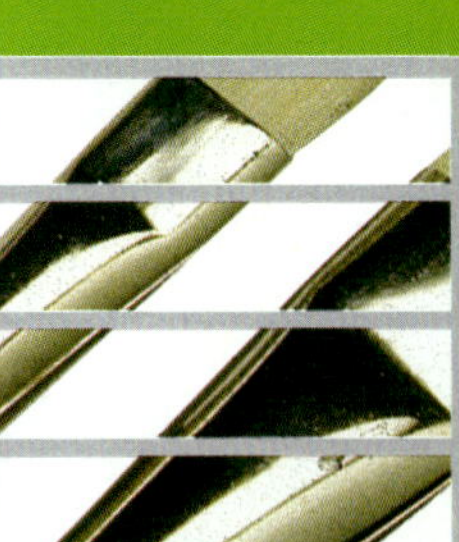

To get to know the properties of oil color there is no better way than using the palette and brush just for painting a simple picture. For example to paint a flower, do a few free fan shaped strokes in yellow. The buttery quality of oil color is visible. Afterwards, use green paint to do the stem (if the brush is not too heavily loaded the bristle marks will be visible on the support. Give a few blue touches to the base of the flower. Afterwards do a few carmine strokes, dragging part of the yellow. The way it blends is a clear indication of the oiliness of the paint. Finally, paint on the stem some strokes of green mixed with yellow. The opacity of the color allows light colors to be painted on top of dark ones.

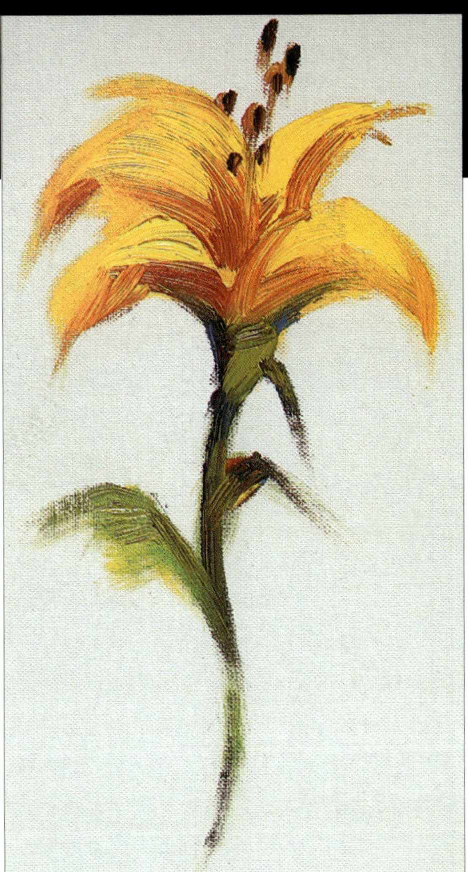

On top of the colors already down you can work quickly. Observe how the color carmine drags part of the yellow because the latter takes some time to dry.

Darkening a color

In the same way that white is unsuitable for lightening a color, neither is black the most ideal for darkening a picture because when it is mixed with other colors it creates a wide range of grays which although they do darken they also take away vitality from the whole.

It is much more recommendable to do the operation using colors from the same range as those in the picture, but with a darker tone, or other colors like blue, carmine or umber.
Continuing with the landscape example, if the left half is darkened with black, and the right with luminous colors the latter will be more vivid because it will not have gray tones that dull it.

The color of the objects

When an artist is painting a picture they must always remember that there are no exact colors which identify a concrete object, even though unconsciously we often do identify one with another. For example, when thinking about an orange, this color often comes to mind. However, it can be misleading because any surface of an object is in reality composed

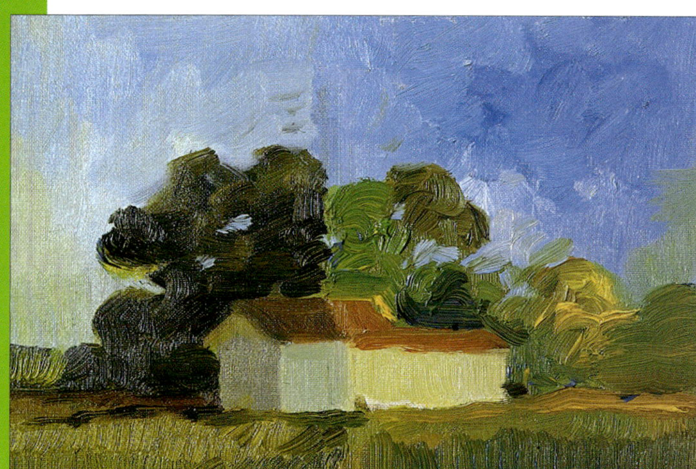

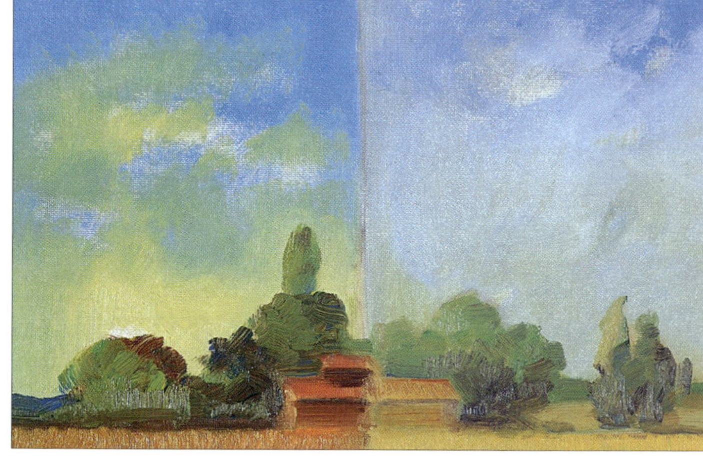

The left part of the picture has been lightened by tones more luminous than the original. On the right the lightening has been done with white, unfortunately spoiling some of the luminosity and vividness.

On the left the painting has been darkened by using black. On the right dark but vivid colors have been used, so maintaining the luminosity of the picture.

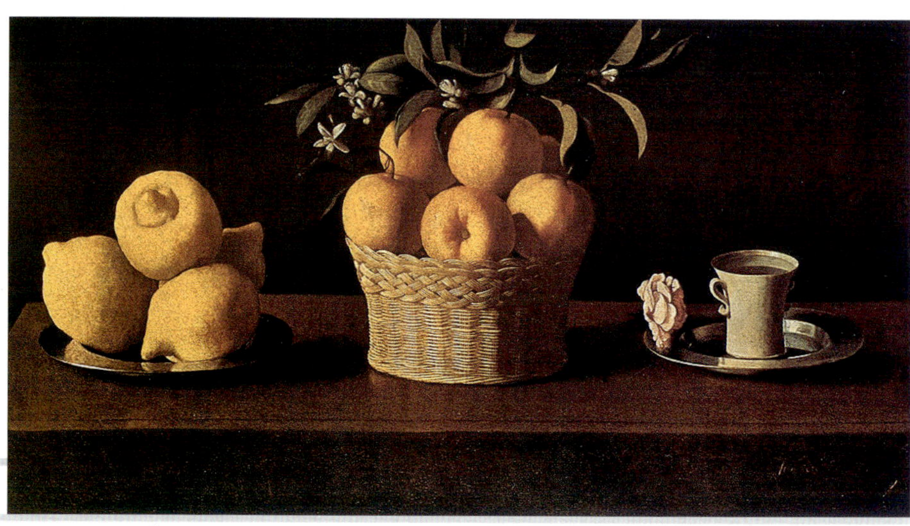

An opaque and luminous medium

Oil color has so many possibilities that it is considered the most versatile and tractable painting medium existing. Since it appeared the great masters have never ceased to be surprised by its richness, creating works which combine opacity with luminosity and oiliness, as you can see in the still life with lemons, oranges and a rose, painted by Francisco Zurbarán (1598-1664) and kept in the Conde Contini-Bonacossi collection in Florence. In this oil painting the crisp contrast between the opacity of the table in the background and the intense luminosity and transparency of the fruit and objects that make up the still life is outstanding.

of various tones if not colors. This is because the light that falls creates the tones. Orange peel can be the color orange but under some conditions, like, for example, when it is next to a blue object, its shadow zone will not be orange but instead it will be shaded with blue, or even violet, tones.

Brushes

The most suitable brushes for oil painting are hog's hair brushes because they are tough and allow the paint, even in dense quantities, to be loaded and handled comfortably. Rounded, flat brushes stand out for their special ductileness.

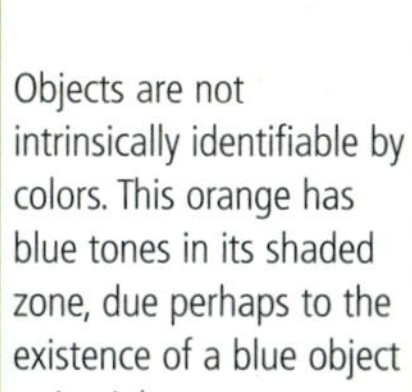

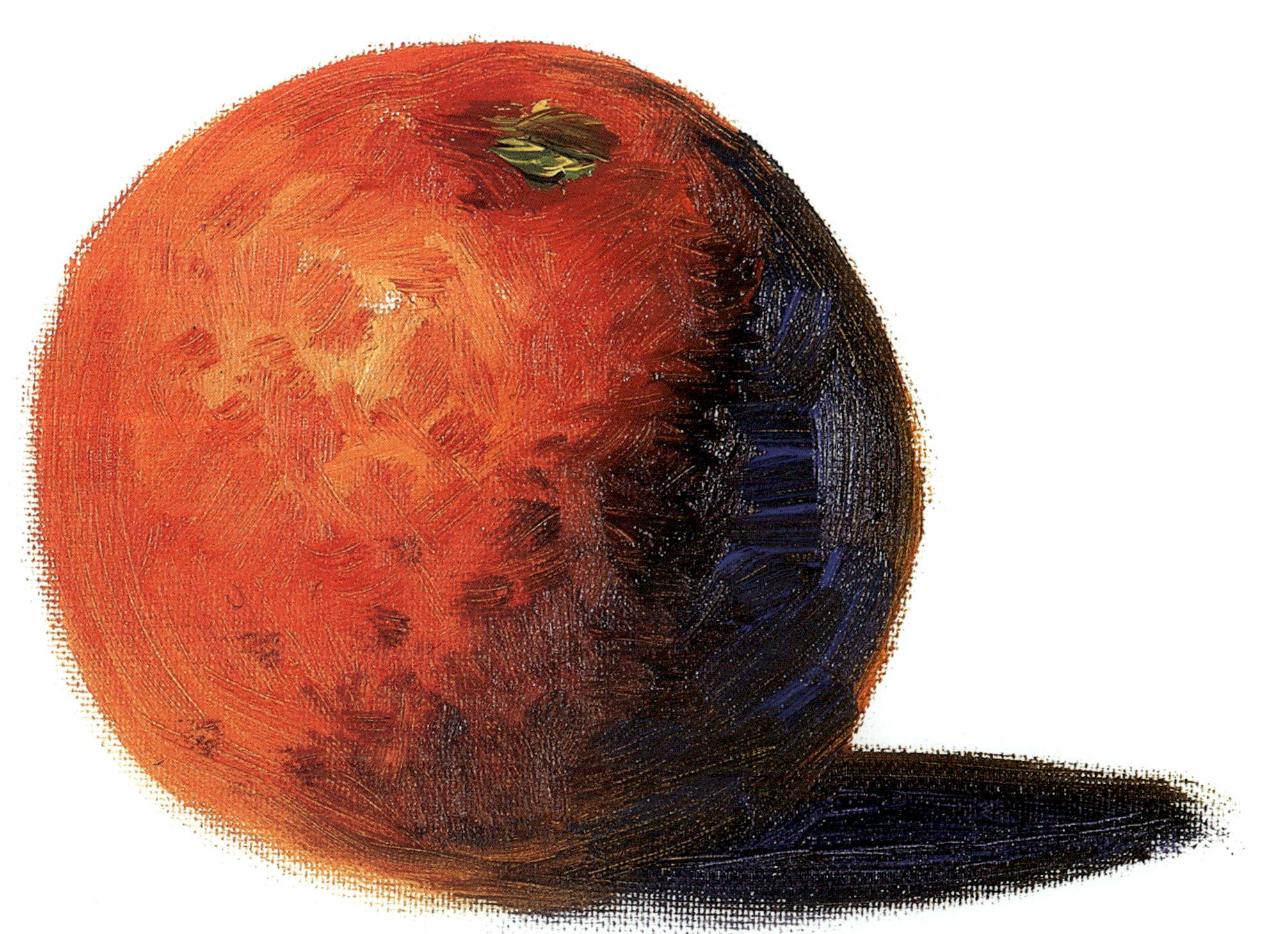

Objects are not intrinsically identifiable by colors. This orange has blue tones in its shaded zone, due perhaps to the existence of a blue object to its right.

Summary

PLACING THE COLORS ON THE PALETTE
To do the mixes comfortably the colors must be ordered by tones and chromatic values.

HARMONIOUS OR CHROMATIC RANGES
The cool harmonizing range is composed of blue colors. The warm range is made up of reds. The broken colors are grays and browns.

LIGHTENING AND DARKENING THE OIL COLORS
The lightening of a color must be done with luminous colors, never with white. To darken do not use black. Dark colors give more vividness to the resulting hues.

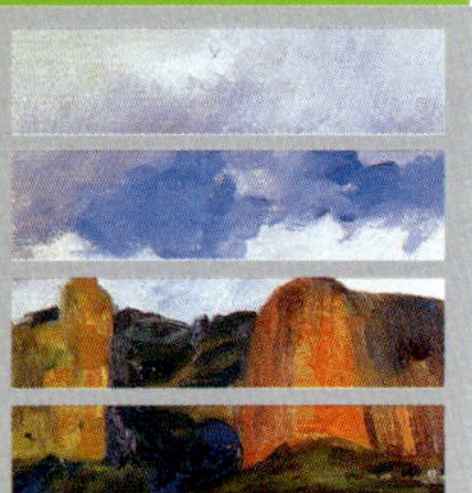

Exercises

THE PRIMARY COLORS IN A LANDSCAPE

Mixing colors is a practice that all artists should do regularly so that they learn to master the theory of color and how to apply it. Just with the three basic colors and white it is possible to obtain all the tones which can be contemplated in nature.

The next exercise consists of painting a cliff scene full of chromatic subtleties. Only the three primary colors and white will be used. When we put down the initial ground it will seem that all the strokes blur together but as the painting advances, each zone will begin to have its own distinct color or tone.

Necessary material

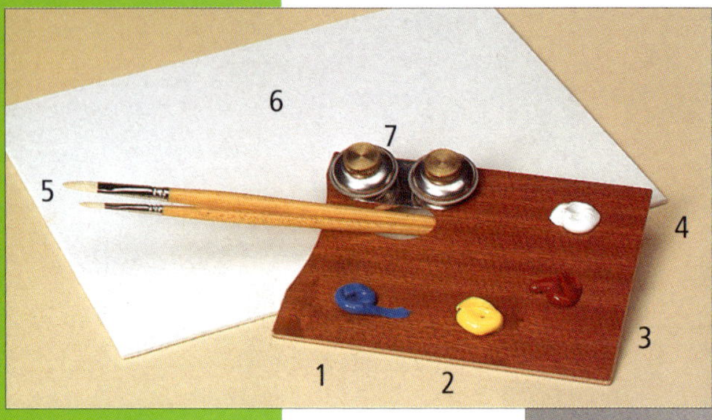

Oil colors: blue (1), yellow (2), magenta (3), white (4), hog brushes (5), primed cardboard (6), linseed oil and turpentine oil (7).

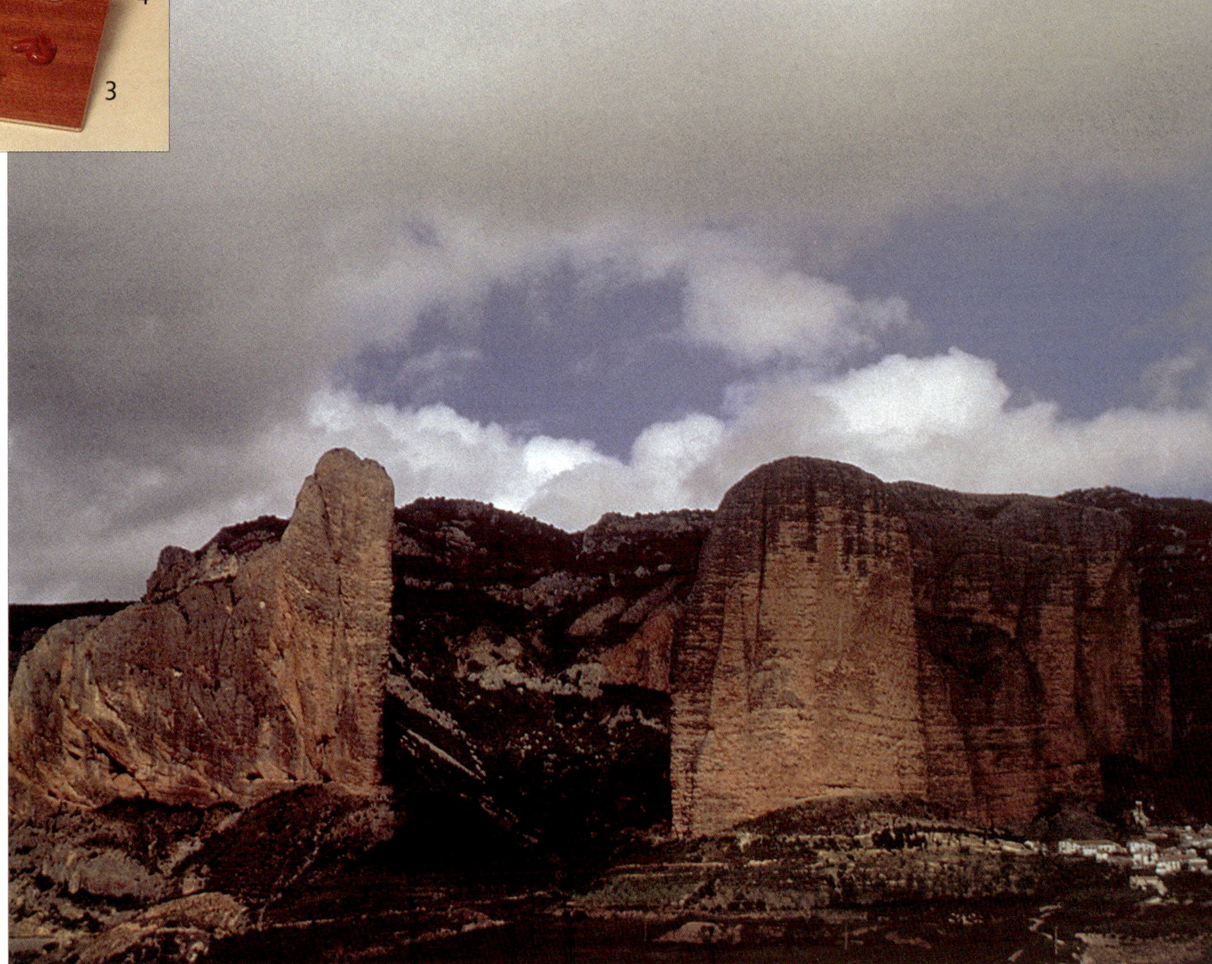

1·Start the painting by wetting the brush in turpentine oil, drain it off against the side of the jar and then add it to the blue (only the tip of the bristles need be loaded). Then start to paint on the primed card.
Paint the lower line and above this schematize the form of the cliffs. It does not matter if you make mistakes and have to do corrections. With oil colors, as many alterations as necessary can be made.
Afterwards draw the edges of the clouds in the sky.

2·Mix blue and white on the palette, using much more white than blue because just a little bit will be sufficient to give the white the required tone.

Start working on the sky, in which the whiteness of the clouds stands out.

As the clouds take shape, add a little dash of magenta. The resulting tone is similar to violet and it is going to be used to paint the darkest part of the clouds.

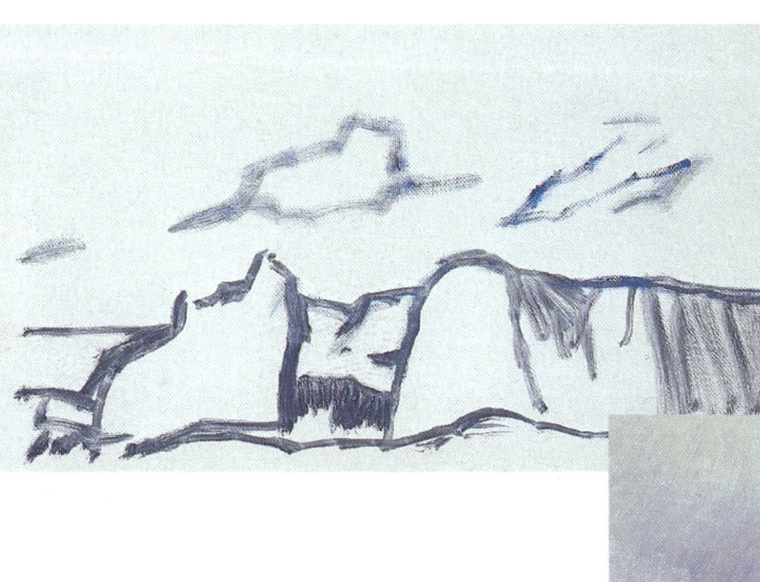

3·Take a little blue and add white to it until you get a cerulean tone -a sky blue also called azure- much more brilliant and denser than the color of the clouds (this mix does not incorporate magenta). Paint the central zone of the sky.

With almost pure white paint the upper zone of the lowest clouds.

Mix magenta and yellow until you achieve an orange tone. Add a little blue to break the tone and then start the painting of the cliffs.

It always pays dividends to do little mixtures on the palette to test the color before doing it in great quantities.

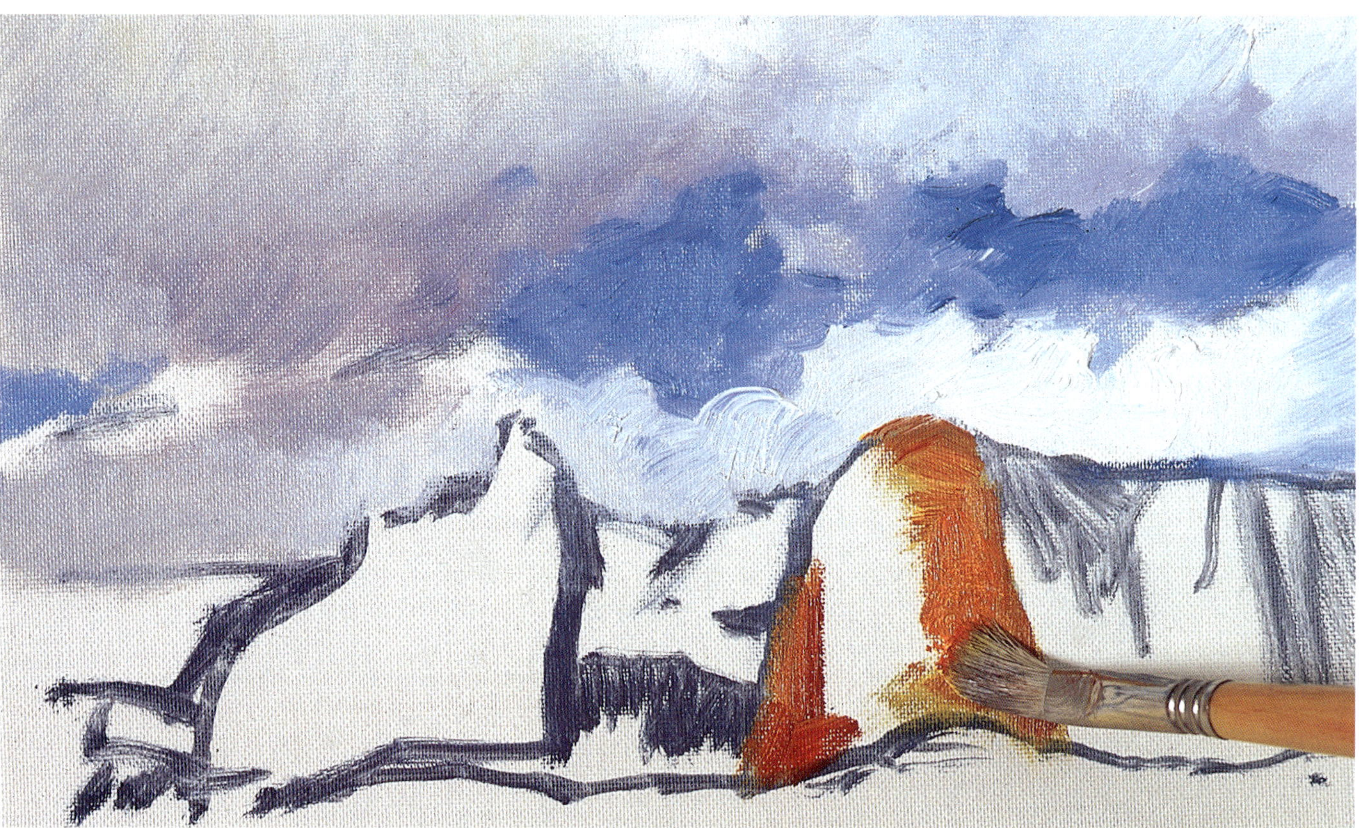

4.·Paint the cliff in various colors, forming different mixes on the palette. Yellow and blue give a green, the luminosity of which depends on the amount of blue it contains (in this case it is 50%). Blue and magenta produce violet. Yellow and magenta make orange.

Add a little violet to the green to give a broken color on the right of the cliff.

To achieve the lighter tones on the left, firstly make yellowish green and then add a little orange. Lighten subtly with white.

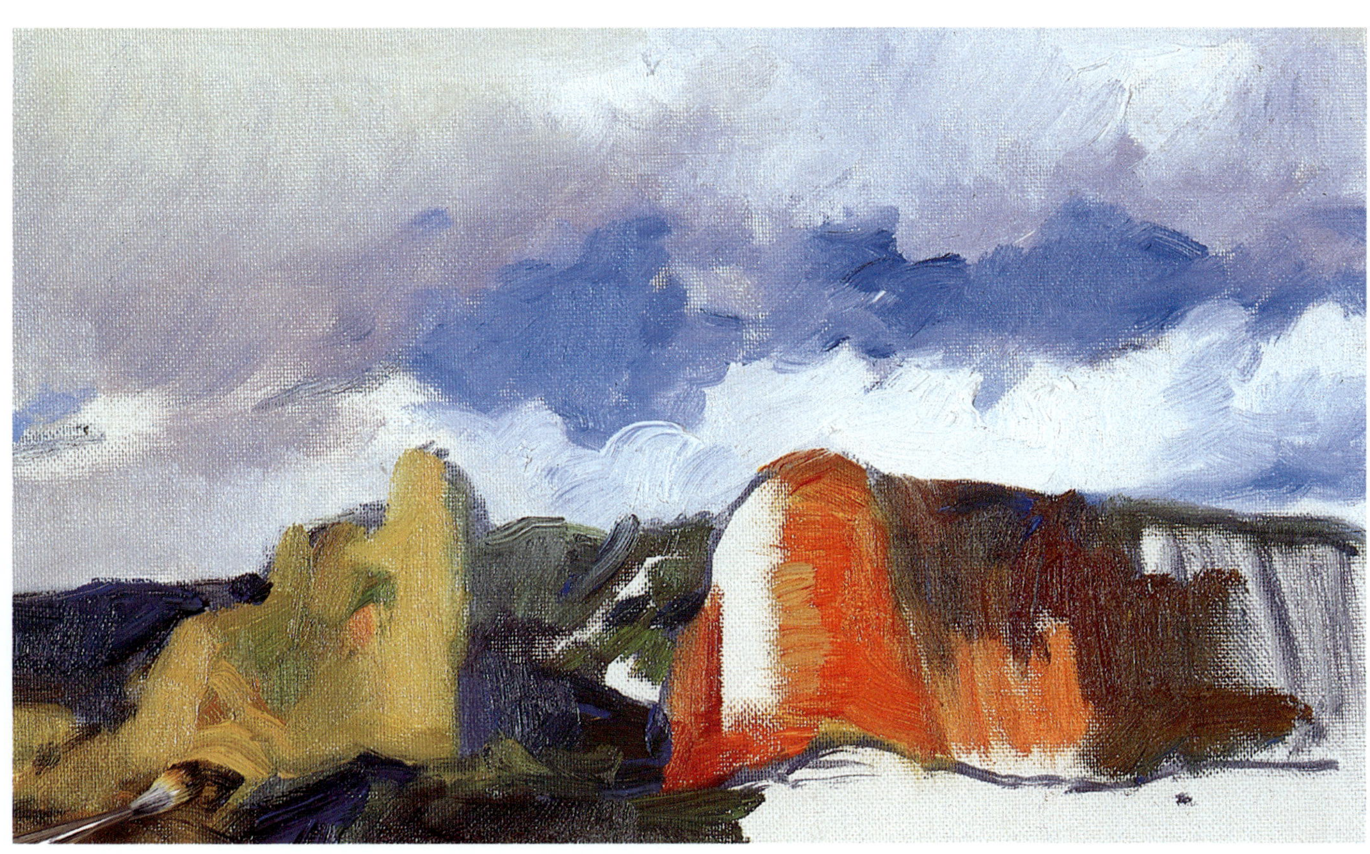

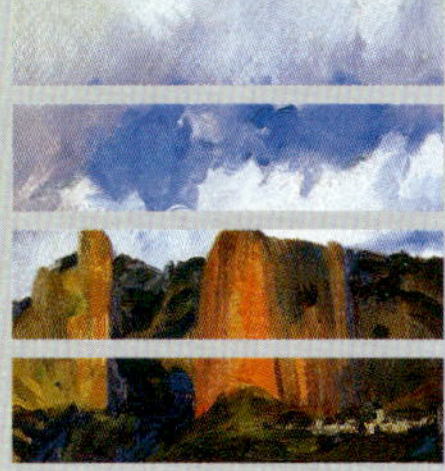

Exercises

5·As we indicated in step 5, the contrasts of the rocky cliff faces are painted with broken tones, darker than the original colors.

The most luminous zone of the cliff is painted in a tone somewhat more pinkish, obtained from magenta, white and a little yellow.

6·Continue to work with different green tones in the lower part. First the green was obtained from yellow and blue, making it pasty on the palette. Afterwards, a little magenta was added to break the color and make it earthier.

In some points, paint with this tone darkened by a bit of blue.

Below the cliffs, depict the houses with little stains of white and dragging the color.

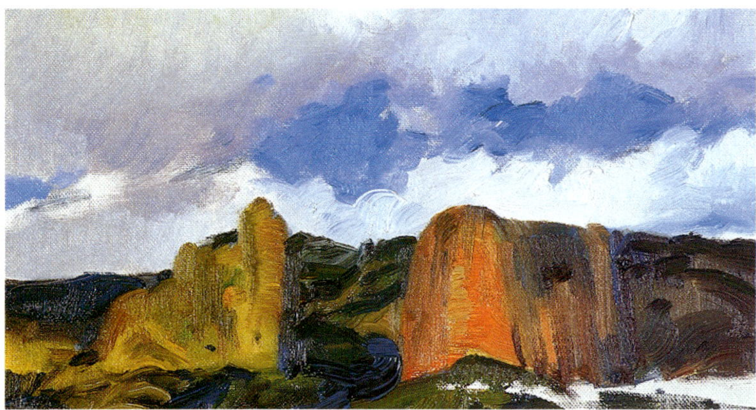

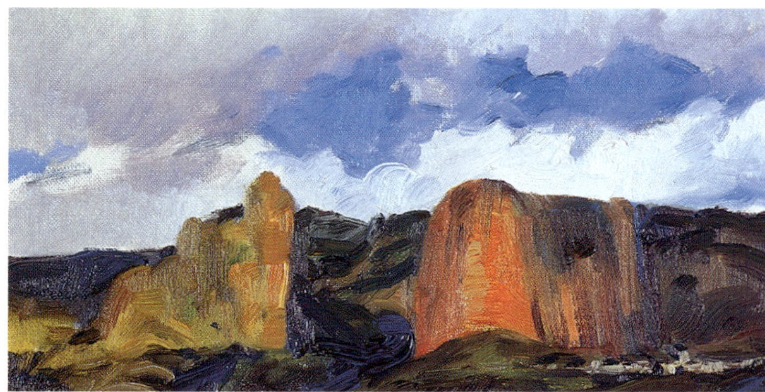

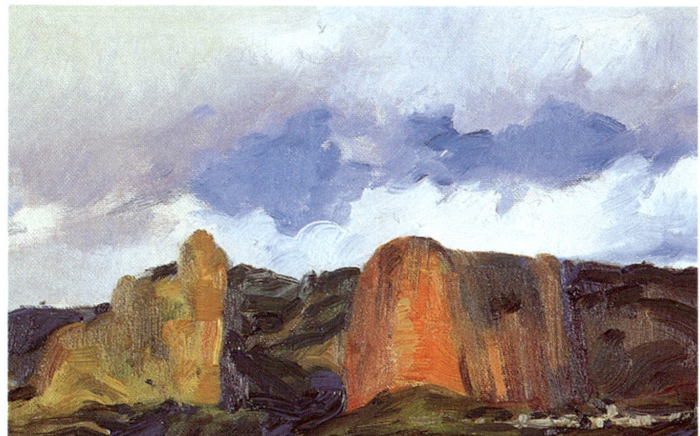

7·To finish off increase the contrasts of the cliffs with dark tones.

Use these dark colors to paint around the little white houses, making them stand out much more.

This landscape is now finished. We have gone a long way in practicing color mixing.

The outline is done directly in blue oil color

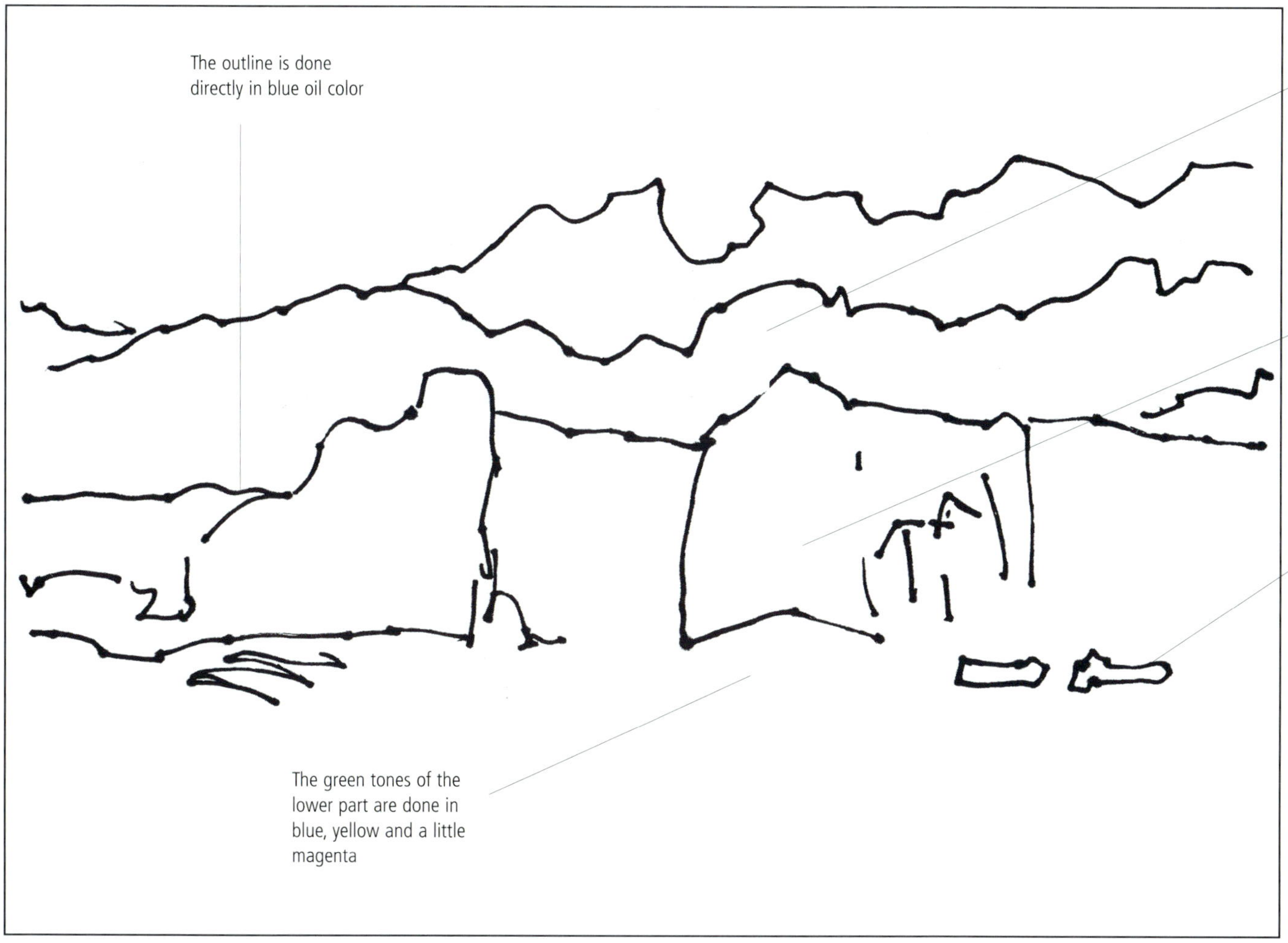

The whiteness of the clouds comes from, of course, a lot of white and a dash of blue.

The orangy color of the cliffs was obtained from magenta, yellow and a touch of blue.

The town is painted with white strokes.

The green tones of the lower part are done in blue, yellow and a little magenta

Chapter 3

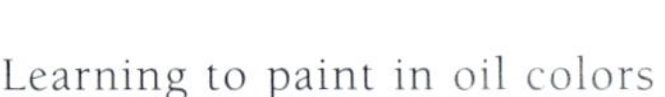

Strokes in oil colors

Oil painting is not only a medium which offers an extremely wide range of colors. It also allows, due to its thickness, the application of strokes that model the forms and give the work a characteristic texture.

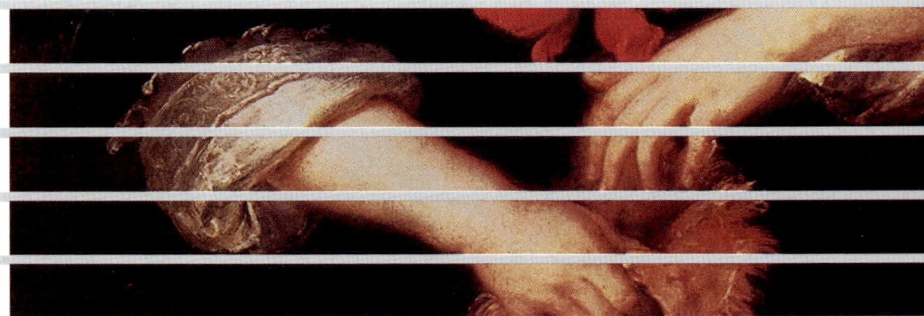

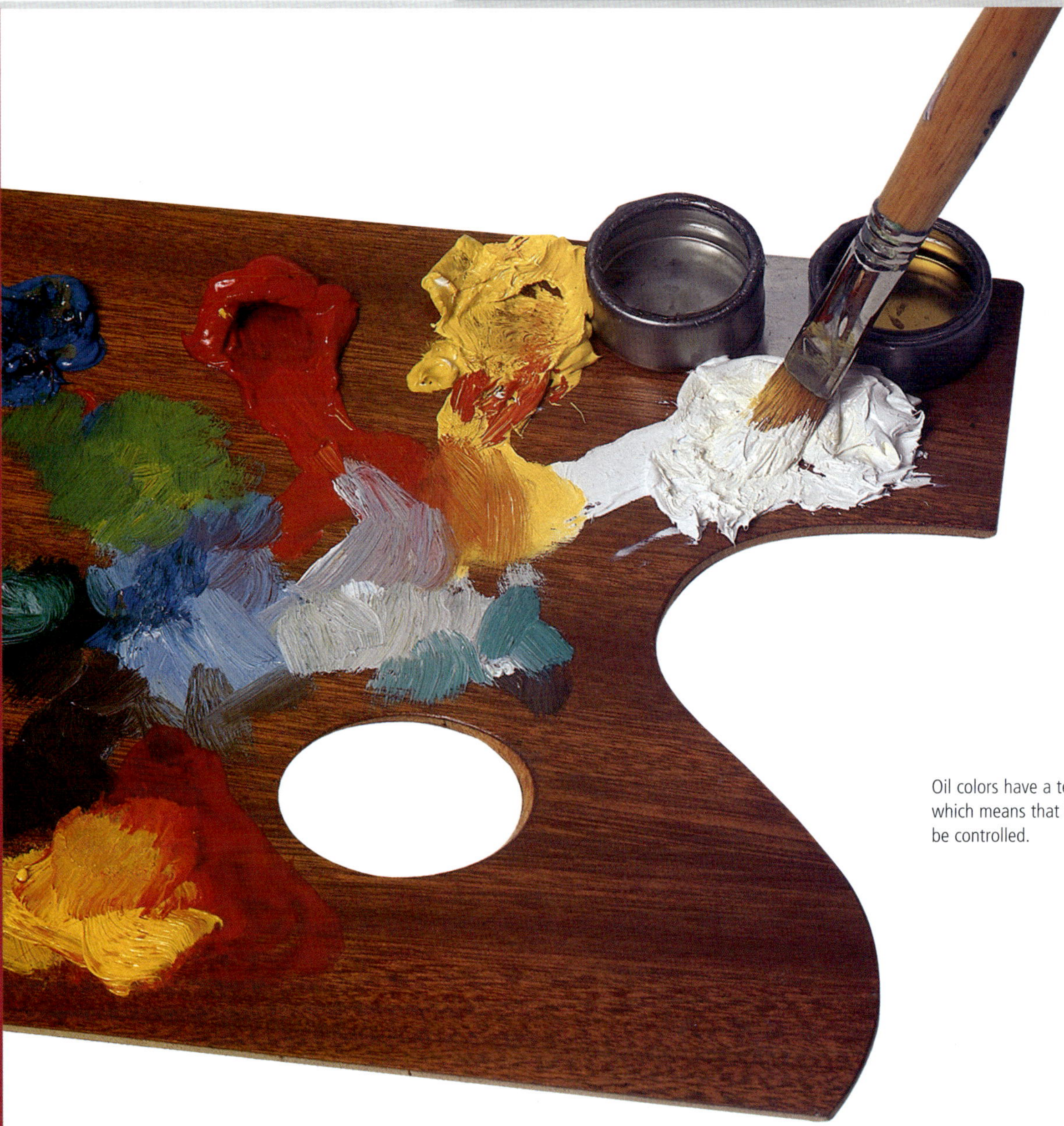

Oil colors have a texture similar to that of butter which means that it sticks to the brush and can be controlled.

Oil color is a pasty medium, sufficiently dense to permit a thick, opaque stroke. Immediately the artist will realize that its texture is very similar to butter. Moreover, oil color has an unsurpassable property: it offers one of the widest ranges of colors that any painting medium can provide. Oil colors are dense enough to be applied in strokes that allow modeling of the form and give the work a characteristic texture. Once it is dry, the oil painting does not alter its form. This quality is added to the possibility of being able to manipulate the stroke, or in other words, to be creative.

In this chapter we are going to deal with different ways in which the paint can be applied to the picture, a question directly related to the way the brush is handled. The stroke is closely linked to the line but they are not exactly the same. A line can be made by a brush, with charcoal or with any of the other drawing media. The brush stroke produces a line and it adds the inherent quality of the mark of the bristles, the dragging. This dragging can be more or less dense, pronounced or simply insinuated, depending on the artist's intentions.

Strokes

The stroke is how the paint is applied to the picture. Oil color can be manipulated and easily modeled when put down. This is why it is important to know how to master the mark of the stroke. Your hand must become accustomed to the feel of the brush. Putting down the paint is very important to all the creative process. In the following practice exercises you will be able to see how the oil painting changes, depending on the stroke style and paint application on the picture.

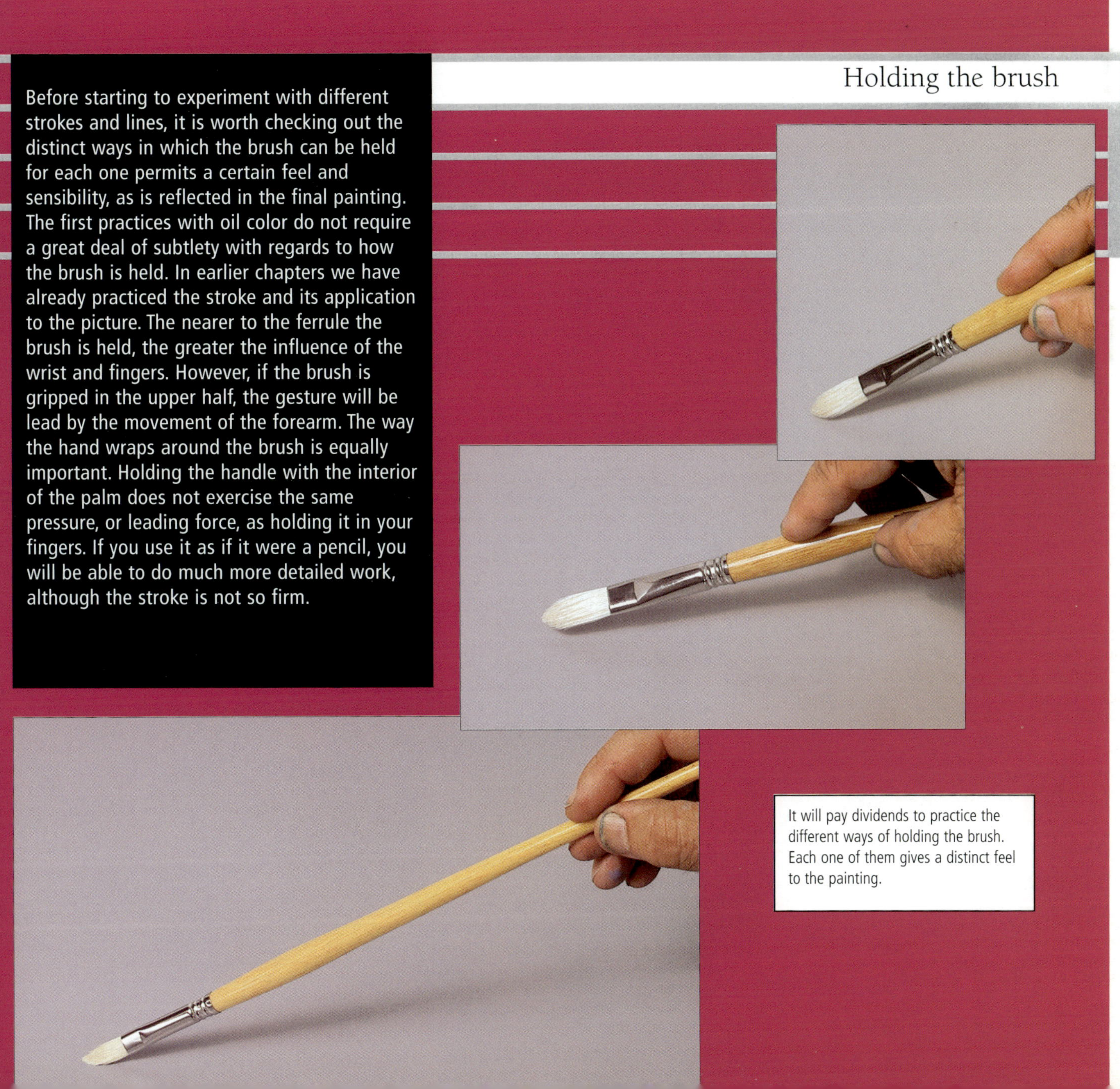

Before starting to experiment with different strokes and lines, it is worth checking out the distinct ways in which the brush can be held for each one permits a certain feel and sensibility, as is reflected in the final painting. The first practices with oil color do not require a great deal of subtlety with regards to how the brush is held. In earlier chapters we have already practiced the stroke and its application to the picture. The nearer to the ferrule the brush is held, the greater the influence of the wrist and fingers. However, if the brush is gripped in the upper half, the gesture will be lead by the movement of the forearm. The way the hand wraps around the brush is equally important. Holding the handle with the interior of the palm does not exercise the same pressure, or leading force, as holding it in your fingers. If you use it as if it were a pencil, you will be able to do much more detailed work, although the stroke is not so firm.

Holding the brush

It will pay dividends to practice the different ways of holding the brush. Each one of them gives a distinct feel to the painting.

The drawing lines

The drawing lines are necessary to get linear strokes, without texture, similar to those obtained from charcoal or any other drawing media. However, here the line can be done in a much more continuous form. In general this type of line is done once the initial sketch has been done in charcoal, pencil or sanguine. To do it, dip the brush in turpentine oil and using a dark color, the tone is not too important, go over the previous drawing, unifying the model being developed.

If the brush is too heavily loaded, the fluid stroke could run over the picture, so be careful to control the amount of color loaded. The brush must not be too thick, in fact, for this opening phase of the painting it is important to use a thin hog's hair brush. Why must hog's hair brushes be used? The reason is simple: they do not absorb a great deal of paint and are therefore not soaked in turpentine oil either. In this way the stroke on the picture can be more easily controlled.

The first strokes

The first strokes correspond to the initial staining of the picture. There is a basic rule that must always be respected: oil colors must be applied thick over thin, which in practical terms means that the first strokes must always be more diluted with turpentine oil than the later strokes.
Turpentine oil makes the oil colors much more fluid and transparent so when the strokes are made the brush hardly leaves its characteristic mark on the picture. These first layers of color

On top of the charcoal or sanguine sketch, go over the picture with a stroke very thinned in white spirit.

The pasty color is applied on top of the first thinned layer. This time the strokes acquire the properties of the brush strokes.

Paint the first strokes very diluted in white spirit. It does not matter too much if, as in this example, the color runs over the picture because it can be corrected later.

offer the possibility of covering any area very quickly. Although you should try to avoid the paint running down the picture, it is not too much of a problem because in oil painting this can always be corrected in later layers. On top of the first color layers you can paint with somewhat more opaque oil color. This will give the stroke more texture and feel, the properties of oil painting. The fluidity of the thinned first strokes will have gone. Use the brush lightly loaded with color to start to paint the dark nuances of the tree bark. The color painted first moves into the background.

Straight strokes

The first strokes applied onto the stained picture must be very neat, more than anything so as to avoid chaos and confusion. This neatness when doing strokes must be respected, at least in the first practices until you get used to color application. Later on we will see how the stroke order and the direction of the strokes can be changed completely. To do the staining of the picture start with straight strokes, one next to the other, so as to insinuate the forms you are developing.

Staining strokes

A thin line next to another one forms a wider stain. Bearing this idea in mind, paint all the background of the picture. Use a blue color and straight strokes to fill all the background. On top of this great mass of color, finish the painting of the tree form. Finally, use dark tones to do the details of the branches. The strokes become color masses, or stains, when they are grouped together. These stains need not be made up of great quantities of paint. In fact, when you are starting out and learning to paint in oil color, you should not use pasty paint as what is important is to learn how to manipulate and guide the stroke on the picture.

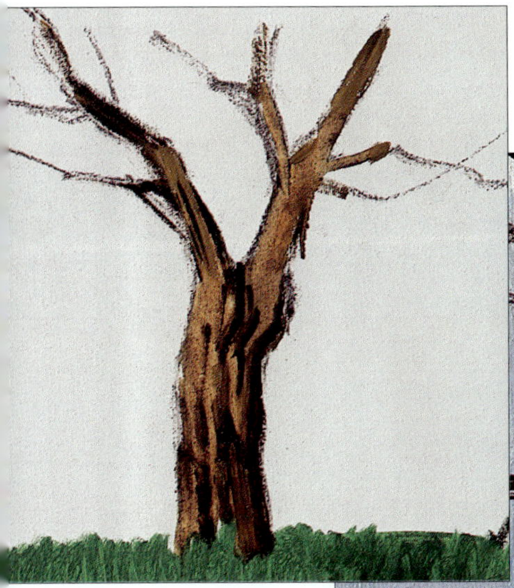

The background of the picture is painted with straight strokes which together form a great blue mass. On top of this the tree is finished with straight strokes which depict the branches.

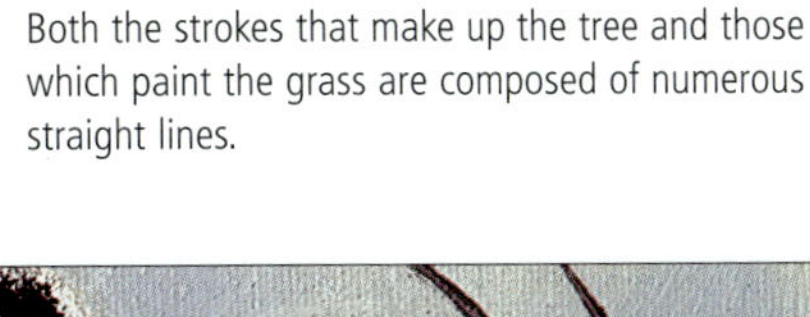

Both the strokes that make up the tree and those which paint the grass are composed of numerous straight lines.

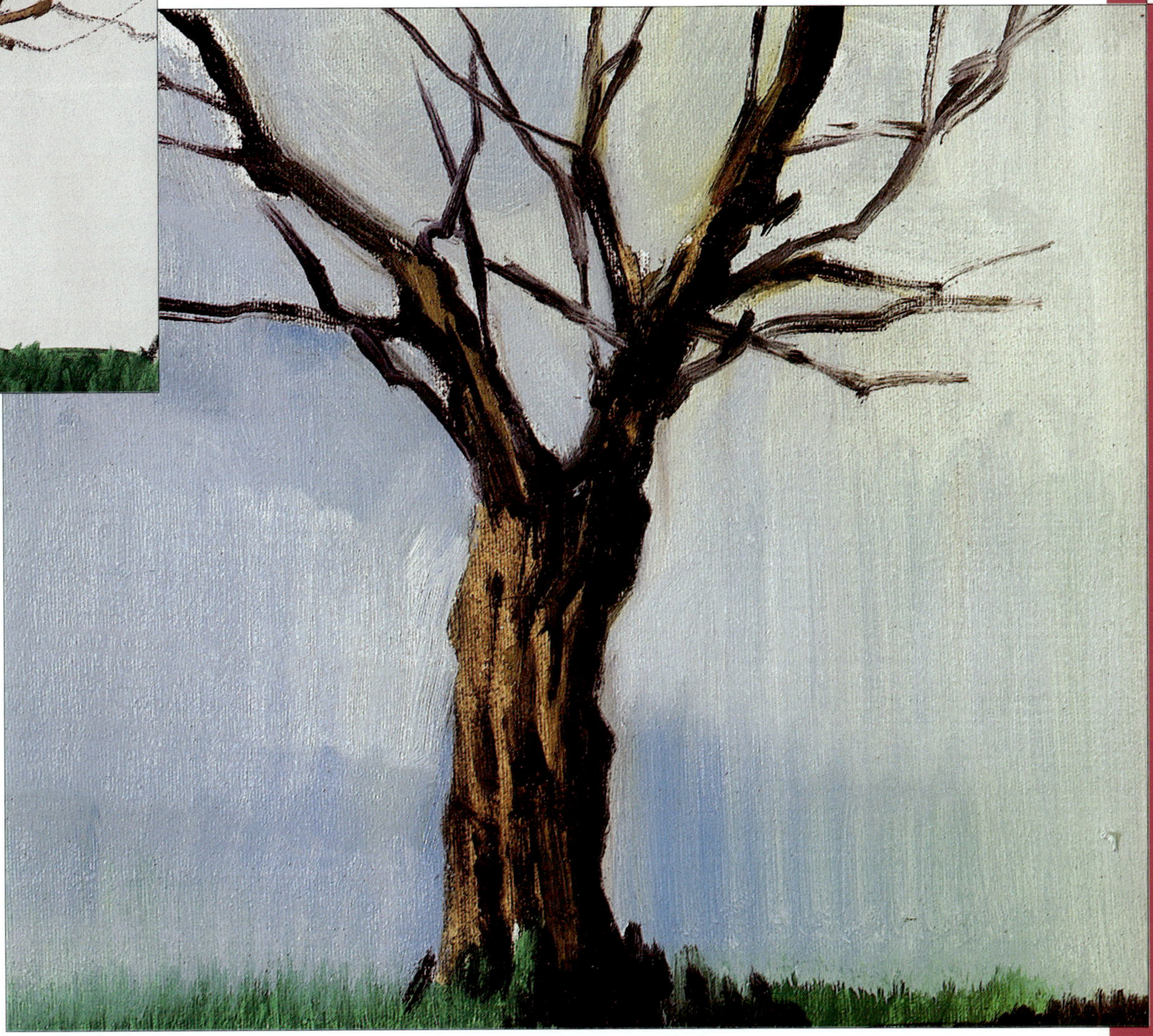

Different strokes for each zone

In the last practice exercise we studied how the principal processes take place in oil painting. First the brush strokes, on top of these, the thinned strokes, the staining, and finally the finish. The order of the strokes is important and it is also fundamental that at times each zone has its own stroke, or line, which defines it. If we go back to the last exercise we can appreciate that the sky painted in the background is correct but it has turned out a little monotonous. What would happen if the strokes were laid down crossing over each other, with distinct color nuances, instead of going in the same direction? This is the next suggestion: each plane of the picture must be composed of its own lines..

The first stains

Although the way the strokes or colors are done is modified, the picture must always be started in the same way. Firstly, a thinned color is applied that stains as much of the picture as is possible. It must create a base solid enough to be able to take up the denser colors that will follow.

The master of lines

Rubens (1557-1640) was one of the great masters in the history of painting. His drawing, present in all his works, comes through in the vigorous lines of his brush strokes, even when the piece is completely finished. In this magnificent portrait of Helen Fourment, kept in the Monaco Art Gallery, you can perfectly appreciate how the line that defines the form of each part of the figure drags some of the color next to it. This can be appreciated clearly in the strokes that define the woman's left hand.

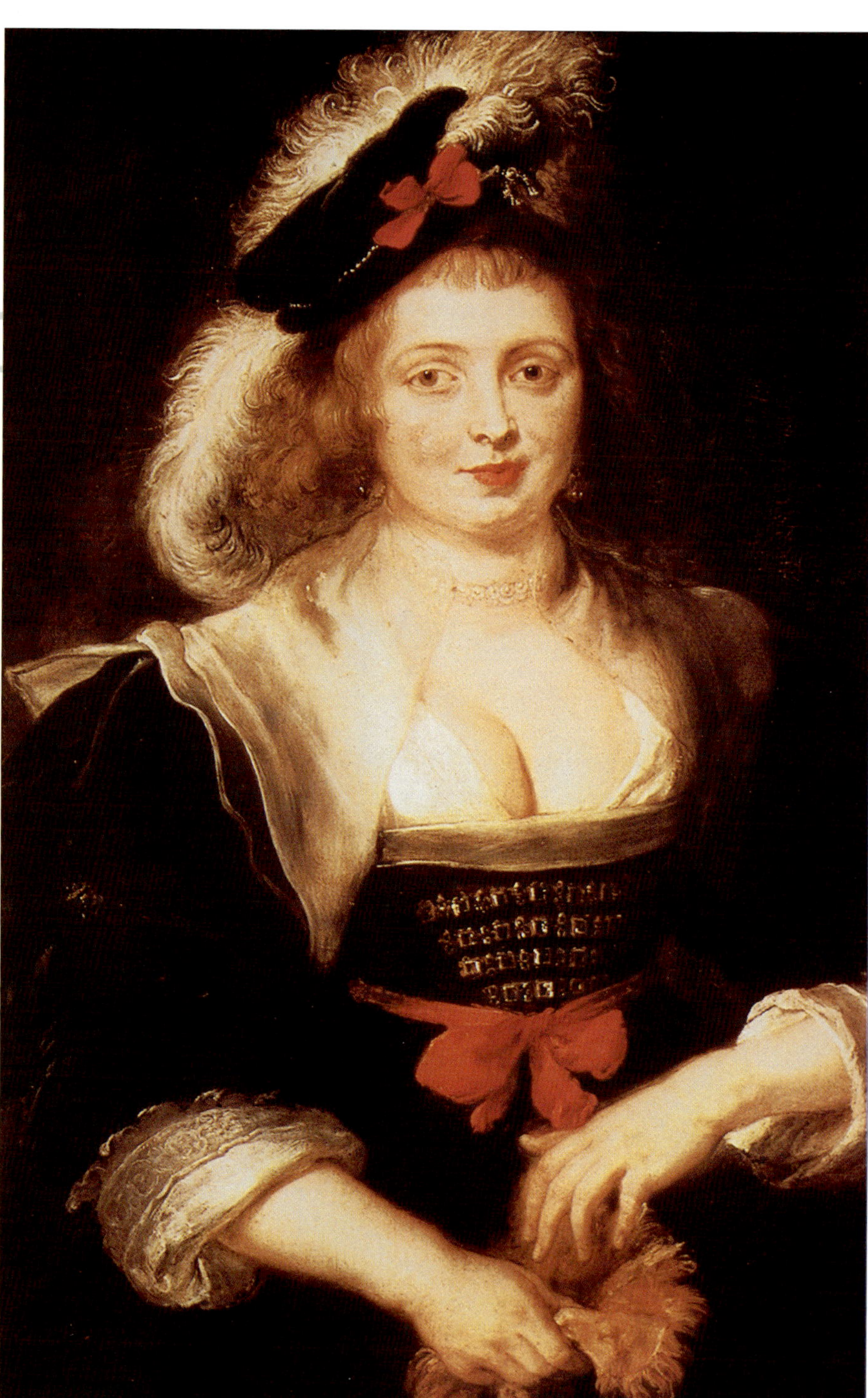

Another important question is that although in these chapters we are always starting out with pencil or charcoal, there are times when this is not recommendable depending on the complexity of the subject. Sometimes we start sketching directly in very thinned oil color.

To paint the first stains, thinned oil color is still used. However, with some quite complex subjects, like the one being done now, ordered and parallel strokes are not employed in the entire picture. Instead each zone treats the lines and colors differently. In the sea area the strokes must be straight and long. In contrast, in the rock zone, the strokes are neat and follow the plane of the rock face. Each plane is enriched by the diverse directions of the lines. The sky, too, is composed of free strokes, but here it is not judicious to mark off the planes in such a pronounced way as in the rocks.

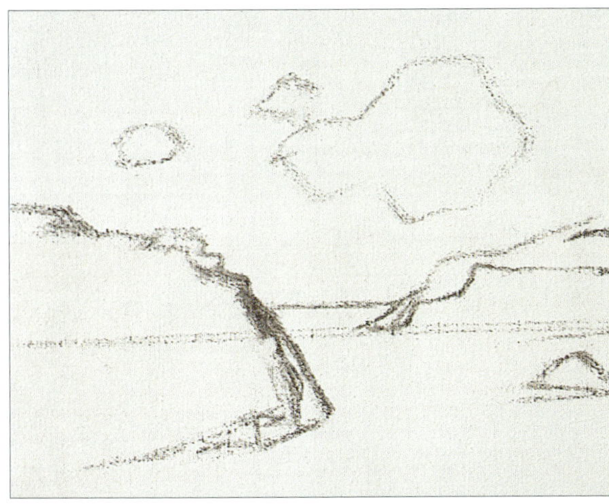

The first sketches are always drawn in charcoal or with pencil. However, later on they will be done directly in very thinned oil colors.

Looking for the color range

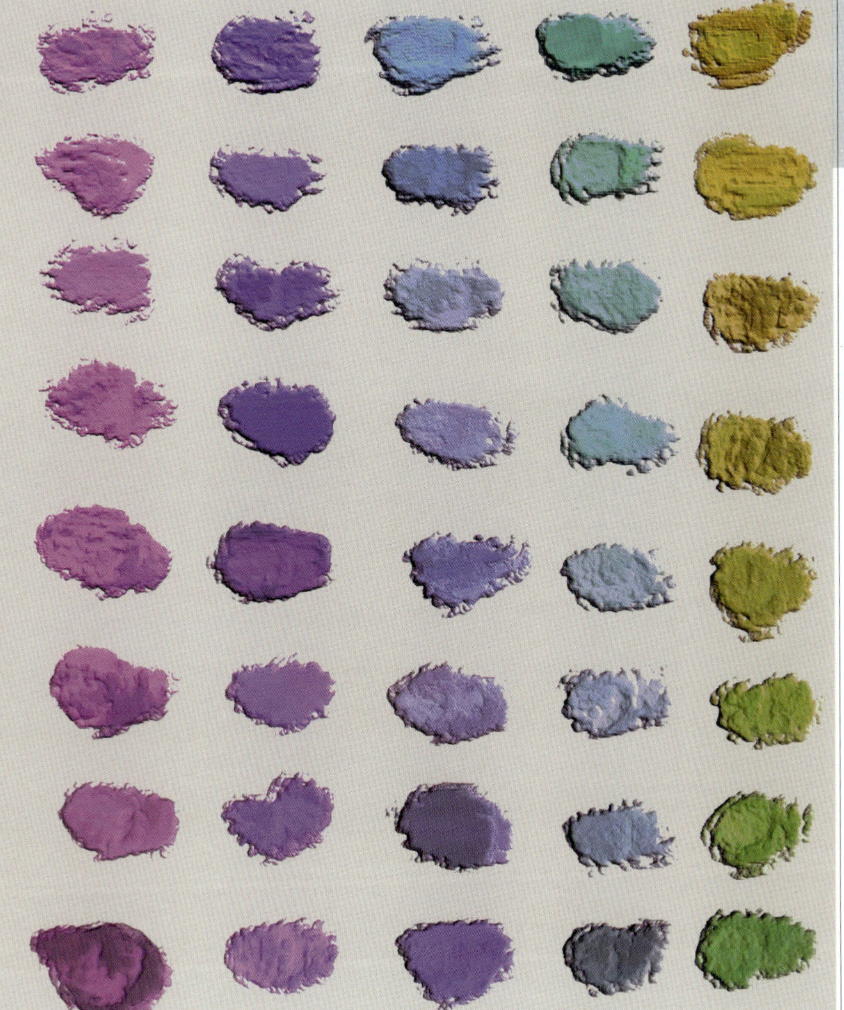

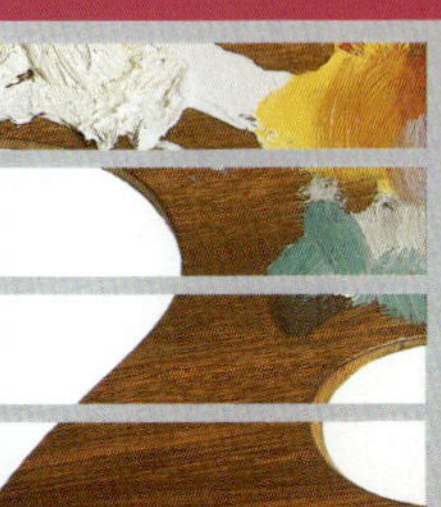

The color range is one of the most important questions when starting to paint. Doing a color range like the one presented here below is not a complex task, however it will help you to understand how colors are built up and which tones go into them. To paint a range like this one, start with yellow on the palette and add a little green, each time a little more. Afterwards, get to work on the blues, mixing in darker tones. And finally, do the violets, adding carmine progressively to the blues.

Contrasts and dense strokes

On top of a perfectly constructed color base, more pasty strokes can be applied. This time the line is much denser and the colors are superimposed on the first layer. Logically when the new color is applied part of the lower color is dragged, provided that it is still fresh. Bear in mind that the thinned oil color dries much more quickly than the thicker paint. Although we are now working with denser strokes, it is still not time to use completely pure color straight out of the tube. For the time being it must be thinned by adding a little white spirit or turpentine oil, but not so much that it becomes runny. The contrasts on the rock faces are done using groups of straight lines that vary in direction according to the plane they occupy. The water is resolved with lines clearly distinct from the rock area.

Horizontal lines predominate and the strokes never quite cross over each other. The curved lines in the sky are formed around the clouds, painted in white.
A key detail to be observed and noted is the difference in the blue color of the sky and of the sea. The former contains more white, which permits a more atmospheric hue and feel.

Each of the zones in the picture is done with different line and stroke styles.

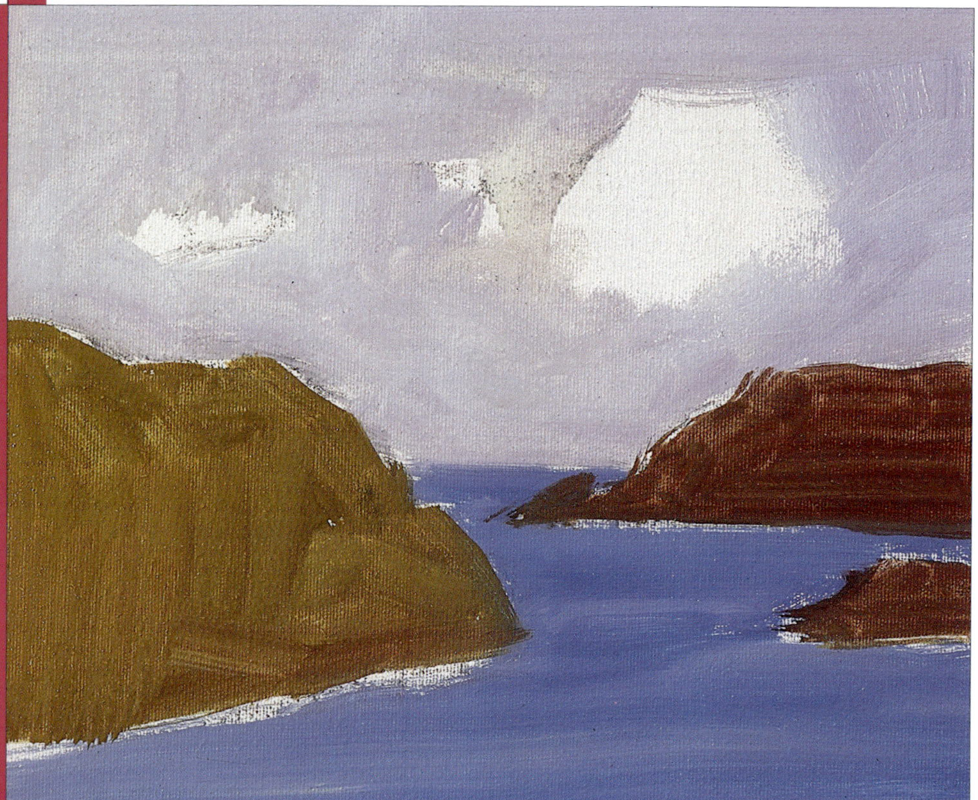

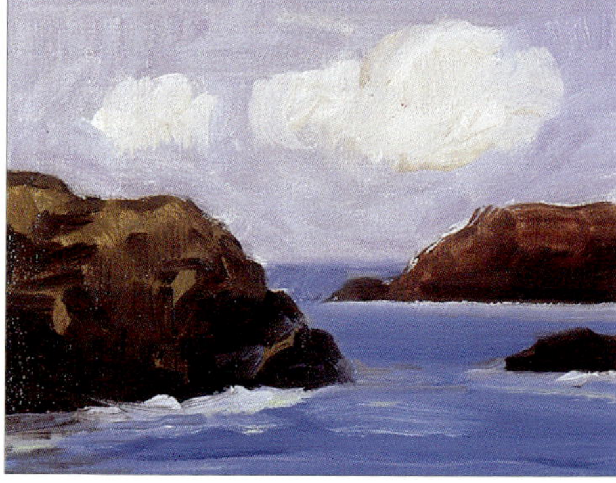

The contrasts are applied with a denser line than in the first layers.

Pure colors and controlled strokes

The stroke becomes denser as the picture advances. It is less necessary to mix the oil color with white spirit and the line is more evident due to the oiliness of the paint. The still fresh lower layers allow the new strokes put down to mix slightly with the colors of the picture as they become perfectly integrated. In this type of fresh and spontaneous work, it is not necessary to go over the strokes too much. One line for every color mass is enough because if you repeat the line the colors will blend together, as you will see later.

The finish

The finish must have a fresh look and to obtain it one must know when to stop. It is unnecessary to insist all over the picture, in some parts the paint will only be what was laid down at the beginning, while other parts will be fresh, some of the paint much denser than the previous layers.

It is important to know when to stop painting. It is question learnt with practice.

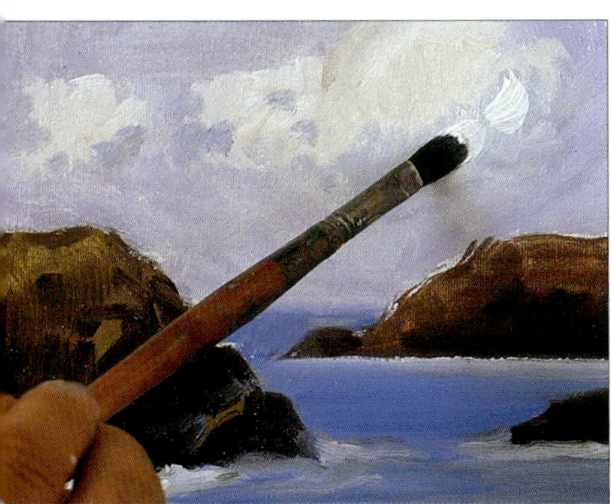

Look at the foreground. The stroke drags part of the lower color. In the cloud being painted, the stroke is direct and striking.

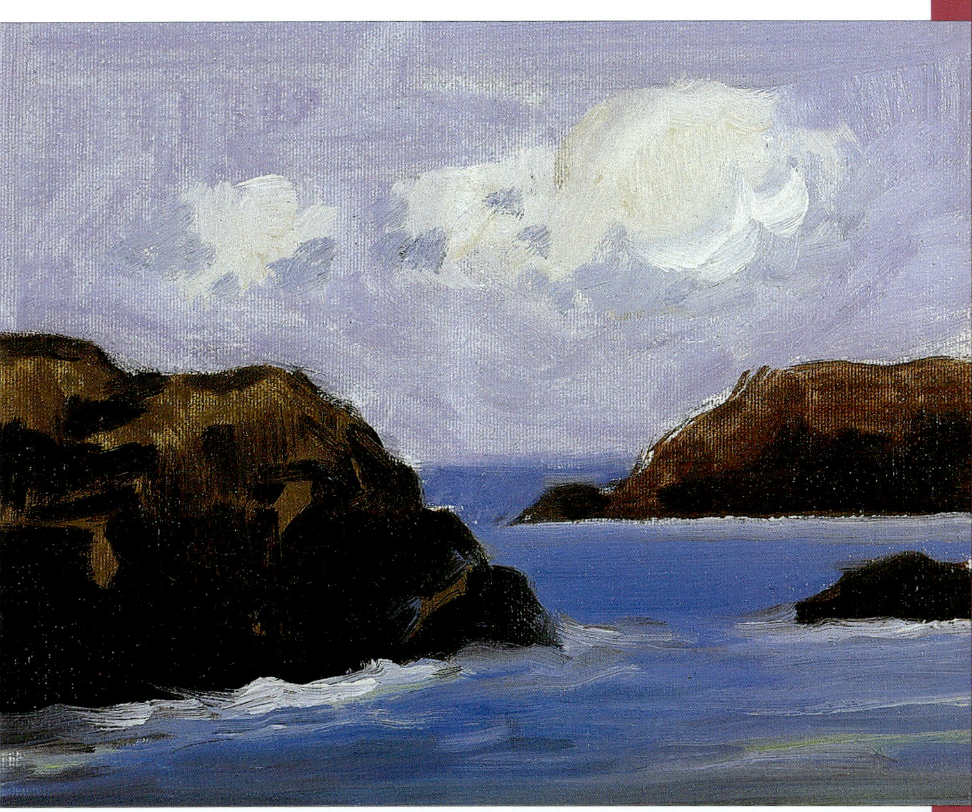

THE STROKE AND THE LINE
The stroke is the way the paint is applied to the picture using the brush. The line is the mark left by the stroke.

DRAWING LINES
These are the lines that allow a linear stroke. They are usually used to do the initial sketch of the picture.

THE FIRST STROKES
These strokes correspond to the initial staining of the picture ground. They are always more thinned with white spirit than the later strokes.

COLOR MASSES
Strokes become color masses when they are grouped together.

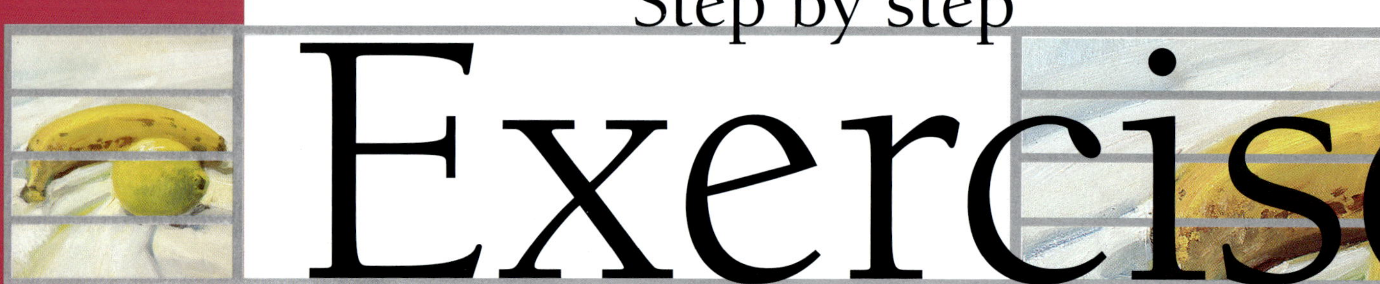

Step by step
Exercises

A BANANA AND A LEMON

We are going to do a straightforward still life composed of two pieces of fruit: a banana and a lemon. It is not a complicated exercise because the color range chosen is very limited: it is based on variations of the colors yellow, green and sienna. Neither the composition nor the drawing will be complicated. However, as we stressed before, it is important to pay attention to this preliminary stage to get the painting right.

Necessary material

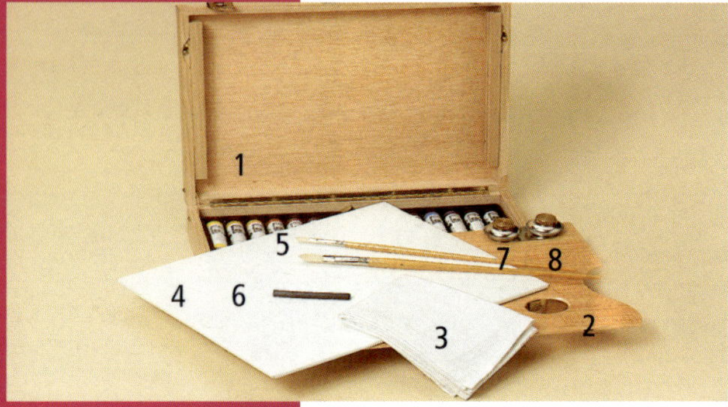

Oil colors (1), a palette (2), a cloth (3), primed card (4), brushes (5), charcoal (6) linseed oil (7), and turpentine oil (8).

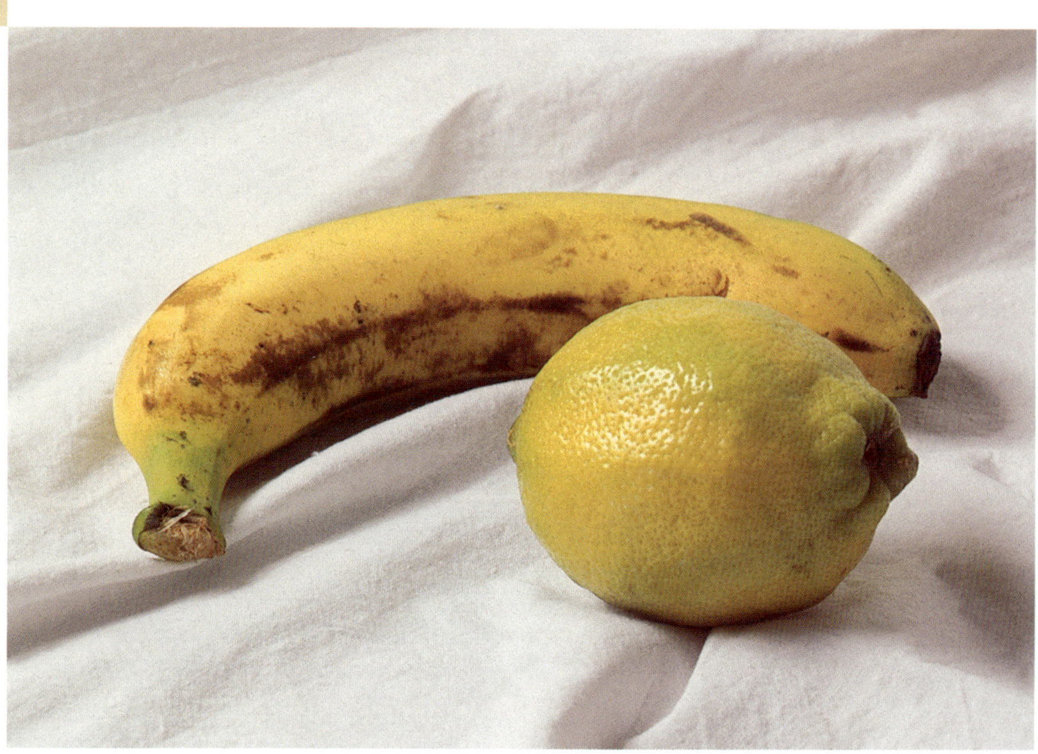

1·The initial sketch is done in charcoal because it allows the picture to be quickly and easily corrected in any of the stages. Just passing a cloth, or even your hand, over is enough to eliminate any zone considered sub-standard.

It is important to work from a perfectly constructed drawing. The more perfected the initial sketch is, the less corrections that will have to be done later. A finished charcoal sketch means that all the zones are perfectly defined, and any possible confusion between distinct parts of the picture is avoided.

2·The colors are started working with very thinned oil colors. Mix white spirit or turpentine oil on the palette to get a low oil paint.
So that you do not soak the picture with turpentine oil or white spirit, add them little by little to the paint.
Drain off the brush so that the color does not run over the ground of the picture. Start to paint the yellow of the banana. Follow the form of its surface, using a stretched, long stroke.

Start to paint the background in a very whitish blue. Here the lines are much longer and are realized insisting with the brush so that the strokes blend together.

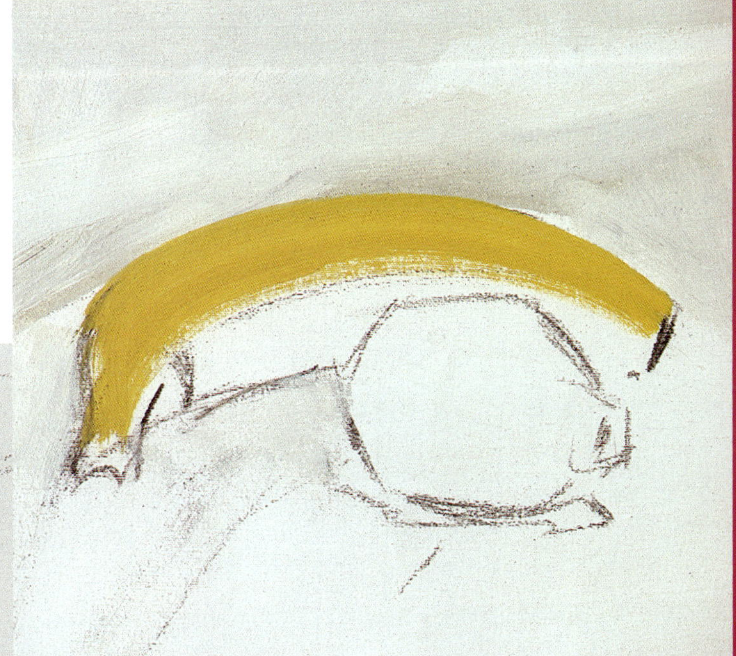

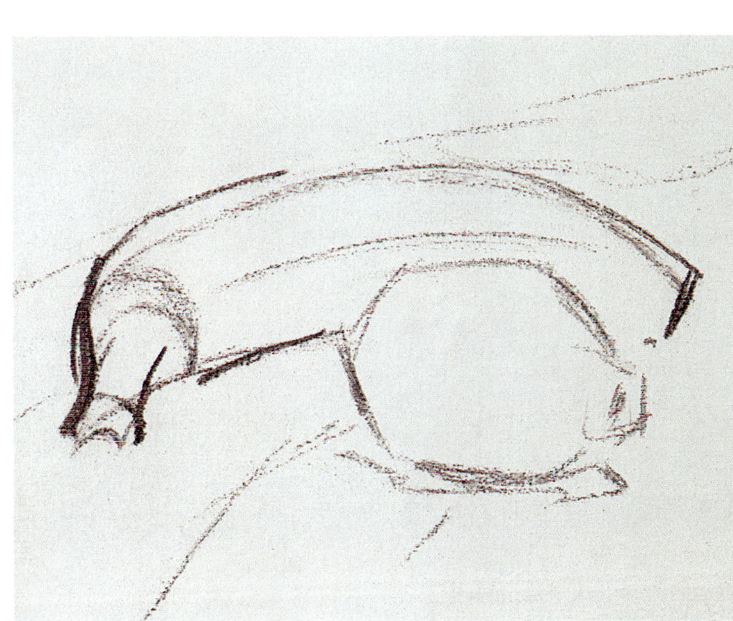

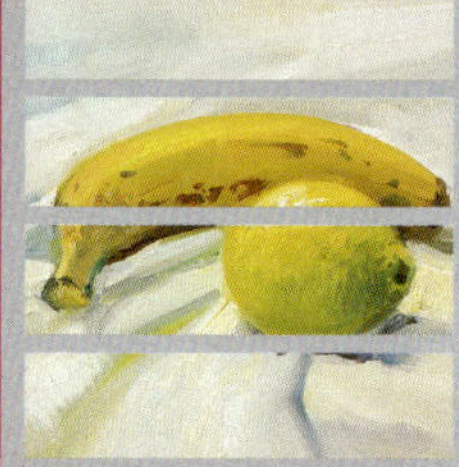

Exercises

3·Continue painting the banana yellow. However, when you come to the part that is to be darkest, add a little sienna, just a dash, enough to lighten the color a shade. This mix is done on the palette and when you have the necessary tone, paint the dark part of the banana. The stroke line is the same as has been used until now: elongated and following the form of the fruit.

In the zone in contact with the most luminous color, insist so that the tones blend together, but without forgetting the intention of the stroke. Start to paint the lemon in a very bright yellow.
In the zone which is to be darkest, use the same yellow mixed with a little green.

4·To get a complete idea of all the colors, paint the picture background. You will then be able to appreciate the contrast effects on the fruit tones and the space that surrounds them.
In this part of the picture, the direction of the line is very related to the plane it forms part of. The dark folds are painted in a very light blue tone, slightly mixed with a touch of yellow. This gives it a greeny look. In some zones the dark lines are vertical, while in other zones they follow the folds of the cloth. However, the lightest parts have completely white and elongated lines.

5·The lemon is finished with quick, rapid strokes that follow the plane of the fruit. Yellow finally imposes itself on the green tone in the shadow zone.

As we have seen in this chapter, it is not a good idea to go over the background stroke too much for this would take away freshness from the whole picture. Use the same blue tone as in the background, mixed with yellow, to get a new color for the shadows. The shadows on the banana are done with long, fresh strokes. Afterwards, do little spots of burnt sienna.

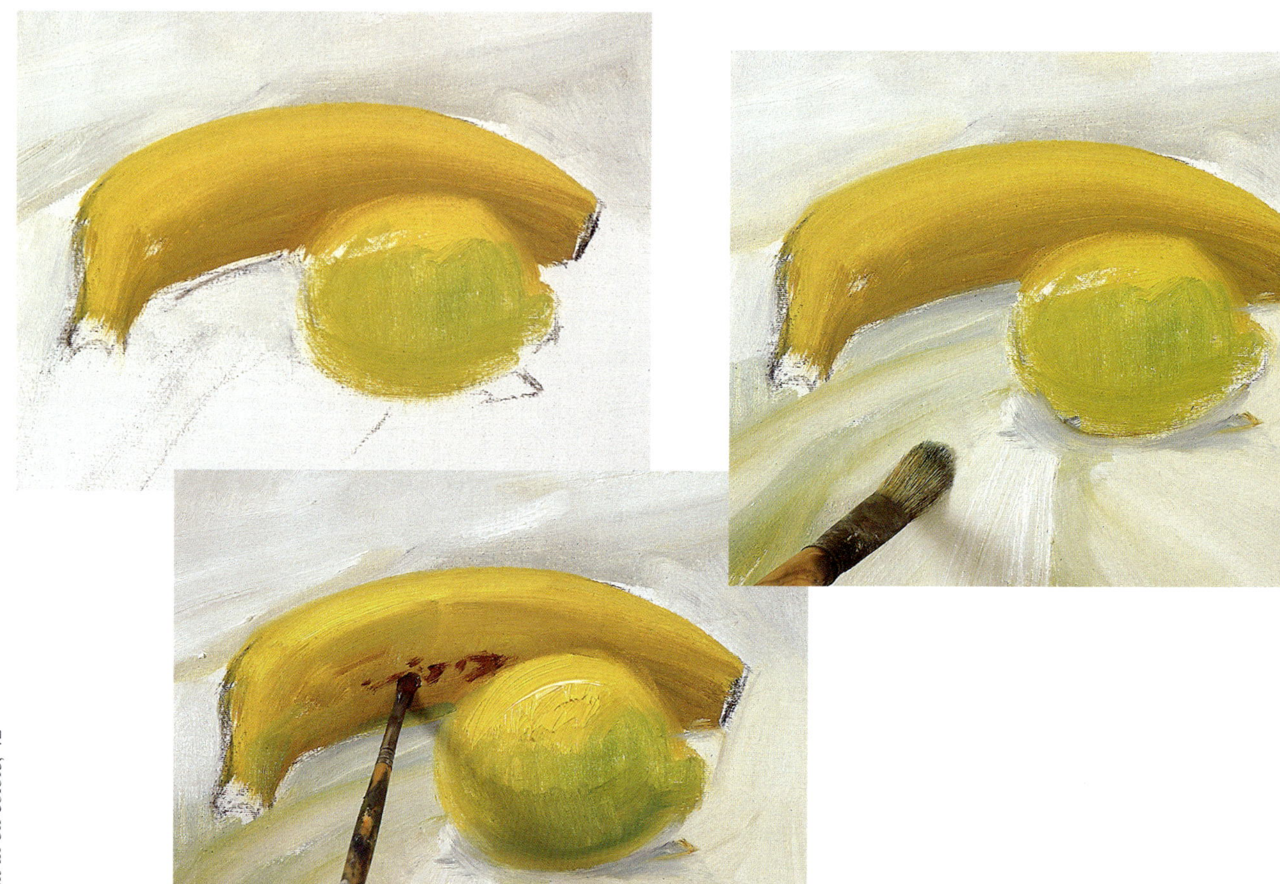

6·The cloth which is the backdrop to the fruit is painted in long strokes towards the central motif of the composition. In this zone increase the contrasts while elsewhere the light tones are left the same.

Paint the dark parts on the fruit, contrasting the most shadowy zones as if they were new planes. You can achieve this by learning how to handle the brush and the stroke. To do the banana the stroke is always long, while for the lemon it is short and follows its own curve.

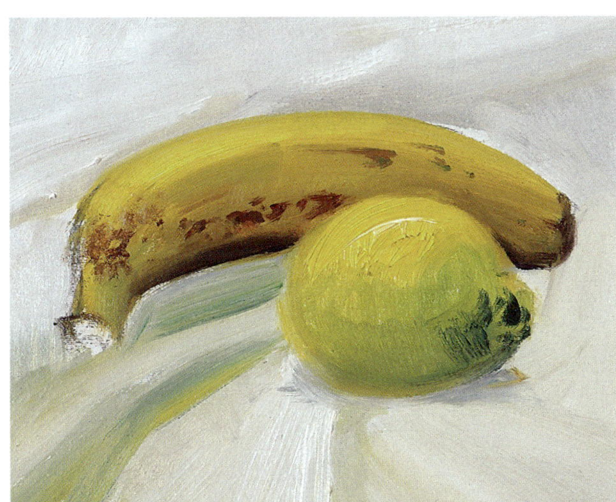

7·The stroke must become tighter as you advance, making an effort not to make the picture too pasty. If there is too much paint, it can be taken away by using a clean brush to put it back on the palette.

The outline of the forms is achieved by small contrasts working in combination with the line.

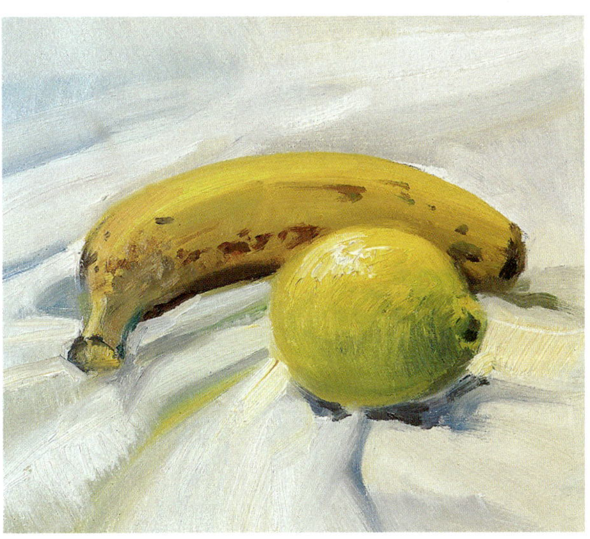

Summary

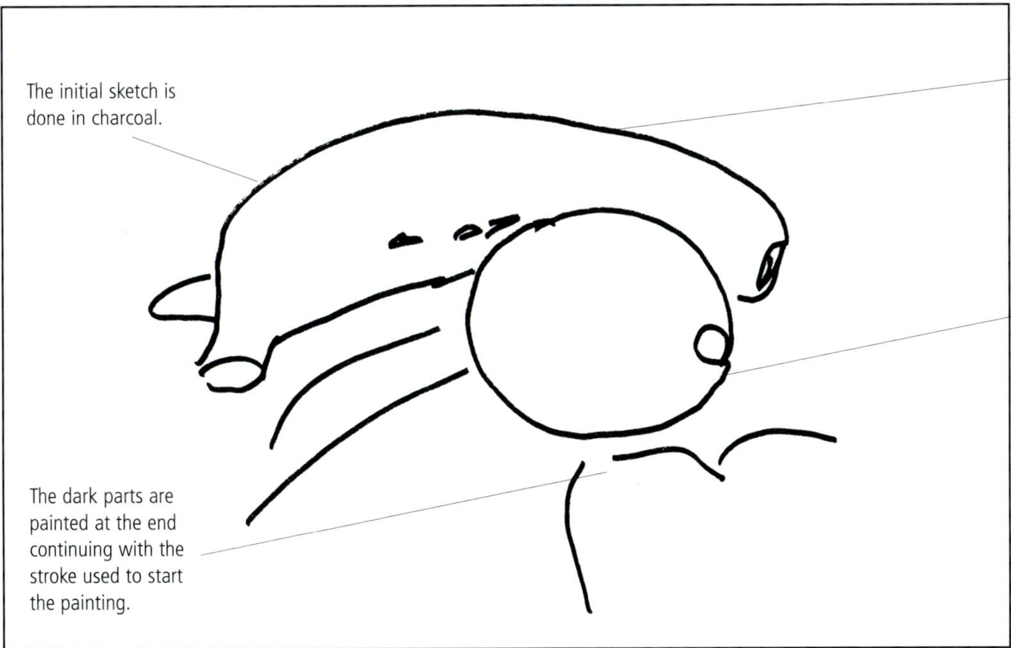

Chapter 4

The properties of the oil color brush stroke

When painting with oil color the picture can require that a stroke allows the blending of two colors. Other colors, however, will have to be superimposed.

When oil colors are applied, as we have studied so far, the first layers are done more thinned with turpentine oil, but the quantity is reduced as the picture advances. From this chapter onwards, not only will we use turpentine oil but also linseed oil will be incorporated as a normal liquid medium for making later layers more fluid.

Turpentine oil and linseed oil together with the containers to be placed on the palette. From this chapter onwards both products will be used.

Turpentine oil and linseed oil next to the recipients. They must be placed at one end of the palette. From this chapter onwards both substances will be used

Thick on thin

In the first tests carried out on oil colors we included turpentine oil as a medium for thinning the color in the first layers. Linseed oil was named as a material but it was never explained how to use it. This calculated omission was provoked by the desire to familiarize the learner with the possibility of diluting the oil colors, above all in the first stages which correspond to the laying down of a uniform field of paint called the ground and then the blocking in of shapes. The following layers are done without any liquid painting medium (like turpentine oil).

However, later on there could arise the necessity to have a more flowing or mobile quality in a layer that does not need turpentine oil. In this case it is necessary to use linseed oil as a dissolvent or a mixture of the two mediums if the work is half way between a thinned color and a thicker one.

Progressive thinning

The new information given in the following chapters will enable you to advance in the techniques and to see how your possibilities are increasing. In this chapter we go back to the subject of thinned paint but with the added interest that during the process we are going to switch to linseed oil or pure oil.

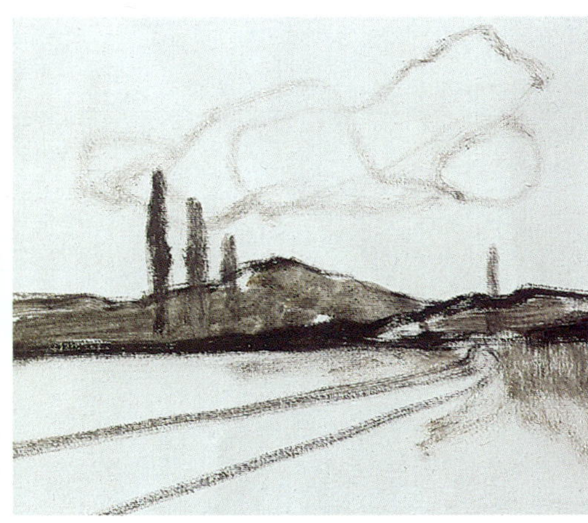

Using the brush dipped in oil color, draw directly on the picture.

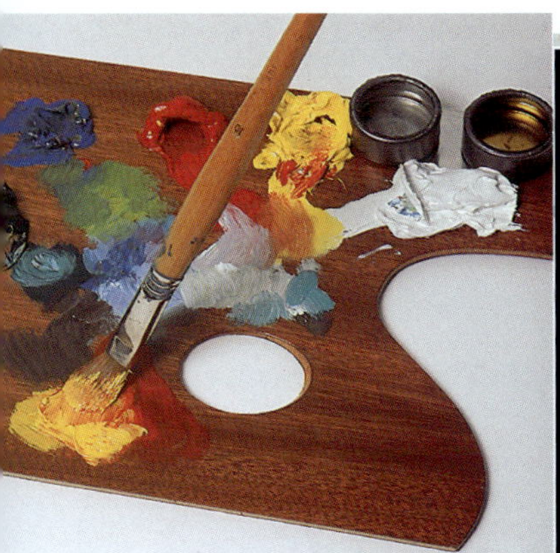

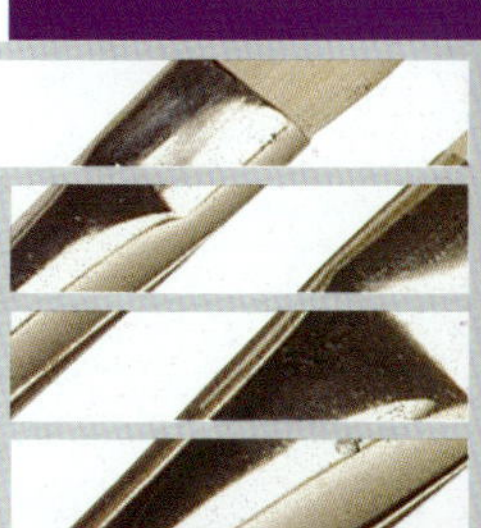

The equilibrium of the mix

You have to know how to get an equilibrium between the use of linseed oil and turpentine oil. At first it may be tricky fine tuning the balance, but with a little practice you will soon pick it up.

The following may be a good procedure: the sketch and the first color field are done as we have been doing up to now, with the color completely thinned. However, it does not soak the picture. The following strokes are done with a dash of turpentine oil and linseed oil. In the final stages of the picture turpentine oil is put to one side and linseed oil alone is used, provided that you want to obtain flowing, mobile colors.

Linseed oil allows the picture to advance with flowing colors which otherwise would have to be applied in a paste like state.

Leaving out the charcoal

The line from the well-drained brush when the paint is thinned can be very similar to any of the normal drawing methods. This means, depending on the subject chosen, the pencil or charcoal can be omitted. This is the case with landscape.

In this exercise we will use neither charcoal nor pencil. A fine hog's hair brush dipped in turpentine oil with a little dark color will suffice. So that the picture is not soaked, absorb some of the moistness on the brush by squeezing it with a cloth. When the brush is drained you can start to draw, redoing and correcting the lines as many times as necessary. If you want to rub out an entire area, apply a cloth wetted in turpentine oil. Do not soak the picture.

The thinned field.

On top of the sketch done in oil colors, paint with thinned colors but not too flowing to avoid them running over the picture surface.

To thin a color it is not necessary to make it totally flowing, or to prepare a great quantity. The simplest way is to add the turpentine oil as you go along, as it becomes necessary. Thinned colors do not shine once they have dried, and their chromatic effects compare unfavorably with pure oil colors. This is why when doing fields with thinned colors the best oil colors do not have to be used. Cadmiums, for example, are expensive colors and it would be a waste to do a ground with these colors. The best plan is to use simple tones and colors to do the ground and then begin building up images with colors less thinned and of higher quality.

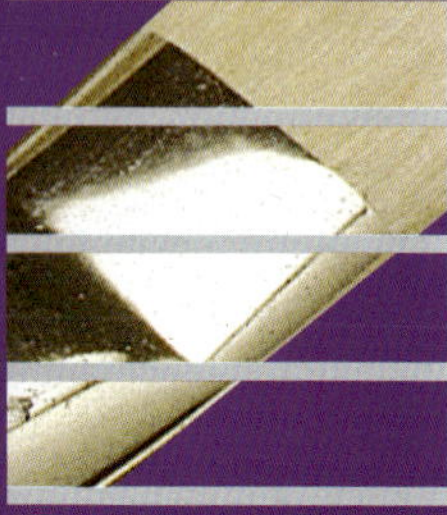

How to thin and make the color oily.

The containers for the linseed oil and the turpentine oil are clipped to one end of the palette.

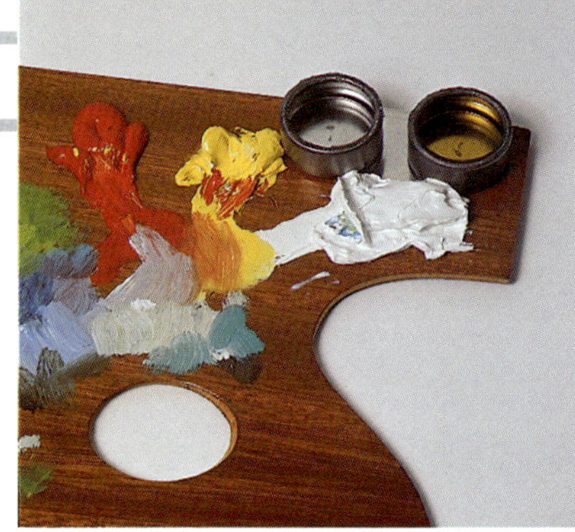

To thin any color with turpentine oil it is sufficient just to dip the brush and apply it to the color deposited on the palette until it is diluted.

In previous chapters we have studied how oil colors are soluble in turpentine oil, and that the first layers have to be painted using this product on the paint. This can be a quick process: all you have to do is dip the brush in the turpentine oil and mix it with the color until it is sufficiently flowing or diluted. As you advance with the painting, the colors are mixed less and less with turpentine oil, and its place is taken by linseed oil, which is the most widely used oil in oil painting as it allows the colors to be flowing, mobile and transparent, but maintaining the drying style of the paint.

Some of the linseed oils commercialized include a siccative -this is a liquid drier which accelerates drying. It is recommendable to use well-known brands sold in fine arts shops because they guarantee the purity and transparency of the oil, and if they include siccative, the right quantity of this too.

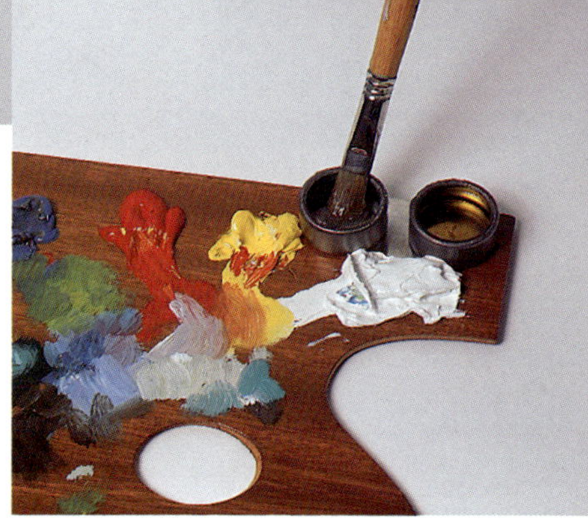

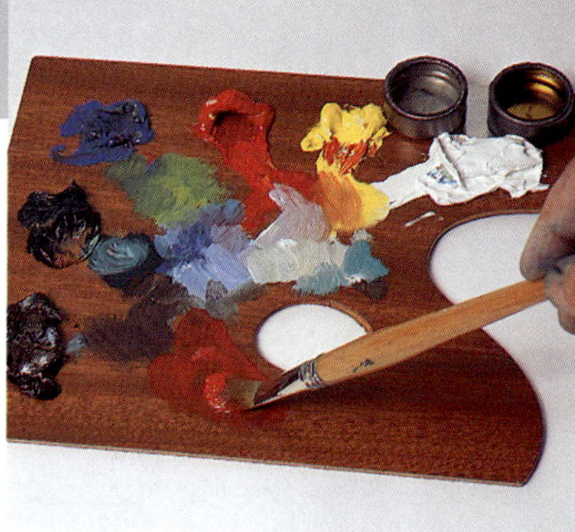

After dipping the brush in linseed oil the color immediately becomes more flowing and mobile, just as is required after the first thinned layers.

Applying the thick brush stroke

You must calculate the quantity of thinner sufficiently well so that on top of a layer of oil color from the tube (paint without adding either white spirit nor linseed oil) you do not have to paint any stroke of thinned paint. As the ground is put down on the support, the quantity of turpentine oil will diminish and it is replaced by pure oil color. Neither is it recommendable to lay down layers of pure oil color before thinned paint because this would break the rule of thick on top of thinned. If you want to do a transparent layer immediately after the thinned layer, you must obtain a mix of turpentine oil and linseed oil. To do this you only need take a little of both on the brush, put them on the palette and add oil color with the same brush.

One brush stroke next to another

The ground of the picture is an opportunity to work more closely on the strokes. The ground provides a base of gentle color on which to build images. Then there are masses of light and dark colors, and then eventually forms are defined. When this point is reached, if you have followed the process as explained, the strokes can be pastier than before and the colors superimposed purer and more luminous. The final strokes of this landscape are those of the grass in the foreground and the yellow highlights of the clouds.

There is another important question which can be appreciated in this straightforward landscape exercise: if you look at the background you will see that the darks have been painted last; this is part of the correct oil painting process.

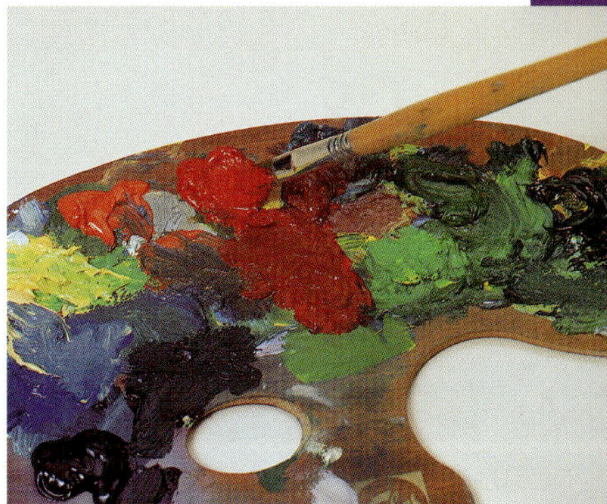

The turpentine oil is only used in the first layers, adding it to the color as needed.

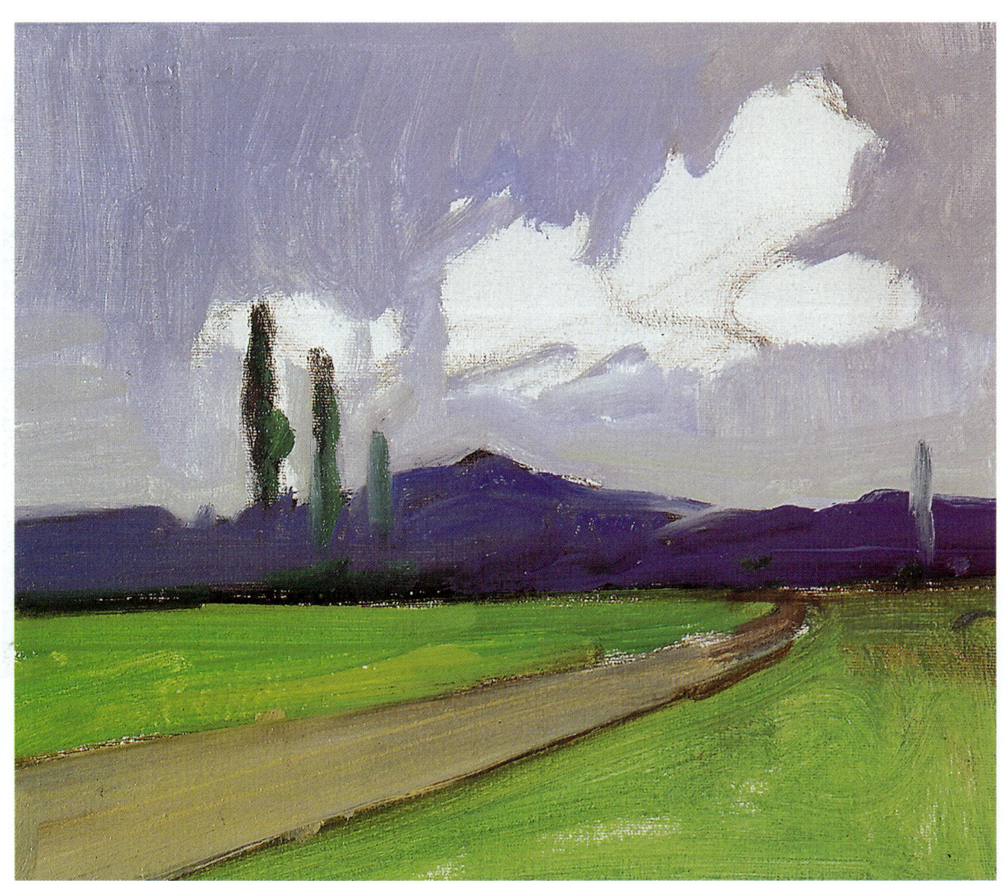

The thinned ground is painted on top of the initial sketch. Even in little quantities the turpentine oil dims the luminosity of the colors, but it will come back when colors are laid down unthinned.

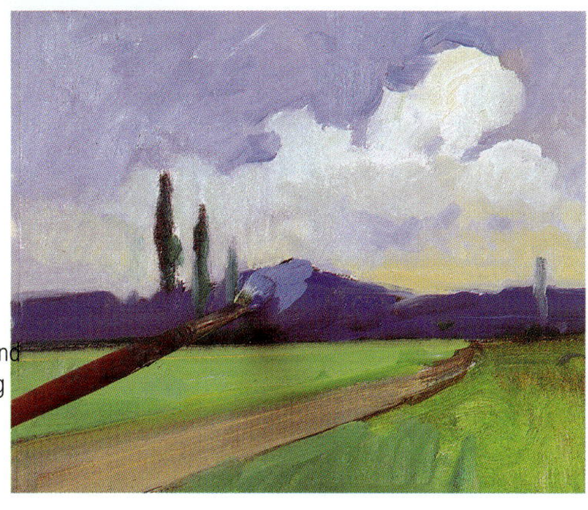

The layers that come after the thinned ground get purer and more luminous. Before adding linseed oil to the paint the colors without additives must be applied.

Dark colors, above all black, must not be painted under more luminous colors. The difference in drying between layers would produce cracks.

Rapid strokes

The transition from the ground to stroke can be elaborate or, in contrast, rapid and spontaneous. Just because you insist on the picture does not mean that the result will be better. Often all you achieve is to spoil the painting completely.

As we have seen before, laying the ground down involves different steps, among which the thinned paint stage stands out and then the application of details. The distinct process should give rise to an intermediate stage in which straightforward techniques are combined to create highly interesting plastic effects. In the last chapter we did a tree trunk to study the line. Now we are going to do a similar exercise but the elaboration will be completely different. The priority is to take advantage of the ground so that it peeks through the strokes.

The picture ground

The picture ground can be done in various ways. The quantity of white spirit used in this first intervention can vary. You can put down the color base by dragging, with the brush almost dry, or you can exploit the humidity of the liquid medium, giving a certain texture to the picture. Thus the painting acquires different plastic values (a plastic value being the expressive capacity of a recourse, like, for example, grounds, lines, or any other effect done on the paint).con otras pinceladas menos aguarrasadas y que contrastan en luminosidad con las primeras.

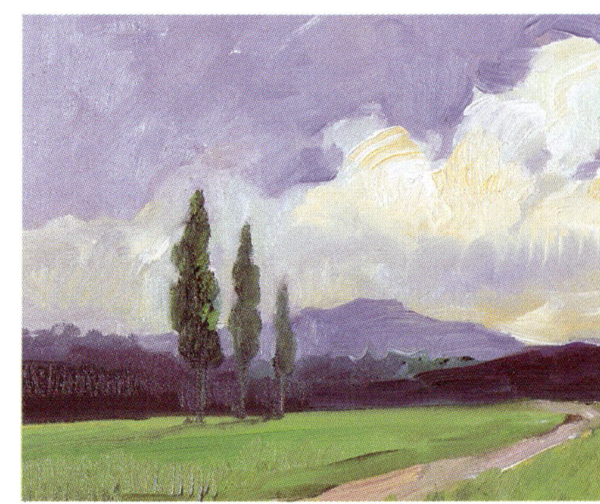

The detailed strokes are the last to be done, once the color ground has been finished.

Be careful with too flowing oil color

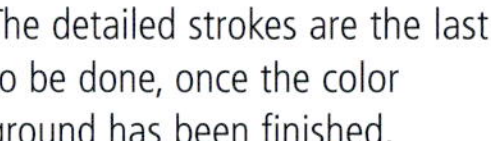

Be careful with too flowing oil color.
Oil colors when liquid are difficult to handle for they lack body and you cannot paint with the brush very loaded: the quantity of oil color put on the picture has to be minimum so that it does not run on the surface.
A very flowing color has to be painted on dry or almost dry lower layers, otherwise it would soak the painting.
When linseed oil is mixed with the oil color it must be done in minimum quantities. Saturating the paint with linseed oil would, among other setbacks, cause the color surface to wrinkle once it is dry. Remember that oil colors already contain linseed oil.

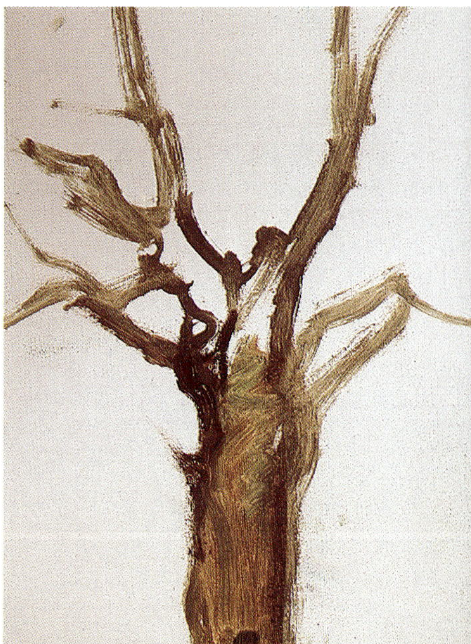

After doing the fundamental lines of the tree, paint its interior with several color intensities; some strokes can be completely transparent and others less so. The colors used will be sienna, sepia and burnt umber.

To paint this tree thinned oil color is used directly but not as a uniform layer of color. It is painted in different intensities, alternating the transparency of the thinned oil color with other more loaded strokes, the luminosity of which contrasts with the first strokes.

Covering all the surface

Just like in previous exercises, as the picture elaboration progresses, the strokes become denser, darker and more compact. Do some dark strokes on the side of the picture and some more luminous ones in the other areas. In all the lower zone the thinned background peeks through.

Going back to the color ground: it is important to cover all the surface so that the true contrasts between the principal color masses and the background can be appreciated. Although the background color is light it is fundamental to paint it because the contrast created will be very different to the completely white original ground.

Detailing strokes

Even the quickest pieces require a well organized process. The series of color layers laid down become increasingly defined and end up as perfectly located strokes that build up the image and the objects.

Burnt umber is used to do the branches of the darkest parts. The strokes can be free but perfectly defined. Now, in this zone, the stroke is no longer thinned but much more dense and pasty as we have studied throughout this chapter. To finish this exercise, different intensities of green are mixed with some of the darkest strokes.

As you can see in the finished result of this exercise, some of the colors painted very thinned at the beginning have been left just as they were on the lower part of the trunk.

Until all the picture is covered you cannot appreciate the true contrasts between the colors and the tones.

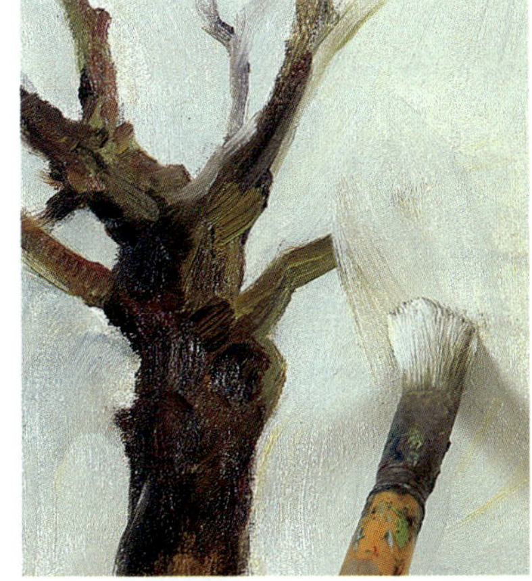

In this close up you can appreciate the stroke style on one of the finished branches.

Although darks have been applied to define and complete the tree, in the lower zone the thinned color painted at the beginning peeks through.

Summary

THIN THE COLOR AND ADD LINSEED OIL
The oil color of the first layers must have more turpentine oil. As you progress with the picture, gradually use less and paint with purer paint. The final layers are painted with little linseed oil.

DRAWING WITH OIL COLOR
Thinned paint allows you to draw directly with the brush.

STROKES ON TOP OF THE GROUND
Once a ground has been painted you can continue with more detailed, defining and contrasting strokes.

DETAILS IN THE STROKES
The highlights and details must be done at the end of the session.

Exercises

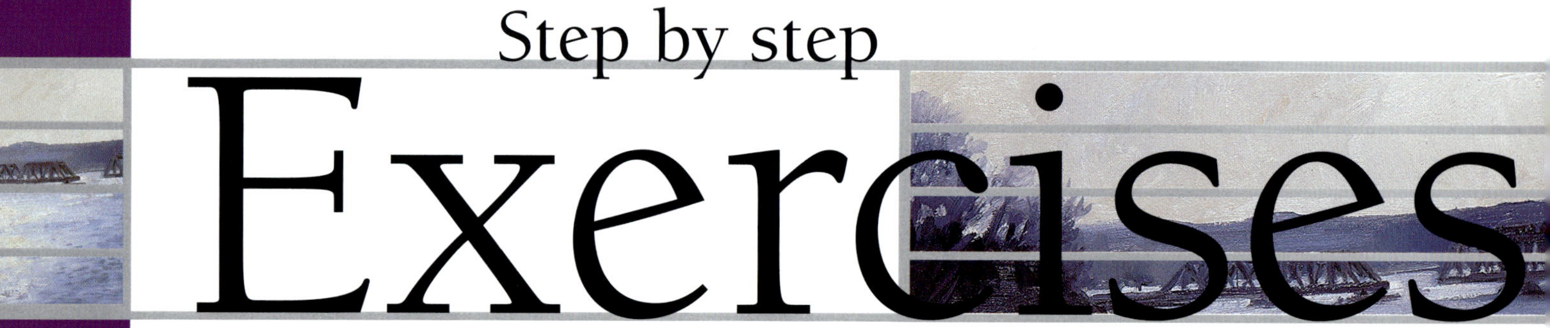

RIVER LANDSCAPE

Now we are going to do a river landscape. It is an exercise so straightforward that it w
be easy to do the diagrammatic drawing and the composition. Choosing a subject
simple enables us to study in depth the technical process of oil painting, from t
elaboration of the initial sketch to the realization of the final details; from the ground
the strokes, or, what is the same, from a general level to the details. This concept will
the guiding principle for later oil color works. Therefore, it is recommendable to p
attention to the stroke style and the application of thinned or purer layers of oil col

Necessary material

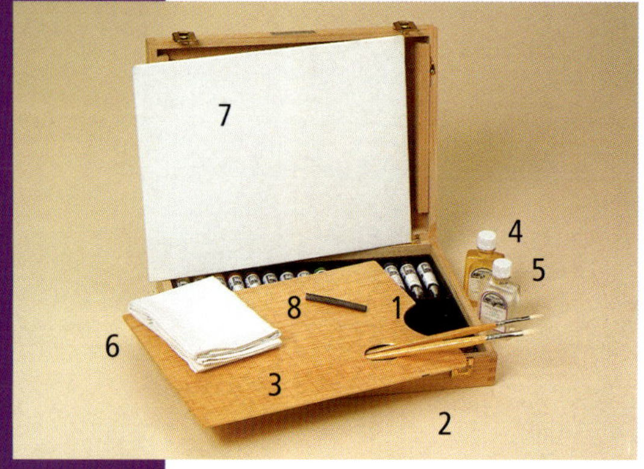

Oil colors (1), brushes (2), palette (3), linseed oil (4), turpentine oil (5), a cloth (6), primed card (7), and charcoal (8).

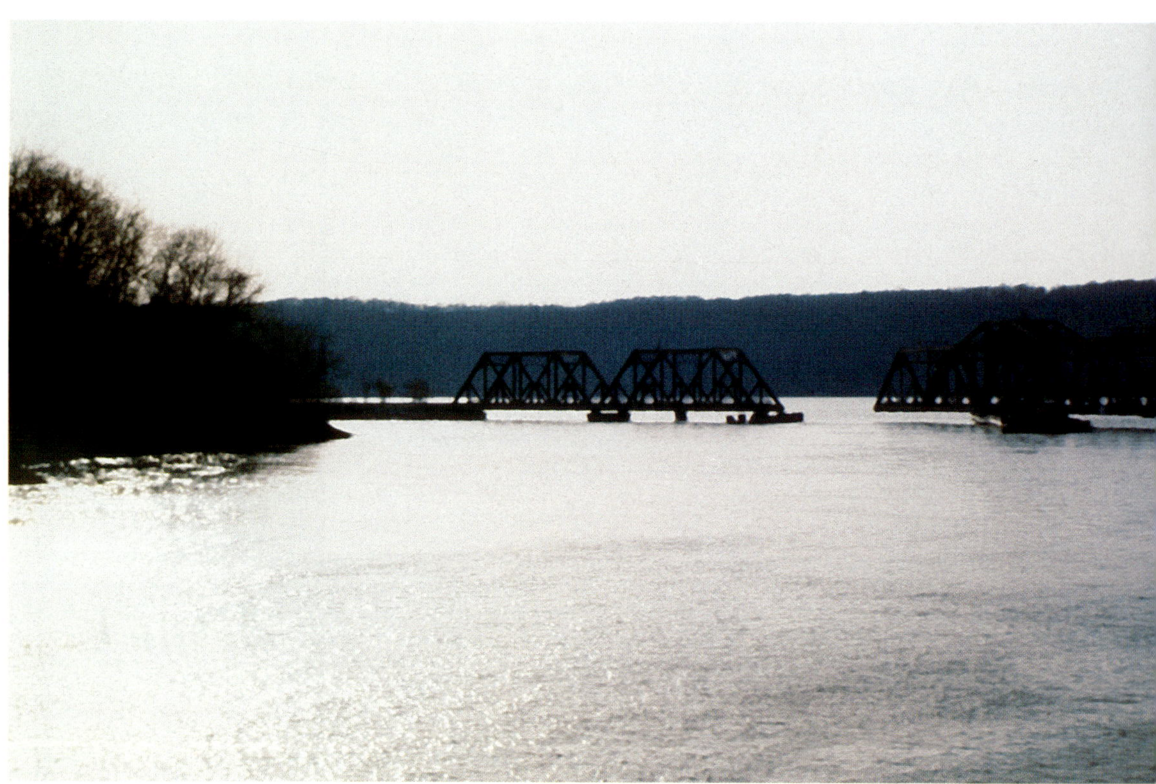

1·Although throughout this chapter we have worked directly in oil colors here we are going to use charcoal to place the horizon line and the mountains in the background. Use the charcoal flat to get a long, completely straight stroke, although somewhat broken. The charcoal point gives the result we are looking for.

Once these simple forms have been sketched, outline the bridges and the trees on the left.

2·The structure of this picture is so simple it permits the ground to be painted rapidly and without complications. From the beginning it is important to bear in mind which contrasts are going to stand out in the painting.

Do the mountains in the background using a thinned but not too flowing oil color because you must avoid the paint running on the surface. The mass of vegetation on the left is done with a darker color, less thinned and flowing. There is also a dark part on the right. This layer of color is superimposed on top of the thinned blue in the background.

All the sky zone is painted in a whitish tone. As part of it is going to remain as it is now, it is painted definitively without thinner. To make the tone more flowing, add a few drops of linseed oil.

3·The contrasts among the vegetation are done in marine blue and cobalt blue tones. When painting this zone part of the white color in the background is dragged by the stroke.

Start to paint the water in a bluish white color. This will be the part of the landscape painting which will experience most changes and receive the most layers of color. The first layer, which effectively covers all the area, is painted quite thinned, mixing different tones of blue, green and white. The strokes must be long and horizontal

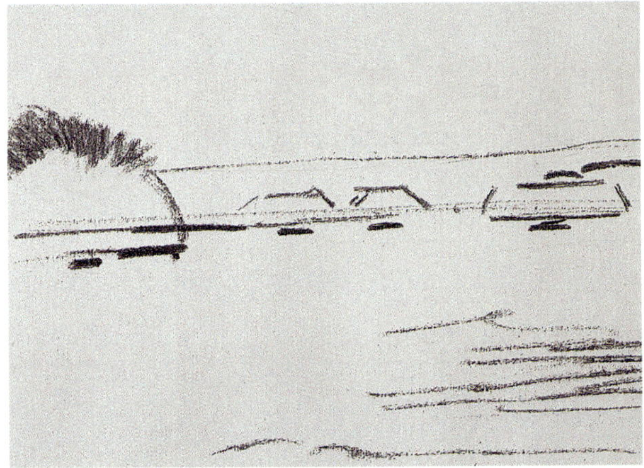

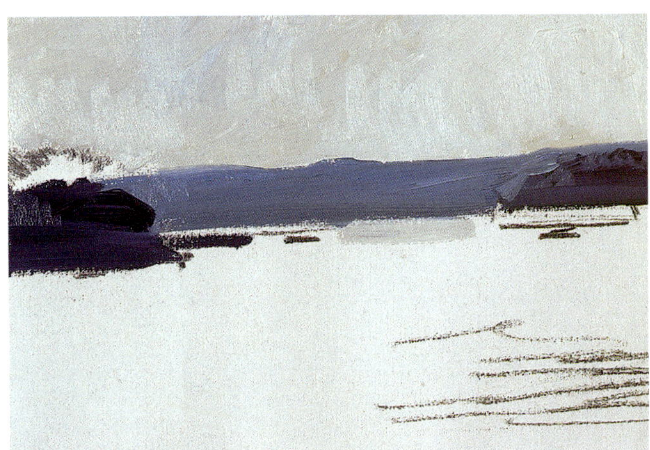

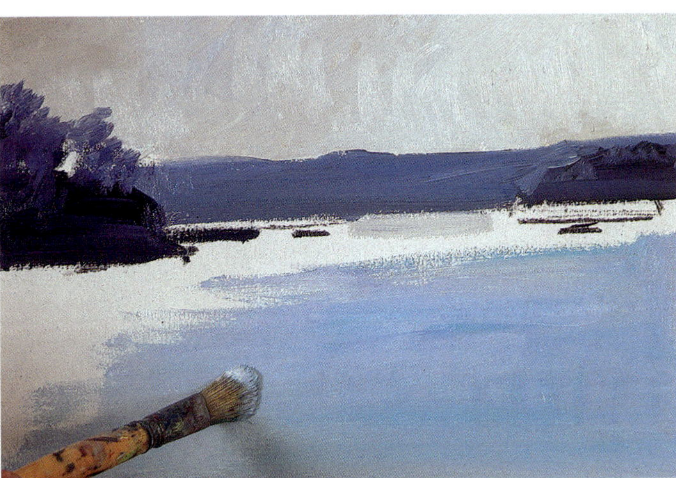

Exercises

4·Let's go back to dedicate some attention to the river and the banks, where the trees are worked on using strokes more defined than the previous ones. The tone dragged in the last application is now usable as a background for these new strokes.

This time we paint on top of water with a much denser, white stroke. Start in the upper zone and go on until you come to the lower, blue, part. On top of the blue ground, paint very dark tones with little thinner. The strokes are mixed on top of the background by doing repeated passes.

5·All the grounds on the picture are now completed. From no on all the color mixes and new additions will not contain thinner but will be painted with the density of the oil colors that come out of the tube.

Do several dark blue strokes, unequal, in the darkest part of the water. Some strokes are short, others long but all of them blend together in the tones of the underpainting. If the color is too thick you can use a little linseed oil: a minimal quantity, however.

6·Continue working on the strokes on the water surface, adding dark and light tones and varying the stroke so as to get an intense luminous, contrasting effect.

The strokes realized next to the most luminous water zone are short and are mixed softly with the luminous background tone. Use the brush loaded with an off-whitish blue to draw the structural lines of the bridges.

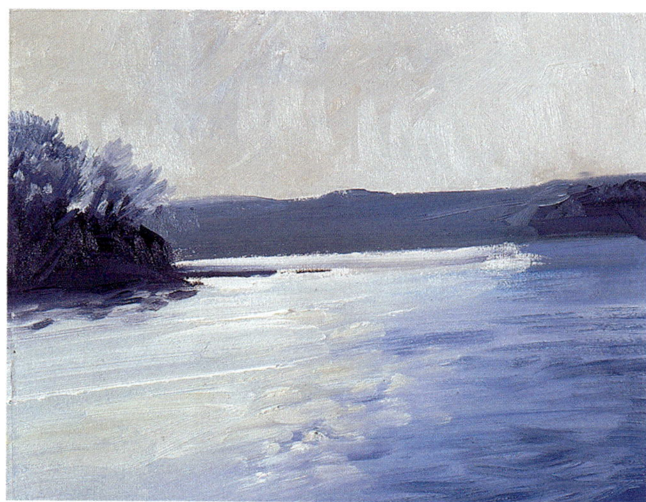

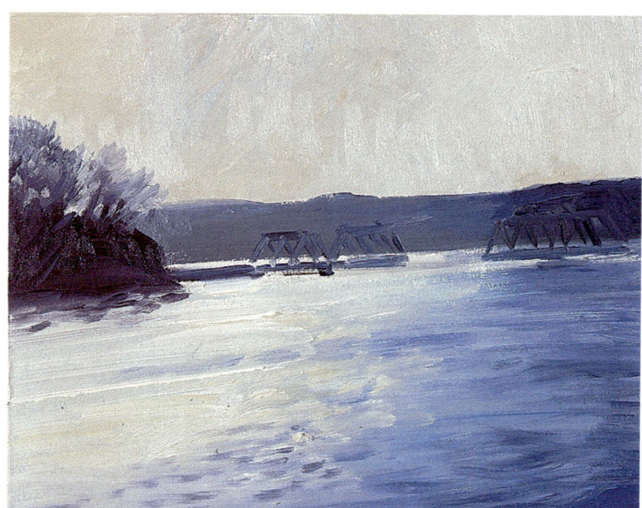

7·Continue working on the water surface. The strokes are now smaller and more detailed, not too loaded with color, just enough so as to slightly change the tone of the layer below.

The bridge on the right is redone with straight strokes depicting its iron structure.

8·The detailed work is now focused on the elaboration of the trees. Do short strokes that mix on top of the background but do not insist too much so as not to obliterate the line. The bridges are finished with straight dark strokes superimposed on top of the previous ones.

To round off this landscape, paint the most luminous zone of the water in a dense white. Place defined highlights that contrast with the blue strokes of the reflections.

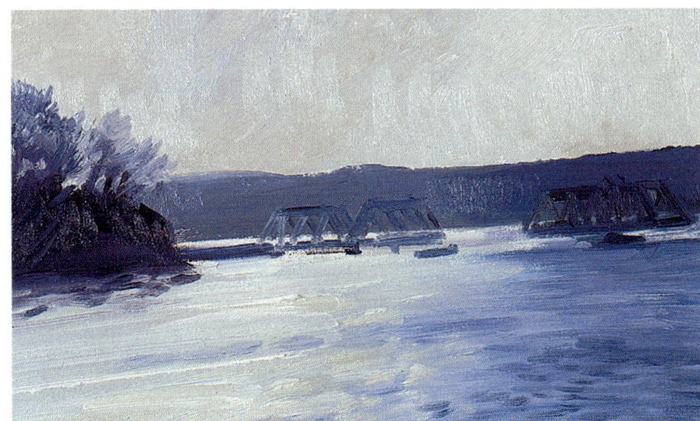

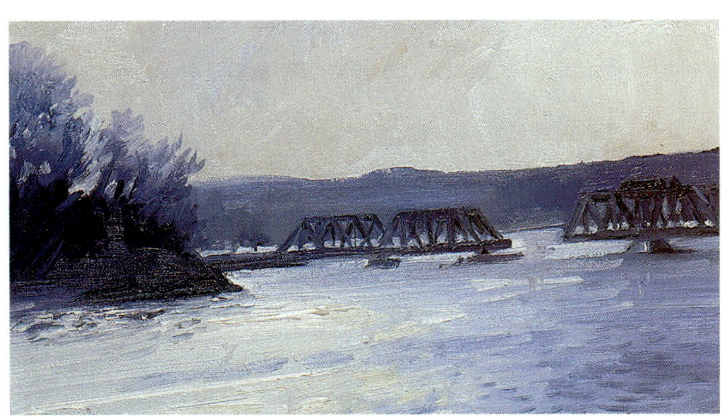

Summary

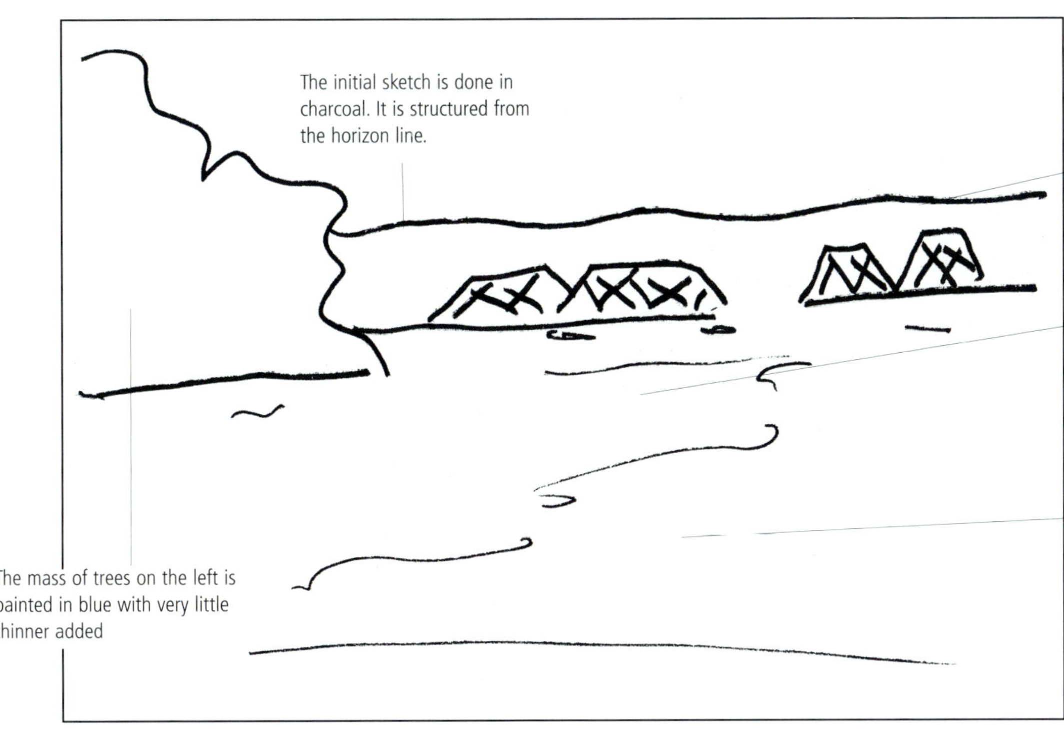

Chapter 5

The cool range

With any range, for example the cool range, you can easily develop the color tones without the colors becoming dirtied.

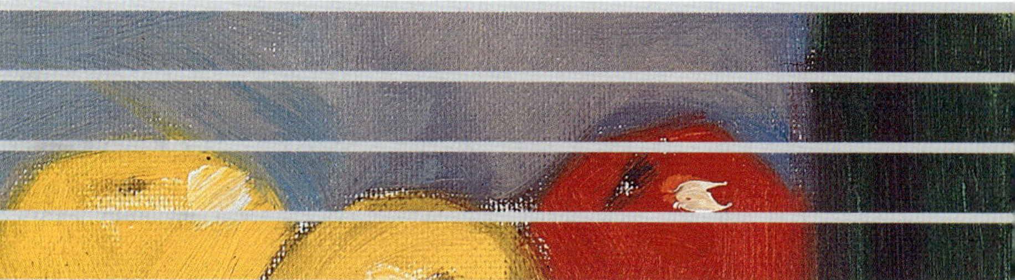

Once we have learnt how to mix the colors on the palette and we are aware of the results of mixing the colors together, we must start to paint. Choosing a particular color range enables us to concentrate on the painting itself without the color getting in the way of our learning process. The stroke and gesture are two of the principal resources on which a painter falls back to elaborate their work and to give it their own personal style. In this chapter we will study the picture ground, the strokes and the use of the colors in the cool range.

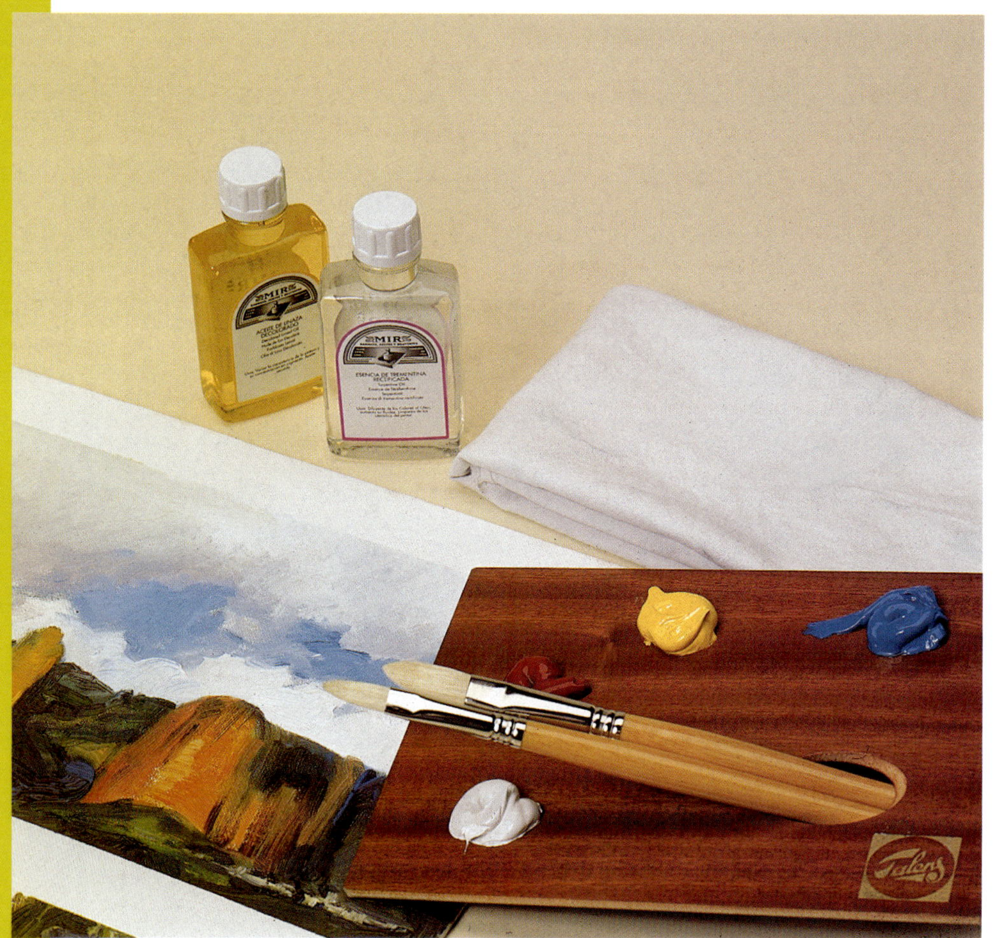

Oil painting is done according to an ordered process. The painter must always have turpentine oil and linseed oil available.

How oil colors dry

Oil color are a dense painting medium, opaque and oily. They are mainly composed of selected refined linseed oil and dry powder pigments. Given its oily composition it is logical to think that a special dissolvent is necessary to thin the color on the palette and on the picture: turpentine oil is used for painting and for cleaning the brushes and palette as well.

Before continuing laying down colors it is recommendable to know how oil colors dry and it will then be easy to understand the correct procedure for effective painting. Oil colors dry extremely slowly because, in contrast to other painting mediums like watercolor, tempera or acrylic, they do not dry by evaporation -they do not contain water- but by oxidation on the surface in contact with the air. Therefore thicker layers firstly dry on the surface and then afterwards the interior dries. Thinner layers more or less dry simultaneously on the surface and underneath.

From thin to thick

You must always paint from thin to thick. This means the first strokes must contain a greater quantity of turpentine oil. The thinning is done on the palette. Firstly dip the brush in the turpentine oil and then drag the color to the center of the palette, stirring it to unify the mix. The thinned color obtained is then used to paint, but be sure to drain it off because it must not drip on the picture. The brush can be drained off over the palette or over a cloth.la pincelada no tiene que buscar la The

Progressive work

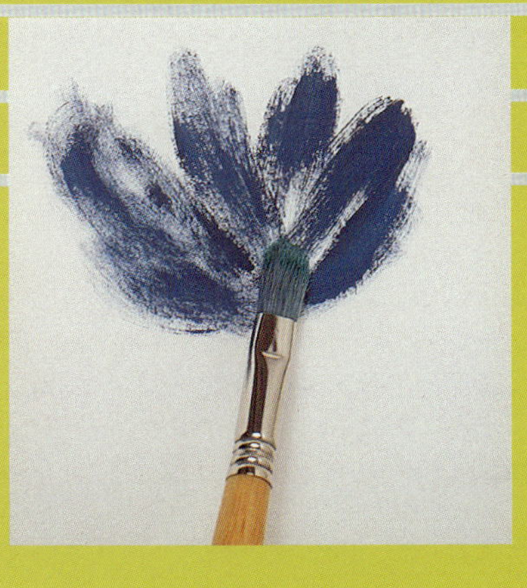

The thinned color must be the first layer painted on the picture.

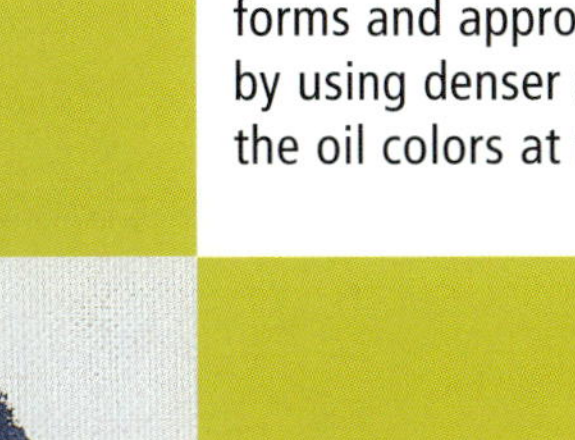

Once the color base has been put down, you can start to define the forms and approximate the colors by using denser strokes. However, the oil colors at this stage still

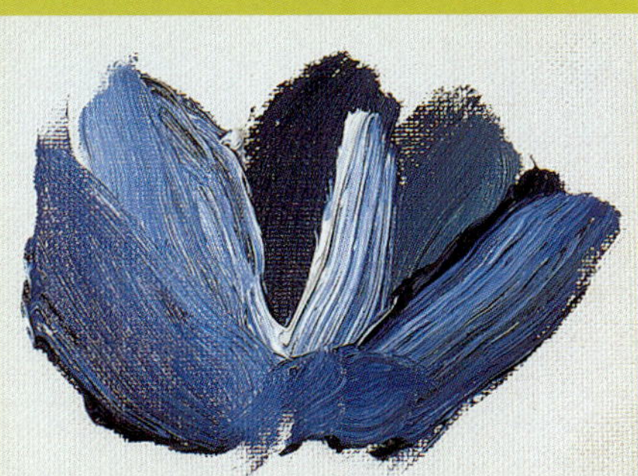

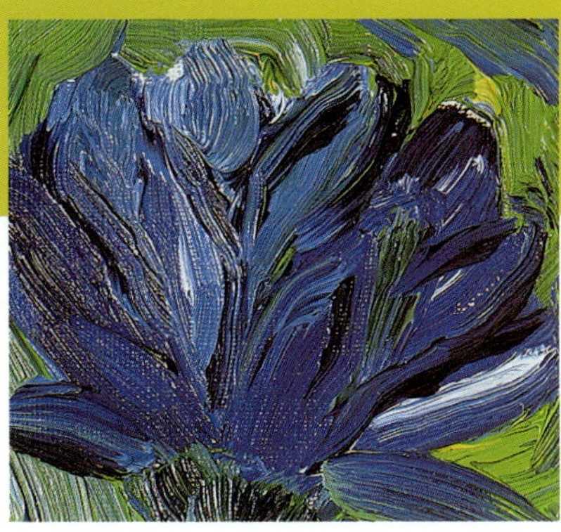

Starting from the color mass define the form with new strokes and apply the definitive tones.

intention of the thinned color mass is to insinuate the form on the picture. The stroke does not have to try to completely define the form but only to roughly indicate how it will finally be. On many occasions an oil painting does not have to be drawn in charcoal first. It can be drawn directly in a very thinned oil color and then on top of this color you start to paint in denser strokes containing less white spirit.

Denser layers

After having applied the first free strokes and thinned layers of color, you can start to apply denser strokes that are closer to the definitive forms. In oil painting the strokes and lines must always be progressive and you should not look for detail with your first touches. Just as the first color masses and grounds are only trying to establish vague forms, the colors and tones applied in the beginning are only approximate and not definitive.

Remember that you can always go back to an oil painting, so it is safer to do progressive work, both with forms and with colors.

Detailed strokes

Forms come most easily by working on the line and color of the previous strokes. On top of oil colors you can add both light and dark colors because, as we have already explained, it is a dense, opaque medium.

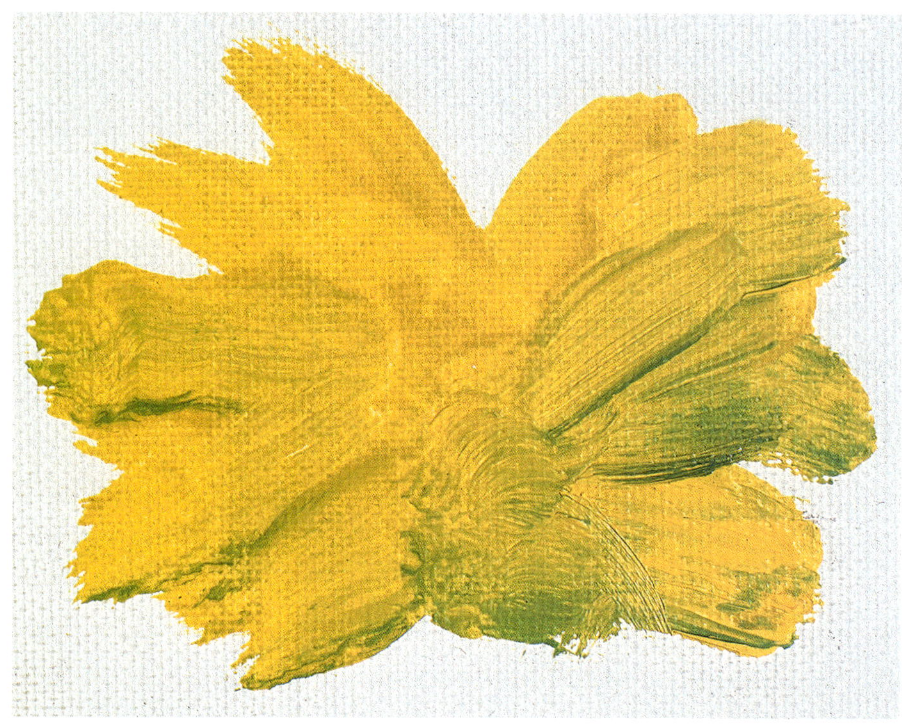

The free strokes define with just one line each plane. On top of these strokes paint in green. If you paint repeatedly the colors will blend.

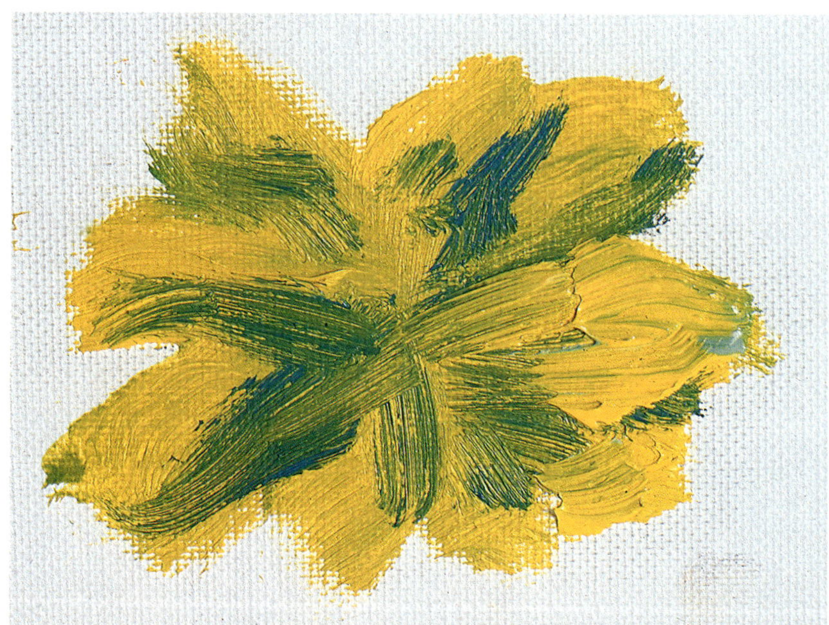

After the color masses have outlined the form, it is important to control the line and stroke.

As the form becomes more complete you can apply more detailed strokes and tones that define the contrasts.

The direction of the strokes and the lines

Given the consistency of oil colors, the stroke is dense and pliable. The brush always leaves the mark of its bristles on the picture surface, which means that depending on how you paint, press the brush and the amount of oil color loaded, you can also model the form at the same time.

When laying down the first color ground the direction of the stroke is not very important because as the oil color is thinned it works superficially. Once the shapes and objects are roughly blocked in, the denser strokes can model the form of the object painted. For example, we are going to paint a simple flower. Firstly put down a thinned color mass and then you can start to paint in a denser color, less loaded with white spirit. The stroke now begins to come into play. Each line, and they can now be superimposed on top of each other, marks a petal.

Lines and tones. As the work advances, new tones are superimposed on top of the initial tone. Here the stroke is just as important. The new lines must follow the direction of the initial strokes and they must also superimpose a new tone. The lower color is stained by the new color. If you pass the brush over the background repeatedly, the colors can end up blending.

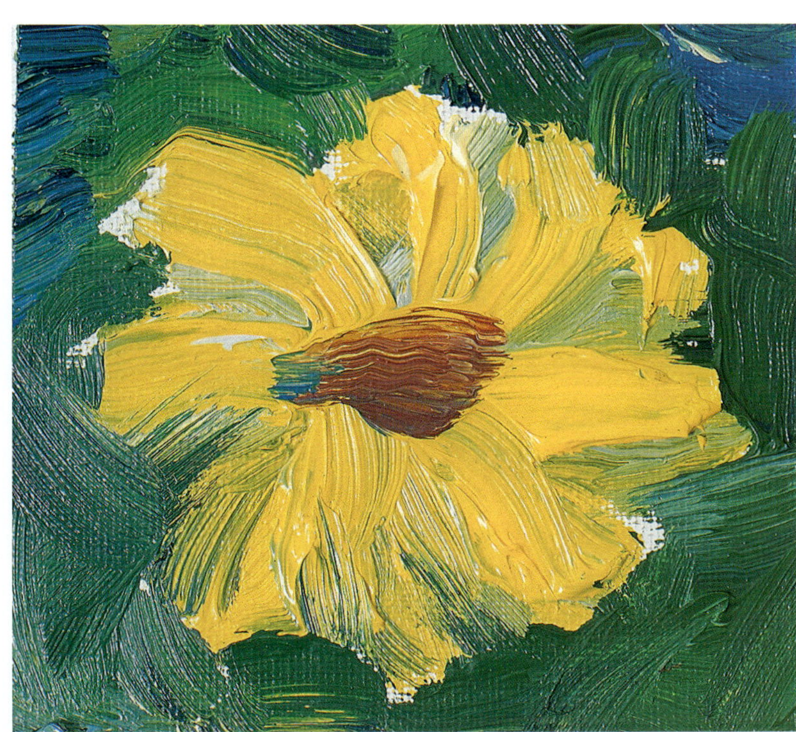

The last strokes give the definitive form to the flower. Finally, use free and oily strokes to finish the background.

How the stroke dries

When a stroke starts out very thick and is continually dragged until the line becomes fine, the drying process begins on all the surface. Logically, the thickest zone will take longer to dry then the thinnest one.
When doing the color ground in oil color it is always important to start the painting with little color on the brush.

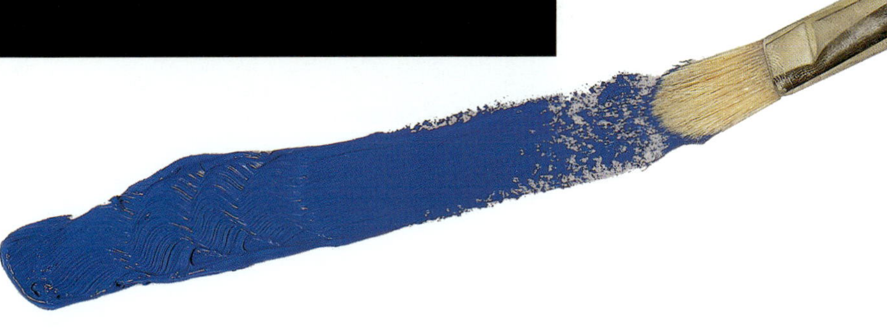

The finish and the line

As the painting advances, the line models the form being painted. Each line defines a new plane. The background is painted with free strokes when it is not necessary that they define a concrete form. These strokes, and the different tones, can contrast with the main colors. Once the ground is down, new colors can be introduced into the picture, the new tones dragging part of the lower colors.

The color masses

So that the forms are painted correctly it is very important to follow a structured process. The first ground put down can anticipate the form but without going into detail. Before we were able to appreciate how the strokes to a large extent determine the definitive form. Colors can be superimposed, blended or mixed directly, but it is important that the oil painting process is always correctly followed.

Superimposing strokes and tones

In oil painting it is possible to start coloring all the picture at the same time. The painting does not have to be limited to working in zones. If the background is elaborated at the same time as color is given to the objects, you can also work on the details of the forms. For example, you can paint the main motif, the top of a tree, with free strokes and at the same time paint the background in a variety of ochre tones.

The initial color ground was painted at the same time as the leaves of the palm tree. To paint these leaves, the strokes dragged part of the leaf color over the background.

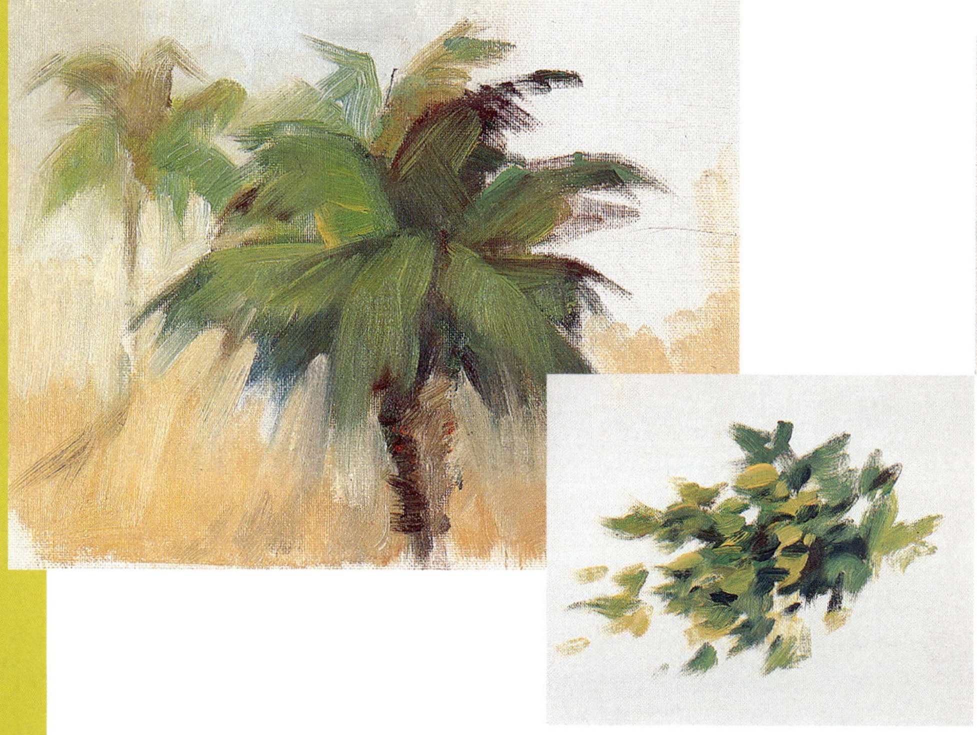

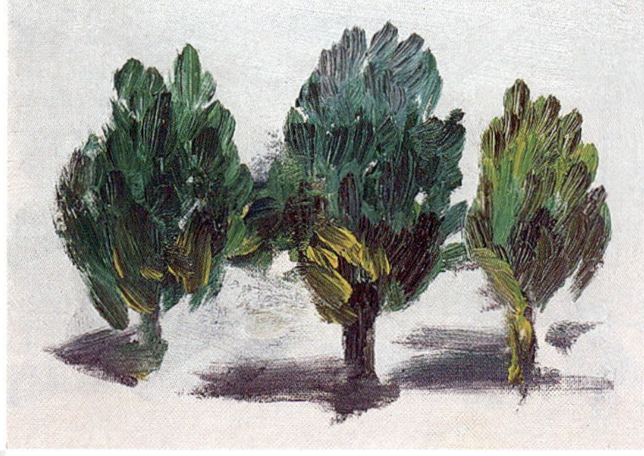

These trees were painted with a ground similar to the previous one.

Superimposing small strokes is alternated with tones from the same color range.

Color nuances in the range

One color range can share colors with other ranges, as shown in this piece called "A still life: pears and melon" by Luis Meléndez (1716-1780), which is kept in the Fine Arts Museum of Boston, United States. You can observe the warmth that comes over despite a great number of cool nuances having been used. This has been achieved by incorporating cool colors softly tinted with earth tones in mixtures done on the palette. The way the strokes have been treated is also important. Here they have been very fine and delicate, avoiding the brush leaving its mark on the surface.

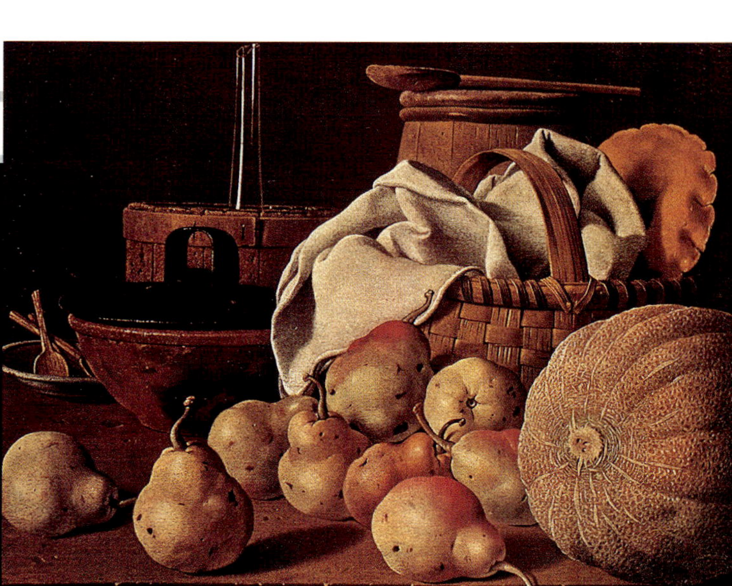

The picture is elaborated progressively. If details have to be added, they can be painted as you go along, anywhere on the surface. If details only have to be applied on concrete zones, the painted background aids the overall vision of the piece.

Elaborated color masses

When you wish to obtain a texture from a color mass the strokes can be superimposed according to the effect you are seeking. The first colors do not have to be rich in contrasts or in color, but as you develop the picture the chromatic variety intensifies along with the density of the paint.

In this simple example that we have just seen, dark strokes have been painted on top of luminous strokes. As you will observe, the color masses are small so as to permit the superimposition of strokes. The tone applied is mixed with the lower one, influenced by the dragging of the brush.

Balance with complementary colors

As we have seen throughout this chapter, working with one color range does not rule out colors from other ranges. In the majority of occasions, cool colors can be balanced against warm colors. Sometimes this is necessary to avoid excessive chromatic monotony. Complementary colors allow strong contrasts to be established between the colors of a picture.

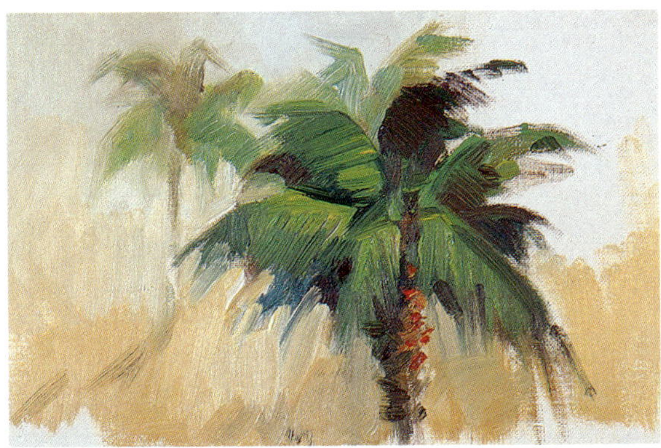

These trees have been painted with a ground similar to the previous one.

The line direction

Each plane receives a line which goes in a certain direction, depending on whether it is inclined or frontal.

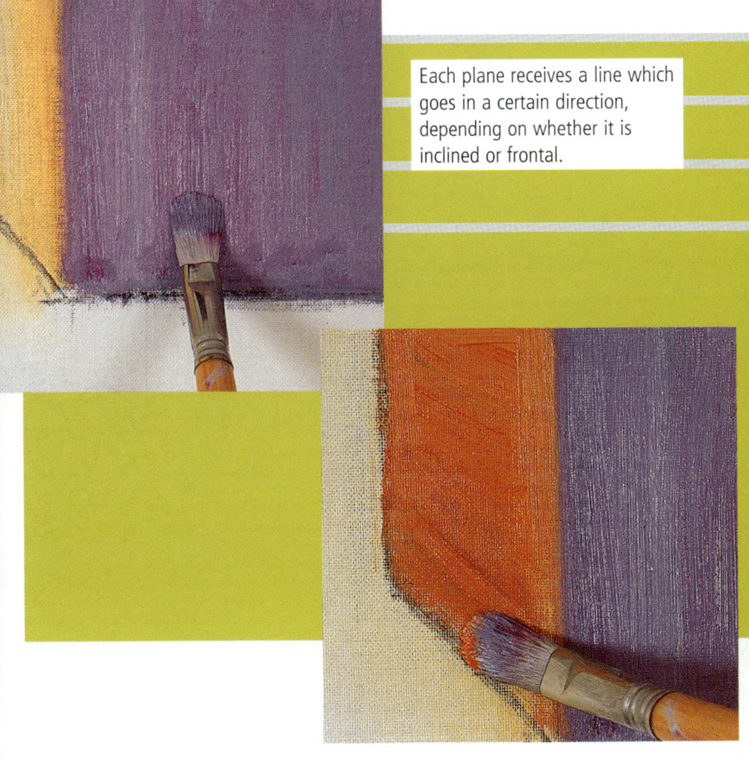

With color masses the direction of the stroke determines the plane being painted. Sometimes a learner does not realize that the objects painted in the picture are composed of planes and they work in the same way in all the picture. The stroke must look for the form of the plane, as we saw earlier when painting the flowers. Among the different painting media, it is oil color which has an outstanding facility for the fusion of tones and colors and one of the richest lines. This is why the form must be studied before starting to paint it. If a plane must appear inclined in the picture, it is recommendable to paint it with an inclined stroke. However, if the plane is frontal, a vertical or horizontal stroke can be used, as is necessary.

Besides the direction of the stroke, it is also important to bear in mind the colors used.

This recourse is one of the most widely used when you want to make a particular tone or color stand out. When you use a complementary color among other colors the result is a very strong reciprocal contrast. In the evolution of the picture you must be aware of the nuances that can help to compensate the contrasts between tones. Here it is very important to correctly apply the strokes. If you work on the forms in an intermediate color among more luminous colors, you will balance the lights and the darks, but the overall effect of the painting will not be compensated.

To get well compensated colors you can paint the background in a mixture of the colors used to paint the principal objects. For example, if the elements of the still life below are painted red, yellow and green, the background too should be painted in a mixture of these. The result will be a broken color which gives unity to the overall effect.

Using color in the plane

In the same way that every plane must have its corresponding stroke, it must also have its own tone. When you paint any object you can observe that the light does not fall uniformly on all the surface. In some zones the light can be direct while other areas will hardly be illuminated. The correct use of chromatic ranges is important in the development of different planes in the picture.

Next to the bottle a strong red has been painted. It complements the color strength. The overall effect is unbalanced by painting the yellow zones.

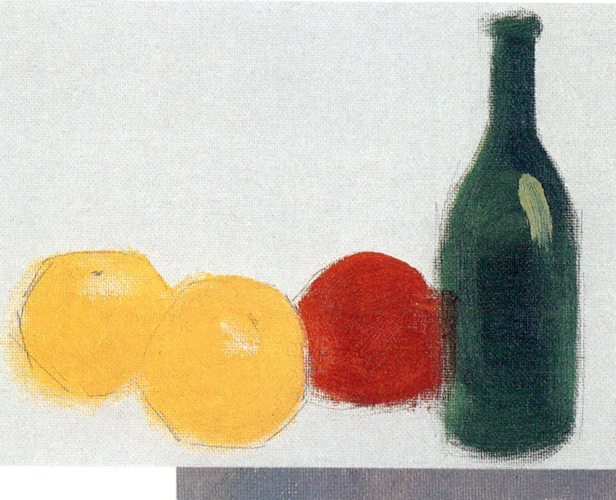

To obtain an equilibrium between contrast and tones, a very bright yellow has been applied to the bottle.

The background is painted in a mixture of the colors used; this balances the overall effect.

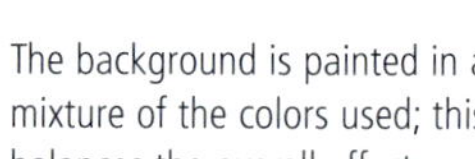

Summary

THICK ON THIN
Whenever you paint in oil colors you must start with the thinned colors.

THE FINISH AND THE LINE
As the color is laid down you must do contrasts and detailed strokes that increase in precision.

SUPERIMPOSING STROKES AND TONES
Progressively coloring the picture allows all of it to be elaborated at the same time.

STROKE DIRECTION
The stroke direction determines the plane being painted.

Exercises

APPLES AND GARLIC
WITH FREE STROKES

When a particular color range is chosen to paint with, the final picture has a logical tendency towards certain chromatic effects. In this chapter we have worked on the application of strokes to depict the different planes of the picture, at the same time as we have explored the possibilities with one color range, concretely the cool range.

The still life tackled now is straightforward. It consists of three simple elements that are based on circles. Pay special attention to the color range in this exercise; basically it is composed of cool colors. Another point to bear in mind is how the picture ground is done.

Necessary material

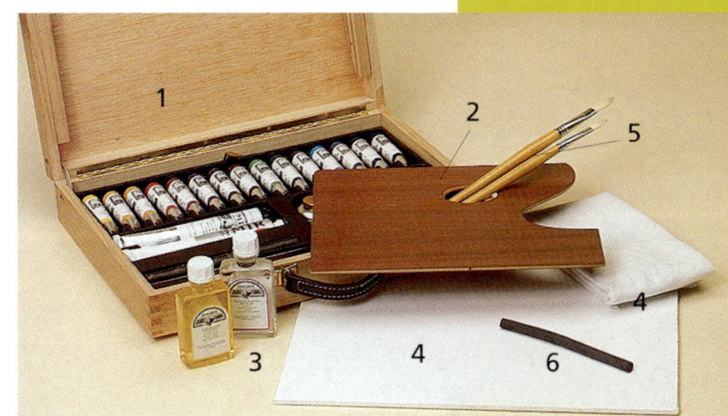

A box of oil colors with a palette (1), primed card (2), linseed oil and turpentine oil (3), a cloth (4), oil brushes (5), and charcoal (6).

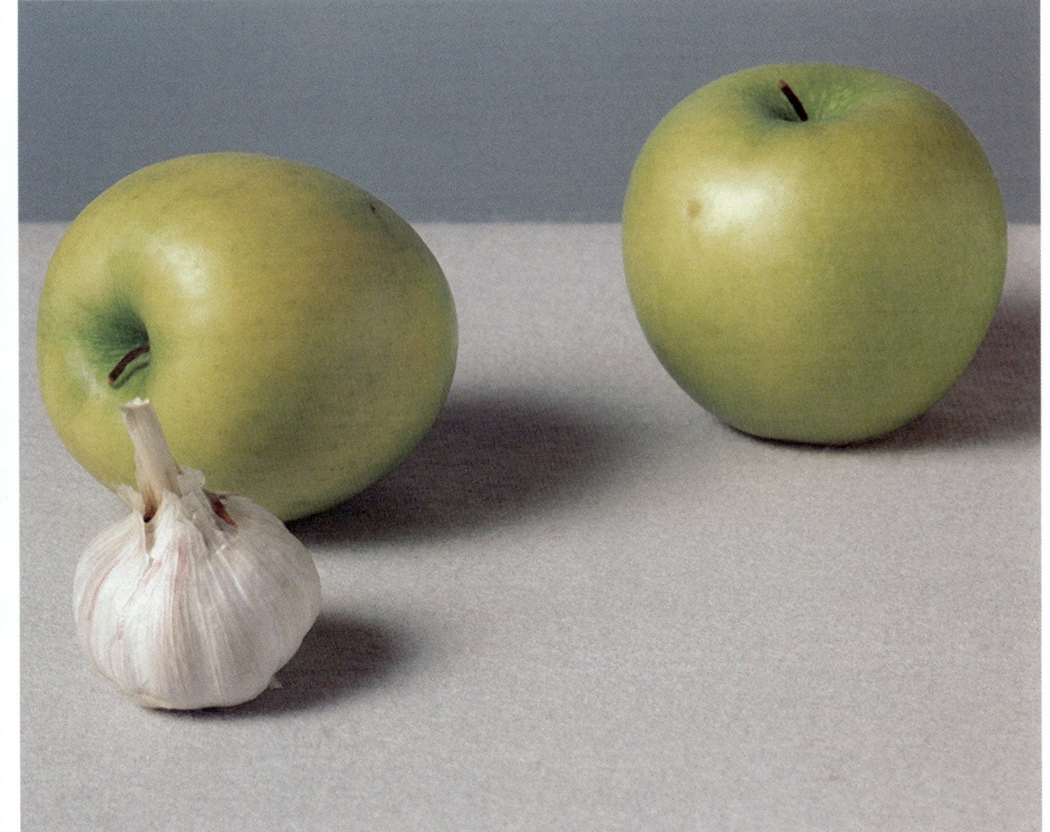

Exercises

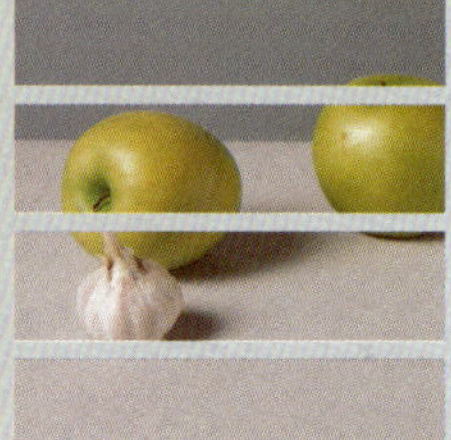

1·As is common in the majority of works done in oil colors, the outline is made with charcoal. The first reason for this is that charcoal is very unstable and can be corrected in any moment. Secondly, it can be painted over immediately without leaving any trace in the oil color.

2·The first color intervention is to do the background behind the fruits so prepare a green mixed with yellow.

Of course, as we are going from thin to thick, this first color is painted thinned, with free strokes and without yet trying to give form to the apples.

In the apple on the right do a few strokes of luminous green without mixing.

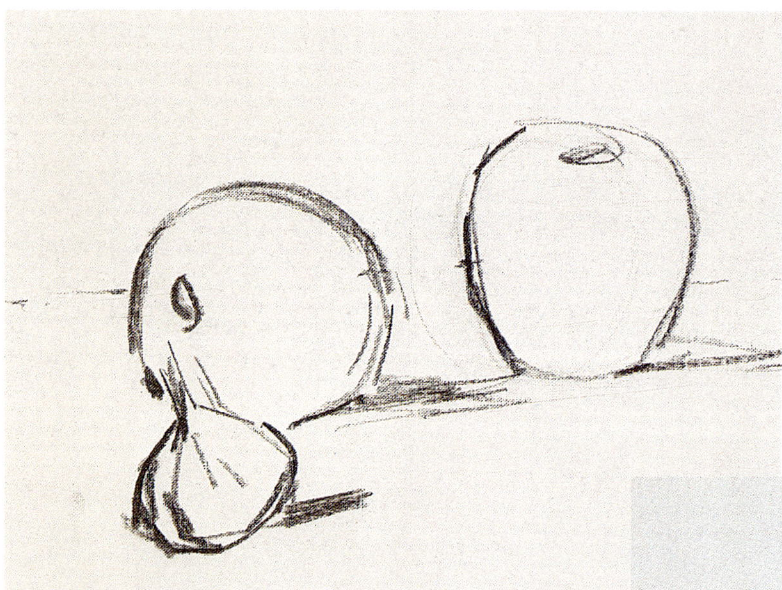

3·Cool colors, the same as colors from other range, can include varied tones and mixes including tertiary colors.

To break a color you must mix it on the palette with a complementary color and then grayen it with white. Here this is how the background tone is made. On the palette start with the color white and add a little blue and a dash of carmine. The result is a gray tone of a certain warmth. This color is applied to the background doing wide, long strokes.

Start the painting on the apples. The stroke direction is important and is realized following the spherical plane of the fruit.

4·The table base is also painted with a very light gray color, nearly white but slightly different to the background. To do this zone load more blue onto the palette. Also paint some green strokes heavily mixed with the gray used before.

The shadows on the apple are painted in Prussian blue, somewhat toned down with white.

The form of the apples is continued working with a much finer stroke. Apply the color in a soft paste and vary the line direction to follow the dark plane

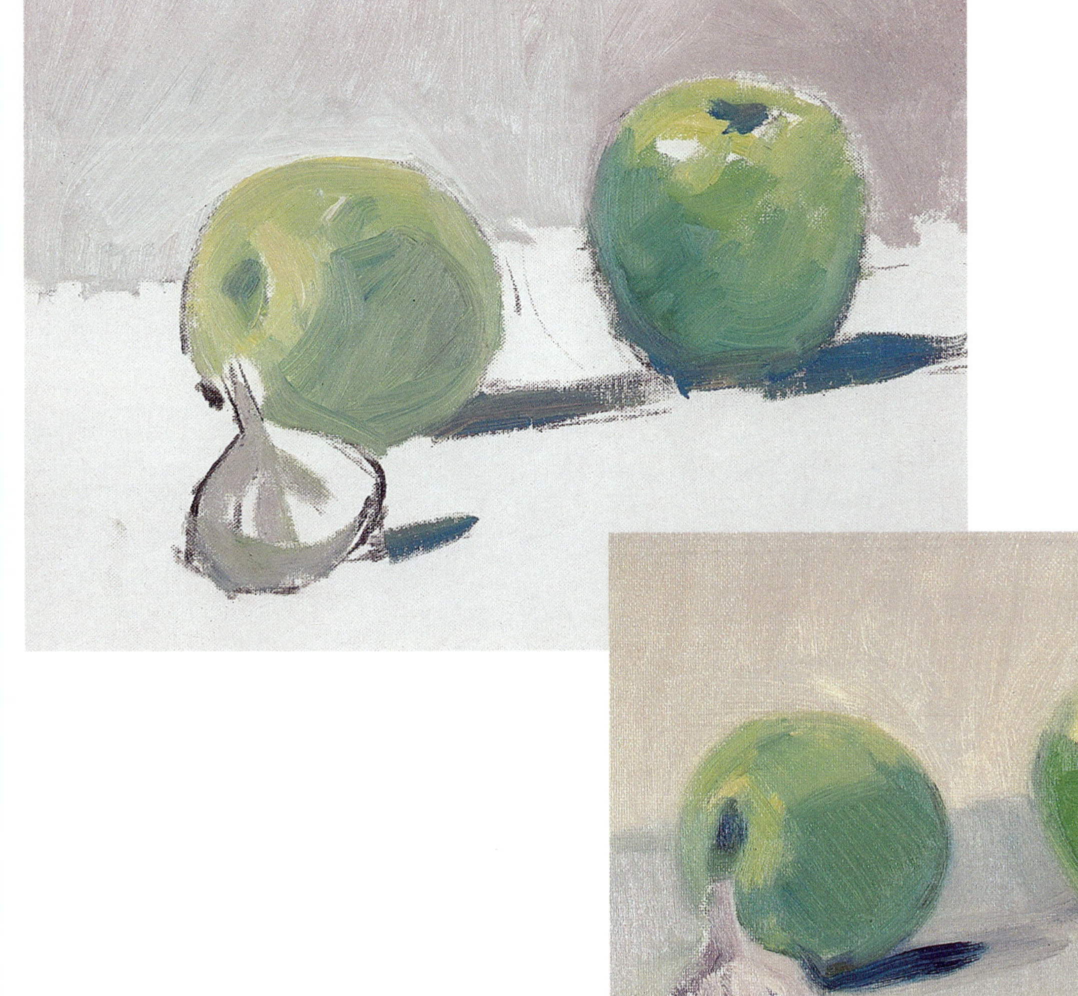

Exercises

5·The garlic is painted starting with its most luminous zones. The strokes are light as they are applied on top of the violetish background.

Make a mix of luminous green and yellow to paint the highlight on the apples.

Dip the brush in dark green to paint the darkest zone on the apples.

6·With yellow straight out of the tube, paint the highlights on the upper part of the apples. These strokes are direct and free, hardly leaving a mark on the surface.

Use Naples yellow, mixed with a luminous green, to paint the transition zone between the highlight and the shadow area.

Use a violet tone, somewhat grayed, to paint the dark areas on the garlic. The shadow of the garlic is painted in the same way that the apple shadow was realized.

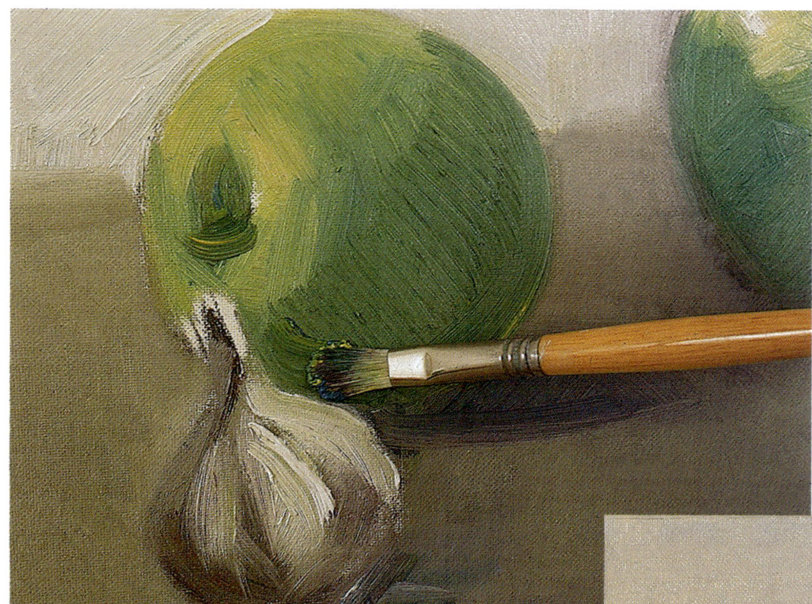

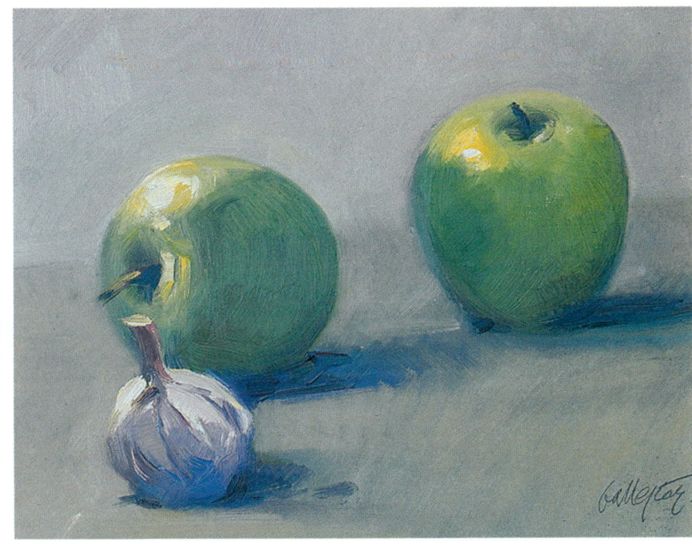

7·To finish off this picture, on top of the colors already down, do a few strokes to blend the tones. These strokes must not be heavily loaded with color, simply pass the brush over to fuse the tones and colors.

Do some very direct purplish strokes on the garlic.

In the lower part, where the shadow is, paint in cobalt blue diluted with white.

Represent the most luminous highlights on the apple in Naples yellow and white.

Summary

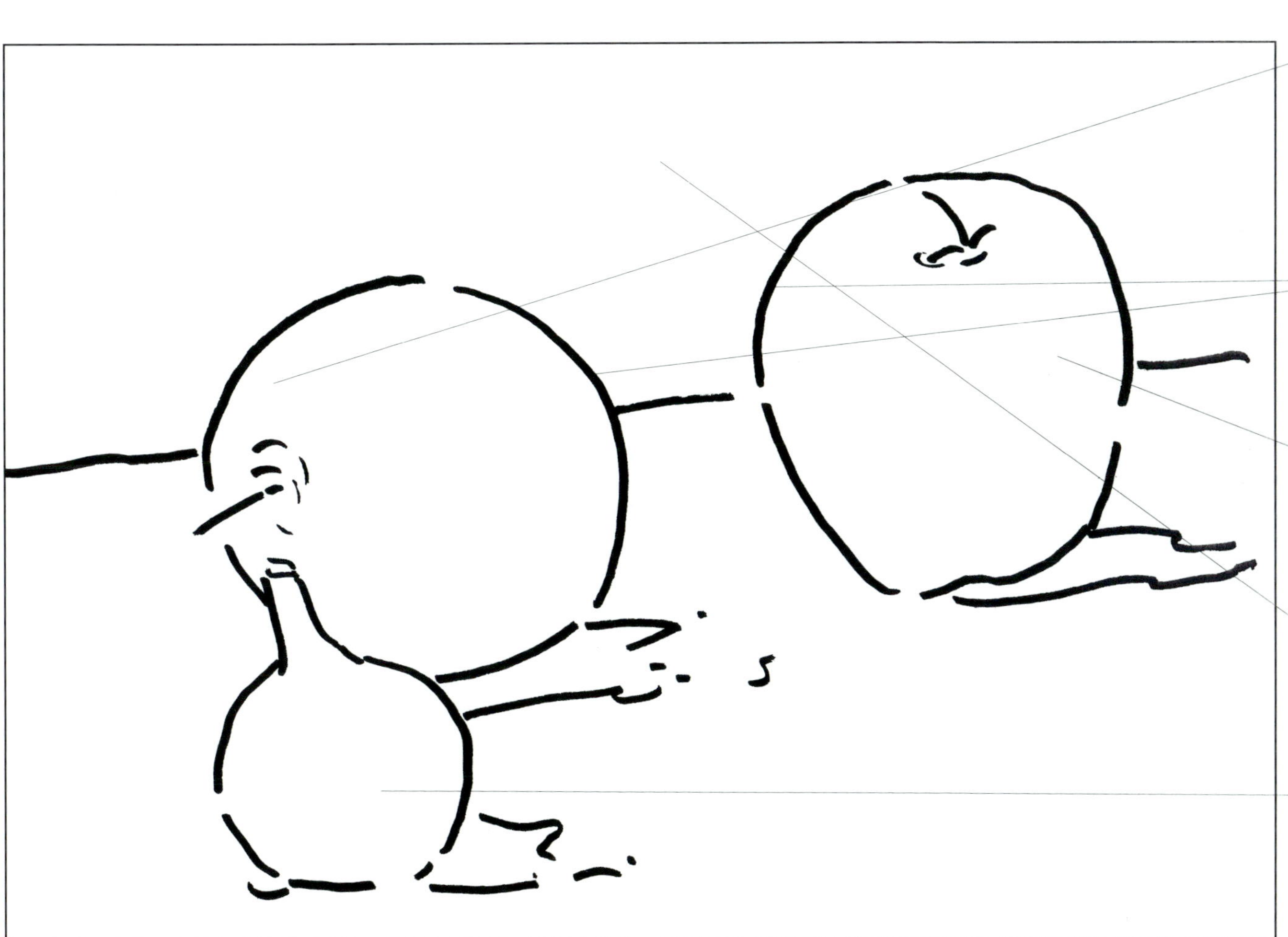

Chapter 6

More about oil color strokes

When painting in oil colors only certain zones of the picture will require a stroke which allows the colors to be blended. Other areas will need a different treatment.

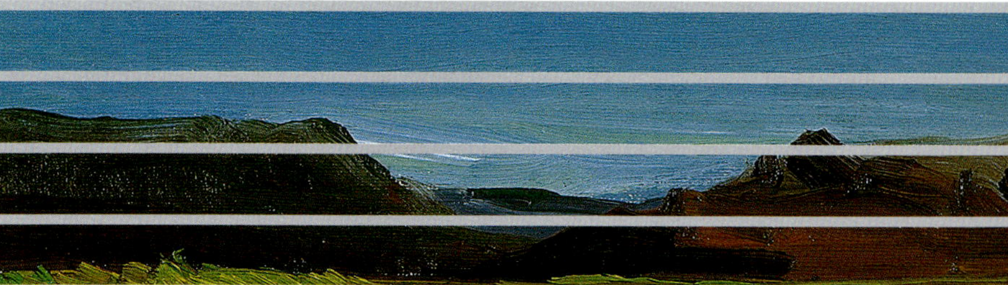

A stroke can be made by stretching or extending the paint deposited on the canvas. Initially its form will depend on the density of the paint and the dragging.

Oil colors have a very soft, buttery consistency which allows them to impregnate the brush and to produce all types of rich interventions: brush dragging, lines, masses. Summing up, a complete series of effects which alone do not mean much but which together allow you to develop any subject imaginable. In this chapter we are going to study how to deal with the stroke depending on what you want to paint.

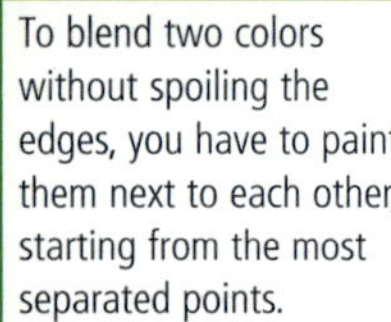

To blend two colors without spoiling the edges, you have to paint them next to each other, starting from the most separated points.

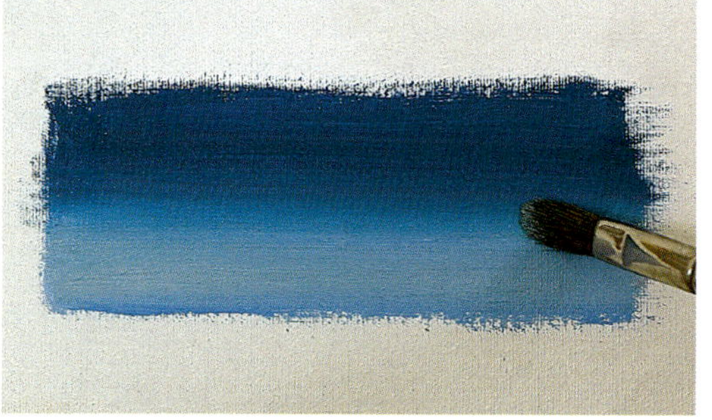

To blend two colors, use the brush with soft strokes as long as the plane that you want to blend.

The form of the stroke

A stroke can acquire numerous connotations depending on how it is dragged across the canvas surface and the softness with which the brush lays down the paint. If you paint with dense strokes on a fresh surface, the dragging stroke will take part of the paint below with it. However, if you paint with precise strokes, without dragging, the mix with the lower color will be minimum. Lastly, if the color Is applIed on top of a dry ground you can do all types of work with the brush without the tones mixing or the color becoming dirtied. The form of the stroke is conditioned by the density of the paint, the dragging and the degree of dryness of the underpainting. In turn this stroke determines how, and if, the colors blend. Opaque, transparent, and translucent painting are all within the scope of oil colors.

Two color fusion

If you paint carefully on top of a freshly painted zone, you can superimpose the strokes without mixing the tones. This is the main guideline to follow for mixing two colors by fusion on the picture. In this way you can add numerous nuances and tints to the colors already down. The quantity of color painted will influence on the first color.

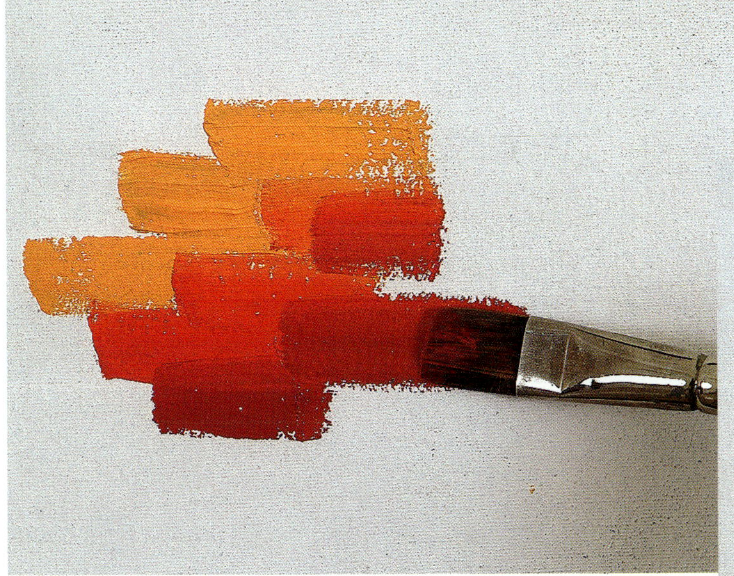

The first stroke is yellow. On the palette add a little red and with this mixture apply a new stroke to the lower layer. Go on like this until you are painting directly with red.

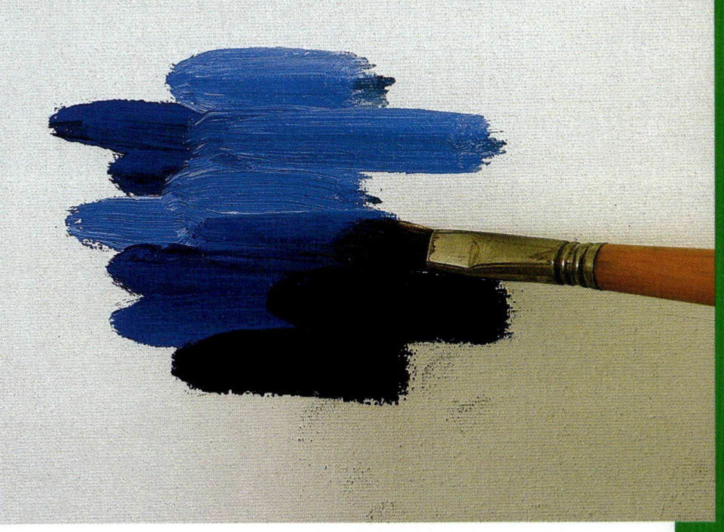

Superimposing strokes permits you to add together light tones on top of dark tones, and vice-versa. The colors do not contaminate each other. Compare the difference between the finish in the first exercise and this one.

Gradating a color with white

White is not always useful for gradating colors. When it is mixed with blues, greens and yellows, it permits whitish tones of these colors. However, when it is mixed with red, the result is a pinkish tone and not a light red nor an orange.

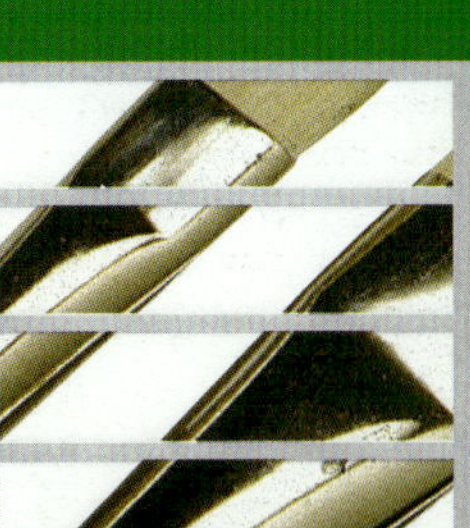

A red gradated with white gives rise to a pink tone. However, to gradate towards an orange it is necessary to use the color yellow.

A soft transition. When the aim is to achieve a soft transition between two colors, it is important that the limits of the two original colors, before they come into contact with each other, are in no way contaminated by the superimposed color.

Gradations. To blend the two colors the process is simple. All you have to do is pass the brush repeatedly over the two fresh colors. Use long strokes that pick up a little of each adjacent color. After going over them a few times, the colors will have blended in a soft and progressive gradation.

Brush touches

Stokes can acquire infinite characteristics depending on how the brush is dragged over the colors. Sometimes the mark will be soft, hardly revealing the traces of the hog's hair bristles. Other strokes, however, will clearly show the brush marks and when the brush left the support.

Progressive color change

With a simple exercise we are now going to show the transition from one color to another by adding one hue over the one originally applied. Use a flat brush. As you can see in the first image, the first stroke put down is yellow. Add a little red and mix it with yellow on the palette. Apply a new stroke on top of the original one, without going over it twice so as not to drag the color underneath. The stroke is finished in a straight line. The other exercise, in the second image, is done with variations of blue, but without there being a tone gradation between the strokes. Firstly paint blue strokes very diluted by white. On top of these strokes, without mixing the colors, paint a very dark blue and on top of this color paint new tones but do not let the lower colors mix. This type of stroke does not finish like the last one. The brush employed must have a round tuft, like a cat's tongue.

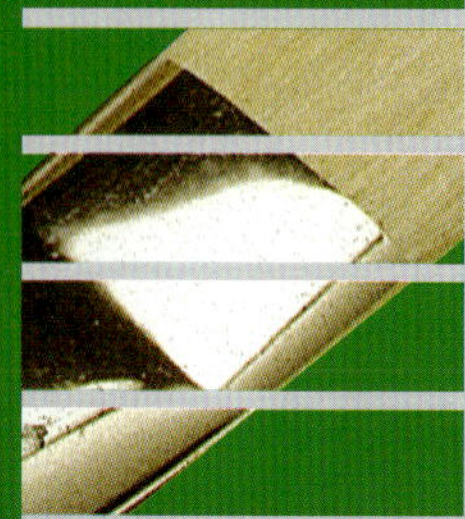

Contrasting color masses

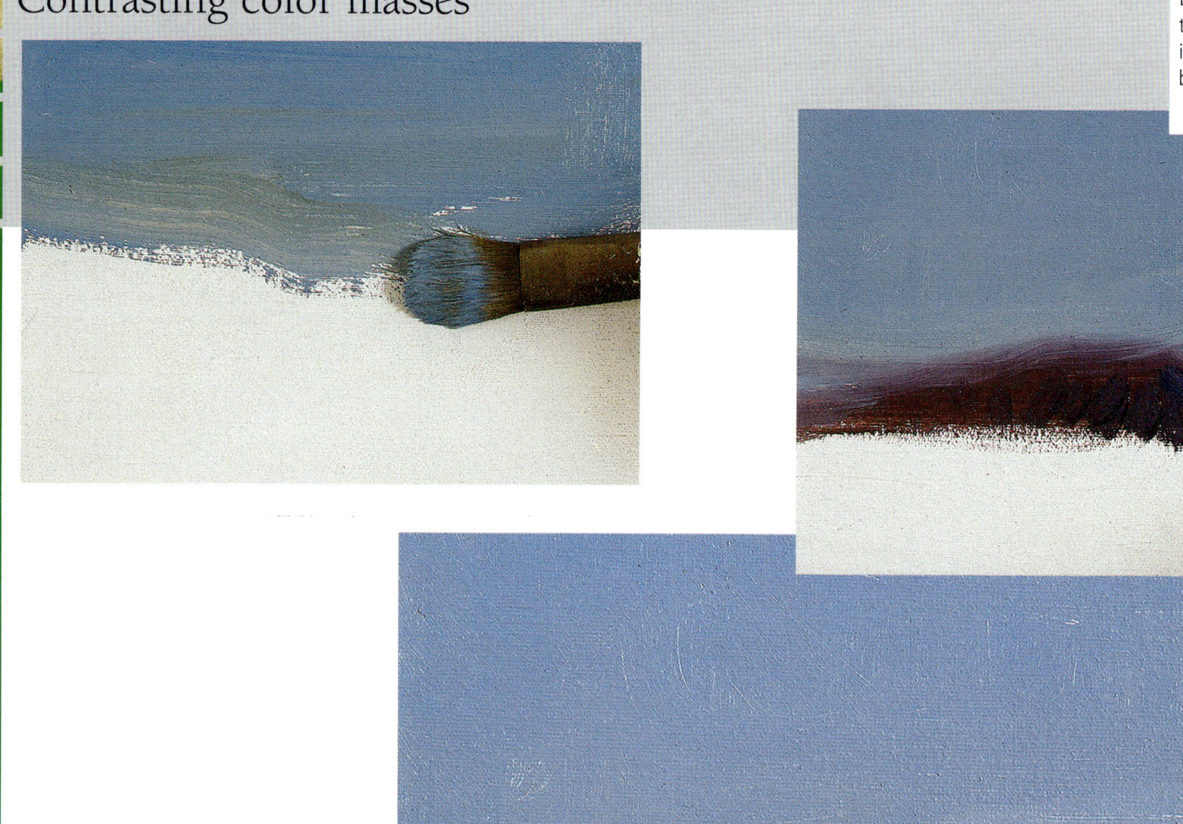

Blend two zones together with the soft intervention of the brush on the edges.

When painting the widest zone bear in mind where the next color begins.

In the foreground two different tones have been laid down. However, as you can appreciate there is no fusion between the tones.

Brush dragging

In this section we are going to offer a brief explanation of this chapter. Three points will be insisted on:
—Strokes to set out a wide area.
—Fusion strokes and intermediate zones.
—Detailed strokes.
Each type of stroke requires a particular brush. Depending on what type of brush is used, a different color drag will be created. The exercise we will now do, which goes from color masses to the fusion of two planes, revolves around the basic use of the brush according to the zone being painted. Firstly the widest planes have to be painted. When painting this zone, although there is no preliminary sketch, you must bear in mind the next plane to be painted so that the right mix is produced between the two planes. If you overpaint and encroach into a zone destined for another color, both colors will be contaminated. In this phase we will use a thick brush.
The next color mass borders on the last one, and it can be done in such a way that it is superimposed or the two masses can be blended. In the latter case it is desirable that the two zones blend along their limits so we will not use the same thick brush but instead a medium one so that there is only a discrete invasion of one color into the other.

Using various brushes

We have just seen how each brush has its own "touch" expressed in its dragging over the canvas or over other colors. Now we will be able to use the different methods of color fusion, as well as the touch of the brushes to elaborate different zones of the picture. In this simple exercise we will start to learn what each brush is meant for: dragging and blending.

Stokes to cover various zones

The large color masses of the picture can be covered quickly if the right brush is used. If a zone destined for a great mass of color is painted with a low numbered brush, not only would it take a long time to finish, but it is also

Drag a few white strokes over the sky until they are blended. The mountains are painted in an earthy color which drags part of the sky.

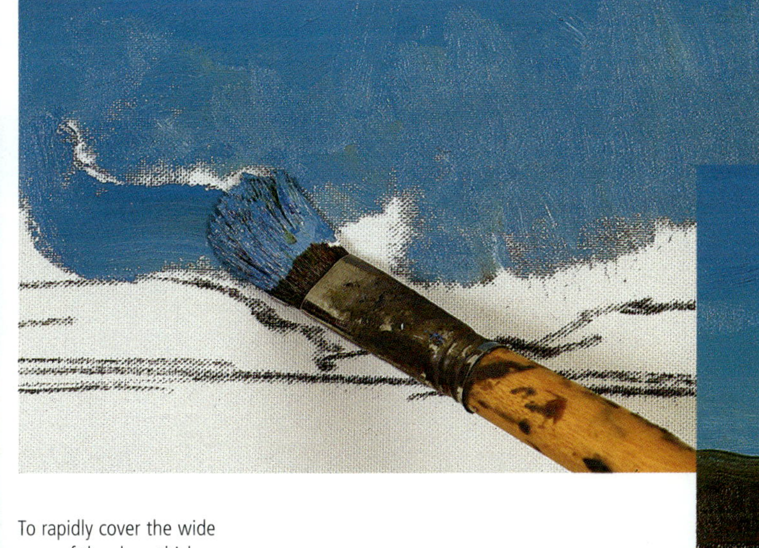

To rapidly cover the wide zone of the sky a thick brush has to be used. A few strokes will suffice.

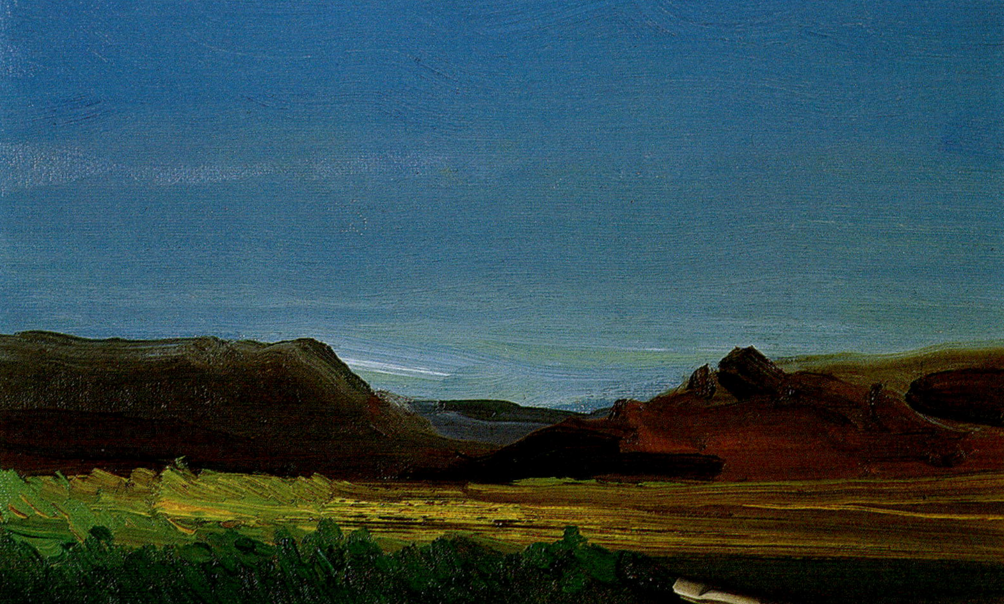

The strokes in the foreground are short and vertical.

possible that the artist's patience would run out.

To avoid this it is recommendable to use as thick a brush as the zone permits. In this exercise after outlining the horizon line, you can see that the sky occupies a great part of the landscape. Painting it with a thin brush would be wearisome, so try a thick brush. Just a few strokes will be sufficient to cover this zone of the picture including the mountains against the sky. The stroke must be long and uniform without the brush leaving lumps in the oil color on the canvas.

Texture strokes

There is a type of stroke, very different to the last ones, which permits not only a color ground to be put down but also gives form and character to tone and color fusion. It is a very varied stroke and aids the creation of textures thanks to it being directly mixed on the picture. The right brush for this work is any of the medium sized ones. A too small brush would not be able to do certain mixes, and its covering capacity would be minimal.

Firstly a clean brush is dipped in white and a few touches are given on the blue background. This white is then blended with insistent long, horizontal strokes.

Start to paint the mountains in the background in an earthy color, for example burnt umber. Here part of the sky color in the zone above the mountains is dragged so that it becomes part of the texture.

Small brush strokes

A small or low numbered brush does not allow large areas to be covered. Its advantage lies in doing detailed textured zones which are normally practiced in parts of the picture close to the viewer, or in very concrete situations or effects. The strokes can vary in length or in width, depending on what you have to represent. In this exercise we will practice different strokes with a small brush.

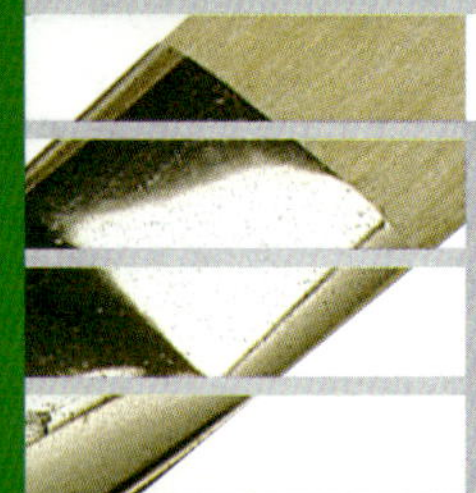

Each brush in its zone

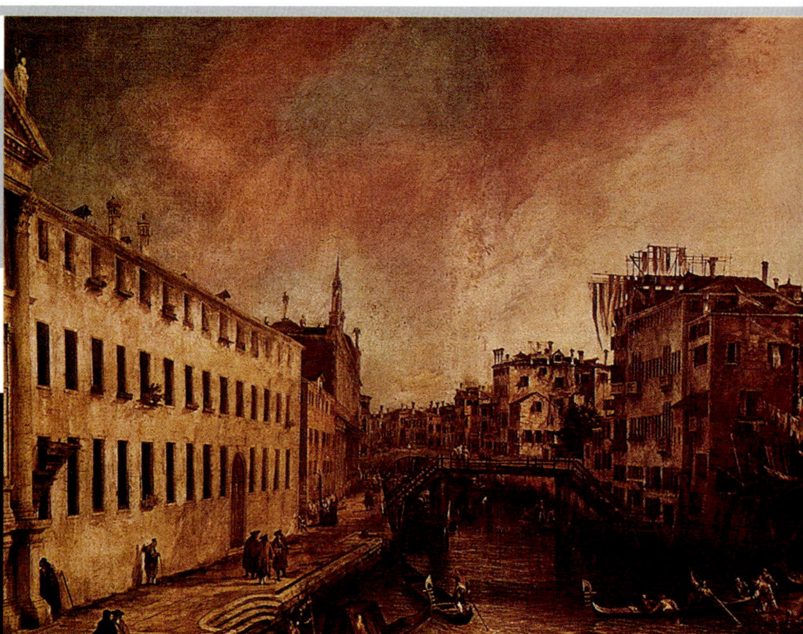

In this oil painting, "The river of the beggars", painted by Canaletto (1697-1768) and kept in the Mario Crespi collection in Milan, you can appreciate how the great venetian artist has applied different strokes in each zone, depending on the texture and the detail sought after. The sky is painted in a wide variety of tones, but there hardly exists any definition between the brush touches. Here he could have easily used a thick brush, insistently dragging over the tones to get a perfect fusion. For the architectural work, brimming with contrasts, it is sure he used a fine brush for the lines and the detail of the ornaments.

Long and short strokes

With the small brush start to work on the most distant earth ground of the picture. To paint this area a long stroke is used in which lines of different colors, green, yellow and brown, are combined. The superimposition of strokes and the dragging caused the fusion of the tones and colors put down. The most contrasted color, a dark luminous green, is painted in the foreground in long strokes with the medium sized brush. In this zone we are not interested in forming a thick layer of paint. We just want to rapidly cover it with color. In the principal ground we start work with a new stroke, this time much more precise and repetitive. The aim is to get a grass texture through short, vertical touches. Paint from the line that marks the limit between the sky and the mountains, making a special effort not to dirty the sky by dragging. The tone employed here is a mixture of carmine, orange and white. The intention to vary the tone is manifested more in the lower zone than in the middle of the sky where the brush hardly takes any color, just enough to get a soft fusion. In this intermediate sky zone although the brush is lightly loaded you must go over the canvas several times so that the long stroke blends into the background.

A succession of strokes to paint a plane

In the last part we were able to see how different strokes permit very varied styles to be applied to a piece. Now we will go into the subject more deeply as we do a complete range of strokes to get one unique plane, in this case the luminous evening sky.

The color masses of the wide zones can include a darker tone which blends with the light tones.

Fusion in the first step

Just like in the last exercise the first strokes, destined to cover the widest surface and to provide a color base on top of which the other tones are going to be painted, will be done with the thickest brush.
The color dragging must be rapid and uniform. In this phase of the work some dark tones can already be applied at the bottom of the sky, but they must be blended with the most luminous blue by going over them repeatedly.

Going over a stroke with another

Before going on with the work on the sky, finish painting the rest of the landscape in dark colors to strengthen the backlight effect of the evening. On top of the base painted blue and the fusion with dark blue, different stroke interventions can be made that notably modify the color. Once again the medium sized brush is used.

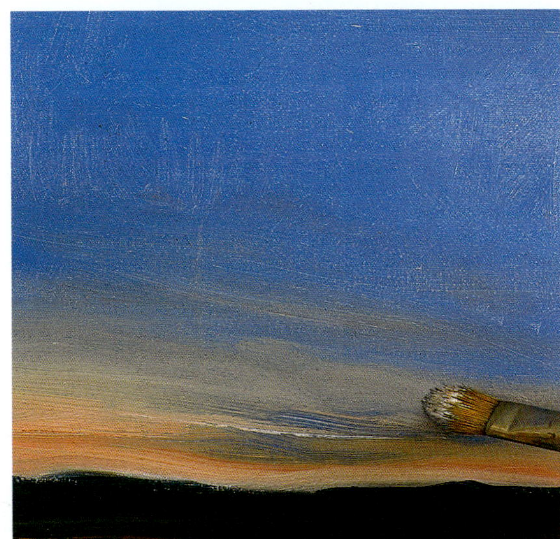

Drawing properties in the stroke

The stroke, when it is realized with intention and the objective is not to achieve a blending, takes on a marked drawing style.
The most perseverant strokes can finally partly blend into the background. However, the most spontaneous and freshest strokes keep their greater expression.
The fresh oil color base can be used to blended the new color, something which could appear to be contradictory when the aim was to achieve a rather direct stroke.
La base fresca de óleo puede servir

The smallest pressure on the dragged brush will take part of the lower color with it. This step requires some attention because we are combining different stroke styles and recourses. First paint with the most luminous color, in this case the yellow below, which must be half golden so that when it is dragged it does not become a completely green color.

In some areas do more strokes which do not blend into the blue background but remain as direct color touches on the initial yellow. On top of this color paint in orange. The process is the same: in the upper zone do long, unrelenting strokes so that the tone blends into the background, and as you work downwards the stroke becomes more direct. At the end do a few touches of pure orange which instead of blending with the yellow make a fusion with the original orange.

Paint a somewhat darker blue tone in the upper part of the sky. This color is added to the original blue base by doing soft dragging strokes which permit a gentle fusion between the two colors. As you paint with this darker blue color, add, going from the right hand side, some orangy tones which when they blend with the blue will turn purplish.

This purplish tone is then softly dragged with long strokes until all the upper zone in unified. The sky can now be finished by adding new orange tones.

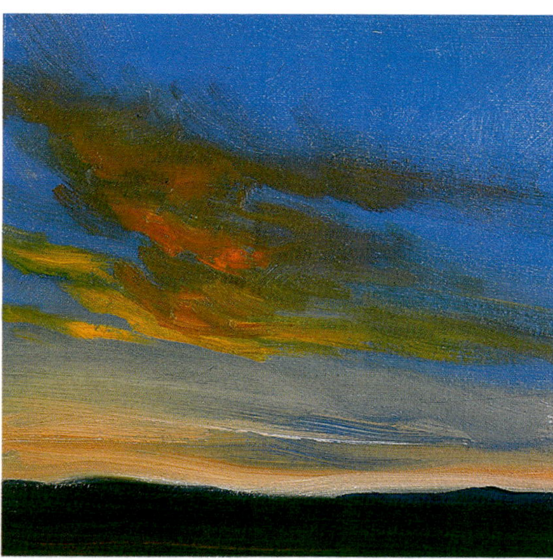

The purest colors are painted as direct impacts on top of a base of tones blended by dragging with the brush.

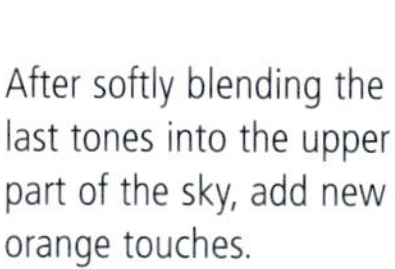

After softly blending the last tones into the upper part of the sky, add new orange touches.

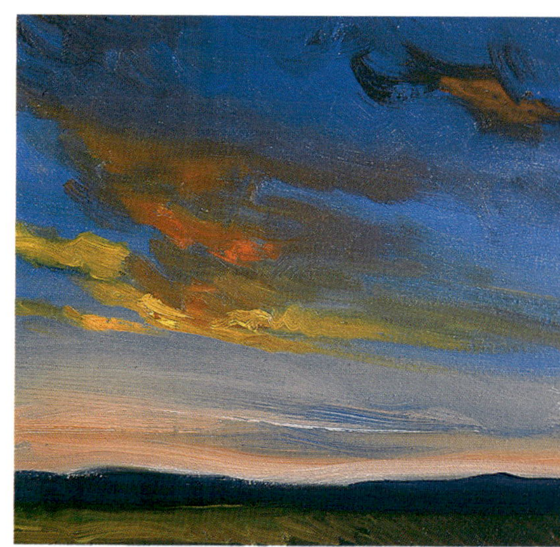

Summary

SUPERIMPOSED COLORS
When superimposed strokes permit the fusion of tones and colors.

BLENDED COLORS
To blend two tones you have to insist with the brush until the edges are blended.

FUSION STROKES BETWEEN TWO PLANES
These strokes are realized with a medium sized brush so that they do not contaminate the two colors. The fusion is carried out softly or just allowing them to seep together.

Exercises

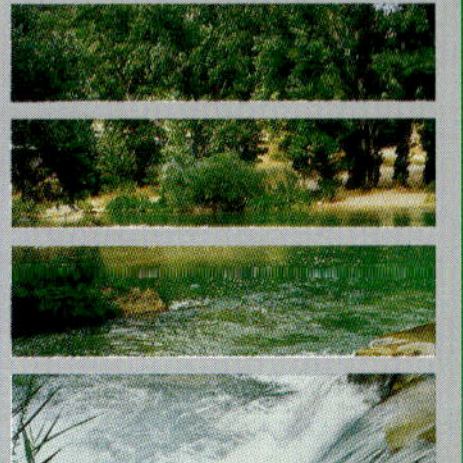

A RIVER LANDSCAPE

This exercise is going to plunge us fully into the marvelous technique of oil painting. We have worked sufficiently on stroke techniques to be able to do a quite complicated exercise. But do not be put off, the process is simple, above all if you clearly distinguish between the different planes of the model.

In each zone of the picture a different stroke style will be used. Observe how the water, leaf and waterfall, in the foreground, textures are represented. Studying the distinct strokes in each plane of the model will be of great help. The slope and the length of the strokes are perfectly marked out as we go through the exercise step by step.

Necessary material

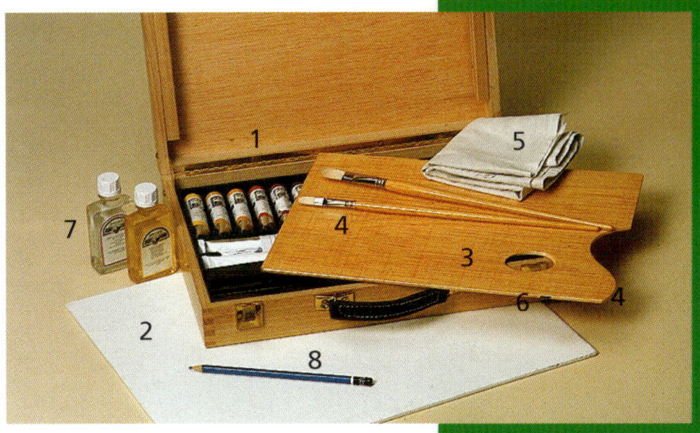

Oil colors (1), primed card (2), a palette (3), brushes (4), a cloth (5), linseed oil (6) turpentine oil (7), and a pencil (8).

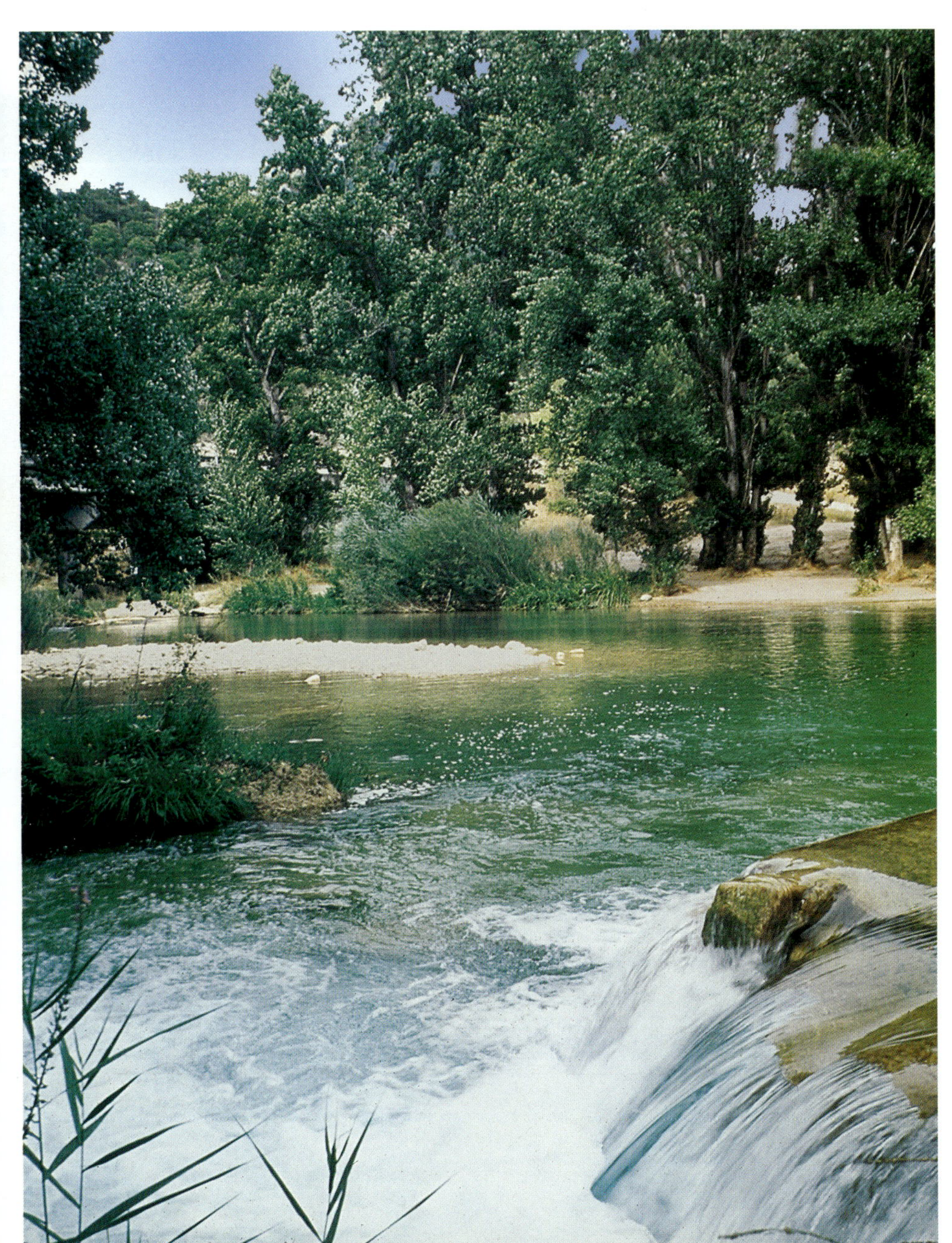

Exercises

1·The initial sketch, in step one, is done in pencil. Its purpose more than anything else is to lay out the principal color masses and to separate the planes of the zones.

Once the landscape has been sketched, go over the scheme with a thinned oil color line. The brush must be sufficiently drained so that it does not run or drip on the primed card. It is important that the shore line is well defined.

2·The initial color masses do not have to be overloaded with oil color. In step two, start to put in the sky ground with a very whitish blue mixture.

The tress in the background are realized with very non-specific color masses that will be the base for much more defined strokes later on. Observe how the picture evolves in its lower zone. On the left hand side you can still observe the green mass, while on the right the strokes are detailed and meticulous.

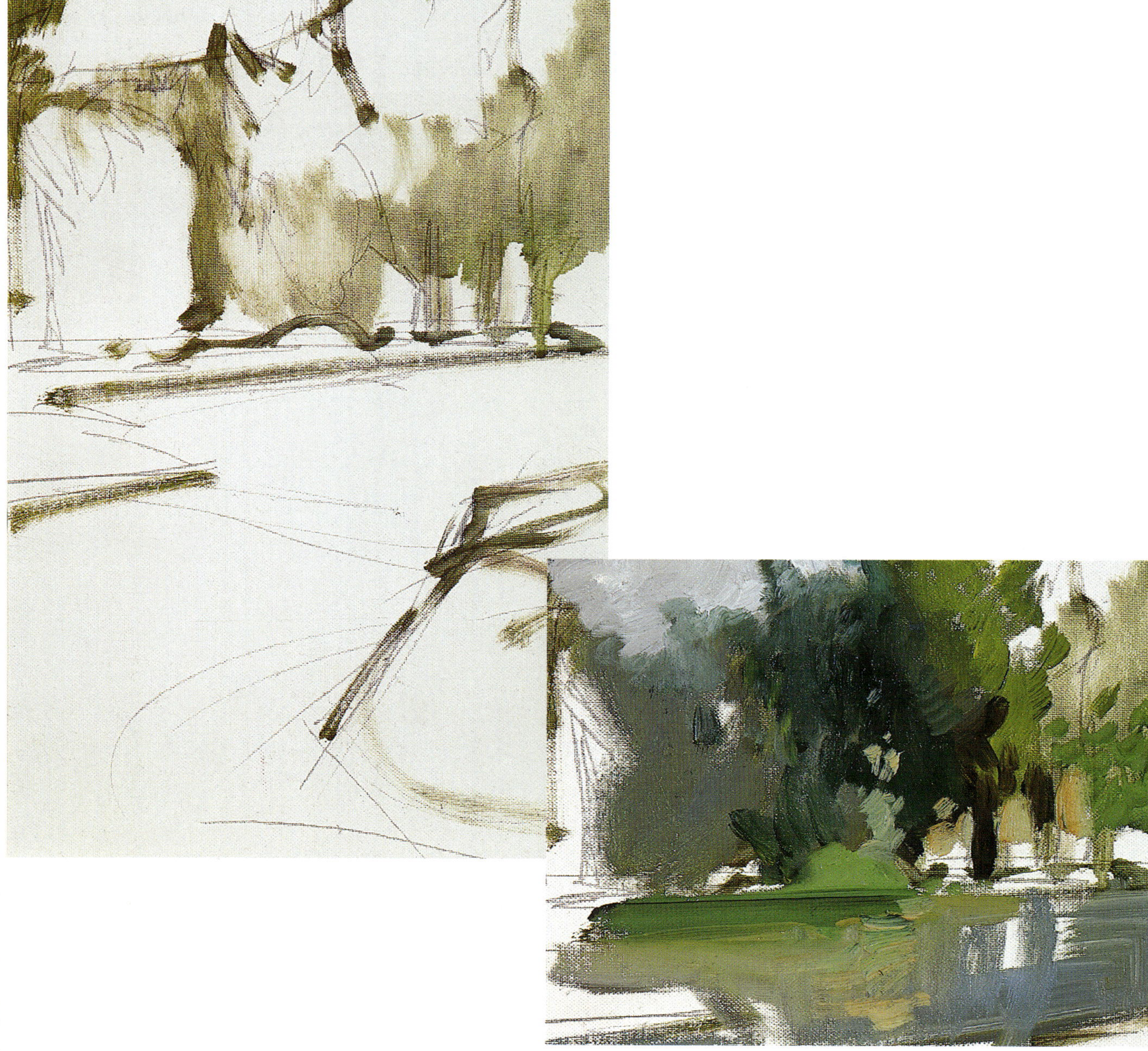

3. In step three, the stroke to form the trees becomes more defined as you go along. On one side small luminous colors are painted and on the other side contrasts.

The difference between the strokes used for the trees and for the water is unavoidably eye-catching. In the forest the stroke is short and superimposed, slightly dragging the base colors, in the water the stroke is long and adds blendings of ochre, blue and gray The cascade in the foreground is realized with a grayish tone

4·Pay attention to the forest zone: the stroke used here is subtle and adds little touches of a very luminous yellow. A fine brush, of course, must be used, making a effort not to dirty the background green.

Use the medium sized brush to paint the colors that form the principal contrasts in the tree zone. As you paint the dark parts in the lower part, insinuate the trunk shapes.

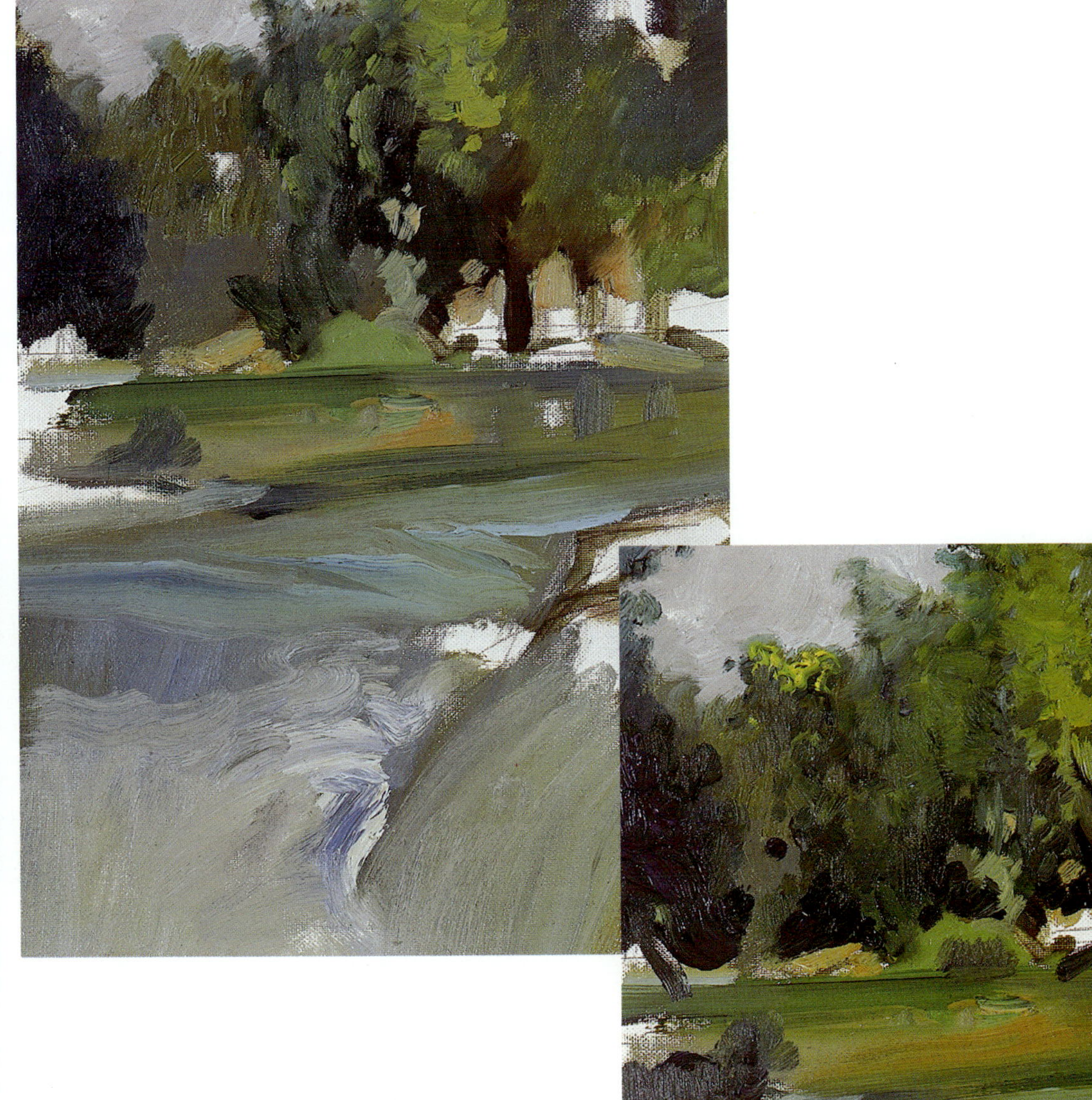

Exercises

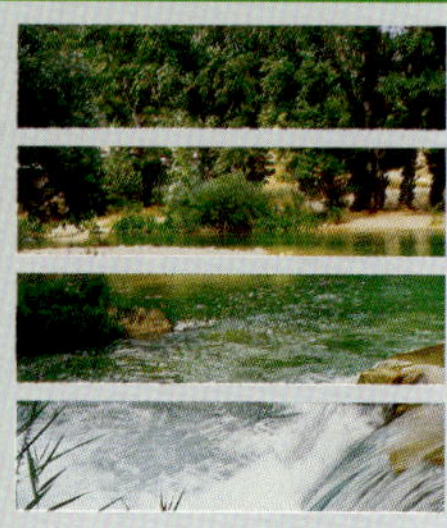

5·In step five, observe how the small dark strokes gradually form the complex tangle of leaves. This point is especially interesting: to give the forest depth the zone of the small yellow dashes is left without hardly any detail.

On top of the water do new interventions to accentuate the dark contrasts along the bank. These strokes are ochre colored and the final definition of this area is achieved with a tone made up of white, luminous green and ochre.

6·The thicket along the shore is done with contrasts between light green and dark green. The tree trunks on the right are defined with the same clear tone as on the shore.

Now the work is concentrated on the elaboration of the water. In reality it is not difficult but it is important to study the line direction and the direct dragging on the picture.

Unlike the rest of the landscape, in this zone white is much more heavily used to represent the foam. It is desirable to avoid fusion and to leave the brush mark visible.

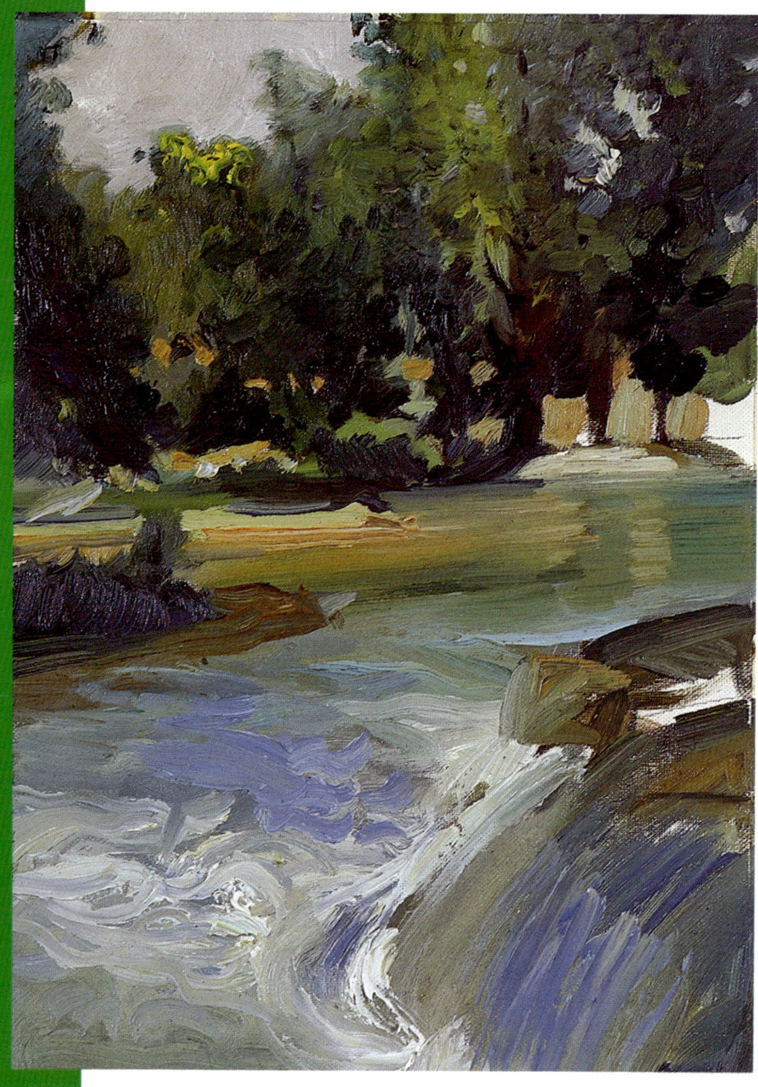

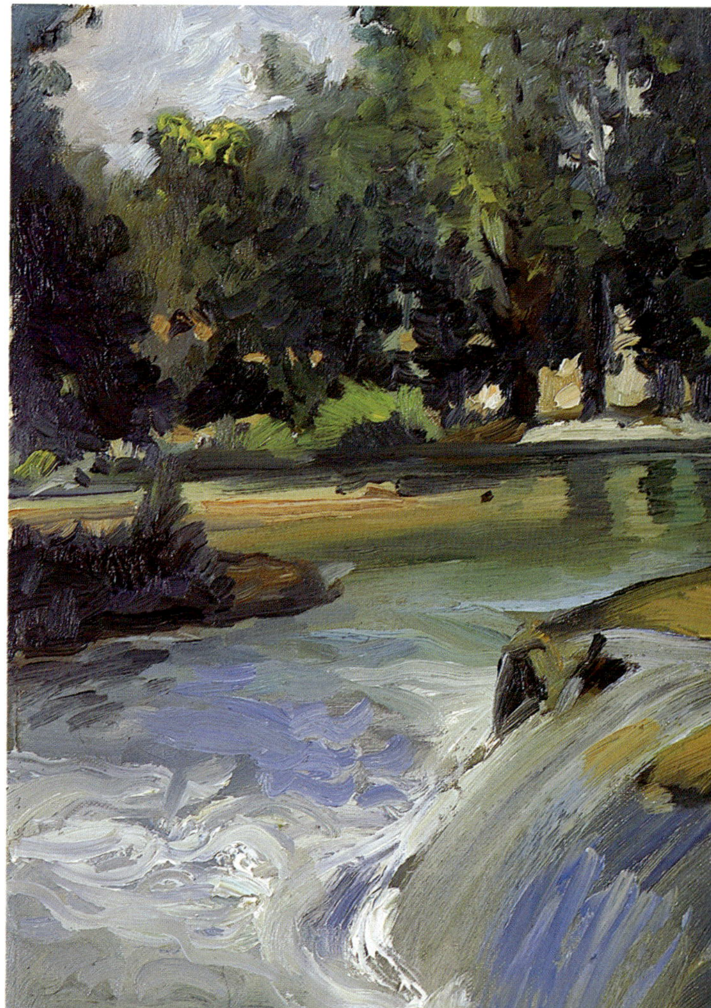

Summary

7·Paint the final contrasts on the trees and some free white strokes on the cascade in the foreground.

You have now finished this beautiful river landscape which has allowed you to practice the different strokes both for blending and for direct touches.

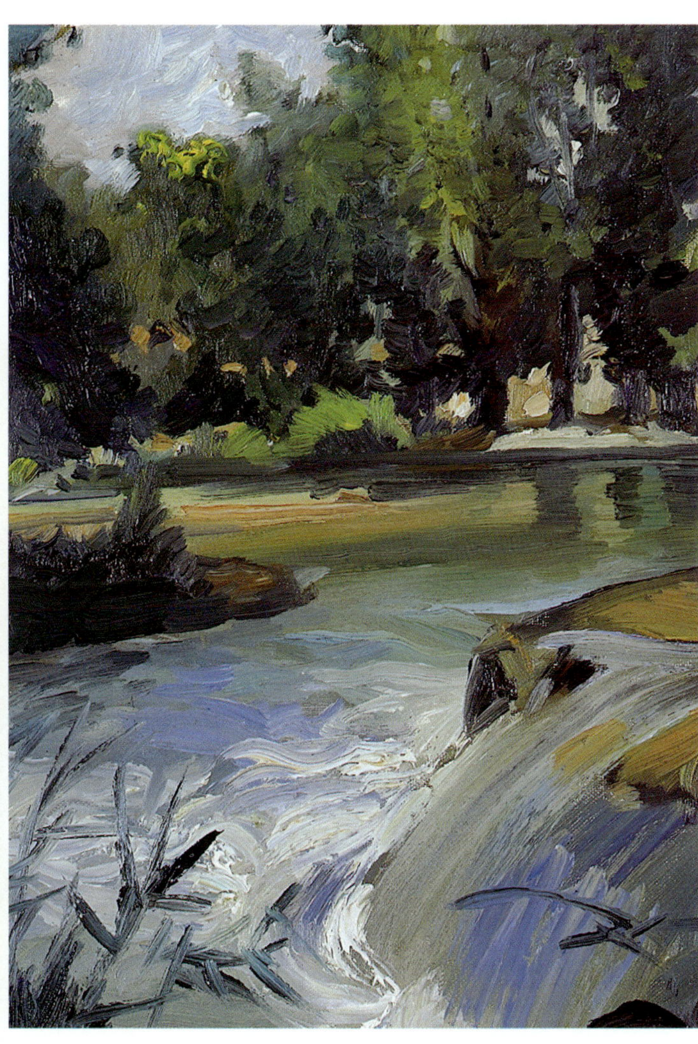

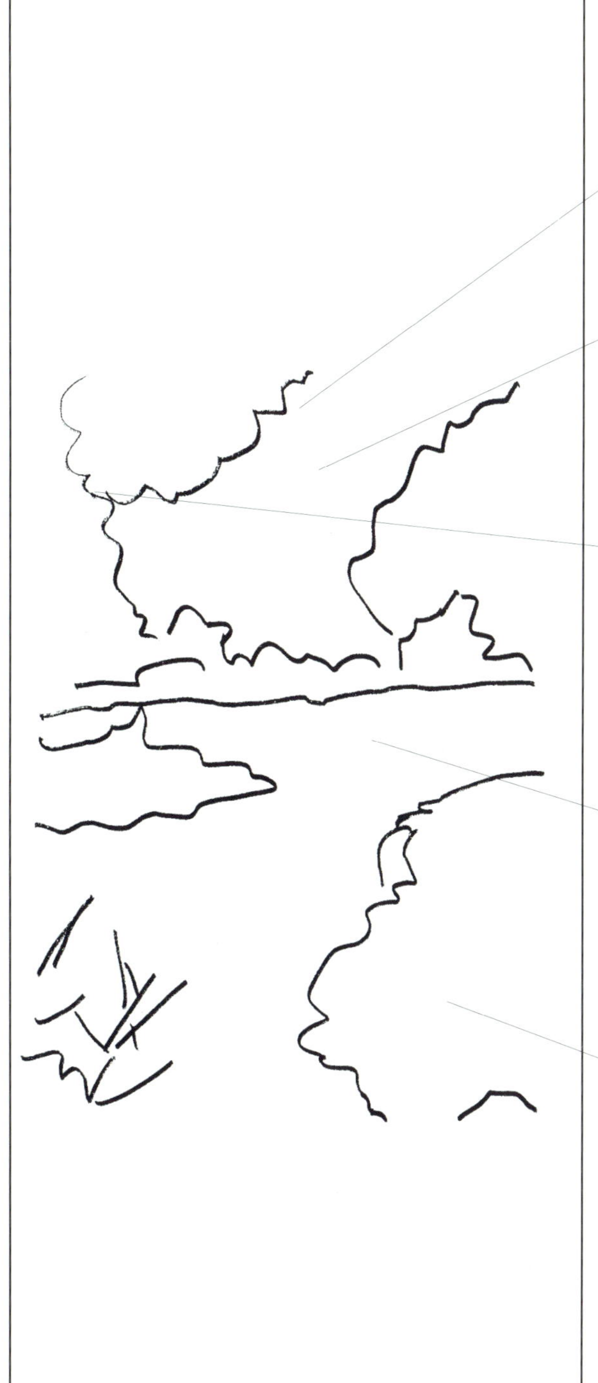

The tree texture is composed of multiple, small strokes.

The trees in the background have varied textures to give an effect of depth.

The initial sketch is realized in pencil and immediately afterwards gone over in thinned oil color to mark out the different planes.

The water reflections are long strokes that blend with the lower tones.

In the foreground the stroke is obvious. It has drawing like properties so that it represents the froth on the cascade.

Chapter 7

Color masses in the picture

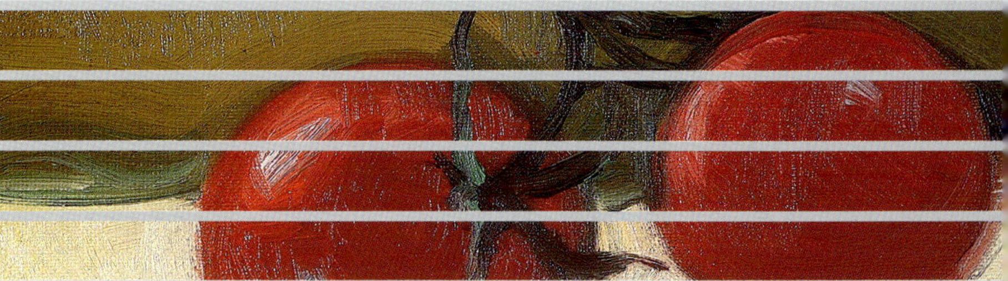

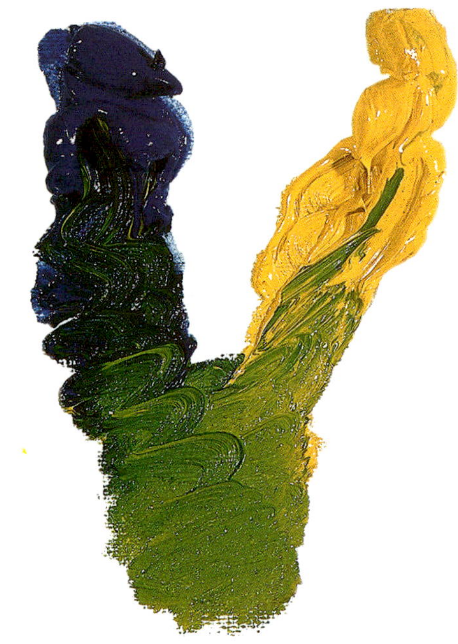

Mixtures of basic colors.

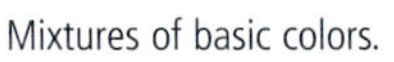

Mixtures of broken colors.

The color masses in the picture are applied progressively as we have already seen in the last chapter. However it is not a technique that is not only applied in relation to the thick over thin rule. Now that the previous concepts have been assimilated, we must practice how to build up the image. In this chapter we will look at a series of exercises which offer us interesting insights into oil painting techniques. So far, in earlier chapters we have practiced different types of strokes and the evolution of color grounds. All these ideas are going to explored in depth. Colors will be superimposed on top of each other. It is recommendable to pay attention to the first color masses and the succession of strokes.

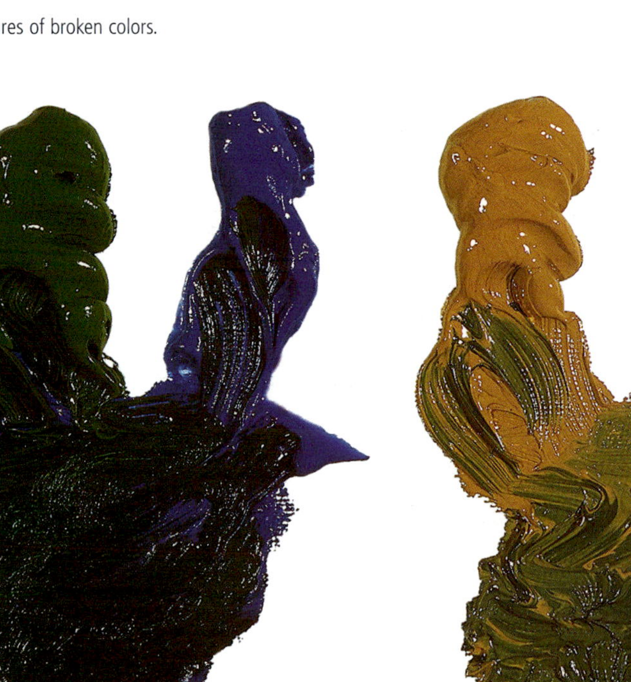

The superimposition of colors

As we have seen in the last chapter, when a color is superimposed on another still fresh one, the superimposed color drags part of the color below which permits a slight variation in the resulting tone. Often this can be a great help to the artist. However, uncontrolled dragging by the brush can give unexpected and undesirable effects if the theory of color is not mastered.

When you are working with different colors you must bear in mind the reaction of the mixes. The basic colors, like yellow, magenta and cyan blue combine together producing secondary colors, for example green and orange. However, if the colors used are already mixed, like brown and green, the result of this mix will be a dirty or broken color.

The first color masses must be rapid and general, without adding detail. What is important is that they cover the base with a uniform field.

Color masses without details

When the artist understands how the colors combine it is possible to do a picture knowing what the result will be of the different masses and superimpositions. The oil painting process must be carefully controlled if you do not want the layers or superimpositions to appear broken or dirty, or to produce new colors by dragging. The first point, apart from following the "thick over thin" rule, is that the color masses must be applied progressively.

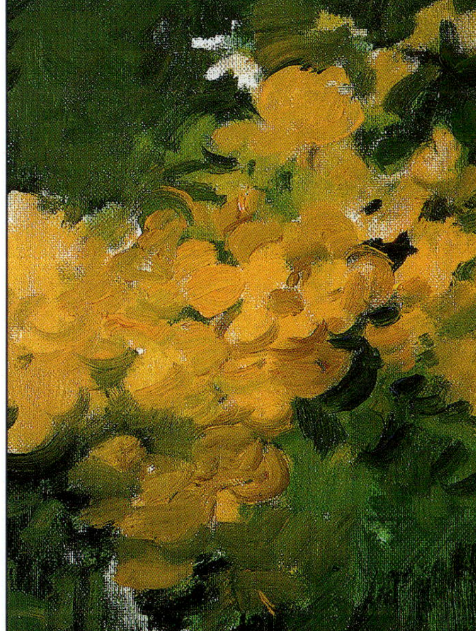

As the color masses are developed, they become a variety of tones of the colors used.

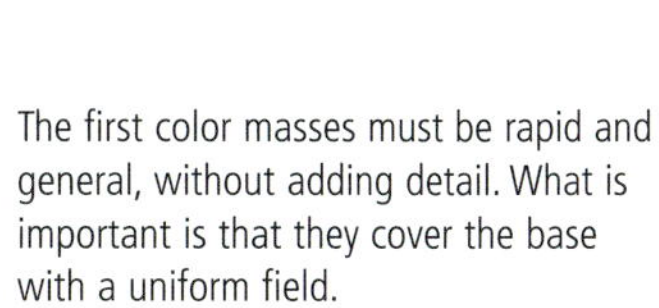

A practical recourse

Oil painting has substantial advantages over other painting media, for example its opacity. However, it also has drawbacks: its slow drying time and the cleaning process. When it is being practiced there are clearly defined stages. The first phase, applying the color fields can be accelerated by using "water-based" oil colors; they dry rapidly. Another plus is that the brushes can be rinsed under the tap with soap and water.

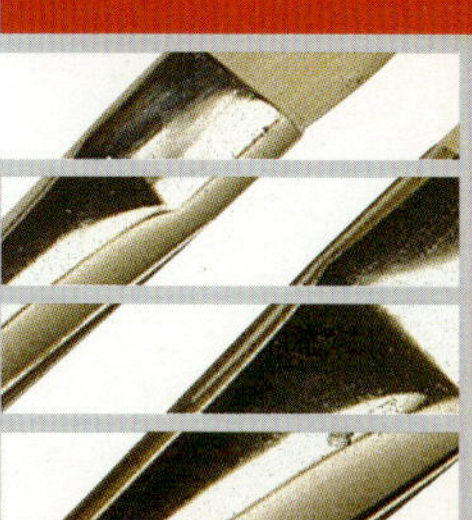

The first color masses will always be general because the details must be left until later when the thickness of the oil color is increased.

Direct mixing on the picture

Details are not introduced into these first layers of color until the picture is quite advanced. All the work done on these first layers is aimed at establishing the tones that will be the base for later colors. When you set about this next exercise it is necessary to repeat that it is important to know how the colors behave when mixed. The first grounds tend to mix the primary colors together; here its going to be green and yellow. The mix, realized directly on the picture, will produce variations in the same color range of the colors used, in this case the cool colors.

The importance of the oil color ground

An oil painting can only be built up correctly and progressively if the color masses are well laid out.
-The first color masses must never be too thick
-The colors must be perfectly ordered so that the minimum possible amount of paint is dragged.
-The small contrasts are realized once the color masses have established a base wide and stable enough.

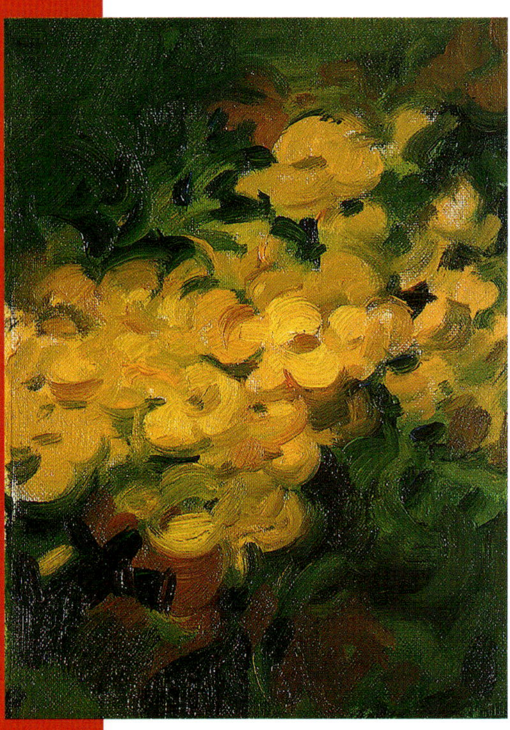

Contrasts are not only constructed by adding darks. The most luminous strokes also allow the forms to be outlined.

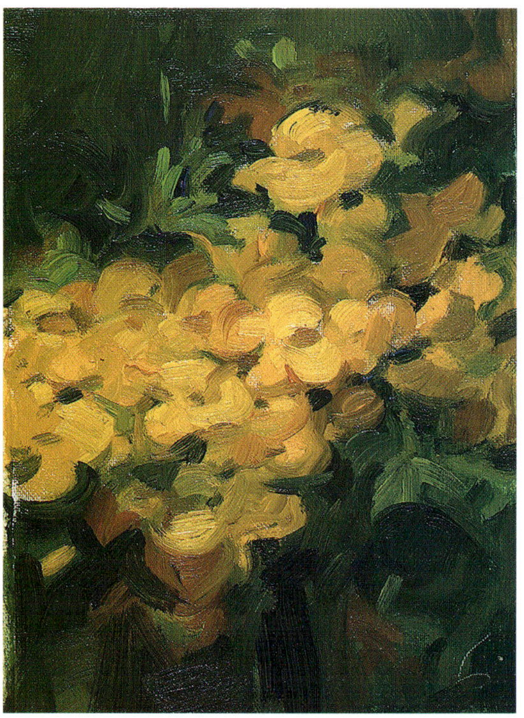

The details can be made more defined when the color masses have been carefully studied.

Contrasts in color masses

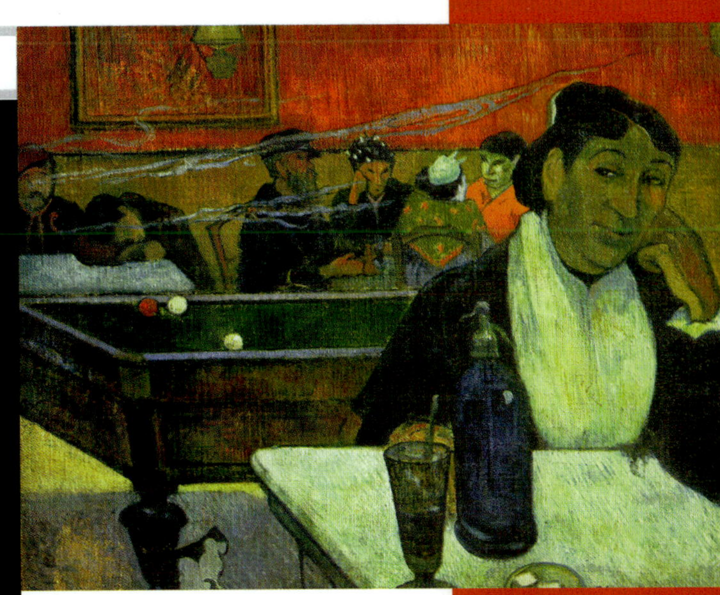

Paul Gauguin's work (1848-1903) had immense personal style and strength. It influenced one of the postimpressionists movements that even today carries weight among artists: fauvism. This name was given to the movement by a critic who spoke of "the wild animals in the cage" ("la cage aux fauves") when describing the pictures on display in one of the rooms in the Autumn Salon of 1905. Originally scornful, the term fauvism became an adequate description for the visual effect that this type of painting produces with its color masses and uncompromising contrasts. This painting by Gauguin, "Café de Arles", kept in the Pushkin Museum in Moscow is composed, like many of his other works, of great masses of color which the artist enriched with numerous nuances. The original grounds were realized around perfectly defined masses. In fact, this is one of the principal characteristics of this great painter's style.

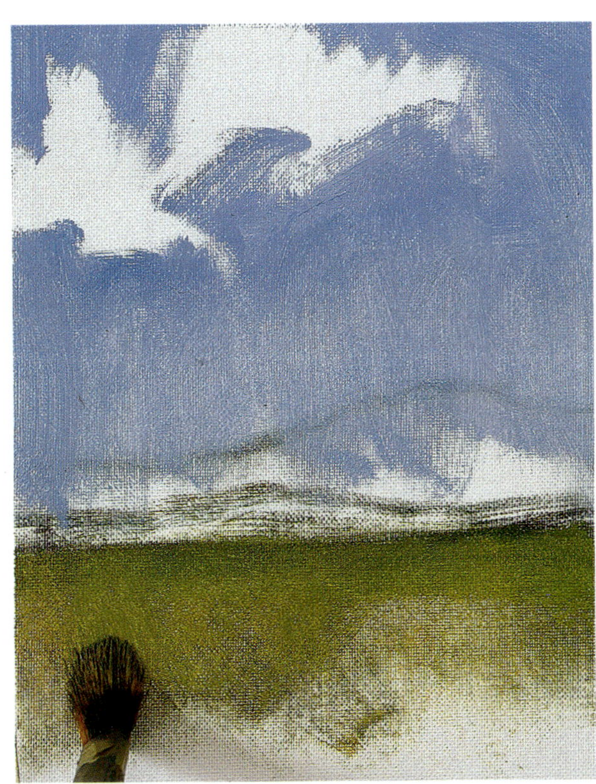

It does not matter if the first color masses cover up the initial sketch. It can be recovered later.

-When the background colors are completed, the forms can be controlled by the contrasts that outline them.

From general to specific

The color masses must be applied progressively, becoming more defined. As the most important masses are placed and the background becomes covered in color, it is possible to incorporate new nuances and tints superimposed on top of the previous ones.

As we have seen in early chapters, progress is made in oil painting by going from the thinned color masses to the thicker strokes, a type of stroke that makes it possible to turn the mass into something much more precise and defined. This point must be born in mind for all work in oil. You always have to develop the piece going from a general level to the more specific details. Two simple sentences sum up how a painting evolves: 'thick on top of thin' and 'detail once the general colors are down'.

The forms lose detail in the color masses

An oil painting is subject to a great variety of changes from the beginning before it is considered finished. Therefore, it is important to know about the properties of this medium if you want the piece to turn out satisfactorily. When a learner starts to paint they come up against a problem: the elaborated drawing they did at the beginning is blotted out by the colors until it becomes unrecognizable.

A learner will have to practice a lot to be able to leave aside the details and to concentrate on the color masses, enriching them gradually as the painting develops.

In the following exercise we are going to do a well structured landscape. It is so straightforward that it will serve as an example of how the oil painting process works.

Rectifying the form in successive layers

The fact that oil colors are painted thick on top of thin means the first layers can be developed very quickly. You have to completely forget about the details when working on the initial colors. This is applicable to any subject. The original sketch, drawn in charcoal or directly in oil color, can be completely covered in color. It does not matter as it is always possible to redo it however complex it may be. What is fundamental is that the color masses are as general as possible and allow the zones to be unified.

The opacity means light can go on top of dark

As it is a completely opaque medium, oil colors not only allow rectifications to be made, they also permit light colors to be painted over dark colors. A white can be painted on top of a blue without the latter showing through: there is no transparency. Because of this principle the layers of color become more defined. The drawing is redone thanks to the color masses and not to the marks. As you can see in this landscape the first masses cover all of the picture and the color blots out the initial sketch. However, it is recovered through the painting, much more concrete in its form. Each little zone can be considered as a picture in its own right where the process 'detail once the general colors are down' is repeated. On top of the background paint the clouds superimposed over the color masses with strokes more precise and defined. The mountains completely define the background. However, if you look closely, even these mountains are not defined definitively. They too are a new zone which must be elaborated.

After painting the clouds, the mountains give form to the landscape.

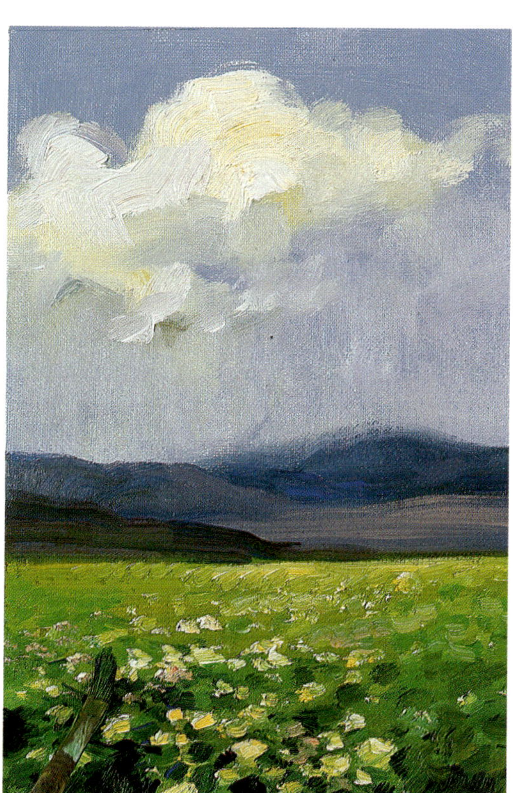

The flowers are not painted until the general forms are in position.

Details at the end

As you can see, in this straightforward process neither details nor small strokes which could have got in the way of the color masses work have been made. Until the piece is completely defined in all its zones no details are painted. When everything else is in place the nuances and contrasts can be added definitively. Pay attention to the details in this example. The mountains are finished off with a much more defined intervention than in the foreground. On the ground start to place dark contrasts that will later be the shadows of the vegetation. This masses are painted with free strokes in the foreground. In the distant background the color is left brighter and more luminous. On top of the colored ground you can paint the defined flowers with short, progressive strokes, going into details.

The form is drawn as you paint

In your early works it will be difficult to follow the rule that the form is redrawn as you paint. However, by doing different pieces with time you will pick up the necessary experience. Understanding comes with practice. The initial sketch is lost in the paint, and in the painting, and then recovered in the process. To practice this concept we are going to do a straightforward exercise in which you can clearly appreciate how the drawing is recovered in the color masses and the defined strokes.

The drawing marks the form

Starting a picture from a well elaborated drawing is the basis of good painting in any medium. However, this does not mean that the drawing is unmovable. In fact, in oil painting it can be altered. The initial sketch is a guide but it will constantly be covered by color.

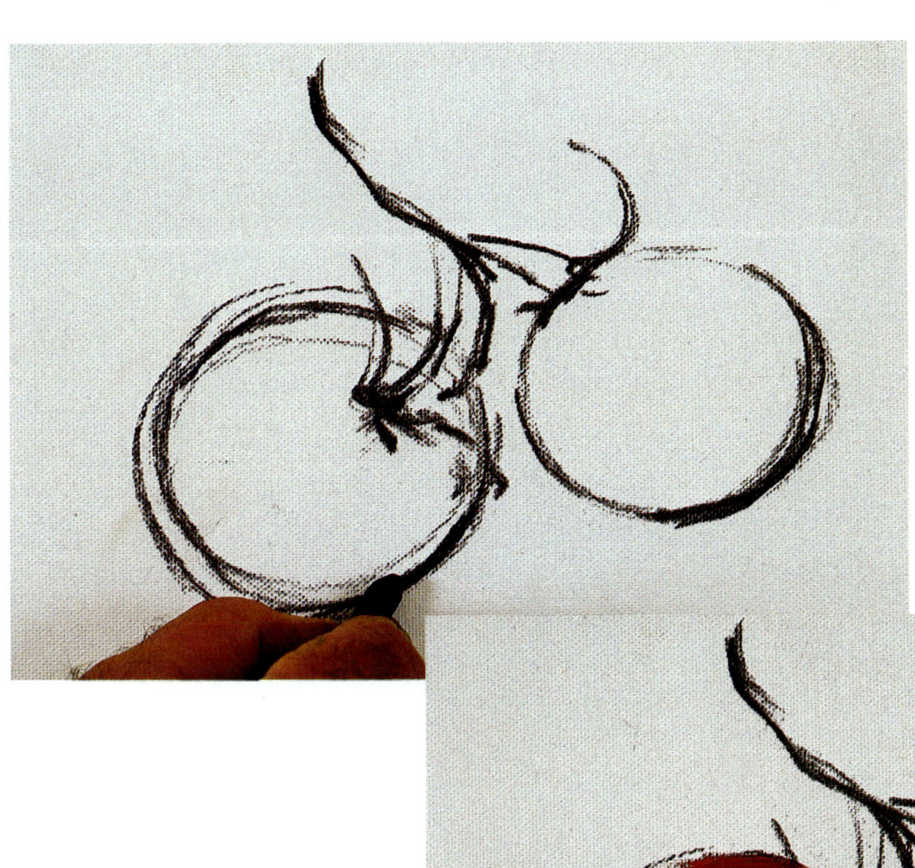

Despite the color destroying the original form, it is important the drawing is done well as it guides the rest of the work.

In the painting process the color masses cover the drawing of the stems.

Do not be afraid to paint

Although the drawing may be well done you must not be afraid to cover it up if it is superfluous. In this exercise a very complete drawing was done, but this should not be an obstacle to the painting of the tomatoes as two red masses. The tomato stems have been completely covered by the color, the great masses of which have priority over the internal forms. Of course, an effort has been made to respect the circles.

Drawing with the paint

Once the principal color masses has been made, you can start to work on the original tomato form and the internal details. If you had done this earlier the colors would have become dirtied. Moreover, detail strokes always work better when there is no obstacle in the way. Here the darkest strokes are superimposed on top of the red of the tomato. The technique is very similar to the last exercise in which the flowers in the countryside were painted over the great color masses in the background.

How to finish the painting

Later interventions with color depend on to what finishing touches you wish to give the picture. It is fundamental to observe the elaboration process of all the zones of the picture. For example, if you want to paint the background so that the tomatoes do not stand out so much due to their color, the stems will be largely covered by the painting. Once the area around the tomatoes has been painted go back and redo as precisely as possible the strokes that depict the stems. The highlights on the leaves are painted in the same way, but only when the colors and the masses have been concluded.

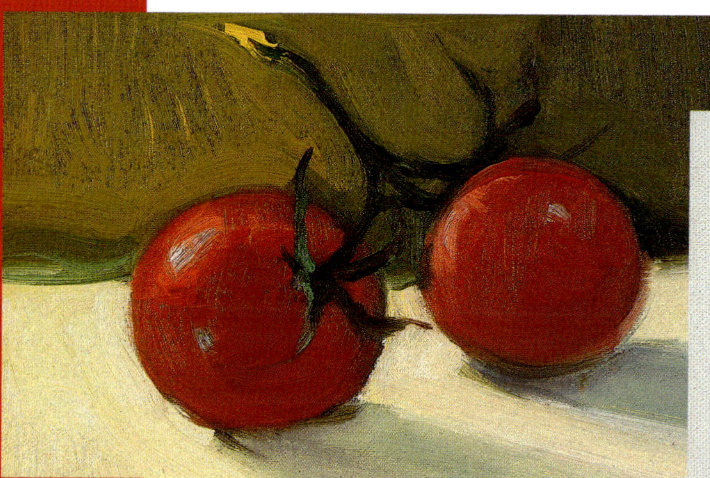

Just like in the last exercise the details are only painted once all the big color masses have been realized.

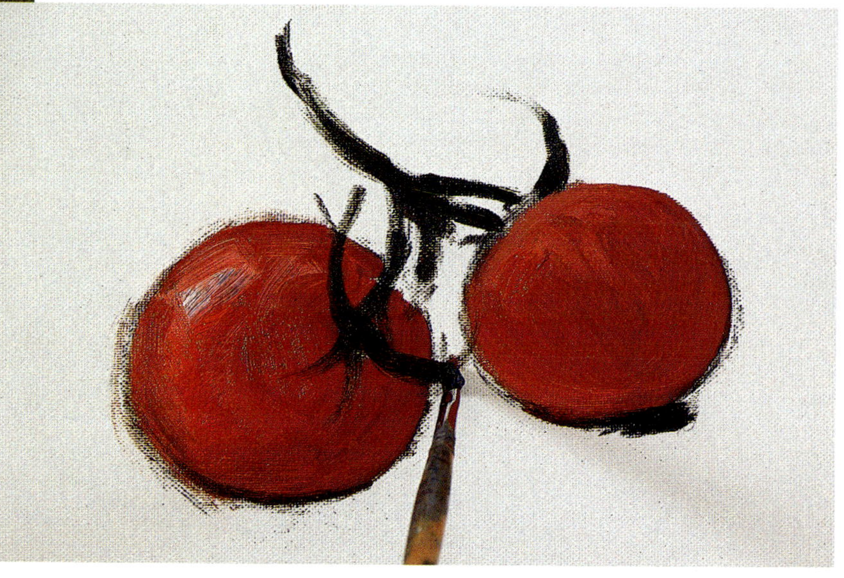

The forms are redone once the color masses are in place.

Summary

COLOR SUPERIMPOSITION. When doing the color masses, the colors are superimposed dragging part of the lower colors when they are still fresh.

COLOR MASSES WITHOUT DETAILS AND DIRECT MIXES. The first colors must be applied in a very general way, without going into details. In this process direct mixes can be made.

THE OPACITY OF THE PAINT. The opacity of the oil colors means they can be constantly rectified and the picture redone, even after it has been completely covered.

Exercises

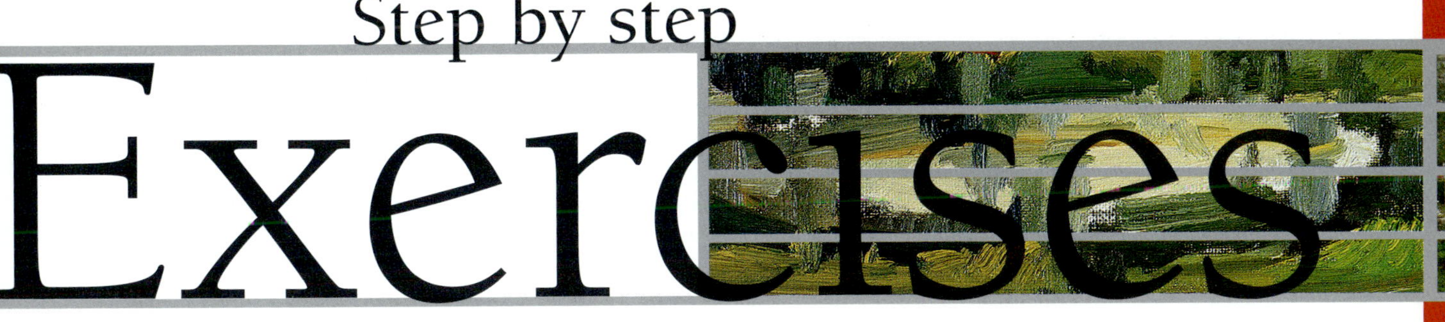
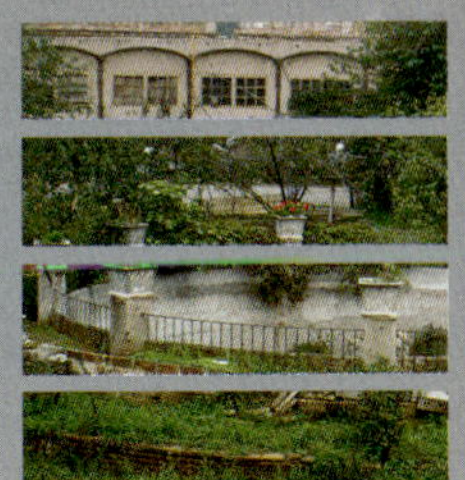

AN ABANDONED GARDEN

The subject we are going to paint in this exercise is a pond in an abandoned garden.

The model must always interest and attract the artist, otherwise they would lose a great deal of their motivation for doing the painting. Here this subject does not involve anything complicated. The composition is simple, completely symmetrical and elliptical. Great masses of green surround the pond making it easier to paint because of the contrasts established.

Necessary material

Oil colors (1), primed card (2), linseed oil and turpentine oil (3), brushes (4), palette (5), charcoal (optional) (6) and a cloth (7).

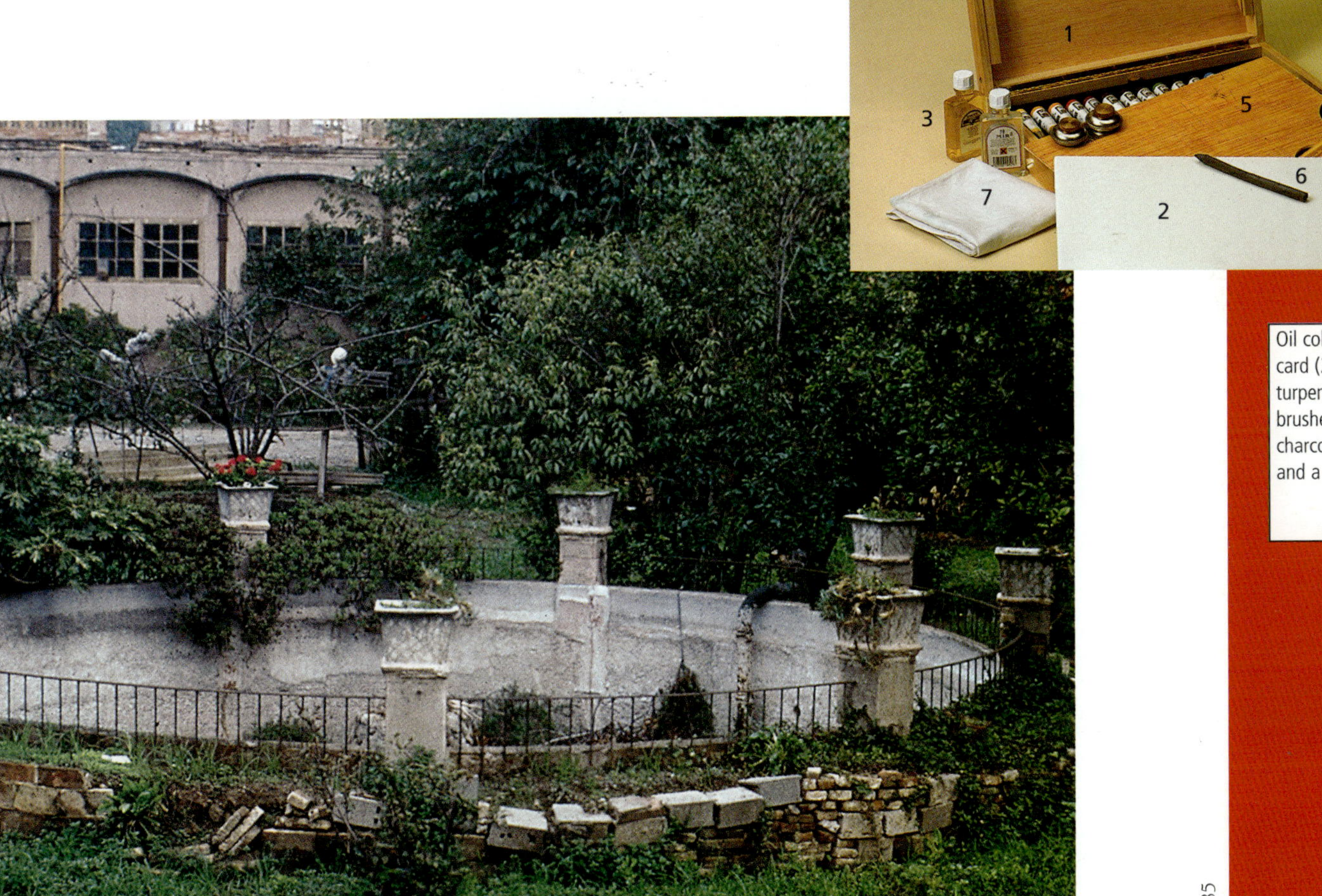

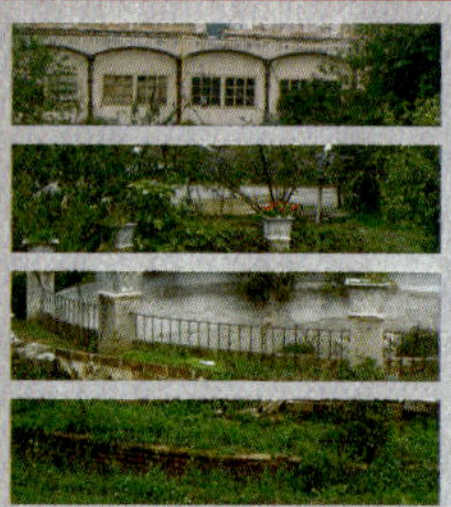

Exercises

1·The outline of the pond can be started in charcoal, to set out the first zones of the picture, but immediately the drawing will be redone in a dark, thinned color which takes away all traces of charcoal.

The pond has an elliptical form due to the perspective. Around it draw the principal dark parts on the columns that run round the pond, and the darks on the trees in the background.

From the beginning the forms are depicted as masses without any detail.

2·Firstly place a large luminous green color mass around the pond.

As you can see, in this first intervention we are not interested in obtaining textures nor in altering tones. All that matters is that the principal zones are covered.

In the same way that the grass space has been covered, color the form of the trees on the right and paint ochre in the background.

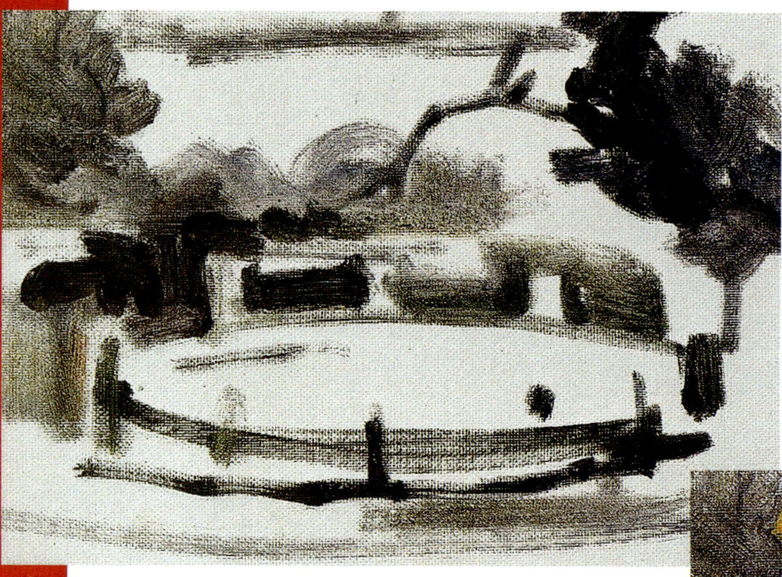

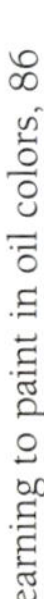

3·Finish painting the trees in the background in a slightly off white. On top of the colored background, start to paint new nuances that are superimposed on top of the first layers, dragging part of the lower color. On top of the ochre, paint in a whitish color. Here the stroke mixes with the original color.

Around the pond construct the trees with numerous strokes. First dark and dense ones for the trees on the right, and on top of these paint in a very light green. The form drawing is recovered thanks to the paint.

4·As we have explained throughout the chapter, the details are not painted until the great color masses have definitively covered the background. Once the tree tops have been painted on the right, you can paint the small spots of light that come through the leaves, completely superimposed on top of the green color mass.

Complete the coloring by doing the vegetation on the left. Continue by starting to paint the grass on the floor in small strokes superimposed on top of the general color. Some short strokes paint the white in the background. Start to paint the pilasters of the pond in a yellowish green. Inside it, paint in a greeny ochre.

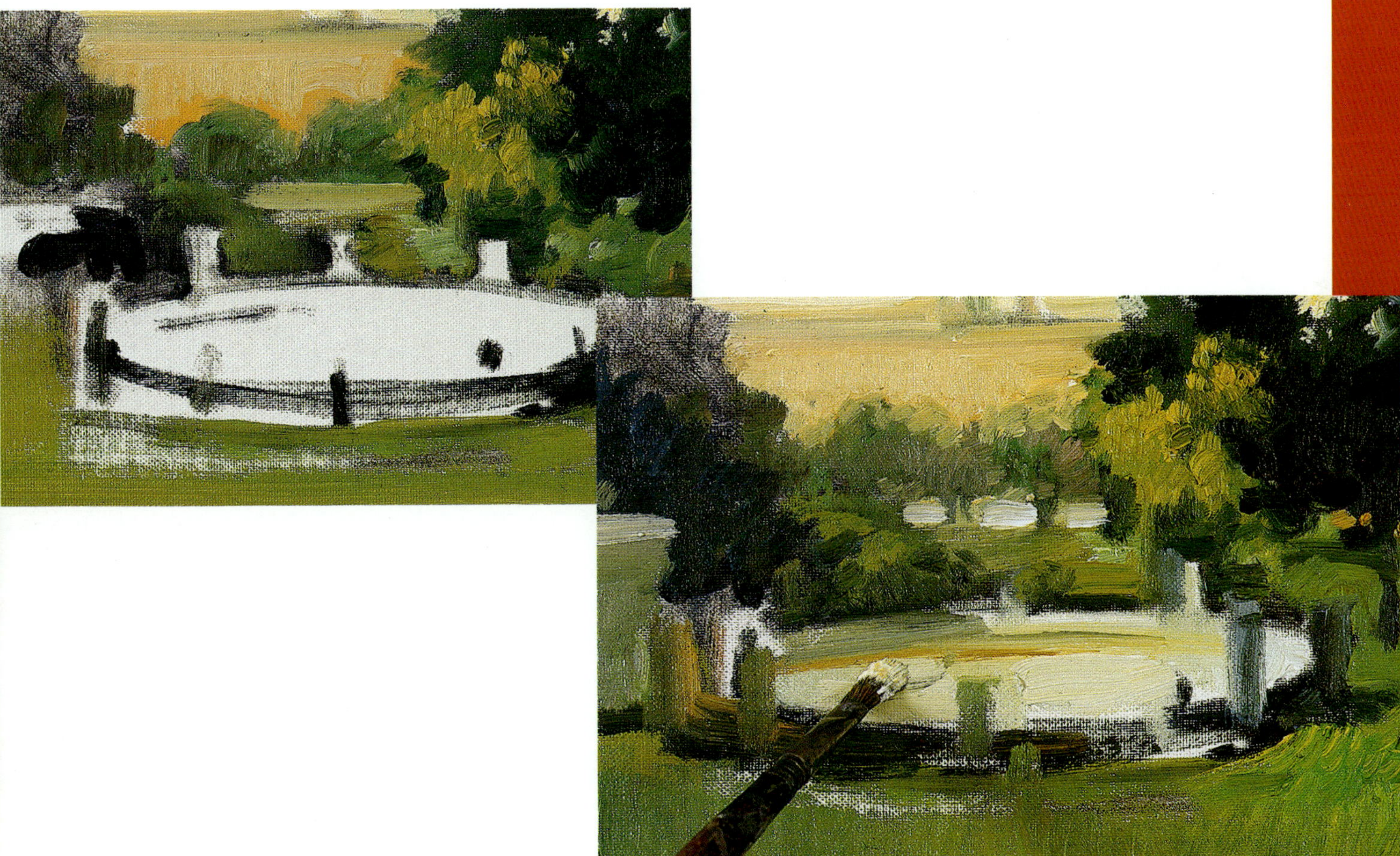

Exercises

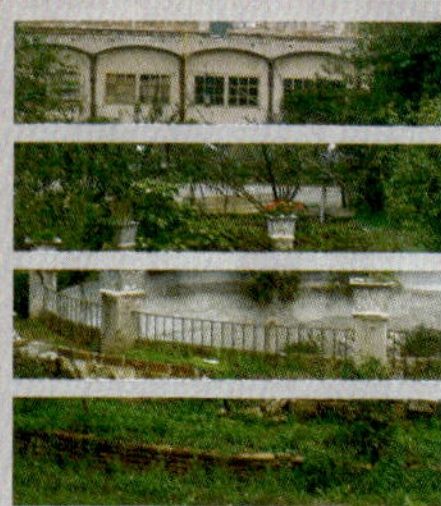

5·As you can see, a detail is never painted unless the lower zone is already sufficiently described by the color masses. Once these color masses depict the background, you can go on to superimposing strokes which give the desired texture or modify the form, the contrast or even the color.

On top of the most luminous tree on the right, paint in an almost pure yellow in little strokes that drag part of the color below. On the left, too, small strokes are made but this time with very dark colors.

6·Oil colors can be redone in any moment so go over the color on the pilasters of the pond until you get the form right. You must be extremely careful not to smudge the inside of the pond. There we want the ochre color to remain pure.

Once you have finished this zone, paint the wild flowers over the last pilaster with touches of red.

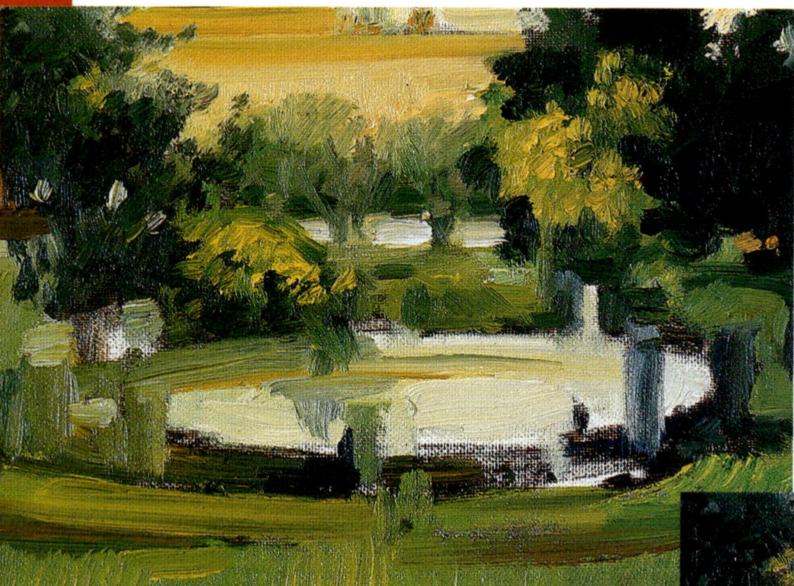

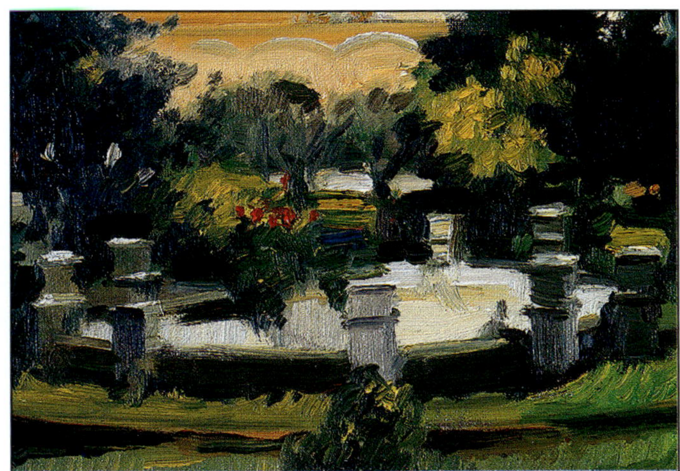

7·Paint the definitive contrasts of the pond. First, the pilasters on which grayed colors come into play and blue colors for the shadows. The highlights are painted last of all with very defined strokes.

The edge of the pond is painted in a dark tone that contrasts strongly with the interior which is left luminous.

Finish the contrasts on the ground and in the vegetation in the foreground.

Finally, the arches in the background are painted so as to redo the architecture.

Summary

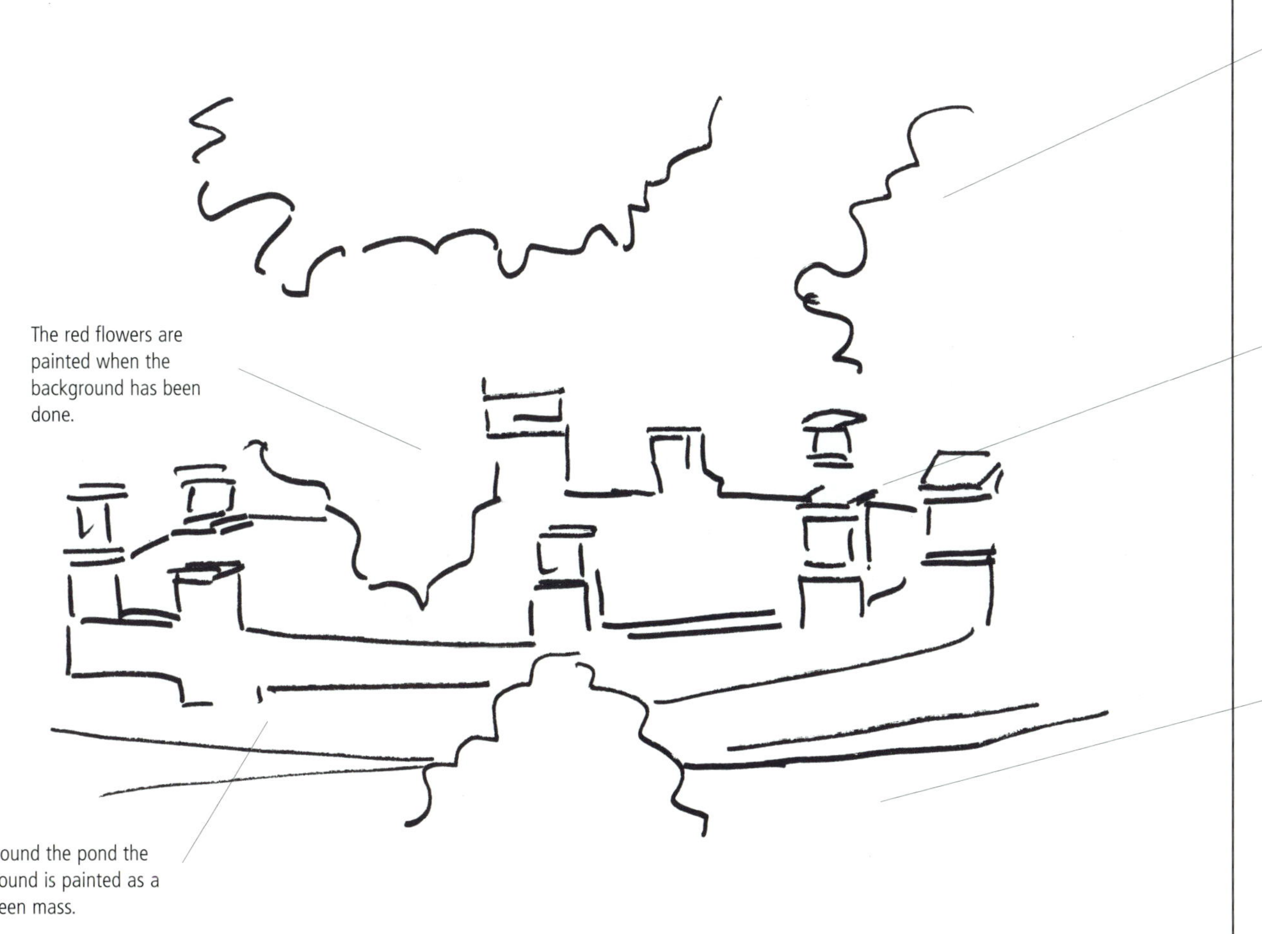

Chapter 8

Light and shadow in oil painting

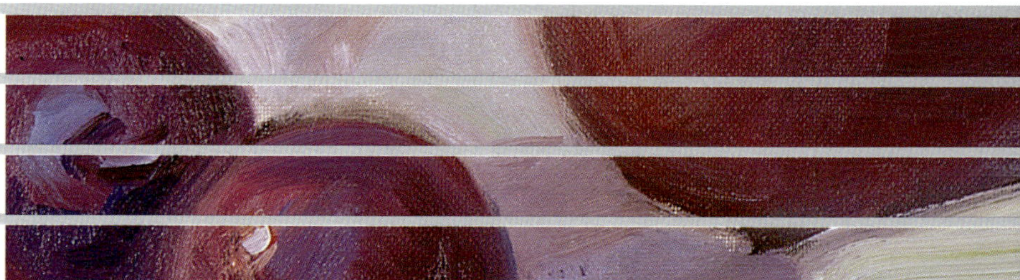

In oil painting the color tones can be expressed through the quantity of light. This means that less light corresponds to a darker tone.

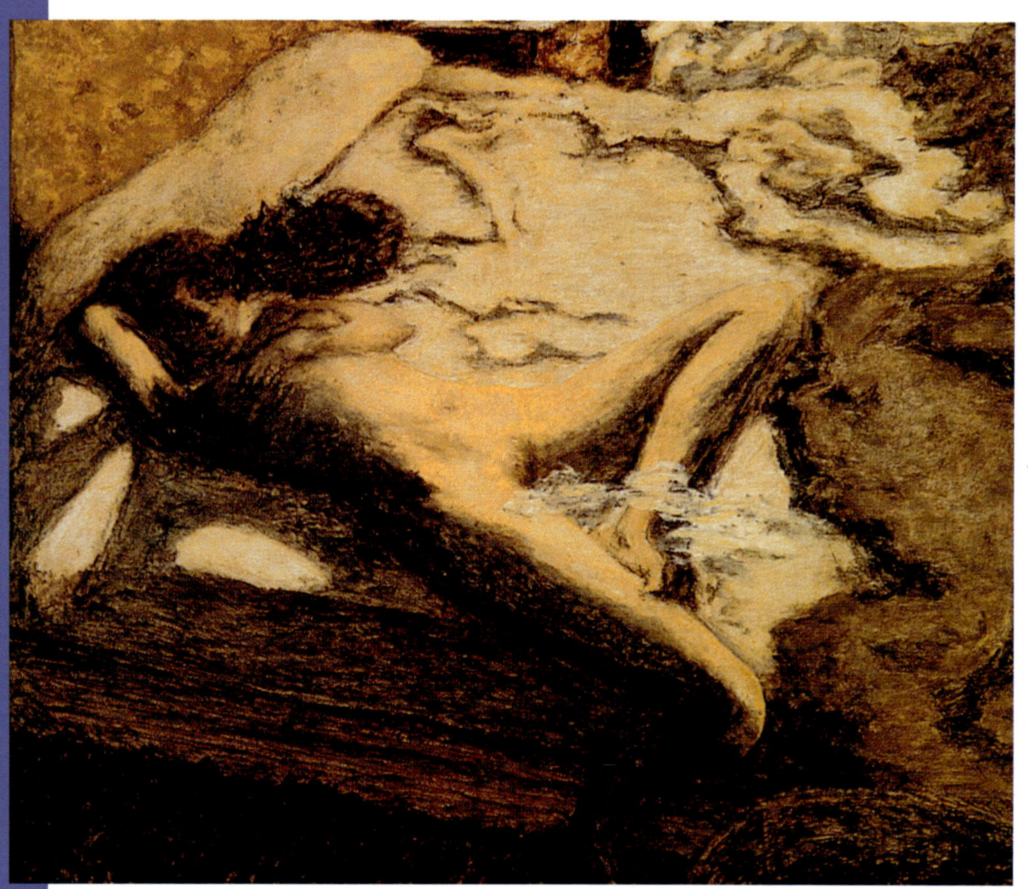

Impressionism, and the artistic movements that came out of it, allowed lights and shadows to be depicted as direct color impacts. In this picture you can see that the limits of light and shadow are not in the black and white but in the intermediate tones of the earth colors.

The reasons why oil painting completely replaced tempera painting are very evident: firstly its slow drying process allowed a much more meticulous work to be done and facilitated the study of the objects and the people being depicted. Oil colors also aid the fusion of colors enabling the artist to achieve tone gradations so subtle that it is impossible to make out where one color ends and the next begins.

In this chapter we are going to study the effects of light on the objects painted in oil colors. It is a complex question that will take up many hours of dedication. When we start out, although you may already master color a bit it is recommendable to temporarily leave it aside so as to be able to concentrate fully on light and shadow. Therefore in the following pages the exercises proposed are in monochrome. Special attention will be dedicated to the way oil colors are elaborated from linseed oil and pigments.

Light tones and dark tones

Dark tones correspond to shadow or penumbra (half-light) areas. If in a picture a mixture between Van Dyck brown and burnt umber is used as the darkest tone, the rest of the tones must not be more intense than this color. This tone will be considered as the black reference for the picture. Something similar is applicable to the light tones: the most luminous tone will establish the limits of lightness. Therefore, if an off-white is chosen as the most luminous it will only be applied in the most illuminated zones.

Bearing in mind these considerations it is fundamental to establish the limits of the light tone and shadow gradations.

Study the model.

Before starting to draw or to paint it is recommendable to study how the light and shadows work on the real model - all the zones included. To practice this we can do a simple still life of a fruit, for example an apple. Here the apple has quite wrinkled peel which means that it is not very shiny and it is easier to locate the light and shadow parts. Next to the apple place a white piece of cardboard to act as a screen, reflector, and backdrop wall simultaneously. The model has different light zones. One part is clearly illuminated and the highlight can be appreciated. The rest of the apple presents a more subdued tone

Pay close attention to this apple. The wrinkled skin has several light tones: one point of maximum luminosity, the highlight (1), indirect light (2), the shadow itself (3), refracted light (4), and the shadow cast, also called projected shadow (5).

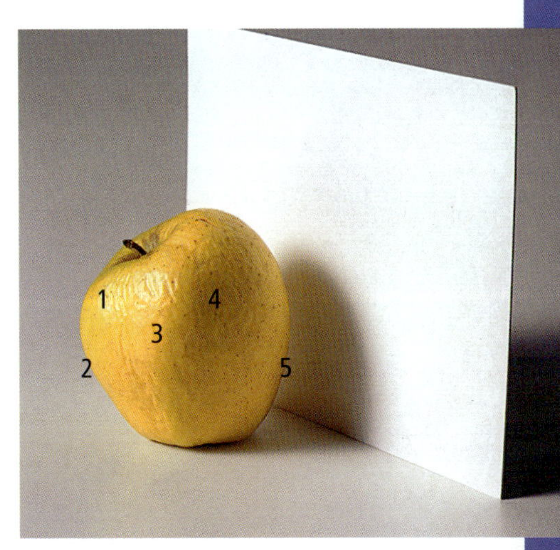

Brushes for oil painting

Oil colors offer endless plastic possibilities thanks to their texture and consistency. Different types of brushes can be used to obtain distinct effects and dragging styles. Which brush is used also depends on the painting phase. To put down grounds or fields the brushes can be flat or rounded. Other smaller brushes allow you to get into tricky areas and do more defined details.

The most commonly used brushes in oil painting are hog's hair brushes and synthetic ones. The texture of the stroke depends on the quality of the hair. The softer it is, the less evident the mark will be. Flat brushes allow straight lines with very defined edges. Thinner brushes permit a finer line the origin and end of which can fade away. Round brushes are useful for doing defined lines or color masses, and even delicate details when required.

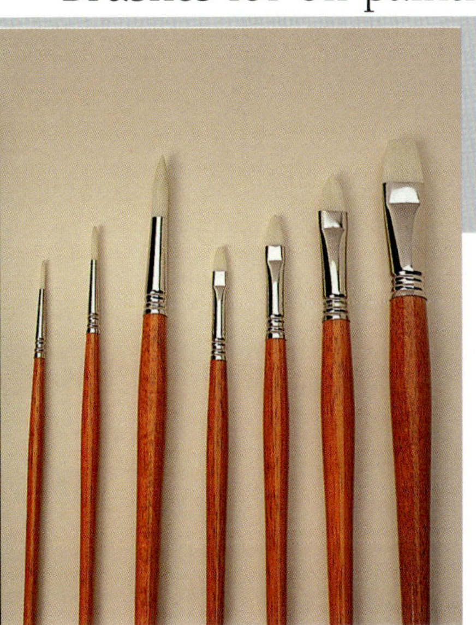

of indirect light. In the shadow zone you can observe various tones. The shadow next to the light plane will be the actual shadow of the apple. By its side, along the edge against the background, a reflection, produced by the light refraction in the cardboard, can be seen. The deepest and darkest shadow is cast onto the cardboard. This is the zone of projected shadow.

Coloring with charcoal

To represent the shadows the most important thing is to know where they are situated, so there is nothing better than starting out with a charcoal sketch which can easily be corrected and allows each zone to be studied before painting. After outlining the apple form and the cardboard wall, draw the shadow that will be the darkest one in this exercise: the projected shadow.

The first strokes

The first strokes should be dense as they are going to paint the darkest shadow: in this case the projected shadow. In this part of the picture you have to define what is going to be the darkest tone in the still life. Using black is ruled out because it restricts the nuances that can come into play. Dark colors like brown or burnt umber are used instead as they offer sharp and rich toned contrasts.

Next to be painted is the shadow zone itself. Firstly the same dark tone was used to mark off the indirect light zone and to intensify the simultaneous contrast effect. Inside the shadow paint in a more luminous tone; the contrast with the background is evident. Color the background with the same color used to develop the shadow on the apple.

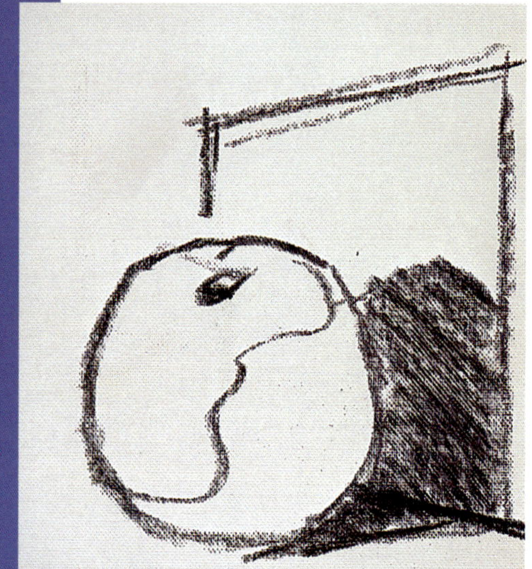

Outline the fruit and draw the projected shadow zone. The shadow outlines the form of the apple. The projected shadow is the darkest zone.

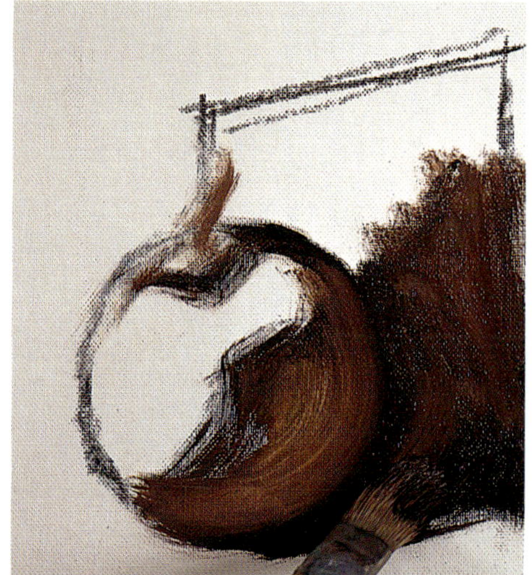

Paint the projected shadow. It is the darkest tone used in the picture. In the beginning the shadow zone itself is painted in this tone but it is later lightened with a more luminous tone.

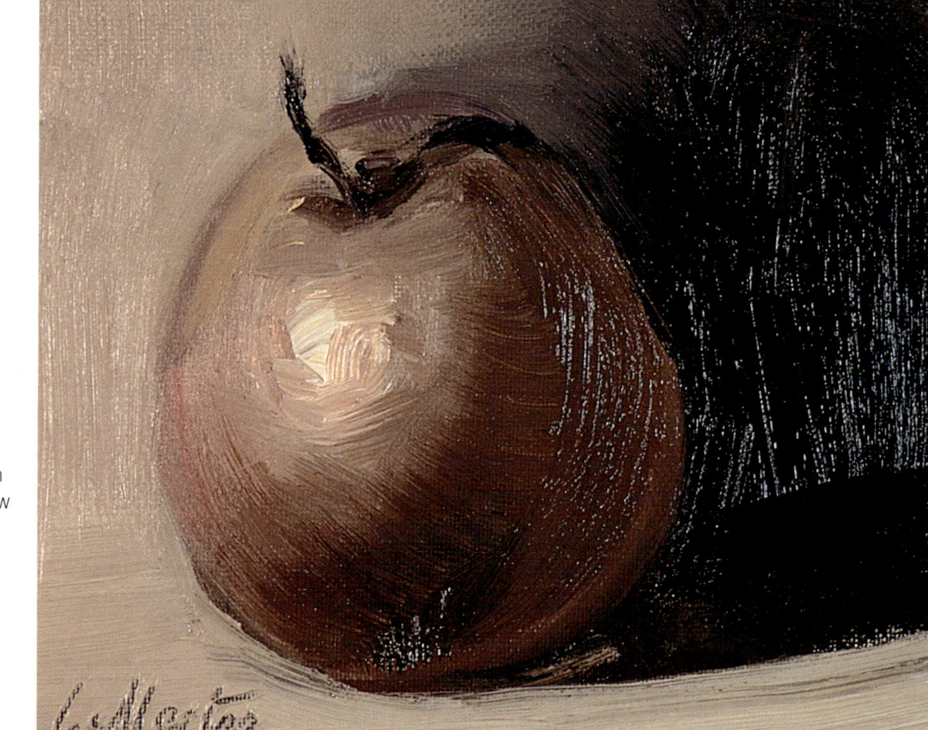

In this close up you can appreciate the indirect light zone and the highlight. When dealing with light and shadow the brush strokes become especially meaningful.

Separating tones

Light and shadow tones are approached in radically different ways. Distinct light gradations can be established in each zone. Logically, the highlight -point of maximum luminosity- is located in the most luminous zone. It is the tone to be painted last to avoid it being contaminated by other darker tones which will be used to develop the rest of the light zone.

The work with the brush and the strokes becomes especially important when painting these zone because one light area comes into contact with a shadow area.

The marks and the lines allow the light zones to be mixed with the shadow zones. If you are not particularly careful when working along the edges an 'invasion' of one tone into another tone could happen. The strokes enable form to be given to the shadows according to the planes in each zone.

As you can see in the image, the tones are softly blended together. Once the principal tones have blended you can place the highlight. Just as we ruled out pure black, pure white is also forbidden. Instead use Naples yellow or other tones close to the luminosity of white.

Differences between the shadows

The diverse possibilities that can be achieved with shadows make for a very realistic pictorial effect, even working from a restricted palette. In the last exercise we carefully studied how light and shadows effect one object but now we are going to work with two objects and their shadow effects.

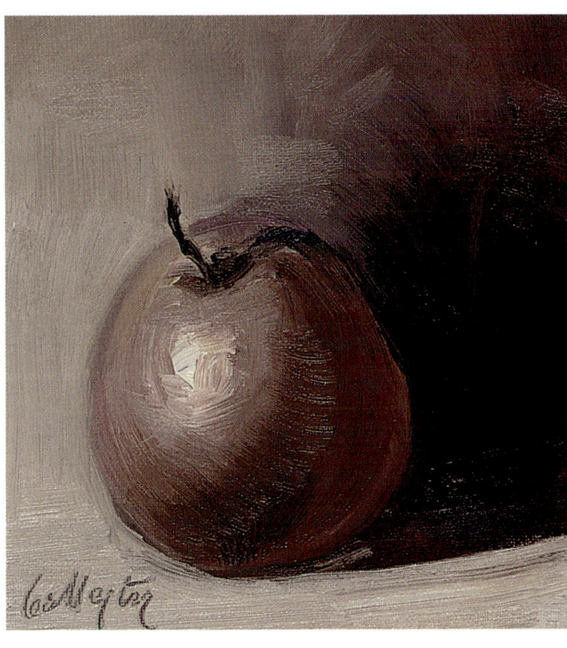

If you look at this finished apple you can see how the zone of refracted light is lightened and gives a volume effect to the rest of the fruit.

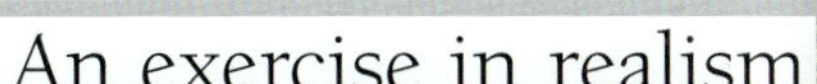

An exercise in realism

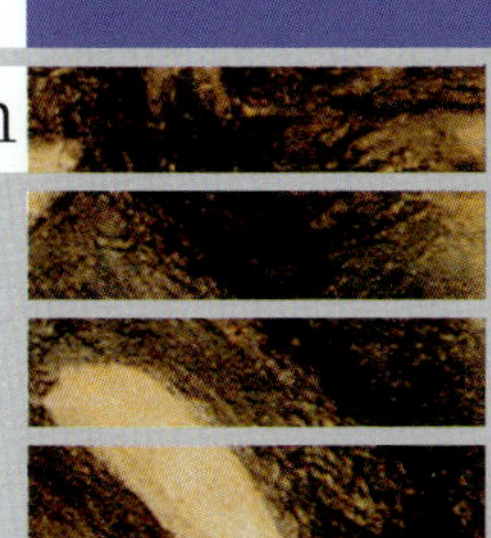

In this simply composed still life the masterly post-impressionist painter Odilon Redon (1840-1916) displays his technical skill. The picture is a completely realistic in depth study of light, the relationship between colors and the complicity in the shadows and reflections. You can observe perfectly how the light source comes from just above the viewer's head on the right. This work of art is kept in a private collection.

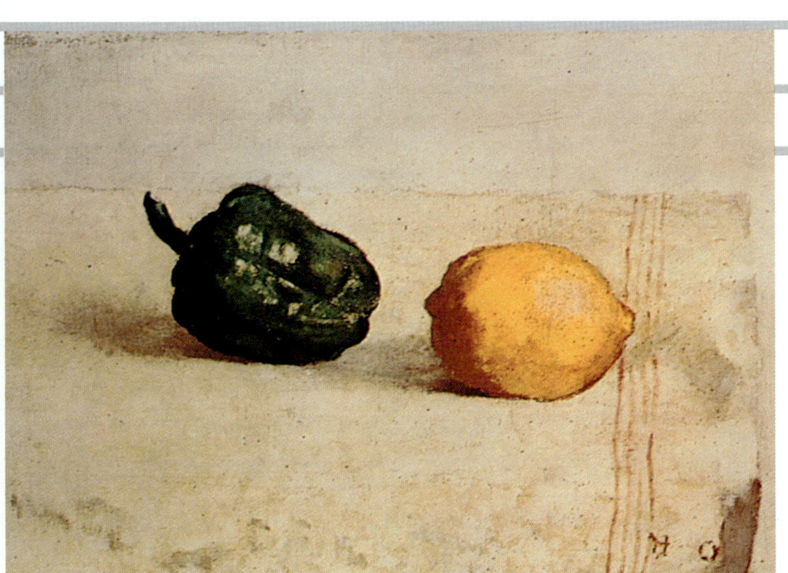

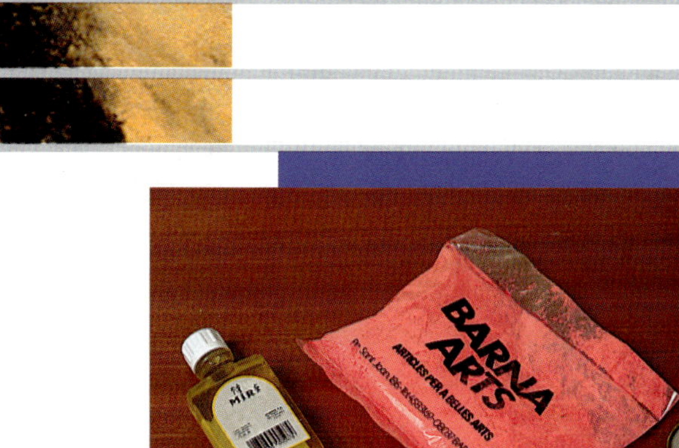

Linseed oil, pigment, a spatula and a palette are the essential elements for elaborating oil colors.

Making a good quality oil color is not simple; it requires technical know-how, perseverance and above all a certain touch so as to be able to control the materials. We will need linseed oil, better if it is refined, colorless and without siccative incorporated, top quality pigment, refined as much as possible, a steel spatula and a clean varnished palette. These materials can be found in Fine Arts shops. Making oil colors at home enables the artist to save a lot of money, but it is only recommendable to make the simplest colors yourself, black, earth tones, medium yellow, dark green and the specialist colors that are not sold in tubes or in any other commercial form, like the fluorescent colors. Many other colors should not be attempted because it would be difficult to get an optimum result.

The quantity of oil colors elaborated depends on the artist's needs, but as it is not a perishable product more can be made than is immediately necessary, especially the commonest colors: they can be stored in screw top plastic pots available in drug stores or chemist's shops. However, even if you prepare more than is immediately necessary, do not go too far: small quantities are better because the butteriness must be perfect and you have to watch out for lumps of pigment.

The method we present here is only one of the many that exist. Following it carefully will produce a good quality paint.

Put a small amount of pigment in the center of the palette and place next to it a few drops of linseed oil, proportionally much less because it is easier to go from thick to thin than vice versa. It is more difficult to add pigment later.

Drag part of the pigment towards the linseed oil with the spatula. Continue dragging over and over again with the spatula edge until it begins to dissolve. Once this starts to happen, you will see that in reality there was less pigment than at first appeared. Eventually the linseed oil absorbs it completely. If it is too flowing, add more pigment until it has a stiff paste consistency. Once it has the right texture you must continue dragging until it is oily, a smooth, buttery paste, not stringy or tacky. When you have finished this process you can add a few drops of dammar varnish or Dutch varnish to increase its shininess or accelerate its drying.

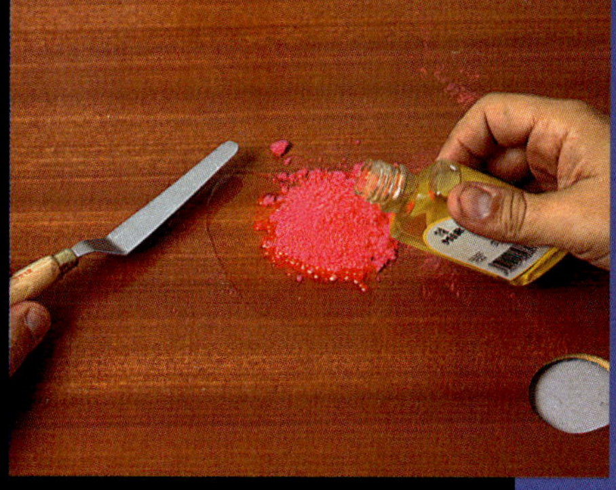

You have to drag the spatula over the paint until it is a smooth, buttery paste, neither too bright nor too pastel colored.

With little oil it is possible to make quite a lot of oil color.

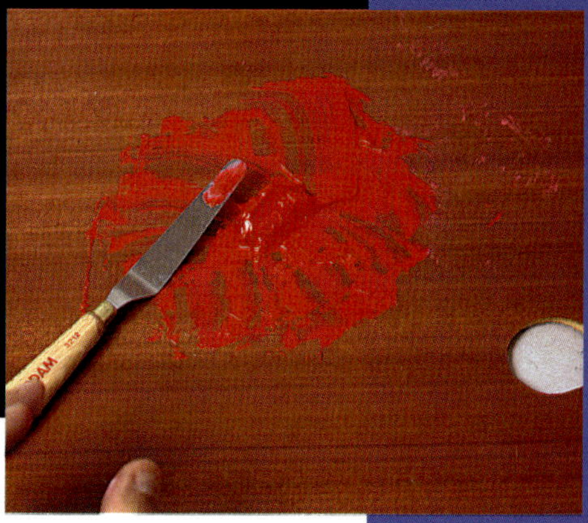

This is what freshly finished oil color looks like.

The compositional study

To do a compositional study charcoal is used because it enables you to position the principal elements as many times as necessary. If you have to correct it, it is enough just to flick it with a cloth or wipe it with a hand. Charcoal is always the ideal medium for drawing before painting in oil color. As you can see, in the initial sketch the forms of each object are defined as much as possible, as well as their location in the picture.

The contrast

In the first exercise, the first contrast could be situated thanks to the charcoal sketch. This is no longer necessary because we will paint directly with thinned oil color. Burnt umber is used for the background which is left perfectly defined marking out the principal forms of the still life and the edges of the table. Use the same tone and a thick brush to paint the shadows of the two elements. When the brush is quite out of paint it gives dry strokes, very useful for creating medium tones, above all when more luminous layers have to be applied and blended with the other dark tones.

Differences between shadows.

The work revolves more around the placement of the shadows than around the highlights because the former offer more options. The highlights are very specific and clearly located while the shadows are rich and spread out over all the surface of the objects. When you paint the light zones, you must bear in

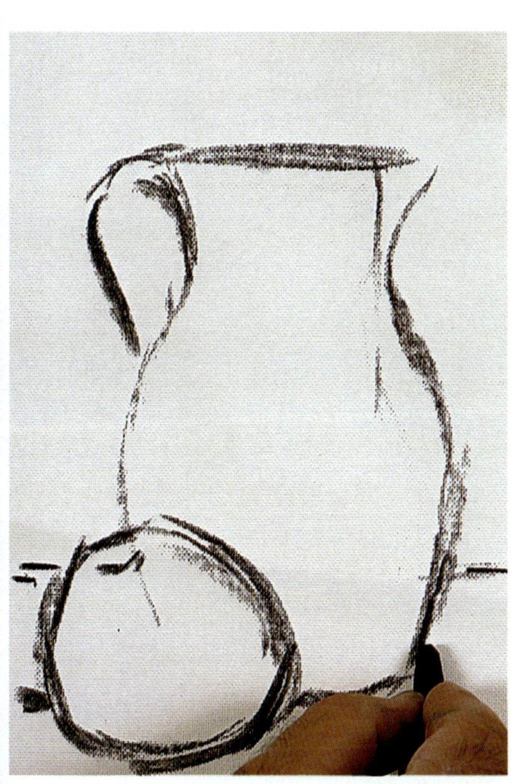

The outline is done in charcoal. Any corrections can be done immediately.

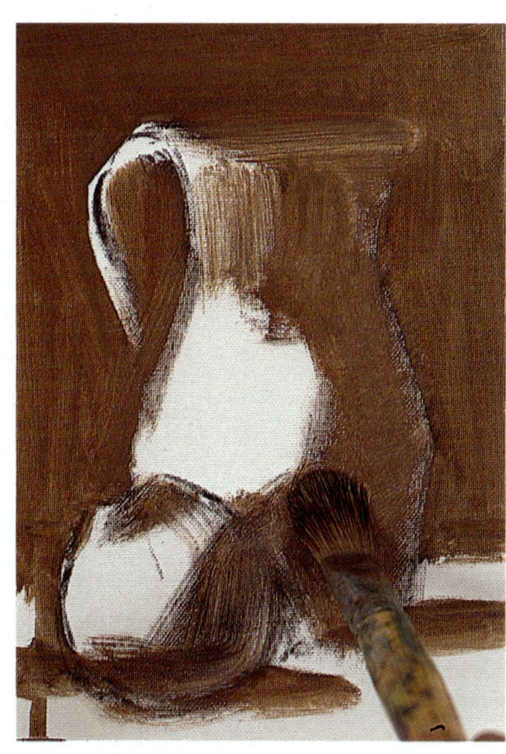

The principal light zone is outlined by its own shadow.

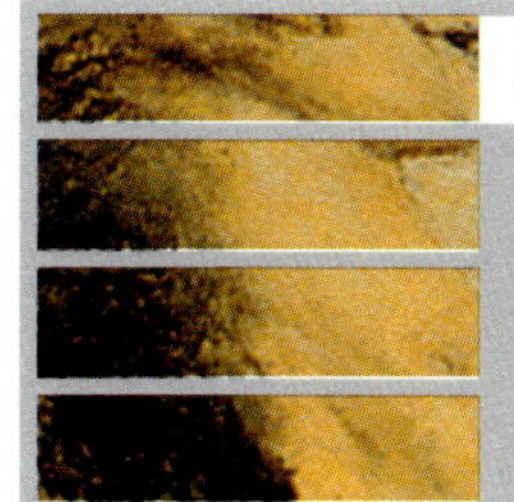

Possible defects in artisanal oil colors

Making your own oil colors can run into certain problems. It is worth knowing the risks beforehand.
-When the paint is disproportionately shiny this is due to too much oil in the mixture. It can make the paint wrinkled or containing airbags when dry.

-When the fresh paint is absolutely lacking in brightness it is because there is not enough linseed oil. This can cause inconsistencies on the paint surface, flaking and blooming of the paint.

mind that the highligh twill have to be applied when the principal tones have been put down. The light tones are worked on the palette, but the nuances are finished on the picture. When you are painting the most luminous tones, the brush drags part of the surrounding dark color producing rich gradations. In the same way, when you want to nuance a dark -for example, in the refracted light zone- paint in a luminous tone and go over it with the brush until it is blended into the background.

The final contrasts.

It is at the end that the most definitive contrasts are developed, the ones that permit a better separation between the light planes and the shadow planes. The great advantage of oil color is that it can be redone in any moment and the work can be progressive. The darkest contrasts are painted in the background, on the shadows of the objects and on the projected shadows. These contrasts define the forms. The

light zones are made brighter. Finis the painting of the most luminous zones and observe how the apple g volume after painting its highlight.

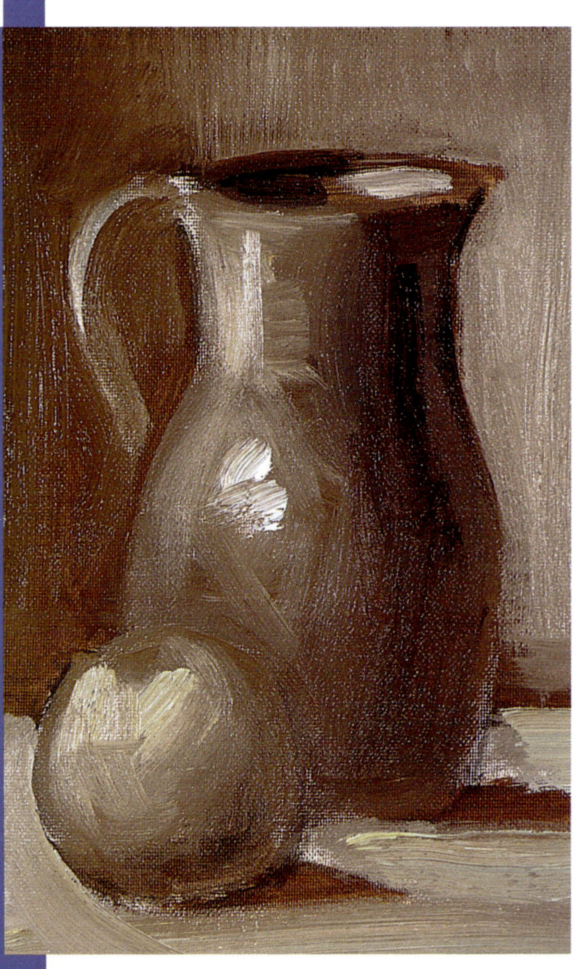

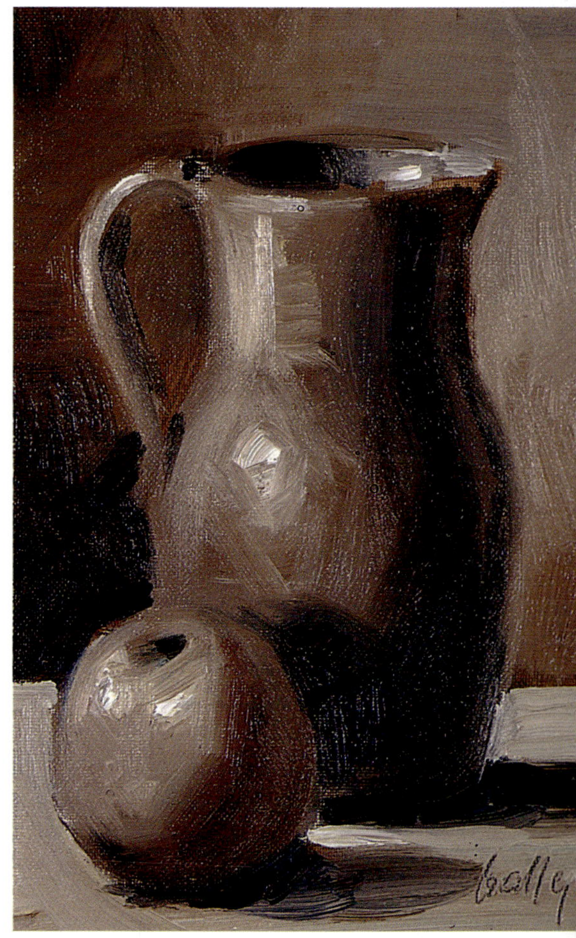

The most luminous tones are alternated with the darks, adapting to the object planes. The shadows blend with the light tones in the indirect light zone.

Summary

LIGHT AND DARK TONES. Before starting to paint you have to establish which tones are going to be used in the picture, and to determine what the limits will be in light and shadow tone gradations.

SHADOW AND LIGHT. The light and shadow parts are the following: the maximum point of luminosity, the zone of indirect light, the shadow zone, the zone of refracted light and the zone of projected shadow.

TONE GRADATIONS. You have to be especially careful when doing the light tones and the shadow tones and when blending them. The stroke work becomes fundamental.

THE FINAL CONTRASTS. The most luminous points and the darkest contrasts have to be painted at the end. These final contrasts are what make the separation between light and shadows stand out.

POMEGRANATE AND PLUMS

Although in previous chapters we have spoken about lights and shadows it was not until this chapter that we dealt with them in detail. The model proposed here is not complex, neither its drawing nor its composition. Its forms are basic, all three of them spherical. The study of the shadows will be elemental and will, at the same time, provide the fundamental notions for understanding the shadows of more complicated elements.

To simplify the color question the palette has been reduced. Therefore if you carefully follow the steps laid out on the next pages it will be straightforward to do the interesting still life composed of three pieces of fruit.

Necessary material

Primed card (1), oil colors (2), linseed oil (3), turpentine oil (4), brushes (5), and a cloth (6).

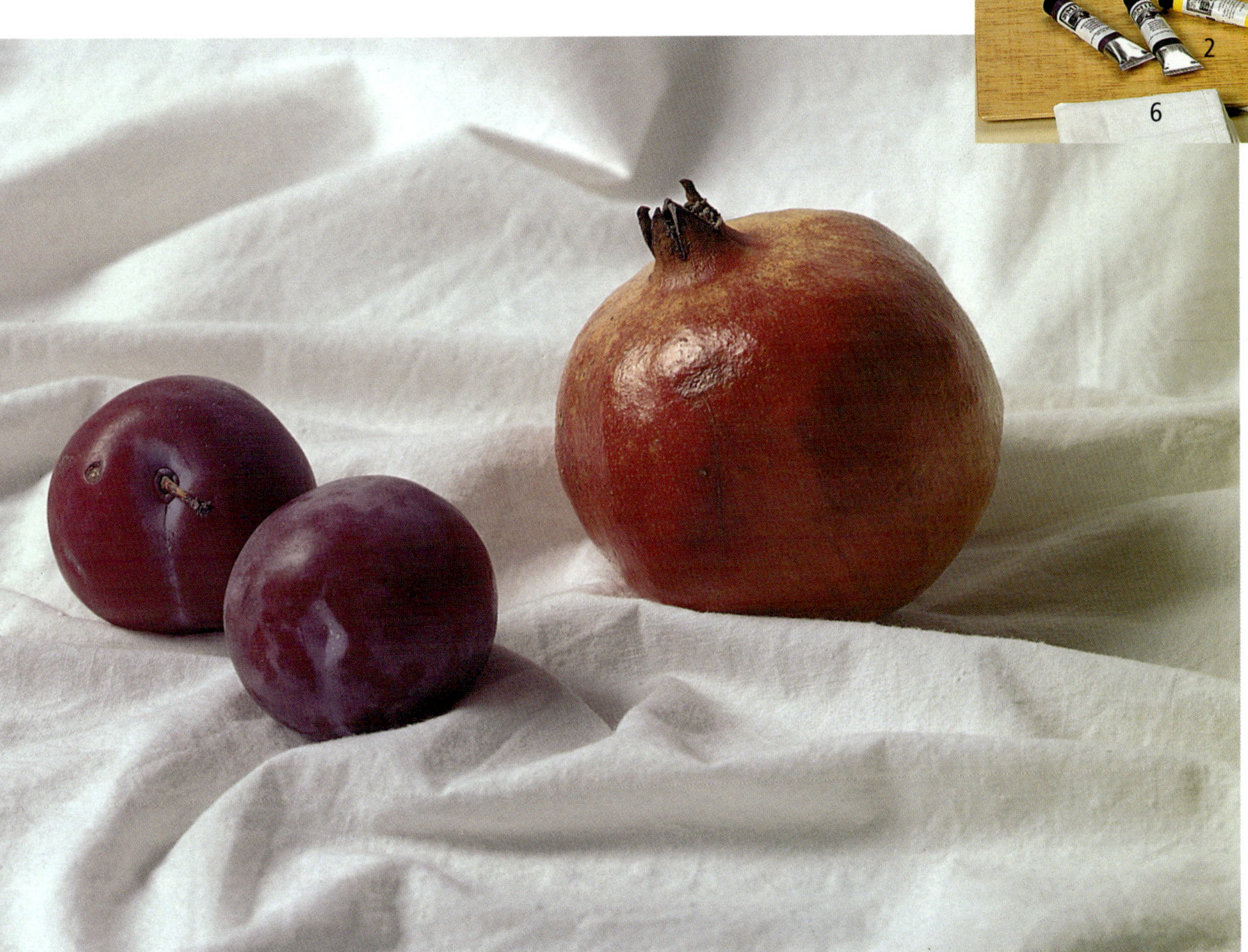

Exercises

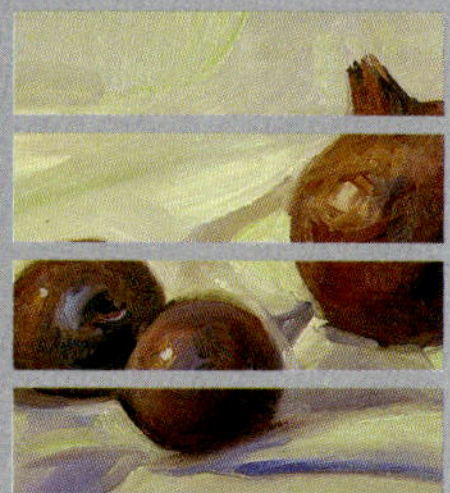

1·The structure of these elements is so simple that the drawing can be done directly in oil colors. If the motif had been complicated any drawing media would have been suitable to sketch the principal lines. However, being simple a quick scheme in oil colors is enough.

The line is begun thinned. In rapid movements, sketch the three pieces of fruit. If it is necessary any correction can be done by going over the line again without having to eliminate color.

2·Once the quick sketch has been done, start to consider the first tones. Put in a general field, in the background; the gray is a mixture of the dirty colors on the palette and white spirit. If the palette is clean, you can get this gray by mixing green, umber and white. The likeness is good enough.

This first dirty, very thinned color is painted where the pomegranate shadow falls, and on the plum the upper portion is painted.
Use violet carmine to paint the most illuminated section of the pomegranate, leaving blank, or in negative, the shiny part.

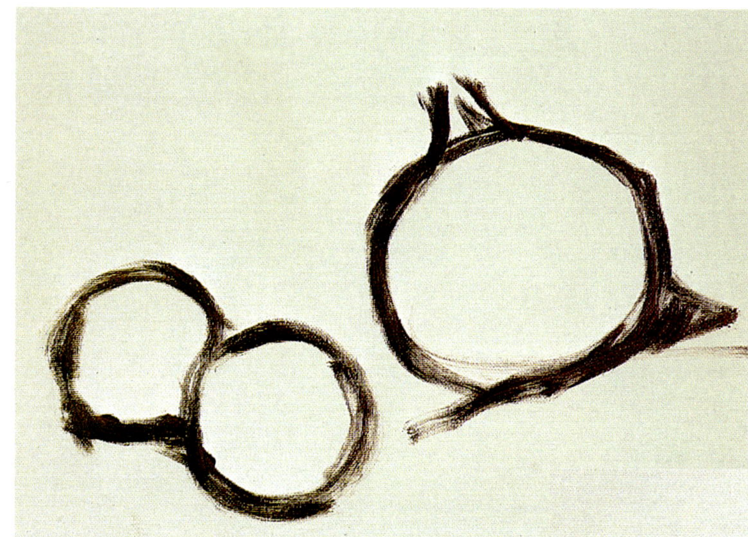

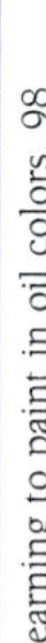

3·Use the same violet carmine with which the pomegranate was painted to paint the plums. The gray zone of the plum on the right is a separation space between the two fruits.

Go over the pomegranate several times to make the colors mix, and then start to work on the spherical form of the fruit.

Make an off-whitish, irregular mix, adding carmine violet, green and blue. Without mixing the color thoroughly on the palette, start to paint the tablecloth.

4·The spherical form of the pomegranate is worked on with curved strokes that define the plane. When the brush is passed over the gray zone, the color becomes lighter. It does not matter because later it can be darkened again.

Start to separate the light zones on the plums with touches of dark violet, mixed with a little cobalt blue. The dashes of blue painted next to the shiny part and in the shadow zone of the plum on the left is fundamental to depict its shadow and volume.

Use cobalt blue and marine blue to paint the foreground of the tablecloth. These strokes drag part of the lower color.

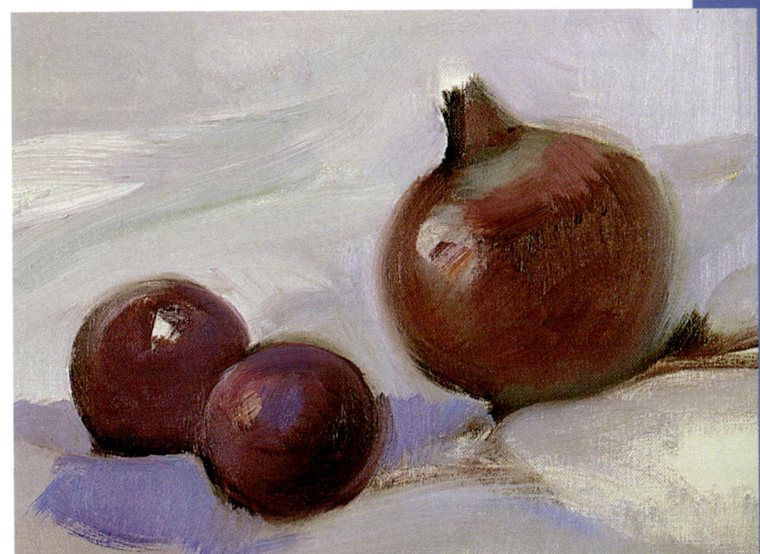

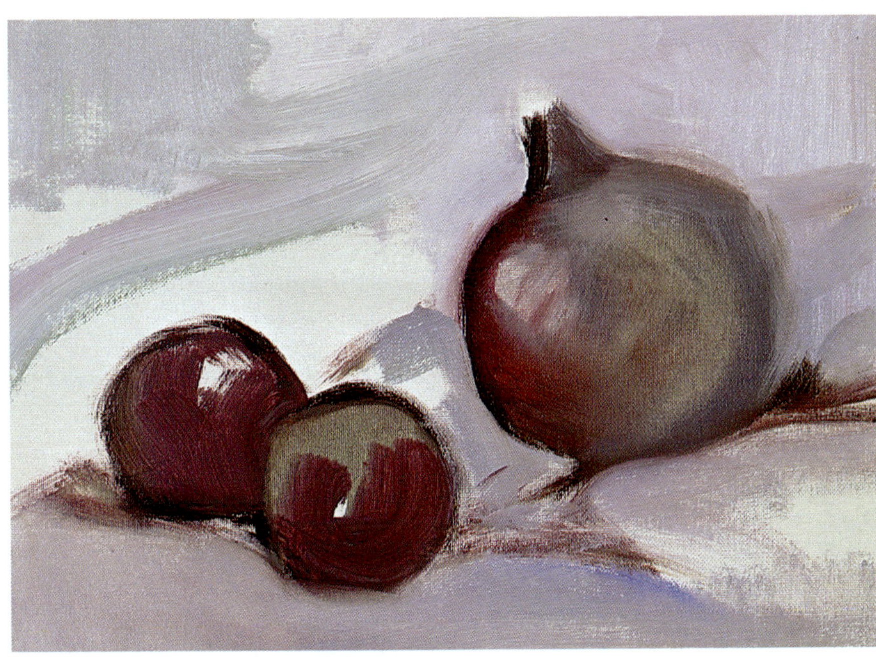

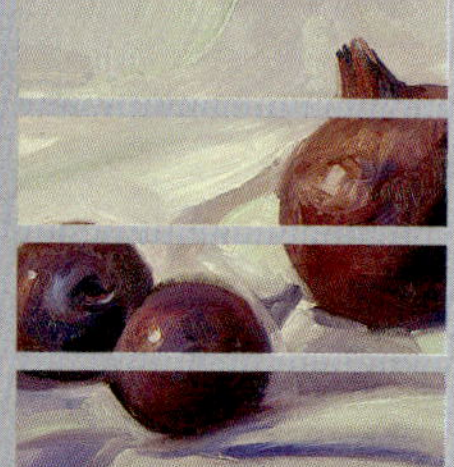

Exercises

5·This step requires a lot of attention because we are going to define the principal differences between the light and dark areas. The light focus source is coming from the left, therefore the most accentuated shadows have to be on the other side. The plum on the left is given a striking touch of carmine in the upper part. On the right of the picture, the colors tend to be cooler and more bluish. On the left they are warmer.

The source of light must be the reference point for situating the shadows. The bluish tones in the light zone are lightened with white. On the pomegranate the most illuminated areas are done in violet carmine toned down with white.

On the tablecloth paint blue lines to mark the folds.

6·In the close up you can appreciate how it is the light tones that define the shadow zones. The most luminous colors of the pomegranate go from white, situated on the highlight, right through the complete gradation of carmine.

Next to the main highlight do a few touches of blue to enrich the spherical form. These strokes are the direct reflection of the plums.

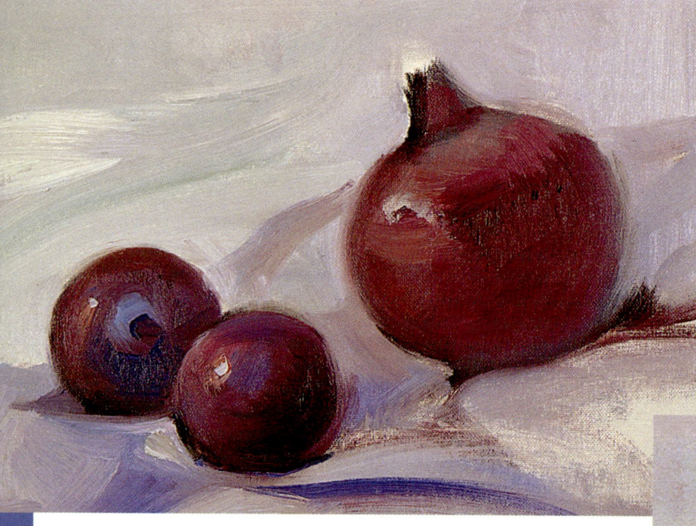

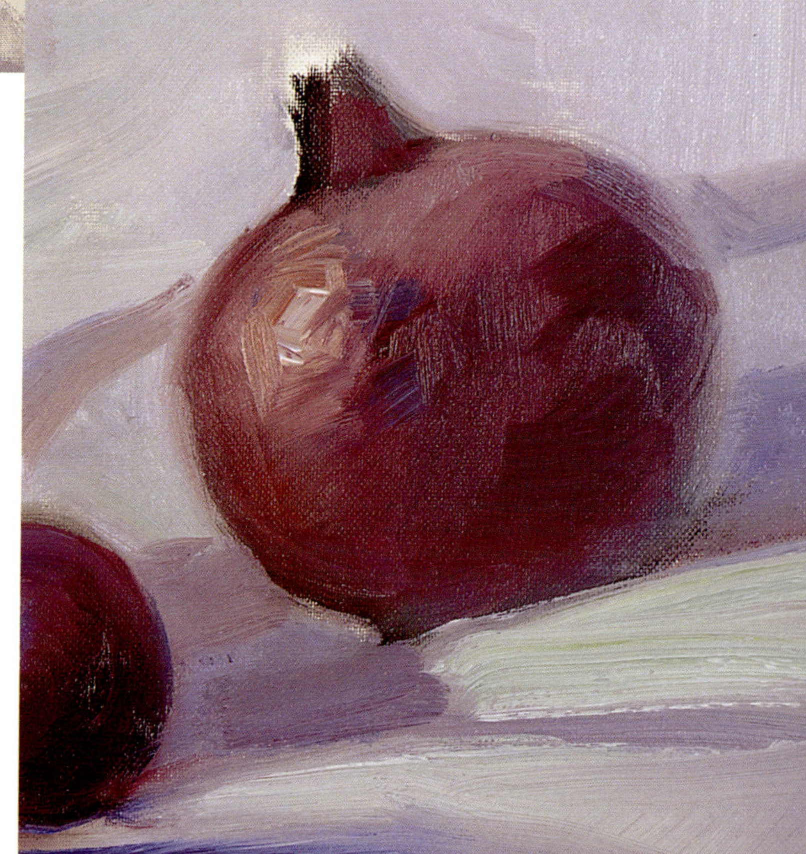

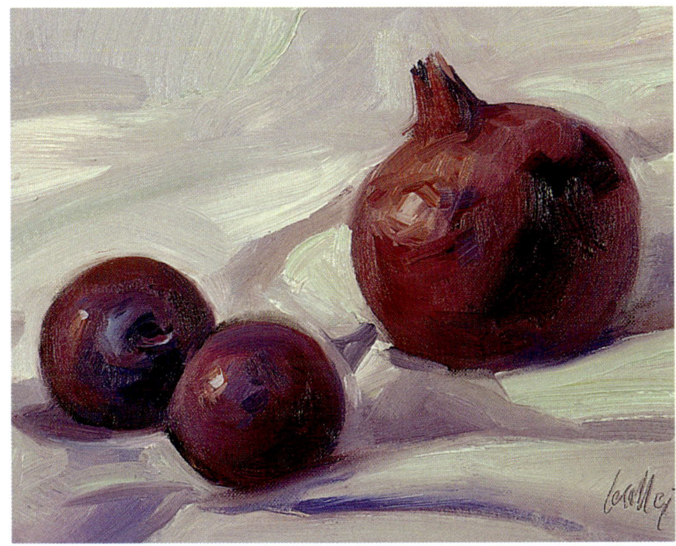

7·Enrich the light zones on the pomegranate with orangy tones that contrast with the pure carmine. To get these luminous tones from carmine and red, without them becoming pink, the tone must be lightened not with white but with Naples yellow.

The dark zones on the plums finish the definition of its spherical form.

Summary

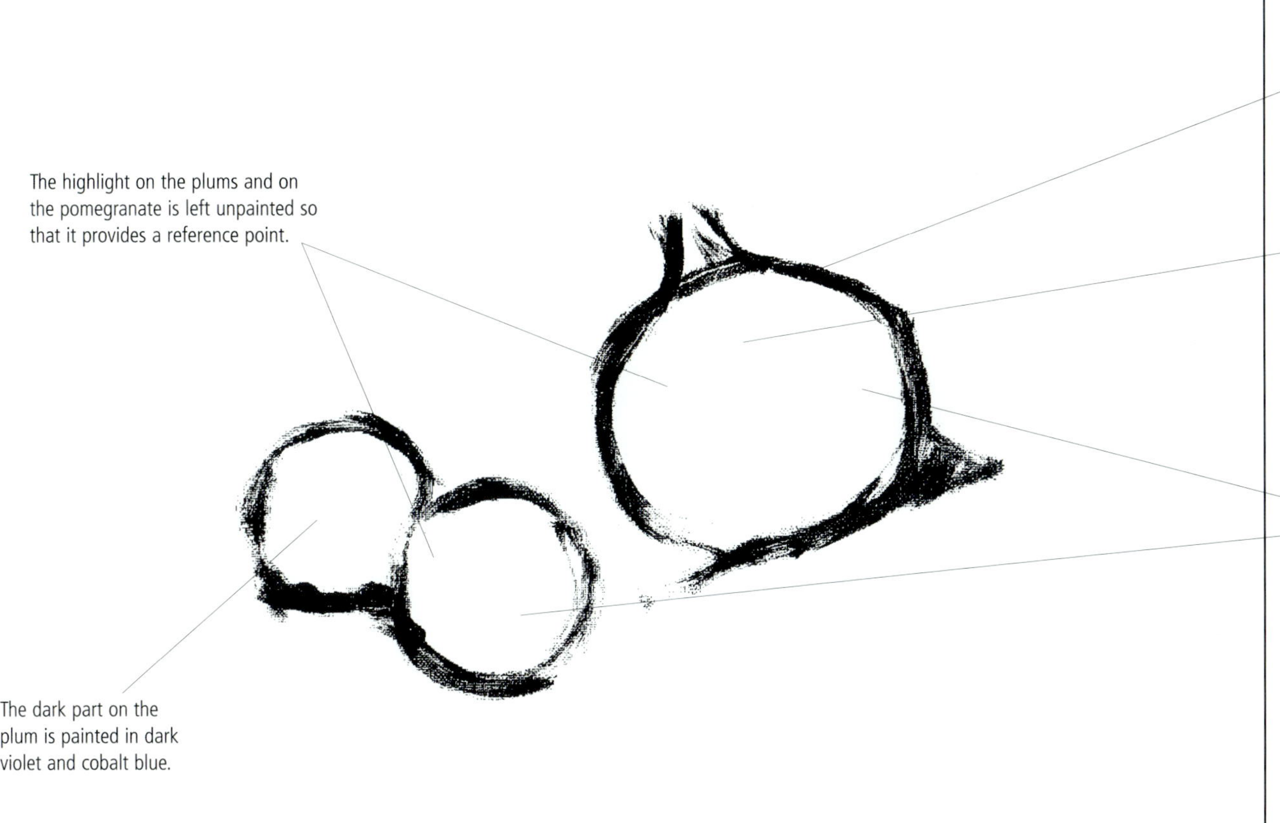

The initial sketch is done directly with oil color and a brush.

The light parts on the pomegranate are realized in colors toned down with white and with Naples yellow.

A thinned grayish color is used on the plum on the right and on the pomegranate.

The highlight on the plums and on the pomegranate is left unpainted so that it provides a reference point.

The dark part on the plum is painted in dark violet and cobalt blue.

Chapter 9

Colorism. Complementary colors

In the theory of color, the color ranges arrange together the colors belonging to the same family.

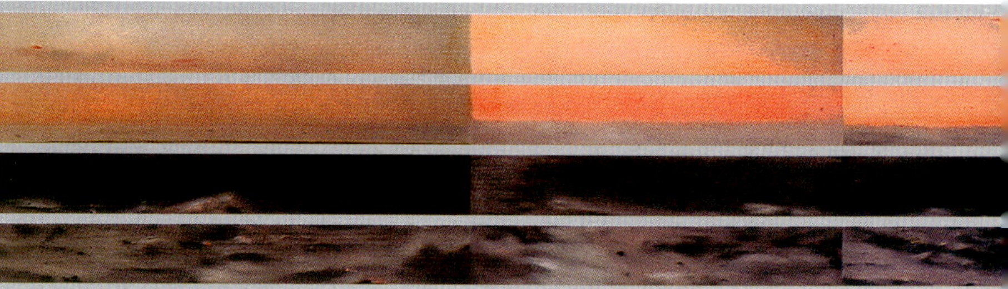

When a picture is painted harmonious colors, from the same segment of the circle, can be used, or, alternatively the artist can turn their back on this and paint in strongly contrasting colors: complementary contrasts. In this chapter we will study that the practical implication of complementary colors is that they provide the maximum color contrasts. You will then be able to paint making the hues vibrate with accents, strong contrasts, and full of chromatic vitality. The great French painter Degas said the art of painting was to surround a patch of Venetian red with other colors so that it appeared vermilion.

A correctly arranged color circle.

The optical effect

Complementary colors are created by offsetting the colors of the color circle. The color circle is nothing more than the primary and secondary colors arranged in a continuous circle. The primary colors are yellow, blue and red. The sec colors are green, orange and violet. The tertiary colors are carmine, deep blue, emerald green and light green.

As you can see, the relationship between the colors in the circle is gradual and harmonious. It is practical because you can see how they act on each other. Thus it is clear that mixing a primary with a sec gives rise to a broken color. Looking closely you will see that the colors opposite each other contrast strongly: the nearer together they are, the more harmonious they are. Colors opposite each other are defined as complementary.

Complementary couples.

The following list contains the principal complementary colors but this does not mean that it is exhaustive. As we have said before, complementary means opposite each other and producing the maximum contrast. Therefore we can use the following pairs of colors to create contrast: purple and orange, and green and red.
Blue is the complementary of yellow, cyan blue is red's complementary,

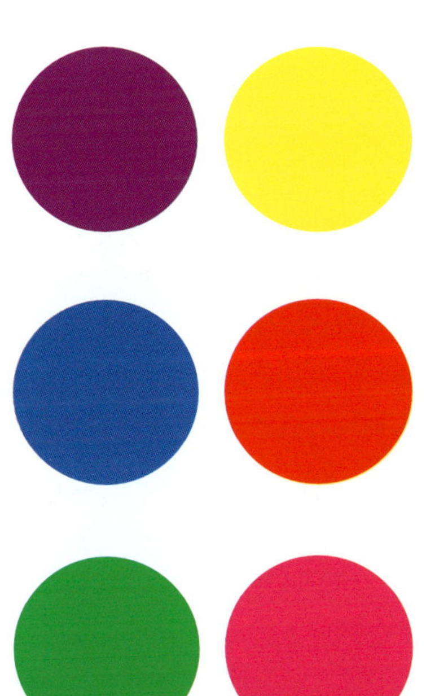

These are the principal complementary colors.

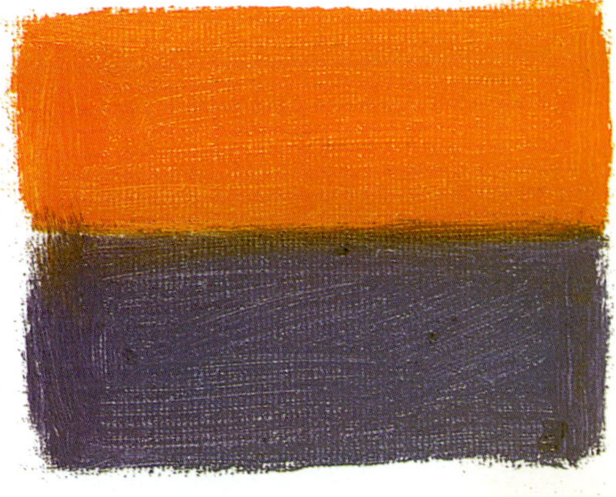

In this straightforward exercise you can see how far the contrast between complementary colors can go.

Making a neutral color

When two opposite colors are put down on a picture, be they complementary or not, it is possible to find intermediate hues by mixing them. For example, if you are working with greens and oranges you can produce a mix of tones to compensate for the excessive contrast.

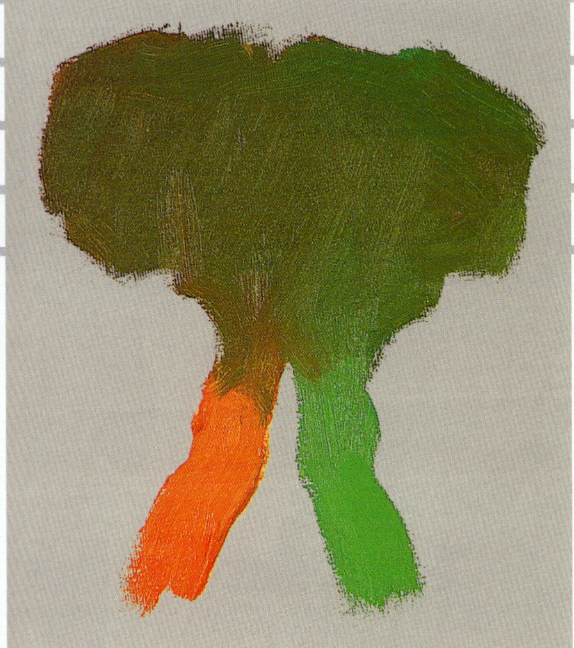

Mixing green and orange gives intermediate tones compensating the excessive contrast.

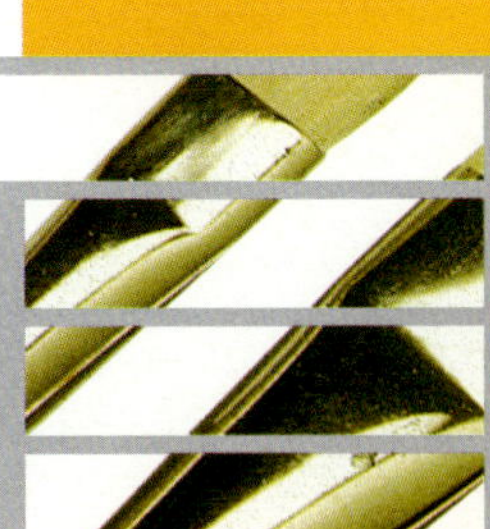

and orange is the complementary of deep blue. Light green is the opposite of violet and carmine contrasts strongly with emerald green.

Complementary contrasts.

The contrasts between complementary colors do not have to follow a strict rule. Contrast can be defined as a strong visual impact produced by the way the colors act on each other. Just doing a little test will reveal how intensely two colors complement . Select two colors from the circle that are relatively near each other -for example green and violet- and paint two blobs next to each other on a canvas. They are different but they do not contrast. However, if two blobs of colors which while not being completely opposite are quite separate are painted -for example violet and orange- a strong contrast is established, not only due to the complementariness but also because one is warm and the other cool.

Planning the picture

When planning the picture we start from the following premise: the complementary colors need not be treated strictly. Instead they must be used as a guide to develop contrasts that give vitality to the participating colors.
Complementary colors can be painted without the necessity to use pure colors as will be demonstrated in the straightforward exercise we will now do. It is a landscape full of contrasts. As can be seen in the image a tree is painted with a clear cool color tendency. It will be sufficient to use

Paint this tree in cool colors: greens, blues and violets. Concentrate here on the color masses.

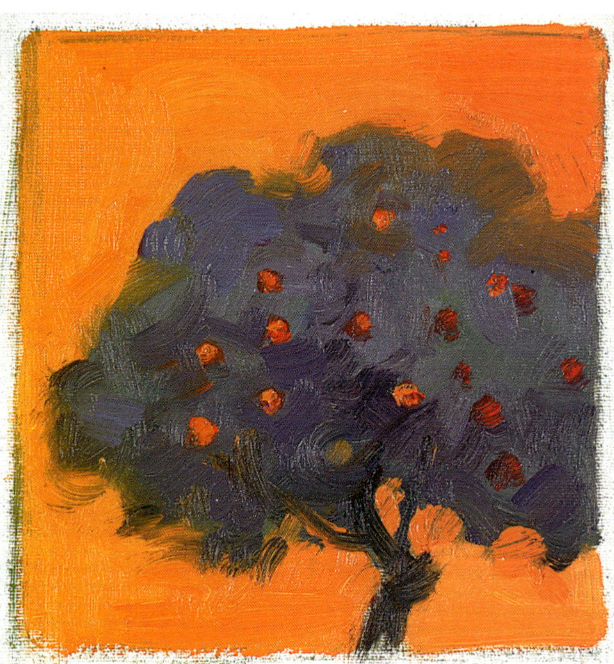

The orange accents on the cool background act as highlights vibrating with energy.

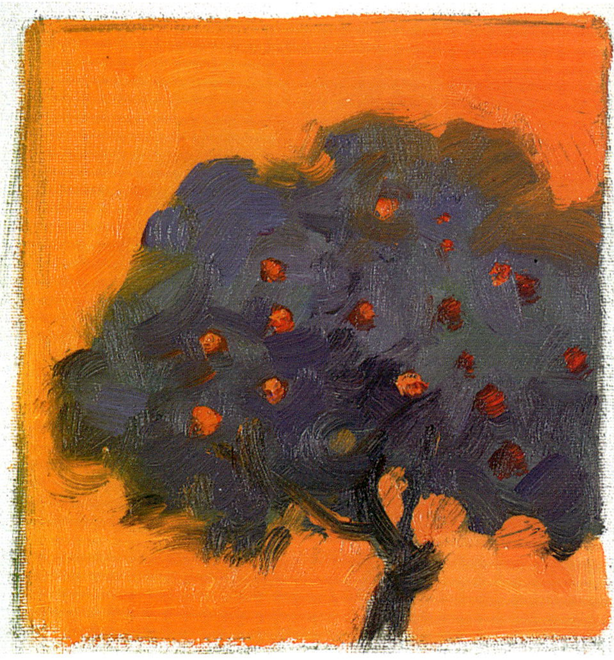

The orange of the background strengthens all the elements in the picture.

greens, blues and violets. In this picture we are not worried about going into details; we want to concentrate on the mass that defines the form. Against the white background, the object stands out reinforced, as if backlit.

Chromatic contrast

The complementary contrast of these cool colors does not have to be found in just one color in the circle. A few hues can make these dark colors vibrate with energy and excitement. For example, you can paint in orange which will produce an image like the one below these lines. If you observe the color circle, you will see that orange is opposite the colors used to paint the tree. The complementary contrast makes both the tree and the background stronger.

Small points of complementary light

We have seen how two color masses intensify each other when they are complementary. We could describe this as the colors vibrating together, a vibration which can increase if the complementary colors are used as small accents. If within the great mass of color that defines the tree a few accents of luminous orange are painted then they will act as exciting points of light.

The color base

When looking for complementary contrasts, the color bases are the key to developing vibrating zones. One color alone can never be complementary: it always needs a partner.

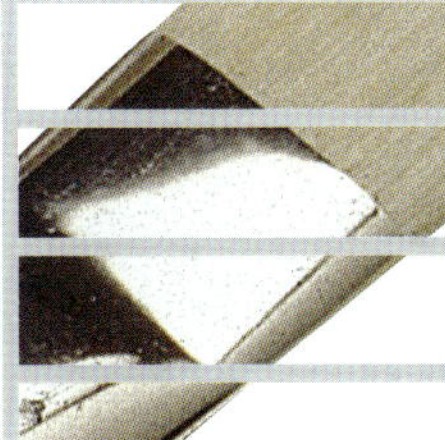

The intensity of the contrast

In this highly striking work, "Sea front" by Eduard Resbier, born in 1967, it is worth pointing out the how the compositional force is combined with a superlative use of color. Without abusing the chromatic recourses, an powerful contrast is established between the cool tones of the sea and the vigor of the reddish sky. The colors used are complementary, which reinforces both zones. To balance the contrast between the two chromatic zones, the brightness of the sea has also been worked on in red tones, echoing the sky.

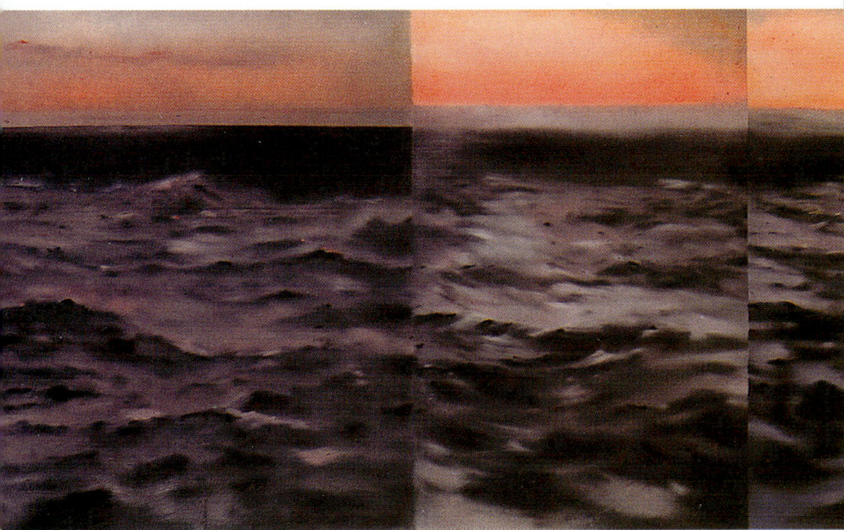

Greens and reds

The color base conditions the search for a complementary color, for the latter must be within a certain range so the initial color limits the possibilities. For example, if green is the base and you want to do contrasting accents from the outset all colors nearby in the circle are ruled out. The complementary colors will be found on the other side of the circle, among red and its variations.

Contrast and tone in complementary colors

As demonstrated so many times, complementary contrasts in some way dictate their own complementary color, but this is not an unbudgable situation. When you have established the complementary colors in a picture you must begin to search for the exact tones.

Going on with the example, you can see that the color base is basically made up of two varieties of green. When red is applied, it vibrates against the dark green. However, it is too dense to be applied on top of the most luminous green. A brighter red will have to be used in this zone.

The form is reinforced by the background

When working with complementary colors the background is very important because it determines whether the colors in the picture create a unified mood or clash against each other. Some of the colors used on the elements will have to come into play in the background. In the example being developed on these pages, green has the leading colorist role. The reds act as vibrating accents.

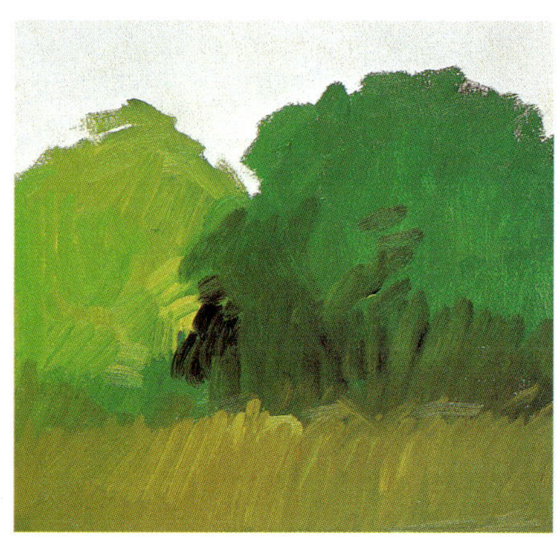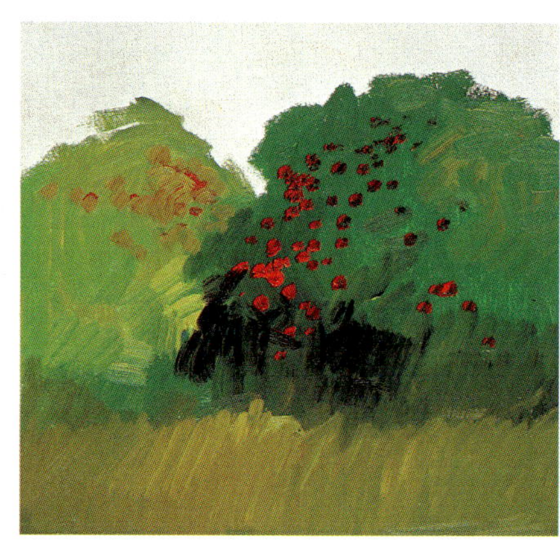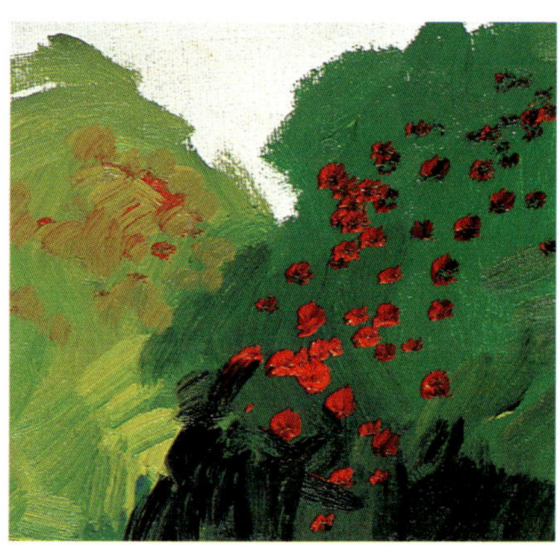

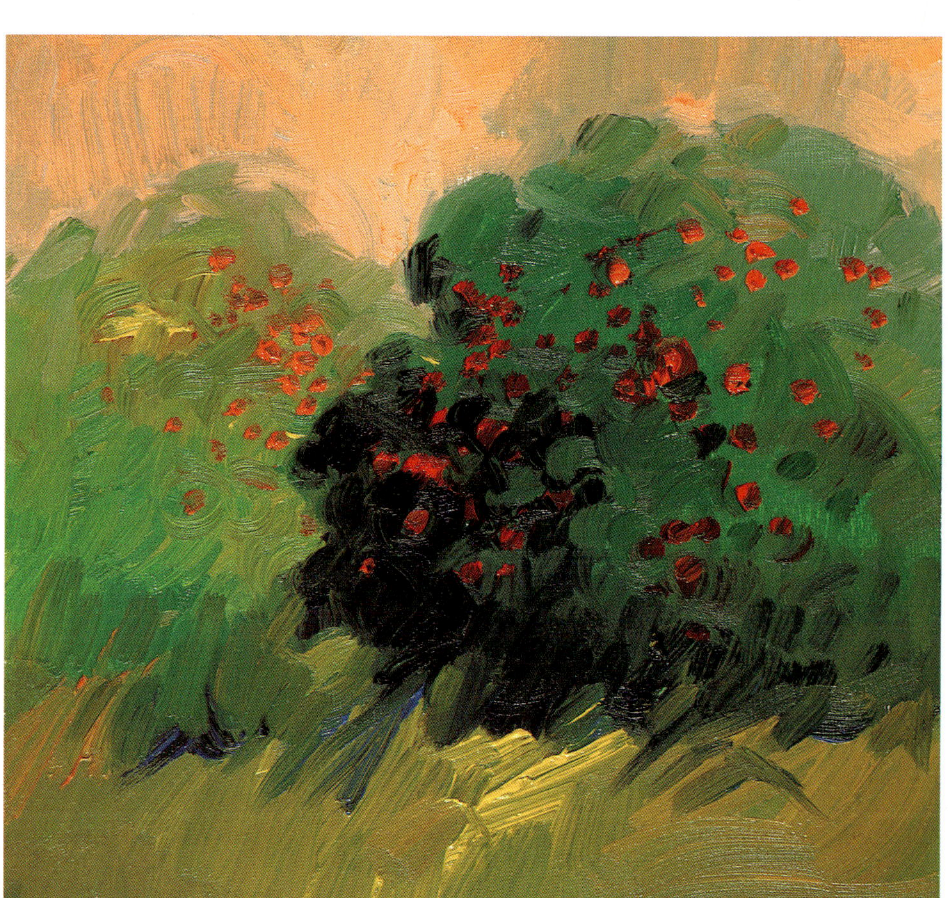

Paint the base -some fruit trees- mixing several variations of green which establish a tone, not color, contrast.

The dark red vibrates strongly against the green base. It has been shown to be the right choice of complementary color.

Do not use the same red to complement the dark green as was used for the light green. You have to find a suitable tone.

The colors in the background are warm so as to break the intense contrast between the dark green and the white.

To compensate for the excessive contrast which the green provokes against the white in the background, the latter has been painted in a warm tone with red, yellow and white.

Alternating color masses

When you work with complementary colors in a complex picture, it is recommendable to develop all of it at the same time to compensate the colors as you go along and control the influences they exert over each other.

Controlled use of the complementary colors

When you want to paint a picture with crisp contrasts you have to find which are the most suitable complementary colors and to ensure that they act on the designated zones. The colors cannot be put down randomly. We are now going to study in more detail how to control the use of complementary by doing a still life with an intense contrast produced by the color orange among cool colors. The color masses must be put in rapidly, situating the colors at the same time as the forms. The aim of the first intervention, however, is not to decide the definitive forms nor colors.

Correcting colors

As all the picture was started at the same time, the colors can be compensated and corrected. The bottle, which was originally painted dark green, is tinted towards a blue tone. On it paint a reddish accent. Both colors are complementary and integrate the bottle and the orange. Mix blue and orange on the palette to do the shadow of the orange. The grapes in the background, much more luminous, allow the foreground colors to be compensated.

The colors work together. Correcting the green on the bottle, now blue, is a better complement for orange.

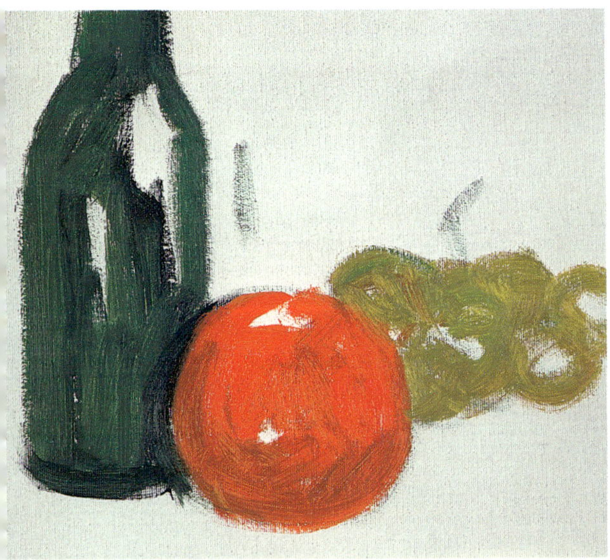

The bottle and the grapes are painted in green tones. Luminous orange is put down as a contrast.

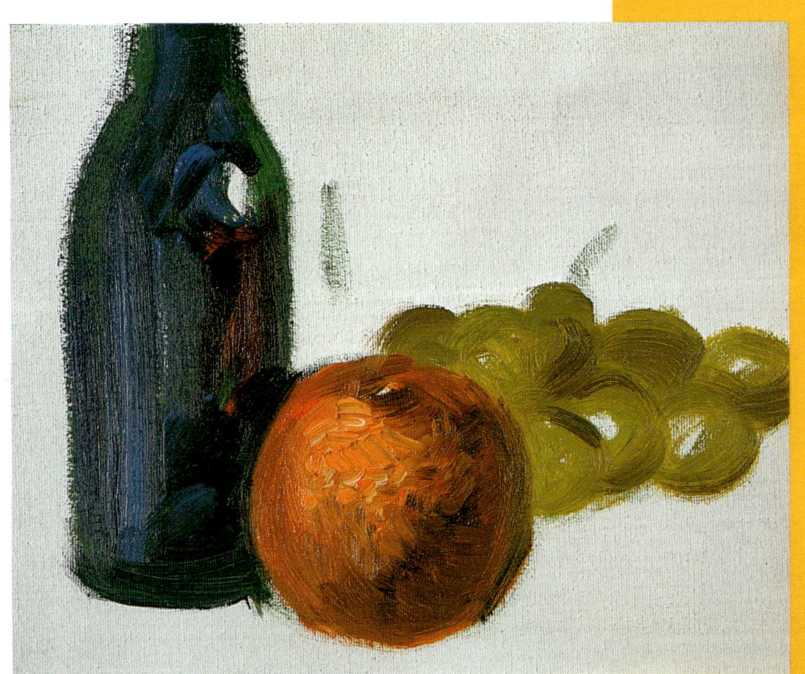

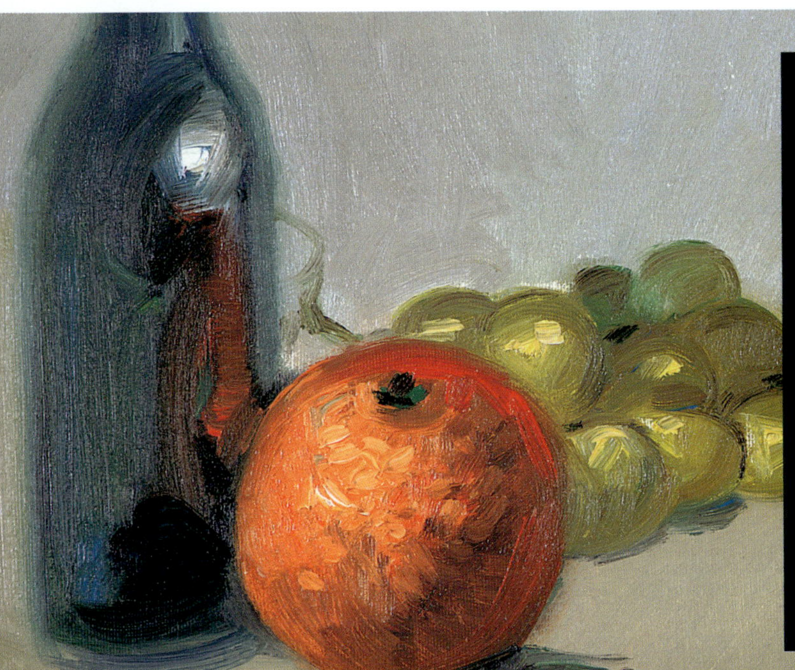

Making a neutral color

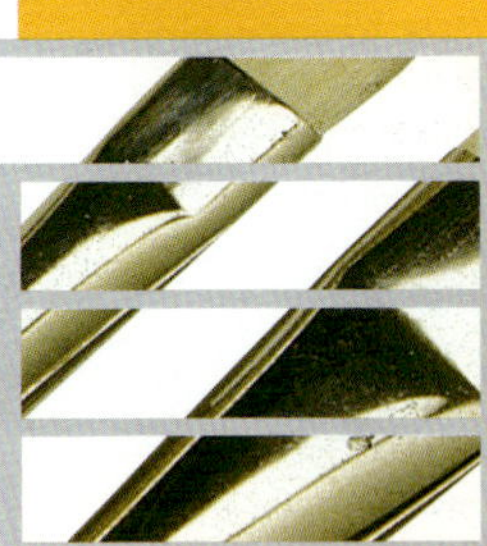

The opportunities offered by the complementary colors is a continuous visual experiment, obliging us to monitor how the colors condition each other and which becomes dominant. Complementary contrasts are legitimate chromatic recourses for any oil painting, whatever the subject.

1. The color orange impacts directly on blue.
2. To get a stronger contrast with the green of the grapes, paint in reddish orange.
3. The shadow zones are done in complementary mixes.
4. he shadow of the orange is painted with its complement.

Balancing the comple-
mentary colors.

When painting in complementary colors it may arise that the elements do not relate to each other because of the dissonance between the colors. To avoid this effect you simply have to ensure that the colors intervene in all parts of the picture equally.
Color gives unity, the feeling of the picture. A painting realized in complementary colors that do not work together will lack unity: the objects will clash and appear to be floating disconnected from the others. Colors must act on each other so as to establish an interdependent relationship between the objects. The reflections of the objects must be done in the complementary colors. These color accents do not have to be mixed together but they must have reference points on the other objects in the picture.

The elements in the picture have been painted in complementary colors but there is no relationship between them and therefore they appear to be floating.

A construction error

It is very common that learners frequently make a mistake when they begin a painting, and they magnify the error as they go along. A painting must never be started in one corner and finished in the other. Everything must be done at the same time, which means that any color can be rectified if next to it a too dark, or too contrasted, complementary is placed. The colors in a picture, for good or for bad, are completely dependent on the others.

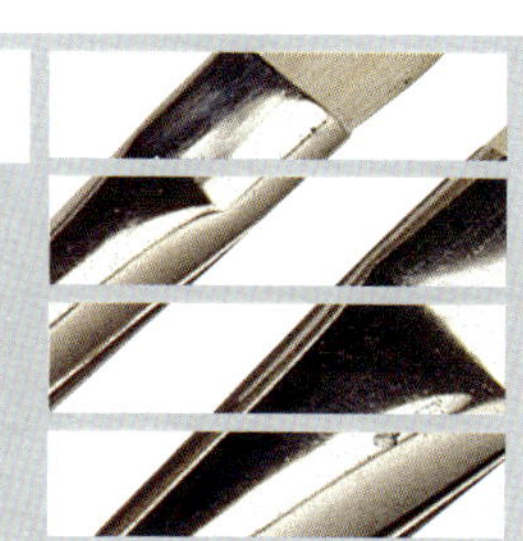

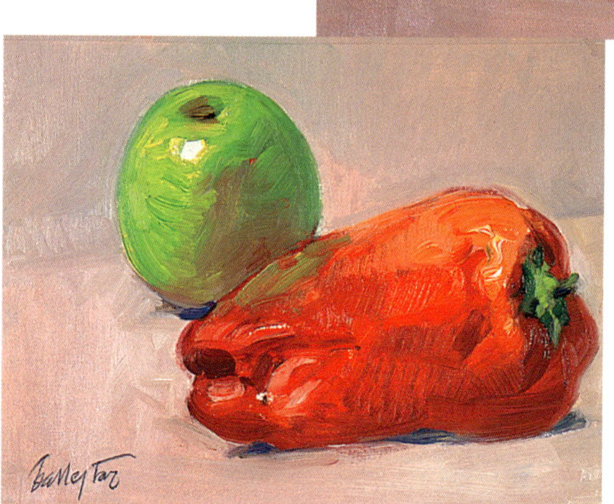

The complementary color accents unify the work and relate the different elements together.

Summary

SUPERIMPOSED COLORS.
When superimposed the stro-kes permit tones and color planes to be blended.

BLENDED COLORS.
To blend two tones you have to insist with the brush until the edges have undergone fusion.

STROKES TO BLEND TWO PLANES.
These strokes are done with a medium brush so that other colors are not dirtied. The blending is done softly or allowing the tones to mix.

Exercises

A LANDSCAPE WITH COMPLEMENTARY COLORS

The excitement of the complementary colors is another reason to justify practicing with this backlit landscape. How you interpret the model is fundamental. The colors painted in a picture do not always have to correspond to the real model. In fact, in the end, the color used in a painting is a matter of individual taste. Anyway, whatever the nuances, the following exercise is a good chance to learn.

Necessary material

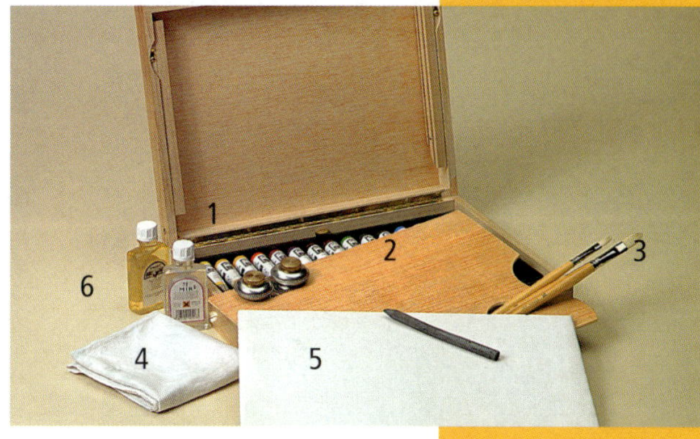

Oil colors (1), palette (2), hog's hair brushes (3), a cloth (4), card (5), and turpentine oil and linseed oil (6).

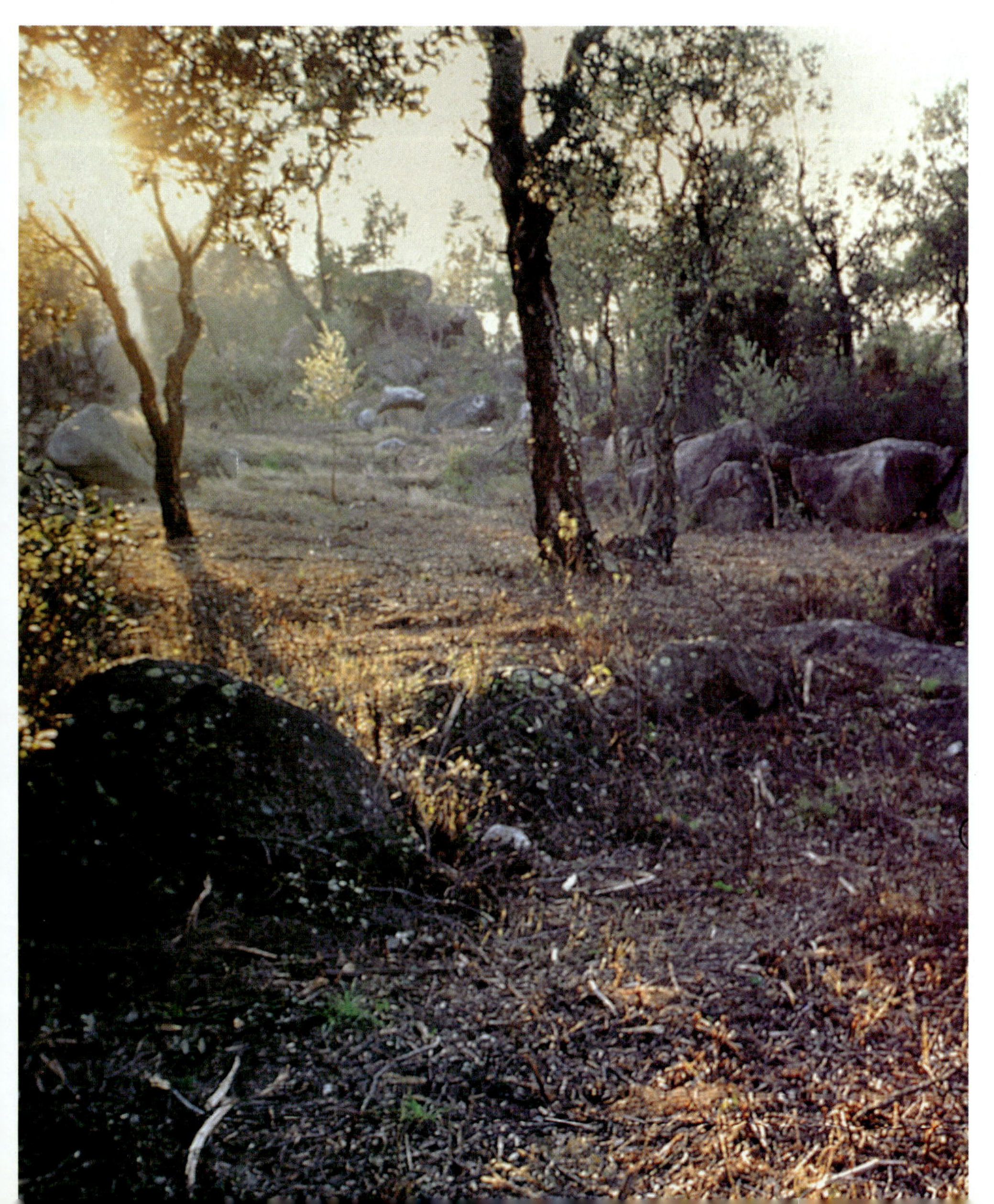

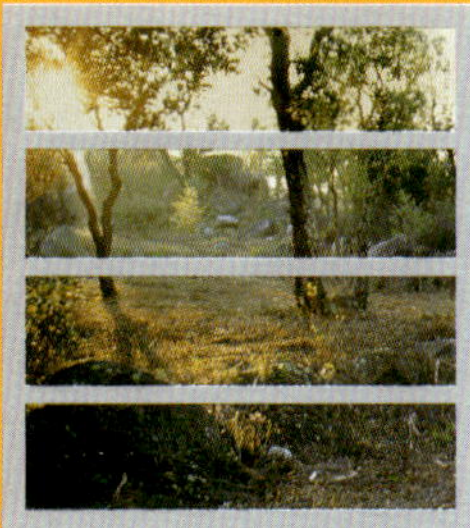

Exercises

1·The oil painting is started, as is almost always the case, by doing a simple charcoal outline. This means that corrections can be done by flicking the hand. Moreover, when you paint over the tone, the fesh paint naturally covers up the drawing lines without leaving traces.

The principal elements in this composition are the trees and the dark volumes in the foreground.

2·Having done the outline in charcoal, the picture can now be painted in a very dark violet. These lines are identical to the preliminary charcoal ones. They define the trees and the fundamental lines of the picture.

Now, while doing the lines in oil color, superfluous details must not be realized. These will be defined in the final stages of the picture.

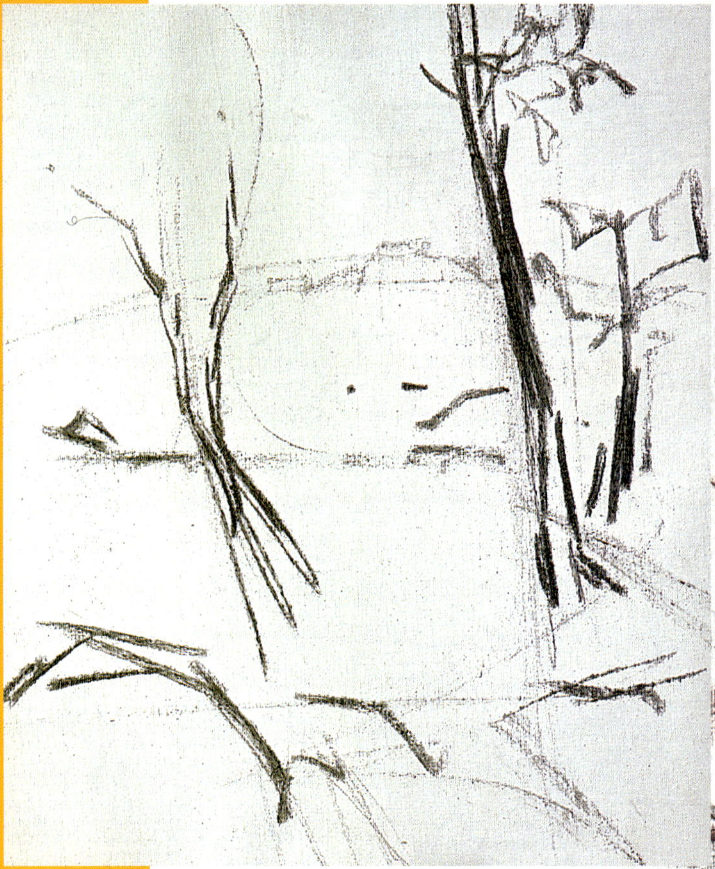

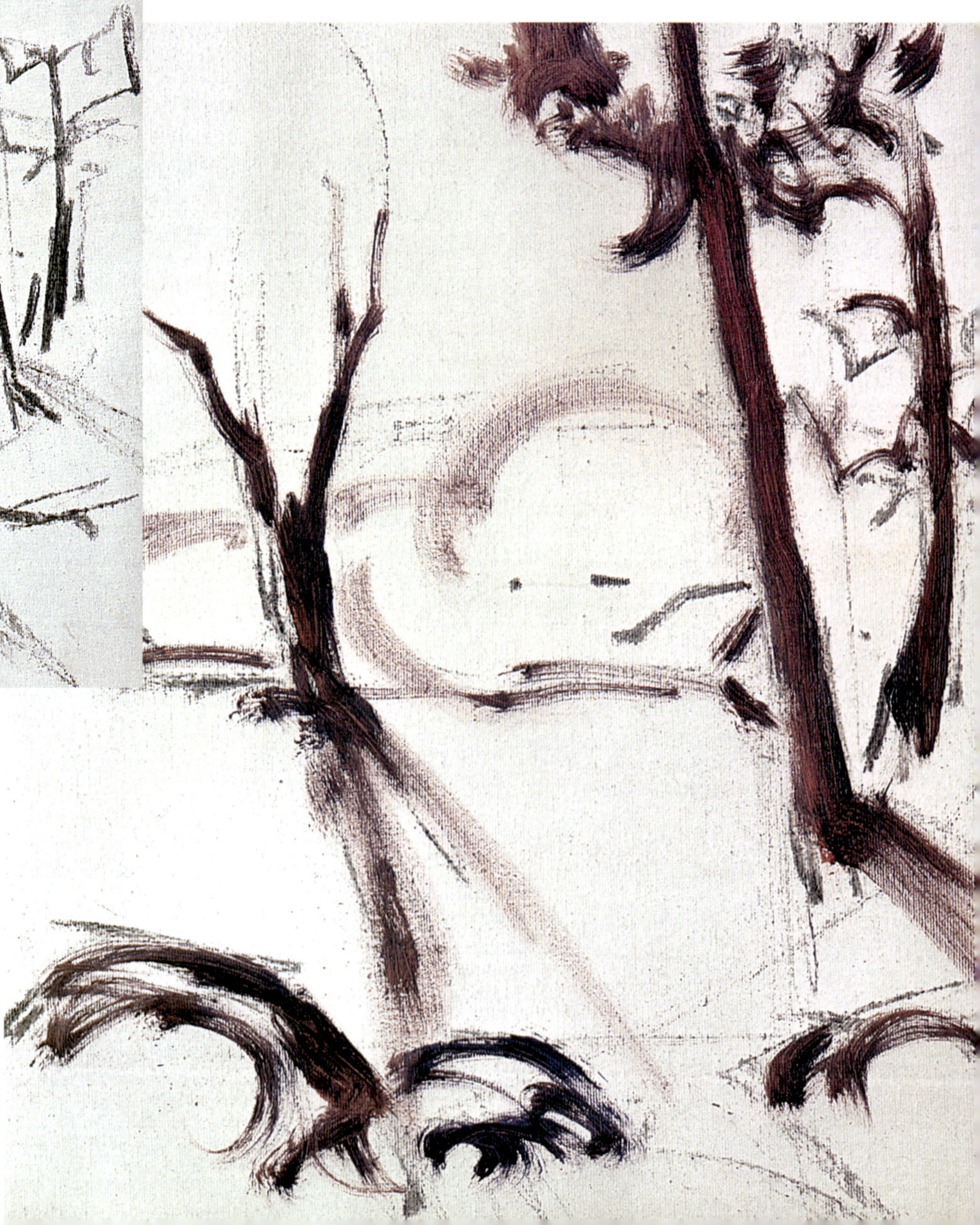

3·In step three the first important contrast is painted; it reinforces the backlight effect. On the palette mix Naples yellow with golden yellow. Without painting too densely fill out all the background, outlining the form of the trees.

Add some blue to the yellow on the palette and start to do the lushness in the background. Use an ochre tinted towards orange to paint the earth. Orange and violet are complementary colors and will be the dominant colors in this representation.

4·In step four we continue painting the earth with long, orangy strokes. In the background the vegetation is enriched with blues tending towards Naples yellow. These colors reach until the darks in the foreground where a little carmine is added. The tree shadow is painted in carmine.

On top of the tree on the right, paint directly in blue on the trunk. Now the colors are starting to vibrate together.

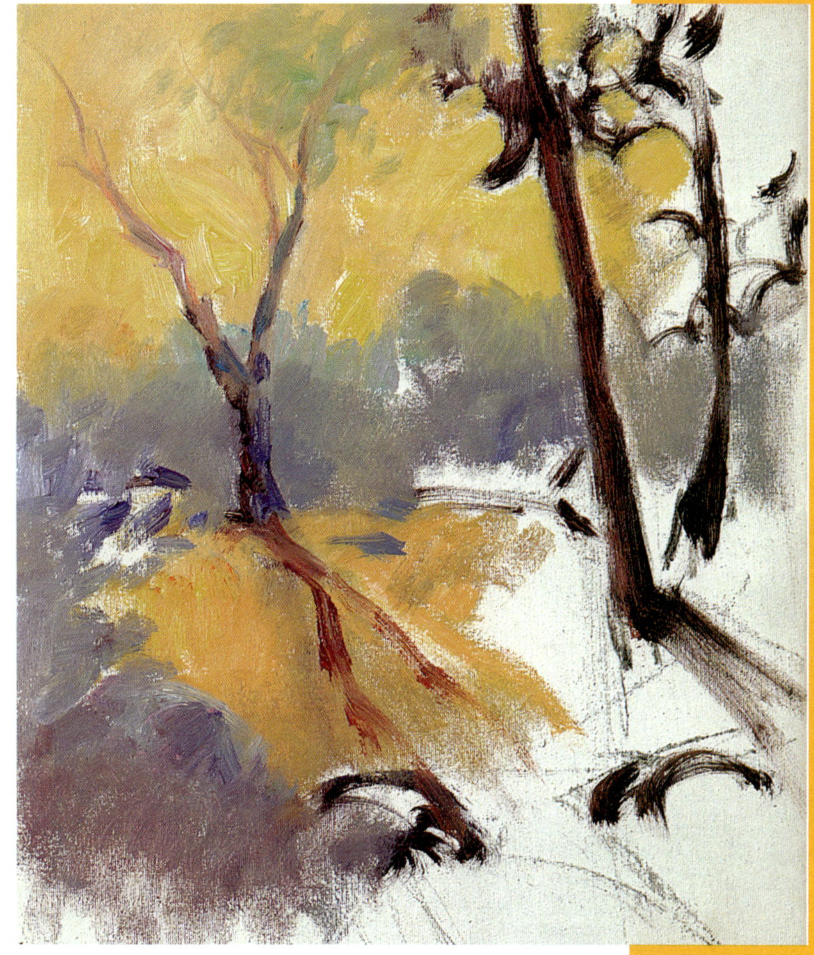

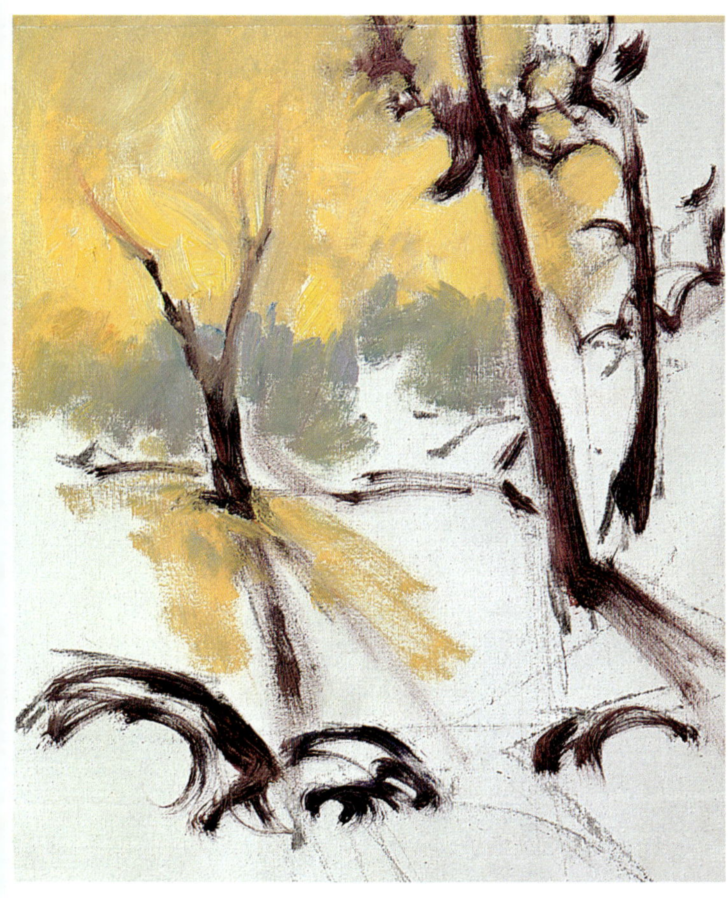

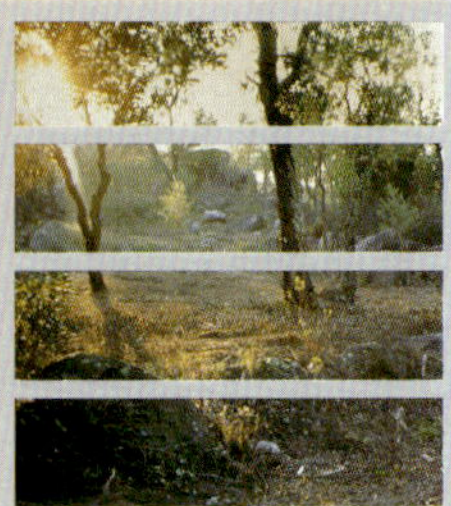

Exercises

5·In step five the illuminated earth is painted in a cadmium orange, the strength of which establishes a very vivid complementary relationship between the violets and the oranges.

In the vegetation in the background paint very luminous violet strokes. When you are putting down complementary colors they work on each other according to the theory of color: a luminous color among dark tones makes the darks appear deeper and the light colors more vivid. Put down red strokes in the trees to sharply contrast the blues and violets.

6·In step six, denser and more buttery strokes are realized as the picture is advancing. On the upper layers, when you want a more flowing color, do not use turpentine oil but instead linseed oil.

The strokes for the grass are short and leaning to insinuate the texture. The yellows and orange variations are slightly dirtied on the right.

In the lower left corner, paint a brownish tone that reinforces the luminosity and excitement added to the picture by the violet around it.

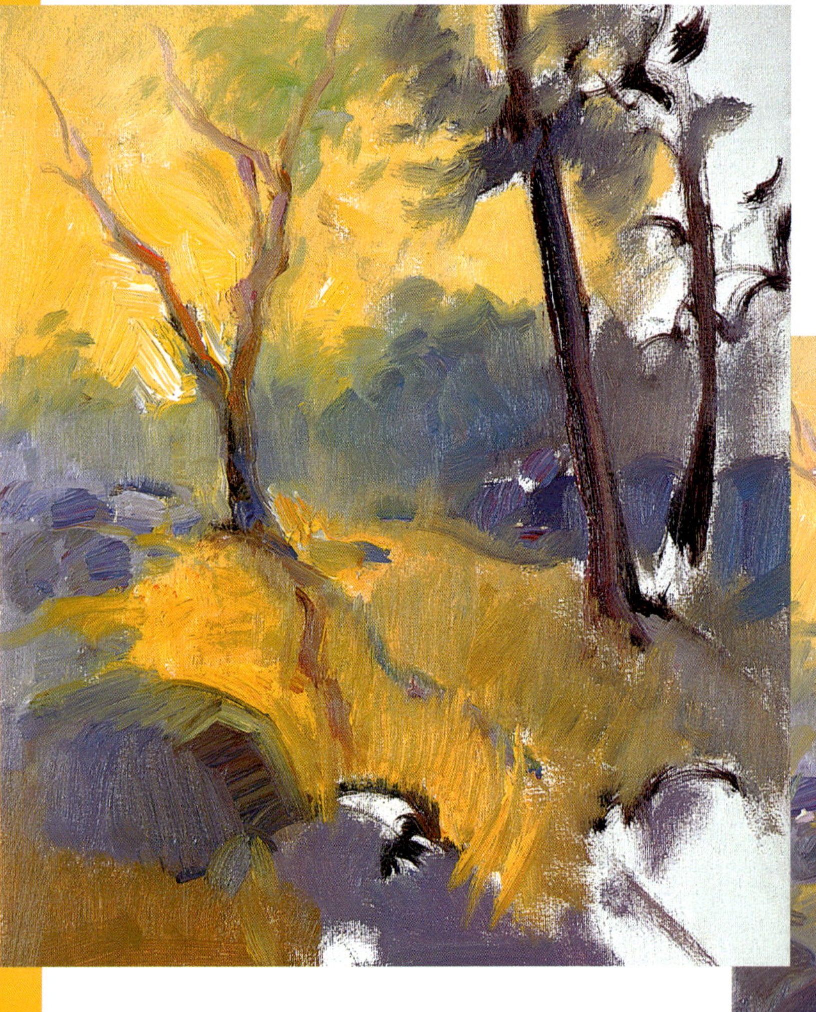

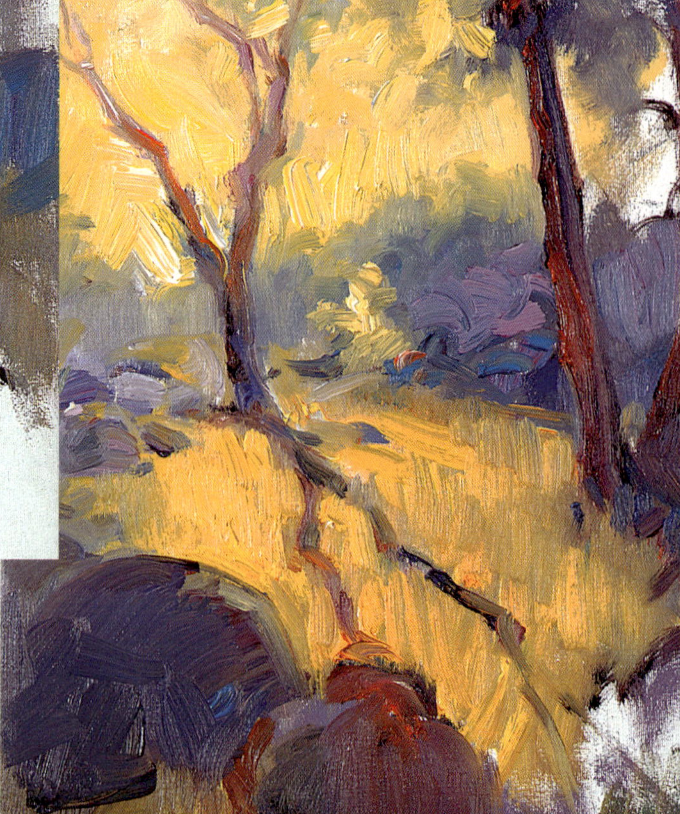

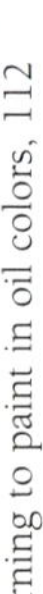

7·In the upper right zone, paint many violet accents which alternate with small orangy, cadmium yellow strokes. Paint dense red strokes on the trunks: they are going to be the complementary color for the greens in the lower part.

Finally, give a few touches of pure orange to finish off this landscape. You will realize that nature's colors have been depicted through complementary colors.

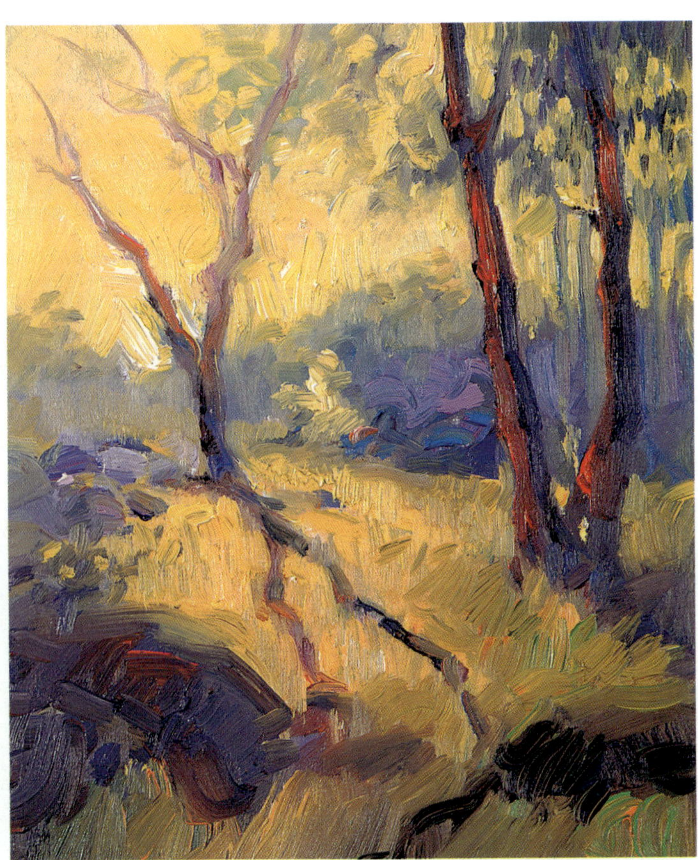

Summary

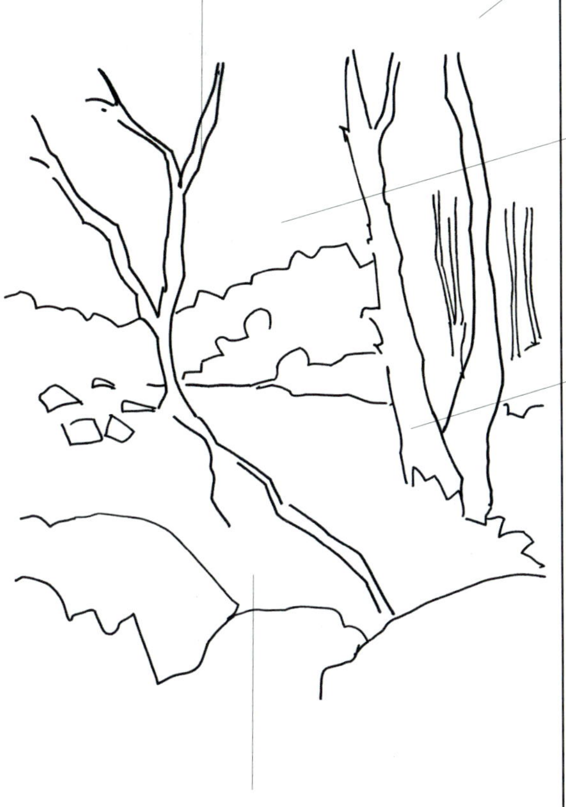

The outline is done in charcoal and afterwards in violet oil color

In the upper right zone paint orangy, cadmium and violet accents

The background is painted in a mixture of yellow and Naples yellow to create the backlight effect

On top of the trees the reds are complemented with greens in the lower part

The earth is painted in orangy colors, strongly contrasting with the violet

Chapter 10

Staining planes

Oil painting permits a great number of recourses which make possible the representation of all types of subjects, offering the artist exceptional facilities and outstanding technical characteristics. Oil painting can also be practiced with a completely flat look.

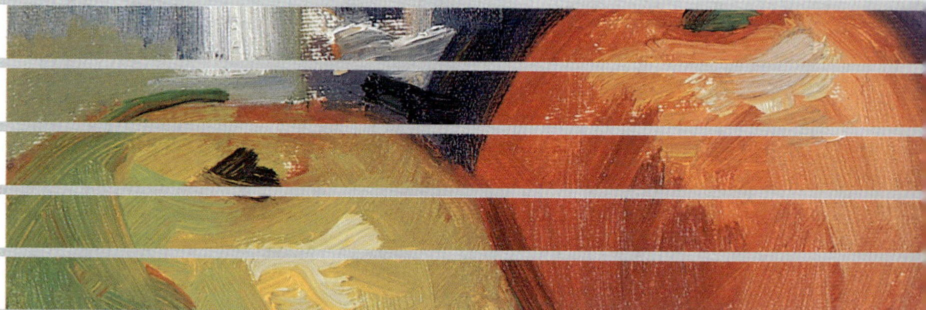

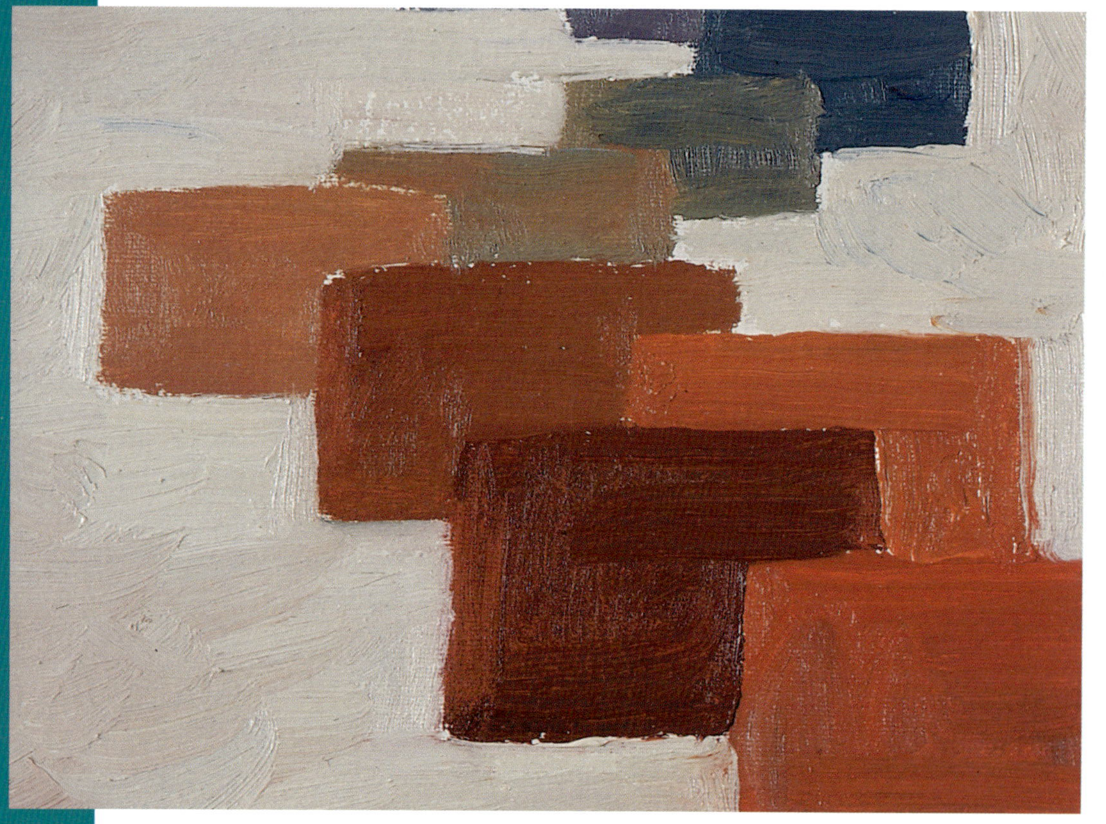

In this picture, painted in oil colors, you can observe a natural ordering of the colors according to the planes in the distance. The warmer tones correspond to the nearest planes.

On the following pages we are going to explain a series of recourses which are very useful for doing paintings the elements of which are placed logically. The notions put forward, starting with the general picture, how to use the brush, the spatial planes and the highlights of every plane, will help to do any later piece.

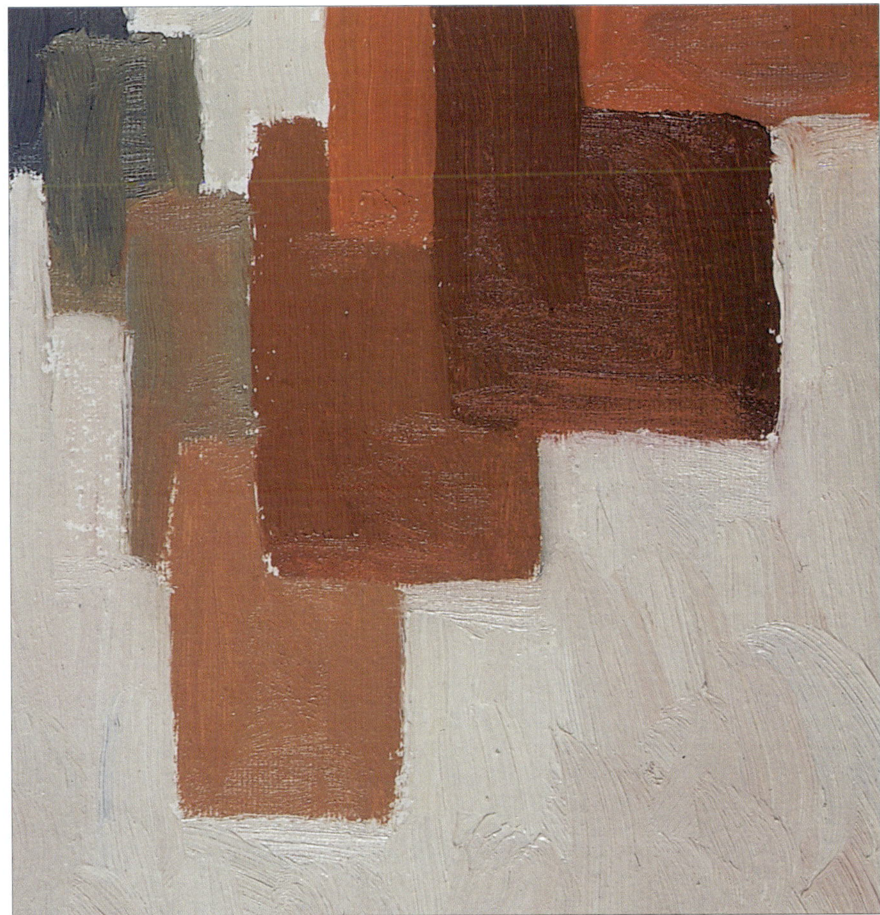

Plane definition in oil colors

Planes correspond to each of the zones that a object occupies in space: They refer to the representation of each of the zones according to the viewpoint of the observer, in this case the artist. For example, in the image shown on this page, each of the zones painted in one color represents a plane and occupies a space in the picture. When an object is painted, the planes are observed in the same way in space. Every one of the faces of the object is represented in a distinct plane, defined by the color and the stroke.

Setting out the picture

A picture is the representation of a series of objects situated in different planes. Logically, in the space occupied by one object there cannot be another. Some objects are near to each other, or to the viewer and some are far apart. Those that are in the same plane are necessarily side by side. Setting out a painting obliges the situation of the objects to be observed from the beginning: how they are placed, the distance between them and the slope of the ground, always according to the artist's viewpoint.

The initial treatment

We now put forward a simple exercise about spatial planes based on the image shown on this page. In this picture the foreground is represented by a red cube;

the middle ground is represented by an ochre cube and the last ground is represented by two earth colored cubes. We are going to paint a still life based on these elements, but converting them into different objects. In the foreground, start to paint in red: the drawing treatment is rapid and direct. Draw a circular form that later will become a fruit. The brush is applied with thinned oil color so that it flows easily over the card. In second plane, above the first one (look at the picture), paint in an orange color another spherical form without going into details. In the background, use an earthy color to outline very schematically two containers. Now carefully observe the scheme just realized: each plane has its own height in the picture.

The principal plane and the background

The principal plane receives more attention than the secondary planes. It does not have to be the most worked on, but it must stand out for its size, color, and brush stroke

Recourses of plane separation

We could see in the last section how planes are separated according to distance, represented by placing secondary planes higher up than the first plane or principal object. The planes of the objects can also be described by color and brush strokes.

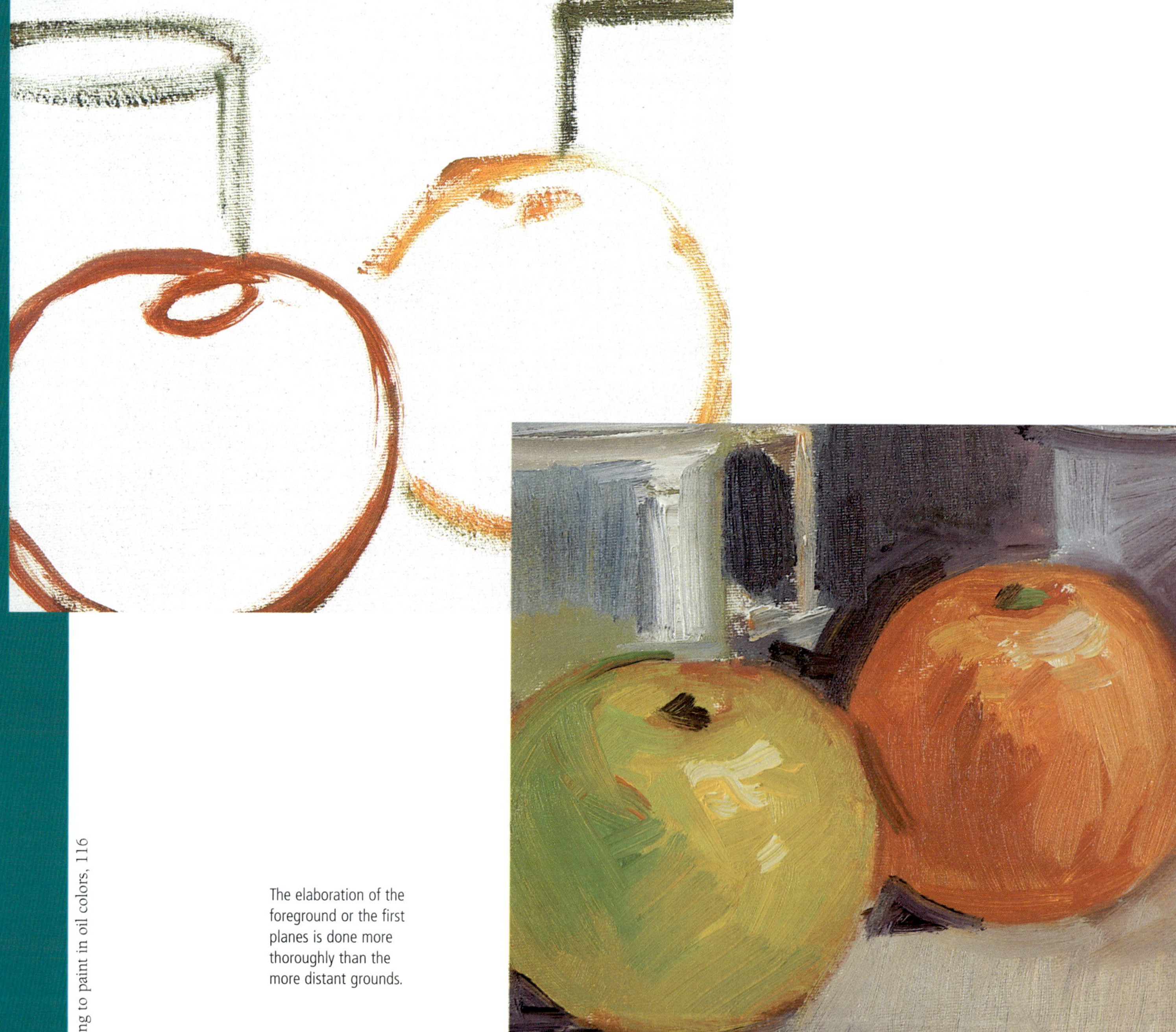

The elaboration of the foreground or the first planes is done more thoroughly than the more distant grounds.

Increasing the contrasts in the principal plane

The principal plane always imposes itself in the composition. The rest of the objects are situated in relation to it. The foreground must always be contrasted compared to the other planes so that they do not appear on top of each other. We are going to do another still life, the foreground of which will be painted firstly and then the other planes will receive distinct tones, establishing a contrast between the foreground and the planes in the background.

The form contours and the color change

The forms painted in oil colors can have a sharply defined edge or simply be insinuated by free strokes that mix with the background colors. Around the foreground paint the posterior planes in clearly differentiated tones. The foreground is thus perfectly defined by the colors and the masses in the background. For example, if the foreground is painted in warm colors, the background can be painted in cooler colors. This is how the contrast strengthens the separation between the planes.

Fading out the forms in the background

To increase the distinction between the different planes of a picture, one recourse can be used which intensifies the effect of the ones previously explained. It is to fade out the forms of the objects situated in the distance. Oil colors are very oily and allow blended strokes to be applied by only caressing a couple of times the paint already down. After several swishes with the brush, you will be able to completely break the form of the background and the planes will have an out of focus look.

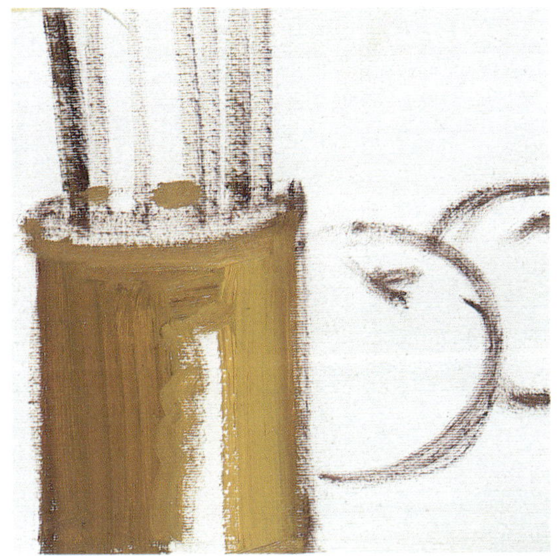

The foreground has been done with warm tones and thick colors.

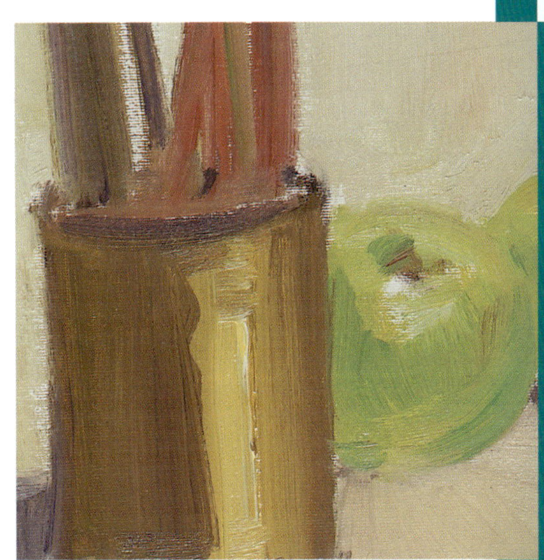

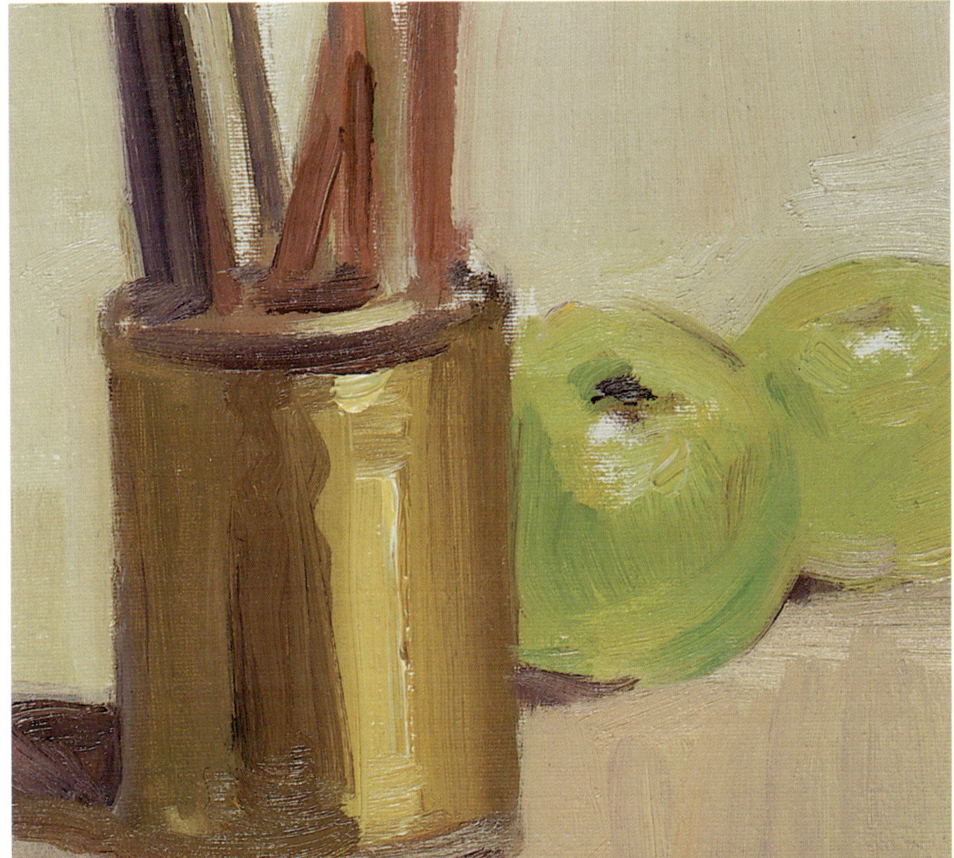

The relationship between the light and the depth of the planes

The situation of the different objects in the picture enables you to consider different options for the points of light. The light that falls on an object can be used as a recourse to favor the nearness or remoteness of the planes they occupy. Although in the model the lights may be similar, they can be interpreted in different ways in distinct planes.

The lights and the foreground

The most important lights are treated as direct accents or pure, bright colors. The accents are applied with free strokes and not mixing the tones underneath. In the foreground the colors are worked on at the same time as the lights. The contrasts are strong, often complementary thereby strengthening the dark tones against the light tones and vice-versa.

Color masses in the middle ground

Before painting the definitive form of the middle ground, you have to establish which is the light zone and which the shadow zone. In this process there is still no separation between the planes, although a much more defined foreground always favors this idea.

In the foreground the general colors are put down and also the most direct lights.

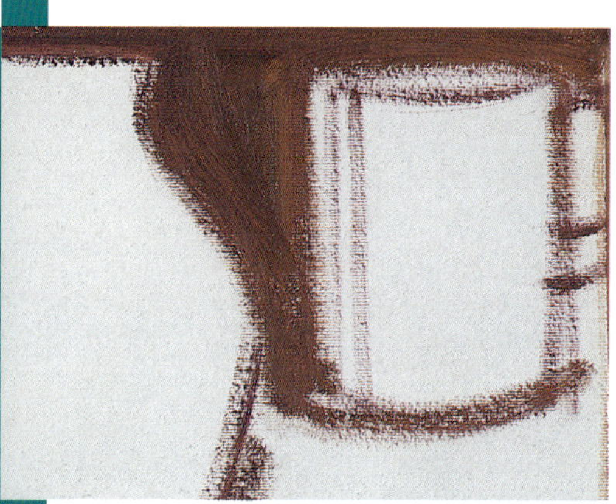

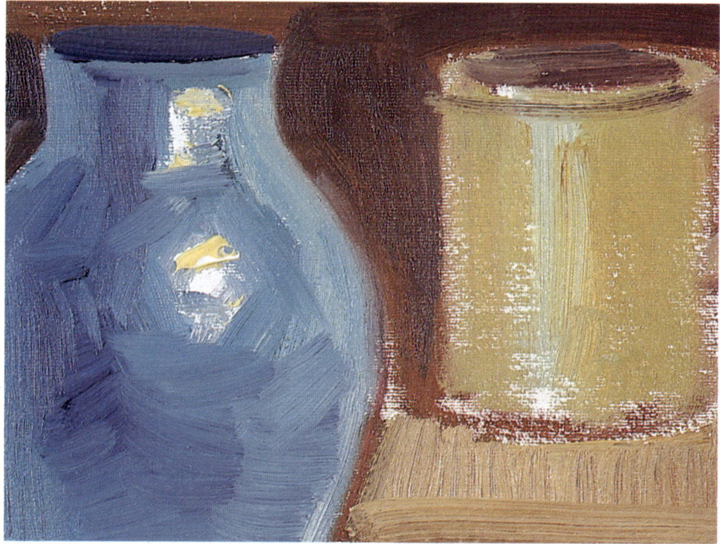

In the background plane you have to establish which are the light zones so as to be able to continue working on the color.

Color masses and the impact of the light.

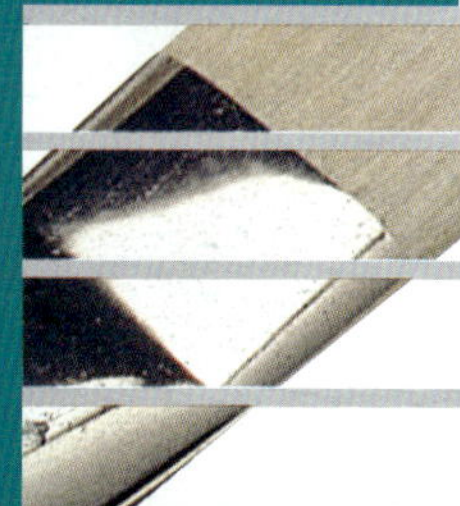

In this masterpiece you can appreciate how the spatial planes are perfectly defined thanks to the two recourses applied. Firstly, the strong light received by the foreground draws it closer to the spectator and separates it from the much darker, background. Secondly, the pictorial treatment given to each of the planes is also different. In the foreground there is a lot of detail while further back there is much less definition.

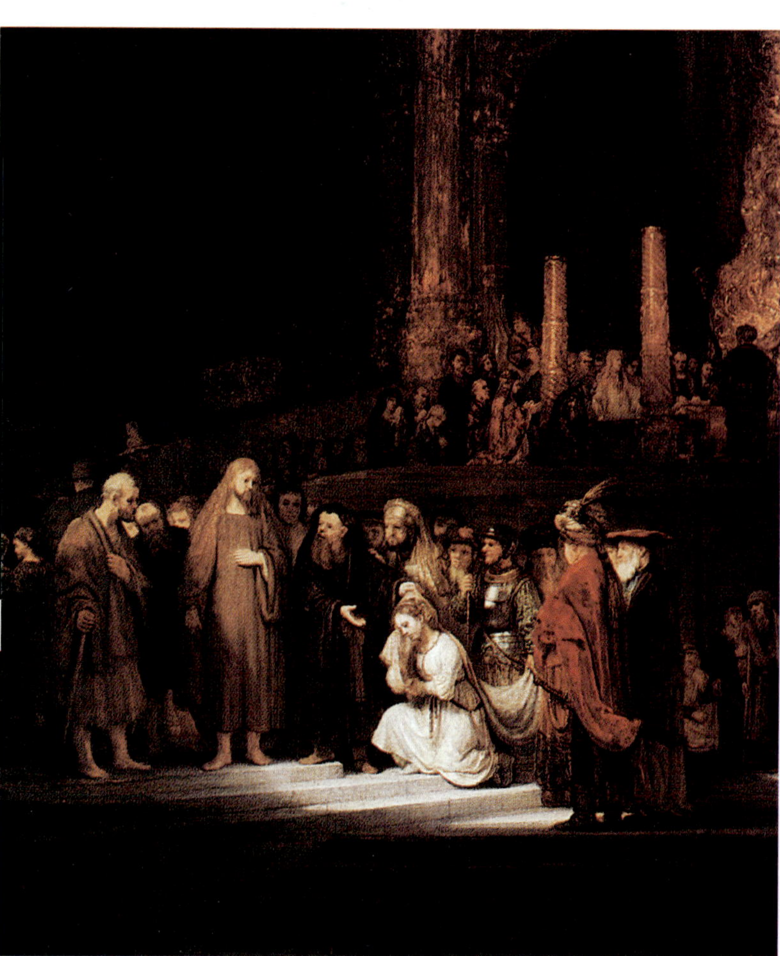

Separation using the highlights

The highlights that have just been painted in the foreground are intense, charged with color and luminosity. Different are the lights painted in the middle ground which are much more monochrome, far from being strong contrasts compared with the other tones of the objects. The light in which the object at the back is painted is dim and full of nuances which subdue its brightness. Pure colors are not used, instead the hues are mixed on the palette to make tones similar to those in the background.

Color in landscape planes

In previous chapters we studied how to create a depth effect using the color white to depict the atmosphere. This was one possibility. However, there is an alternative: create depth by using different recourses from this chapter, eliminating details in the distant grounds and increasing the contrasts in the foregrounds.

With oil colors its easy to insinuate the forms

It is true that with oil colors more than any other medium it is possible to express forms with a single brush stroke. Take advantage of this characteristic and paint the distant planes in a very synthetic way with brush strokes of colors much less contrasted than in the foregrounds. Nevertheless, white does not have to be incorporated into the mix.

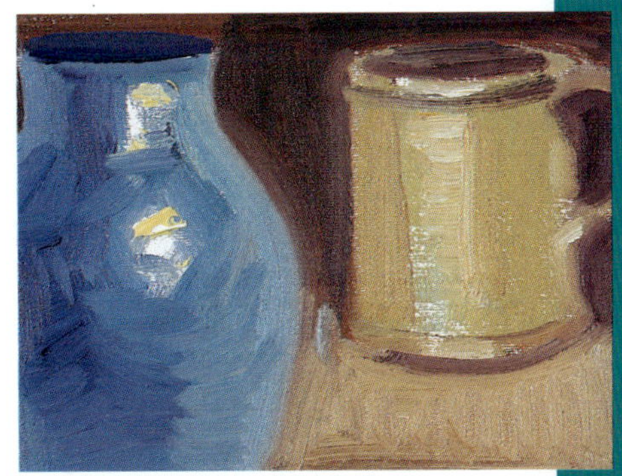

The highlights in the background planes lack the luminosity prevalent in the foreground.

The impact of the brush in important planes

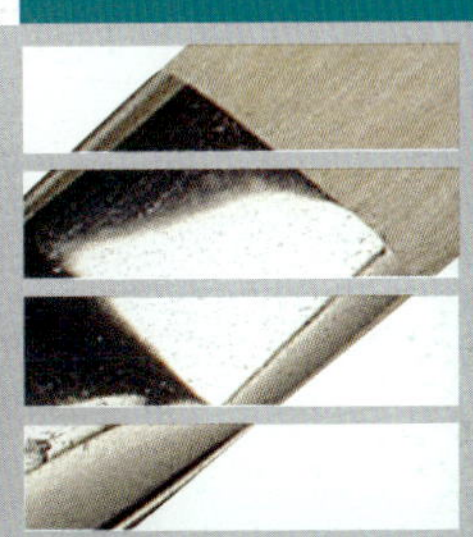

One must learn how to apply the opportune stroke in the right place so as to be able to make more evident the separation between the planes. In this brief exercise we are going to do an example of brush strokes for the foreground.

Firstly, do the forms with color masses, clearly differentiating between the light and shadow zones. On top of the initial color masses, on the front part of the volume, do short, horizontal strokes. As you progress with the construction of form in the lateral planes, apply longer, vertical strokes.

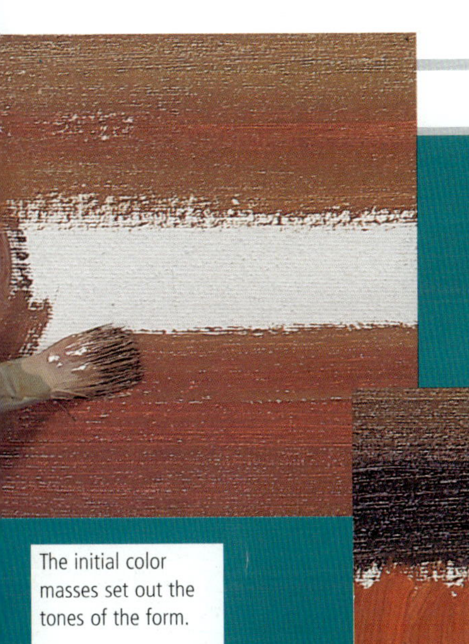

The initial color masses set out the tones of the form.

In the central plane the strokes are short and horizontal.

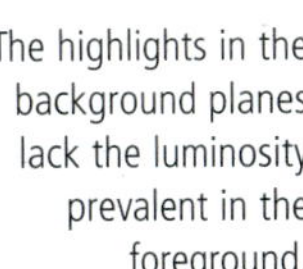

On the lateral planes the brush strokes are long and vertical.

A photographic effect

Just as when you look at a photo there
can be planes in the distance out of
focus, in painting this recourse can be
used to depict the background.
However, the nearest planes are
painted with a higher intensity of warm
tones and contrasted zones.

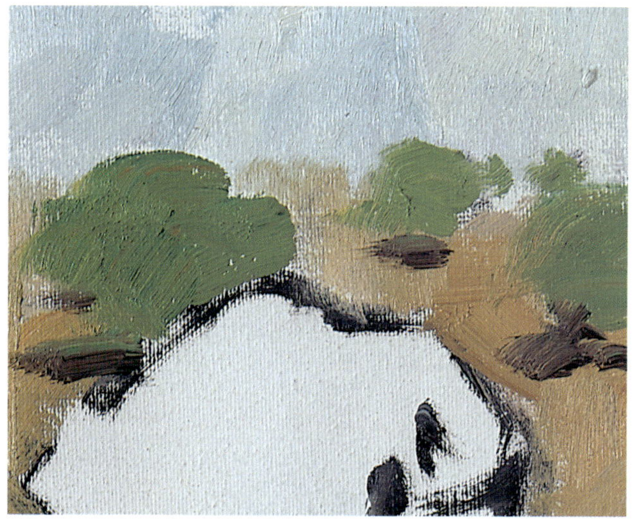

The planes in the
distance are
represented smaller
than the foreground.
The forms are
insinuated with fresh,
direct brush strokes.

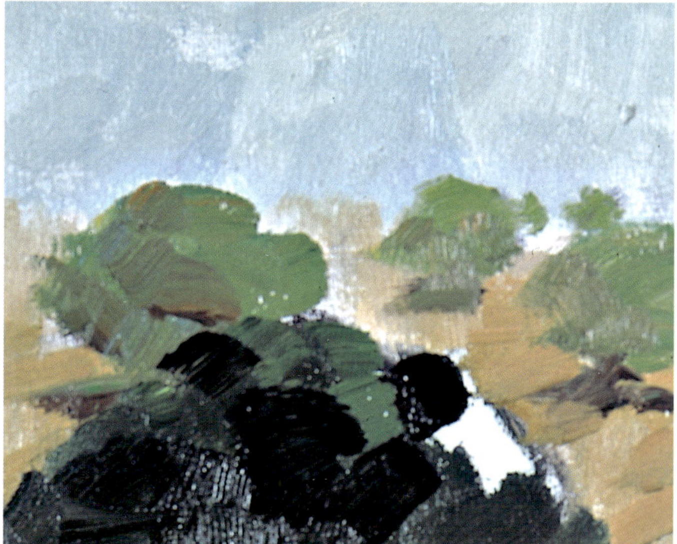

The nearer the trees
are, the more
contrasts and pure
colors that are
painted.

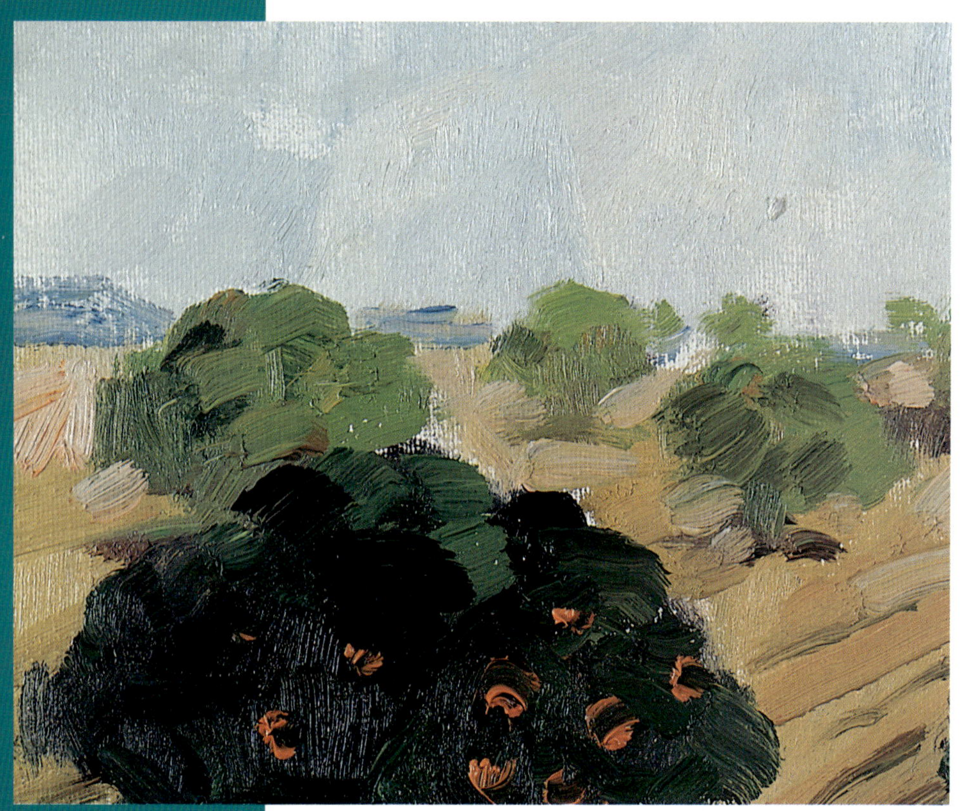

At the end of the
painting process, the
most luminous details
are depicted.

Summary

THE PLANES IN THE PICTURE.
Each zone is divided into spa-
tial planes. The principal
plane is always more defined
than the background planes.

THE OBJECT PLANES.
The strokes are used to define
the planes of the objects.
Plane definition.
The planes in the background
lack detail and contrast. The
forms are more faded.

THE LIGHT IN EACH PLANE.
The lighting in the planes
loses contrast as the picture
goes further back. The princi-
pal planes have more lumi-
nous highlights.

Exercises

BOTTLES AND A TABLECLOTH.

The situating of the different planes in a picture is not a question that can be learned in a moment, but a few practice sessions can suffice to get an approximate idea of the technique. In previous chapters we have studied how the atmosphere was represented in oil painting. Situating the planes in the picture is only related to the atmospheric effect in the technical aspect. The planes nearer are more defined than the ones further off: always bear this in mind. Each of the different planes requires a distinct treatment with respect to both color and stroke.

Necessary material

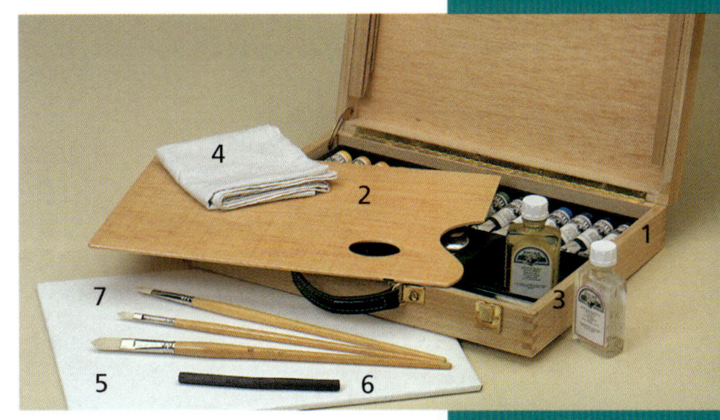

Oil colors (1), a palette (2), linseed oil (3), a cloth (4), brushes (5), charcoal (6) and card (7).

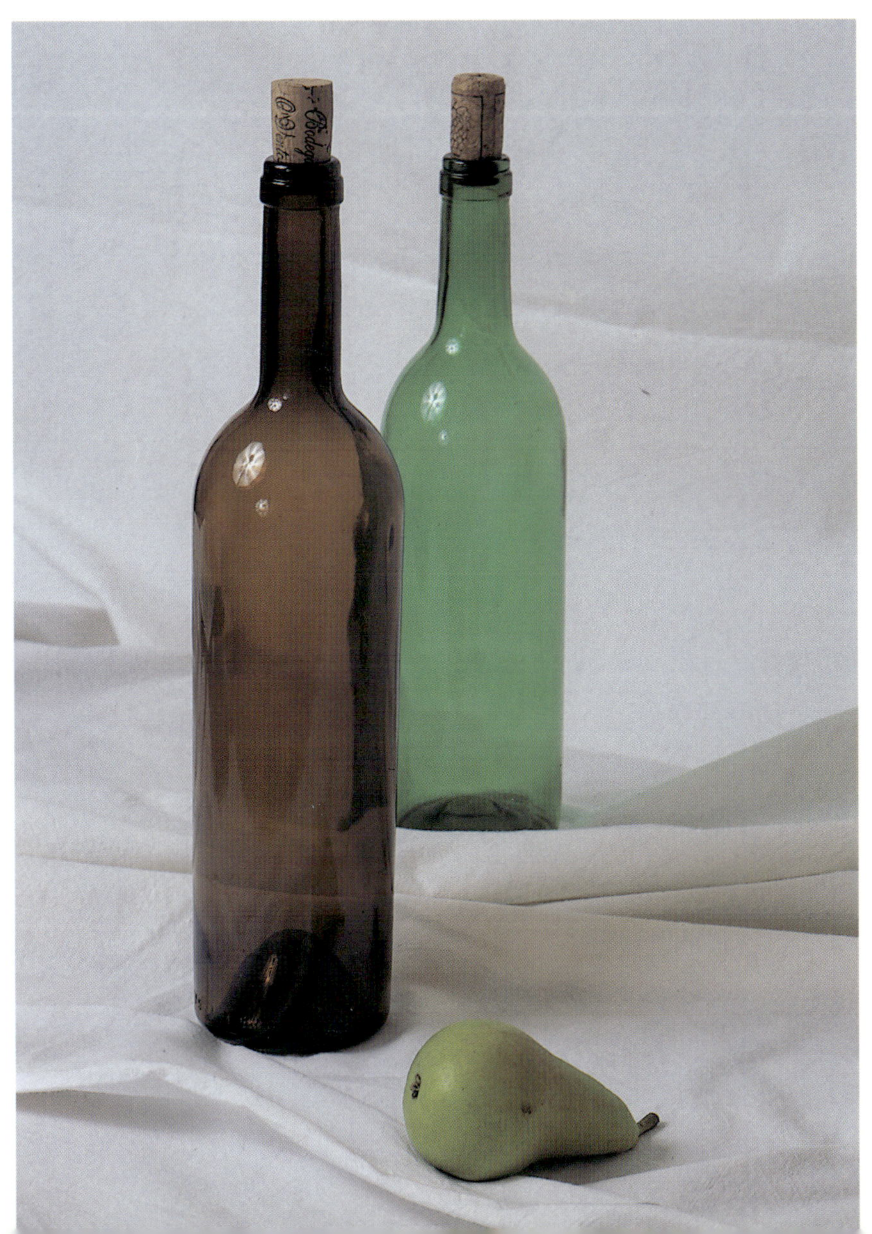

Exercises

1·When you are depicting planes to represent depth, the first outline greatly helps to distribute the different elements in the picture.
The principal elements in this composition are the brown colored bottle and a pear. In the background there is a green bottle.
The outline must be concise and not introduce unnecessary lines.
It is recommendable to define the forms at this stage because symmetric objects, like the bottles, are always complicated to realize.

2·Start doing the color mass on the bottle in the foreground using a mixture of sienna and English red. The mix is not made on the palette but directly on the painting, taking only a little of each color and then dragging with the brush.

While you are painting the bottle, leave reserved in white the zones which correspond to the highlights, although later they will be painted.
The background is painted in blue toned down with a little white.
The tablecloth in the foreground is painted with the brush very dry, only insinuating the shadow zones.

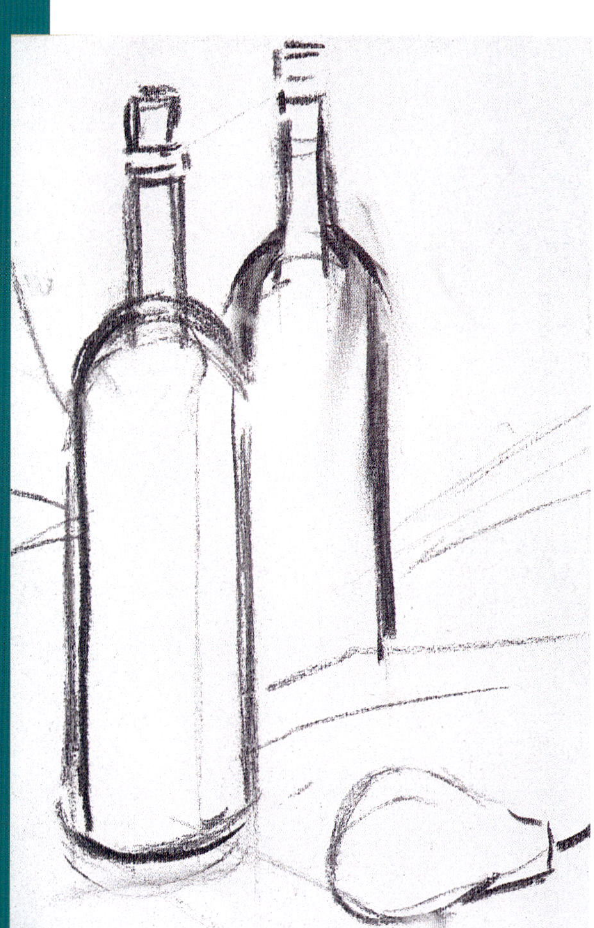

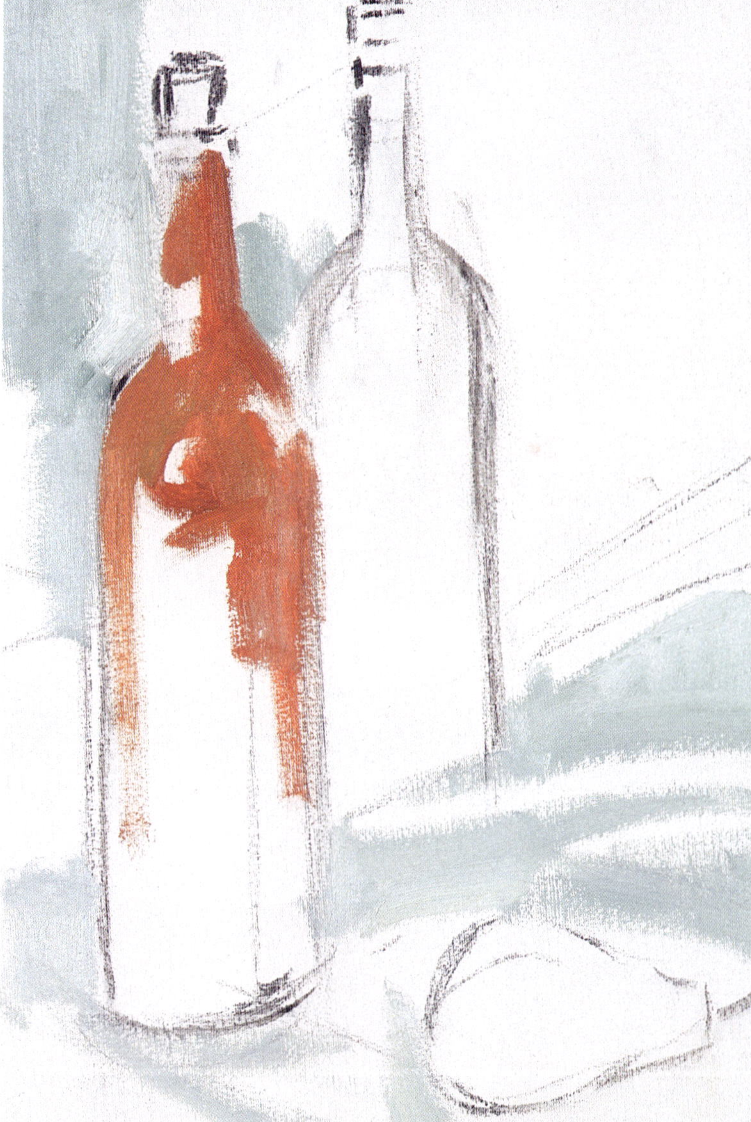

3·Finish off painting the bottle in the foreground in the following way: on the neck and the body the strokes are long and close together. On the left, use natural sienna. In the center, on top of the color sienna, incorporate a little burnt umber, and on the right, paint with a bit of English red, toned down with sienna.

Around the zone of maximum brightness, stick to the English red tone. The pear in the foreground is worked on in a mixture of yellow Naples yellow and green. In the lower zone of the foreground, paint in a somewhat purer green.

The bottle in the background is painted with much less definition. The green tones are very whitish and similar to those around them. Finish painting the background in a mixture of very luminous cobalt blue, white and Naples yellow.

4·All the picture is worked on at the same time, without leaving aside any zone, thus enabling you to compensate the forms and colors of the different planes.

On the principal bottle, in the center, do a descending plane with horizontal strokes, dragging the shadow color painted in the last step. On the right side do vertical strokes of burnt umber. The lower part of the bottle is painted in curved strokes which drag part of the colors already put down. In the background the bottle receives a similar going over but the tones are more limited, green made more pastel with white and Naples yellow.

When working on the planes, the colors have to be used according to the place occupied by all the objects. It would not be coherent to paint the background plane in vivid colors while the foreground is in pastel tones.

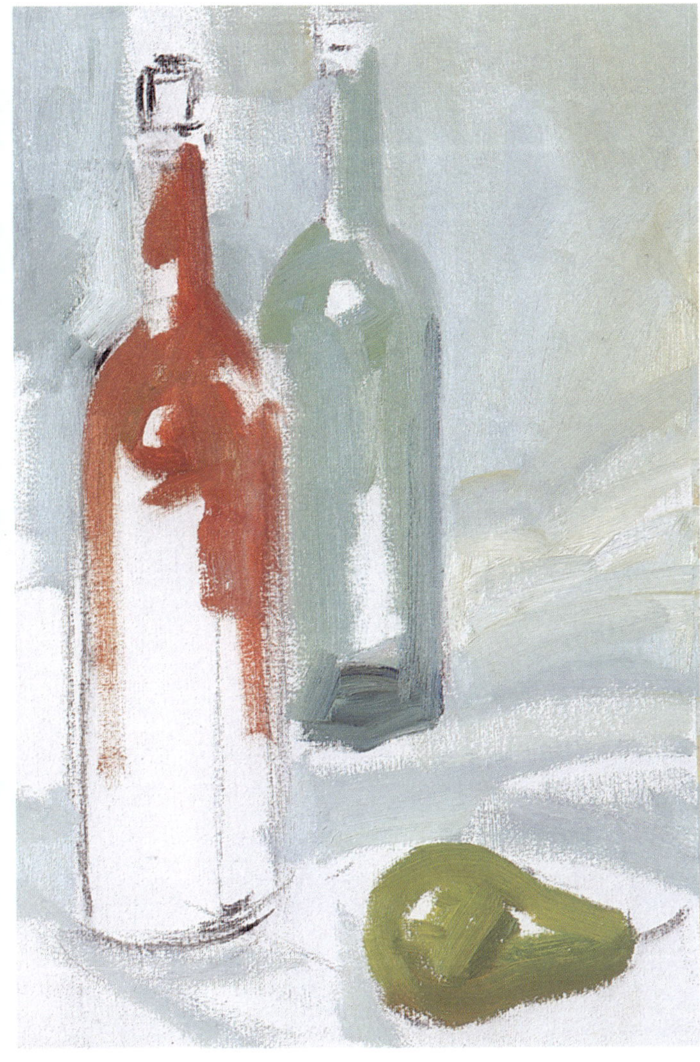

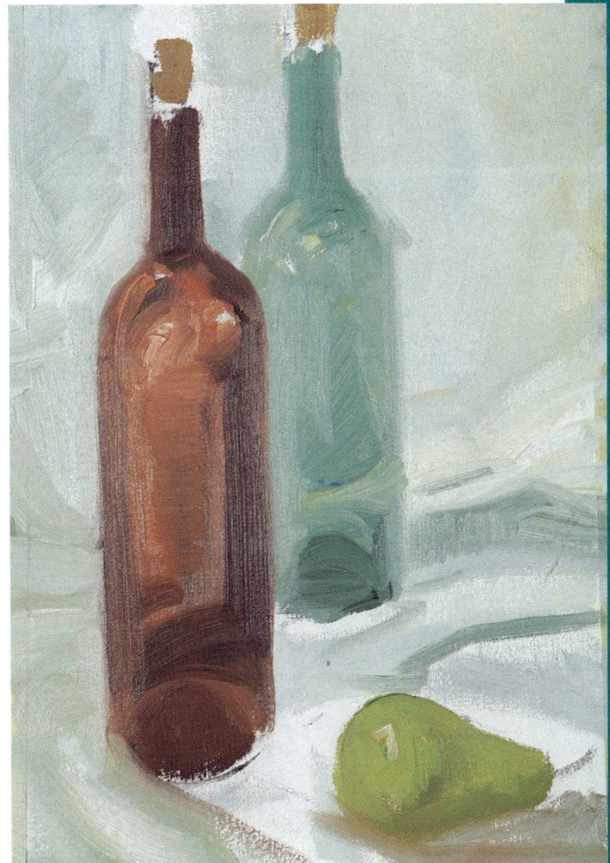

Exercises

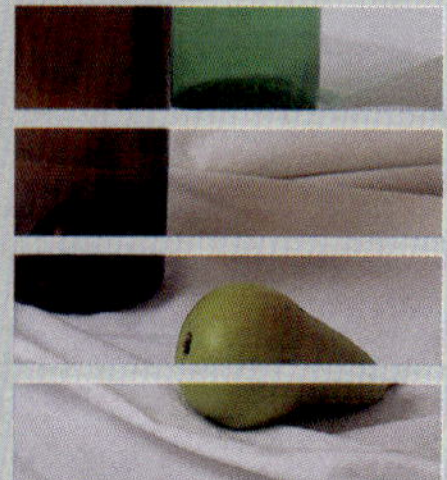

5·In this step you can see the different treatment given to
the planes. While the bottle in the background hardly
receives any extra touches, on the foreground bottle the
color work is insistent. The simultaneous contrasts
between the colors and the tones are accentuated.
On the bottle neck, paint in dark brown with long,
vertical strokes. In the center, the strokes are short and
horizontal to form a distinct plane.
On the body of the bottle, elaborate new planes. In the
center the strokes are short, red and horizontal. On the
curved side, do an orangy stroke the follows the form. The
highlight is painted in yellow.
Observe the way the form of the pear is painted. The
yellow strokes are on top of each other and the green.

6·In this close up you can see the difference
between the treatment given to the two
principal planes. The first one, the foreground, is
full of contrasts and is richer in color than the
middle ground, which practically blends into the
background.

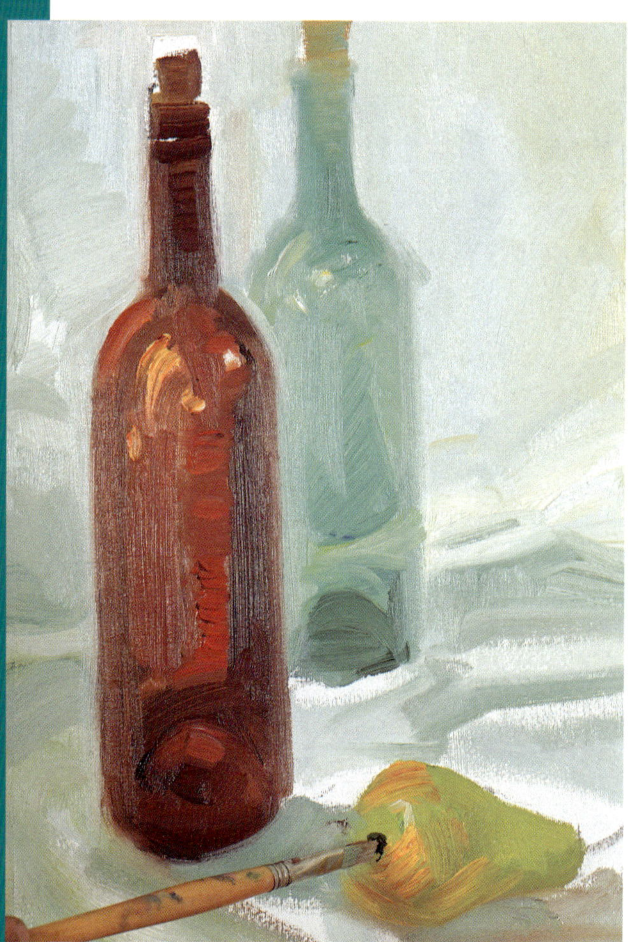

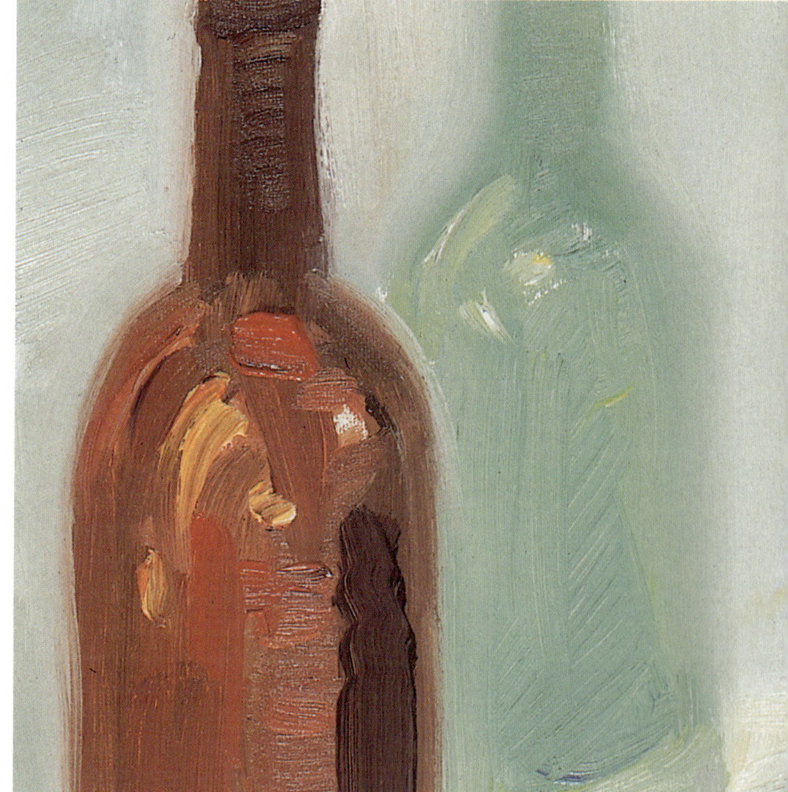

7·The work realized on the wrinkled tablecloth is straightforward and, as always, requires more attention in the foreground than in the background. The light tones in the foreground are much more brighter and the colors purer than further back. Pass the brush over softly to eliminate all the hard edges of the bottle in the background. Its appearance will become almost out of focus. This step will finish off this work dealing with planes in oil painting.

The tones and colors in the foreground are strong and contrasted.

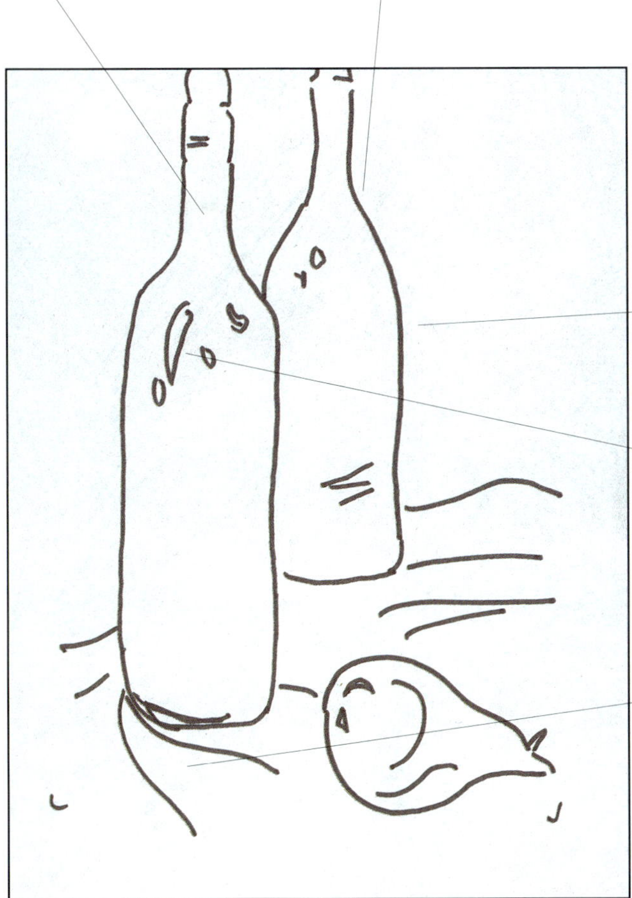

Summary.

In the most distant plane, the colors tend to blend together.

On the principal bottle the highlights are depicted with strong, luminous colors.

The tablecloth is much more defined in the foreground.

Chapter 11

Mixing directly on the painting

Painting done directly on the picture, without too much palette mixing, is called painting "alla prima".

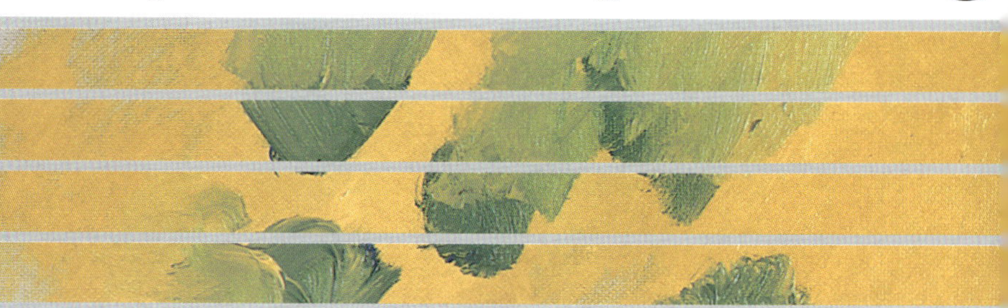

In this chapter we are going to deal with the subject of mixing directly on the picture, something which may require a fresh effort by the learner who has grown used to palette mixes. However, do not be put off, the exercises are not complicated. In deed, they will give the learner the opportunity to acquire fresh recourses that will make it possible to paint without a sketch or an extensive palette. Although this way of working is not the final objective of the learner. Ability comes with experience and practice. This chapter has been included because of the usefulness of being able to sense rapidly and intuitively how direct work is going to turn out.

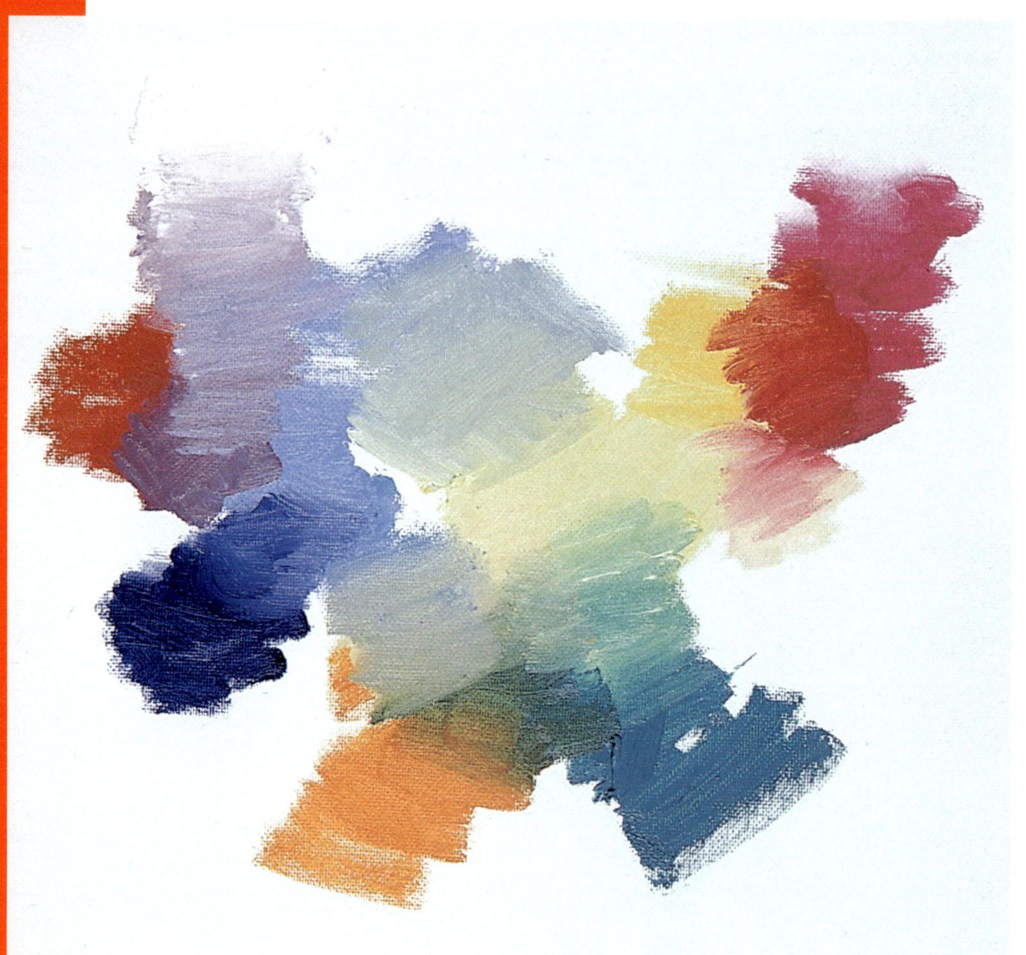

When painting directly on the picture it is necessary to know how the theory of color works so that you get the mixes right.

Test mixes

Any learner who throughout this book has been receiving the message about the importance of palette work is going to be surprised to discover the concepts in this chapter. In fact, the notions about direct painting on the picture are not so different to more studied and elaborated work. Only some questions change, like, for example, testing color mixes on the palette looking for a particular tone. This procedure does not mean painting blindly. Just the

opposite: it is possible to study color and contrasts provided that the fundamental rules of oil painting are respected. The first layers and strokes are thinner than the later ones. Whatever the case, it is not too complicated to paint directly on the picture, something many enthusiasts do because they do not know more advanced techniques.

In the exercises we are going to do, the necessary instructions will be given so that the work does not become a process of smearing paint on the support.

So that the process can be seen visually we will do a simple exercise on canvas or on card. The objective is nothing more than understanding how the method works. In reality if you follow how the recourse works, there is no point in wasting paint by doing color masses.

The first color mass is quite large and must be yellow.

On top of the last color mass, superimpose some direct, blue strokes.

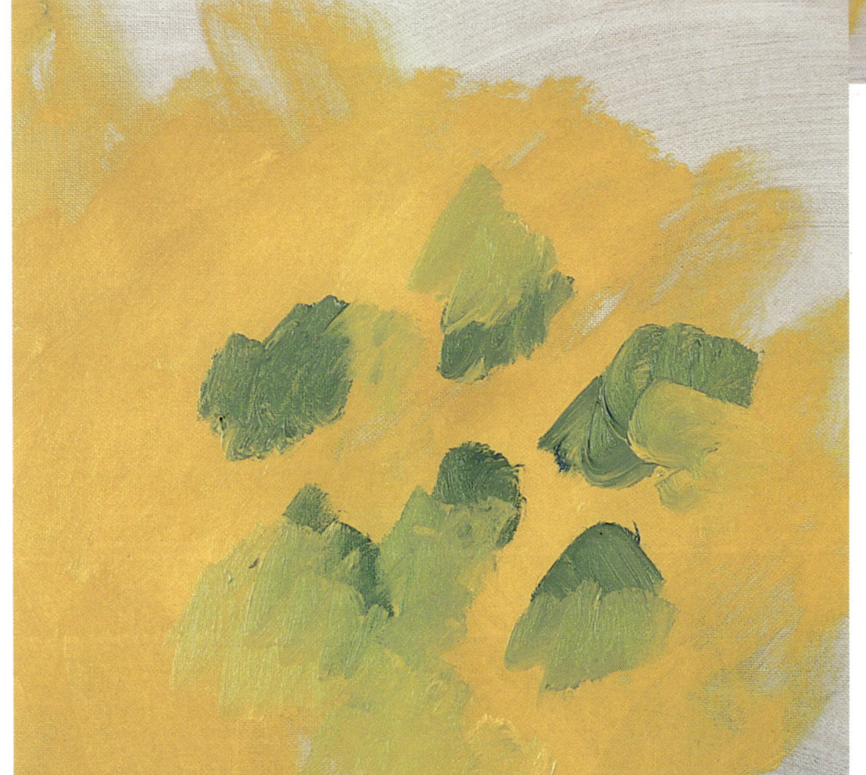

Just pass the brush over the masses many times to blend the colors and to get a luminous green.

Firstly, paint a yellow surface; the form does not matter. As always, the first layer is thinner than the later ones. One of the important advantages of oil painting is that its density facilitates direct mixing on the picture. However, although the paint is used thinned in the first layers it must not be so flowing that it drips or runs. If you need very liquid paint, drain the brush off well, as shown in the last exercise of this chapter.

Once you have painted a yellow mass big enough to be able to work on it, apply direct blue strokes. The paint here is denser than used in the beginning. Do you remember what the color circle predicts about mixing yellow and blue? That is exactly what happens here: green is obtained and this is the process we are going to use in the forthcoming exercises. It is vital to know the colors and the results of mixing them so that we can get the most out of the recourses.

It is easier to darken a color than to lighten it

There are some element rules that must be remembered when mixing directly on the painting. Not all the colors mix in the same way, nor are the darkening processes the same. When mixing on the palette the colors have to be applied according to an order and this holds true for mixing directly on the painting, too. For example, if you want to obtain a particular gray it is always straightforward to mix

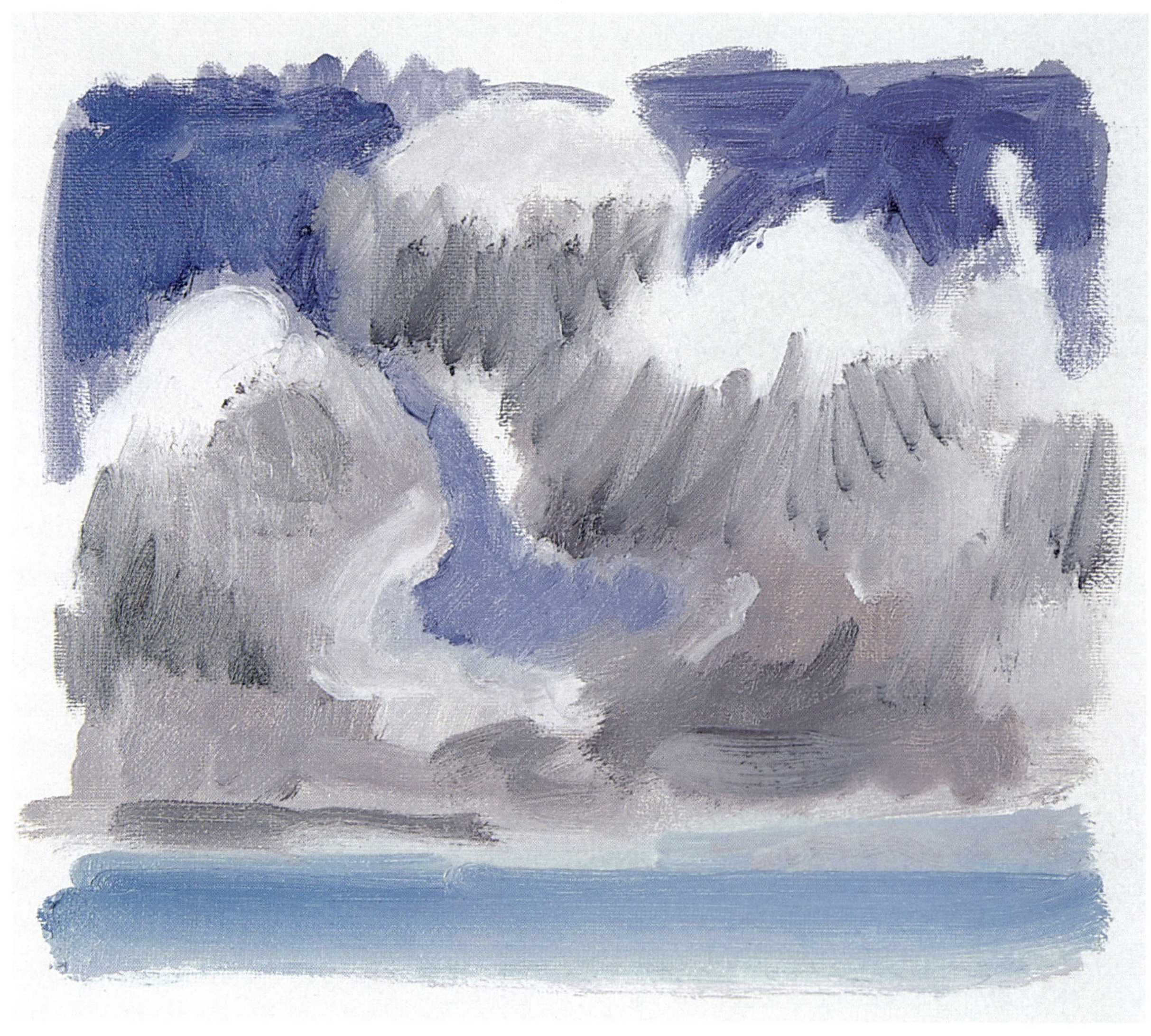

This first direct color mass has been made in quite dark tones. The light zones have been left unpainted.

dark into light, and not vice-versa. To practice this idea we are going to do two exercises in which you can test this first hand. The motif, threatening clouds, is the same for the two exercises. In the first case we are going to do dark contrasts to compose the clouds. The grays will be painted directly on the painting with different black tones mixed directly with white. From this first step onwards it will be necessary to compensate the tones because it will be quite complex to do a soft transition from the darks to the lights.

The form of the clouds has to be preserved because they are the base of the picture structure. To do this apply white directly to the most illuminated zones. Now try to do this same step by dragging the color white towards the darks to lighten them. What happens? The light areas are quickly contaminated by the medium tones and immediately the zones that should stay luminous begin to lose the tone we wanted to keep. Any later application of white only creates new grays. If you wanted to get back the original

tone and luminosity of the picture it would be difficult because the grays developed are not pure colors: they are broken and dirtied. Applying white directly does not help you because it only gives a plain tone with no possibility of relief. The solution to this light onto dark problem could lie in intensifying the darks so that the simultaneous contrasts are increased: the lights would appear much more luminous. Of course, it could also be corrected once the painting is dry but then it would not be "alla prima".

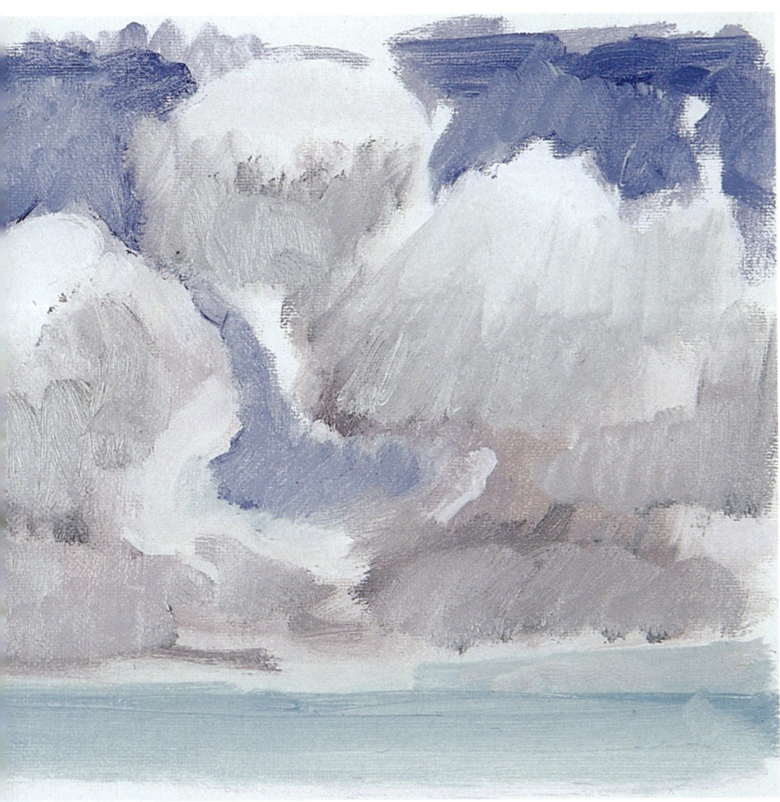

Once the initial dark tones are down it is difficult to preserve the original light areas as they immediately become dirtied.

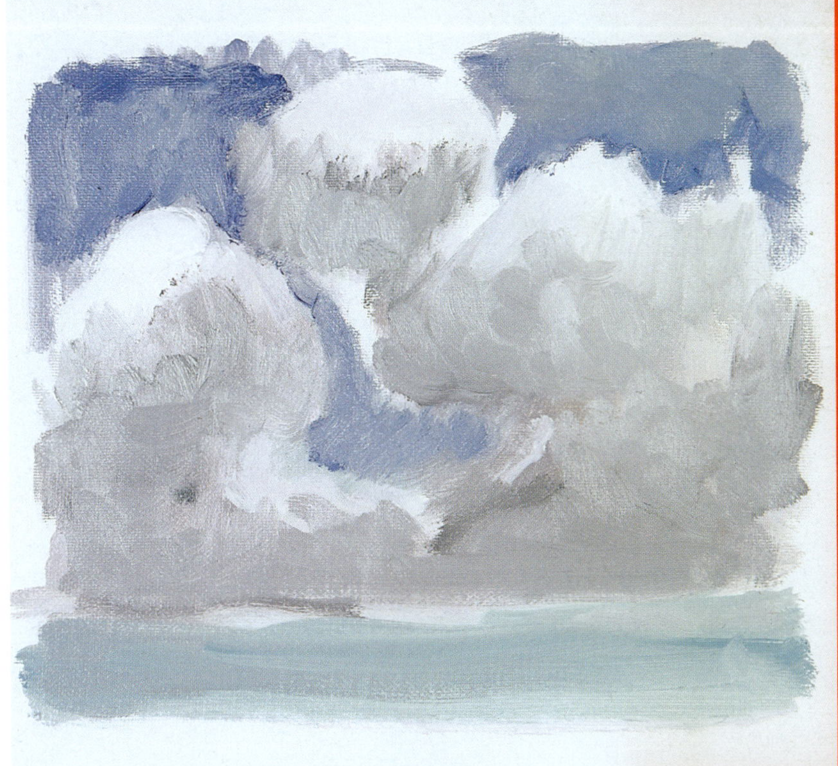

This effort to restore the luminosity has been a failure; the colors obtained are constantly being debased.

Using the brush to mix the color

After the deliberate mistakes we made in the last exercise we can now try again. This time the first tones applied are the most luminous ones. We want some of the cloud zones to remain white without having to go back and rework them. After having done the blues that surround the clouds, paint the whites without excessive insistence and without penetrating into the gray tone zone. Below these luminous tones, do a few strokes of gray. Clean the brush so that the lightest tones do not get sullied and do brush strokes from the light area to the dark to mix directly on the painting. Once the first tones have been mixed, new grays can be applied to the dark part below.

Dragging the brush over the fresh color

Use small additions of dark colors to obtain the mixes which will give volume to the clouds. You need not insist too much because, as we saw in the first exercise of this chapter, any dark added on top of a light tone will cause the base color to contrast notably. Moreover, not only darker tones than the original ones can be applied: as the process was realized very progressively, if any tone is too contrasted, you can compensate with a direct white. This is the method used in painting directly on the painting. It is also important not to clog the painting up with paint so that the tones and contrasts can be corrected immediately.

The first tones painted are the most luminous; on top of these, being careful not to sully them, paint the half grays.

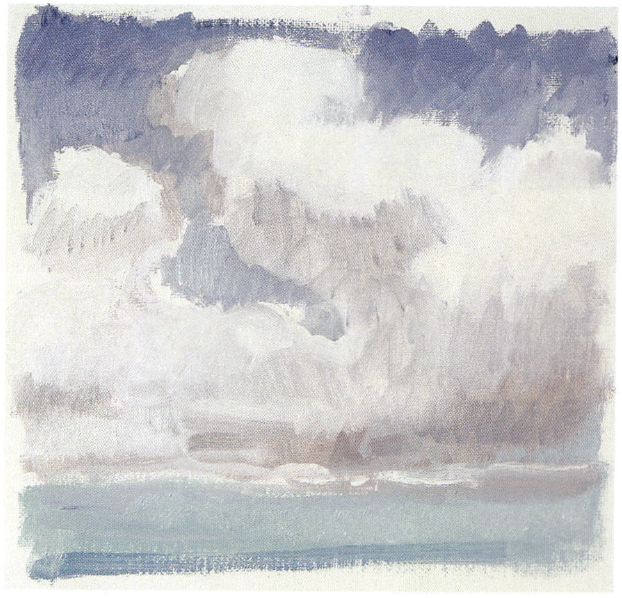

On top of the most luminous tones, other darks can be added without staining the zones that must remain white.

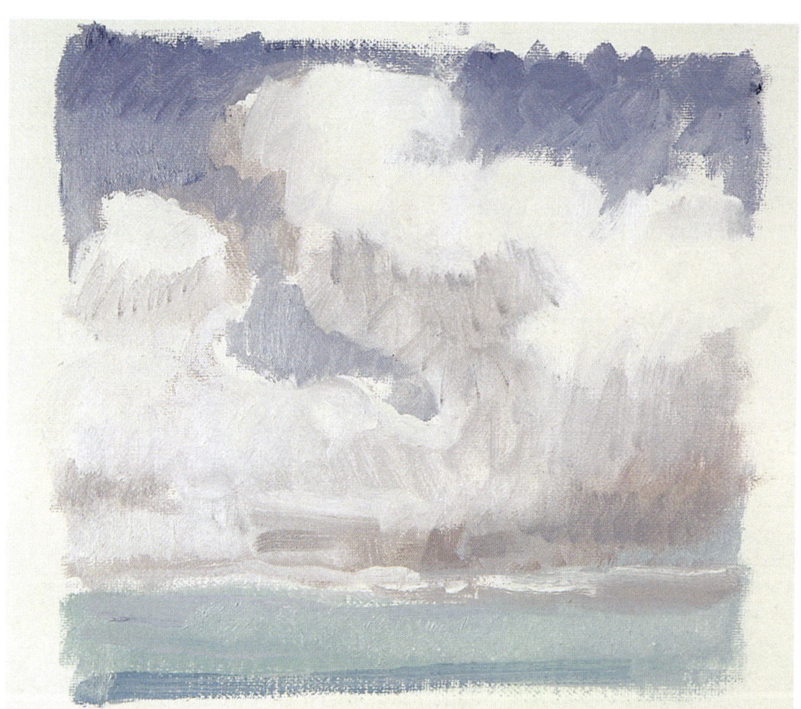

Here you can observe how in the finished exercise contrasts and dark areas have been done, without the cloud areas losing their luminosity.

Control the paint load

As you can see, it is very important to regulate the amount of paint applied directly on the painting. The tones can be darkened or lightened without the paint becoming tacky or lacking in consistency. If a zone is overworked and excessive paint accumulates, the series of dragging strokes would only blotch the colors. To avoid this pitfall typical of learners, it is recommendable to pick up color on the brush little by little. If even so the paint is too thick, drag the underneath color using a spatula.

Darkening luminous colors with complementary colors

There are endless possibilities with painting directly on the picture and many varied recourses for obtaining striking mixes. However, it is fundamental to obtain these mixes without injurious effects for the painting process. The previous exercises were straightforward because all that mattered was to show the procedure of mixing directly on the painting. At the beginning we commented that this direct "alla prima" work was good for any motif and we are now going to apply it to a still life composed of an orange and two lemons. The elaboration process takes in all that was taught before, although on this occasion expressive and luminous colors are going to come into play.

Paint, mix and draw at the same time

Mixing directly on the painting has to be approached according to the subject. It is possible that the picture requires an outline beforehand. Instead of drawing in charcoal, it can be done rapidly in thinned oil color but not too flowing so that we can work with its pliability. The tractable nature of the oil color must never be diluted away.

The outline is done very thinned but without the paint dripping down the surface.

The stroke direction in painting directly on the picture

When we mix directly on the painting we must study the line and brush marks carefully because they define the planes of each painted zone. Often the palette used in this type of painting is very limited and, therefore, the buttery oil color consistency is taken advantage of in the stroke work. Although similar colors may be used in a zone, slight tone changes can define planes.

Each of the zones in the picture is done with different strokes that give subtle changes of form, texture, and color, all of which separate the planes. In the sky the stroke is plain and crossed. The clouds have been realized with soft, long strokes on top of which blue and yellow have been added. In the tree area, the tones are dark and painted with small, defined accents. The earth has been depicted in blue tones.

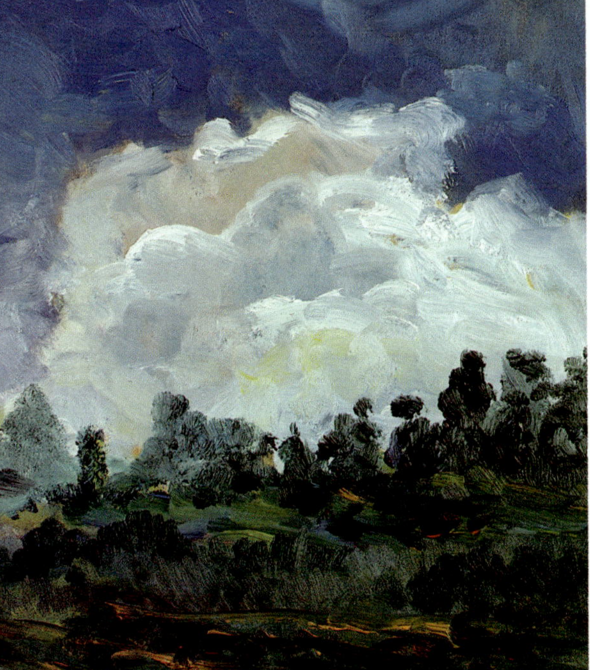

Yellow is used in the foregrounds converting the other colors into green tones. Once the drawing has been constructed the more concrete details can be put in, blending some of the background color.

Colors from the same range

As soon as the outline of the fruit has been drawn, start to paint them. To be able to paint rapidly, without having to use the mixes in the palette, paint the zones according to color ranges. This means the nuances used in the picture can be enriched immediately by tone work. We can observe this effect being put into practice and we will start by painting the lemons in a very luminous yellow, leaving untouched the highlight area. Continue with other, warmer, yellows but without mixing excessively on the picture. Once the lemon tone is resolved, paint the orange. Once again the highlight zone remains untouched.

Before cleaning the brush, paint the lemons again, adding some nuances to the tones. In this process the brush has become stained with the yellow mix and is now highly suitable for using on the orange, raising the key of some luminous zones.

Effects of painting directly

To apply the definitive darks in this exercise, black must not be used; there are always alternatives that do not sully the layers below so much and do permit highly luminous dark areas. When complementary colors are used to obtain darks, the effect is highly contrasting. In this example the colors are a mixture of violet and orange.

The outline is realized directly, with rapid stroke work.

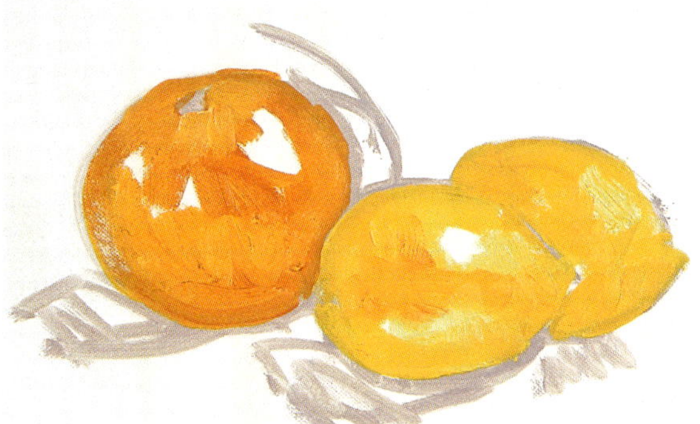

To paint the fruits it is important to use to the full every brushload of paint, to cover the underpainting and to mix directly, forming each element.

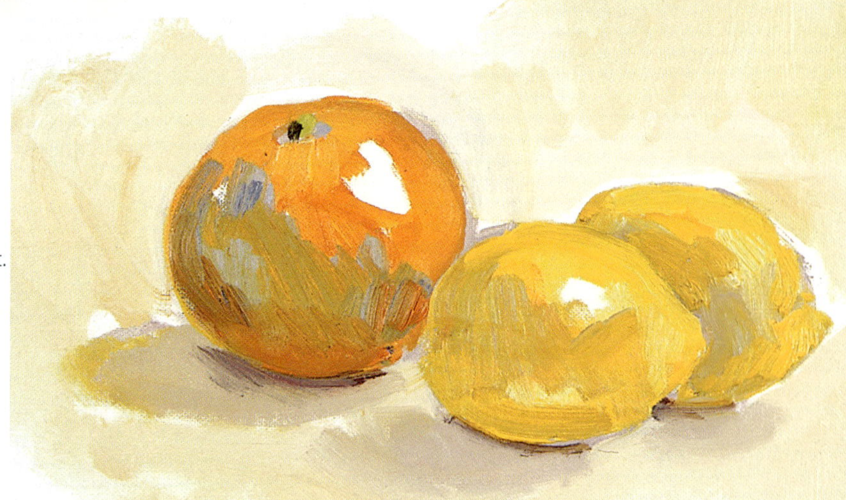

The dark parts are realized in violet. The highlights have been left untouched and appear much more brilliant thanks to the orange and Naples yellow of the background.

Summary

DARKEN THE COLORS ON THE PICTURE.
You always have to start from luminous tones or ones brighter than those used in the contrasts.

THE BRUSH FOR MIXING COLOR.
Color is added directly. Dragging one color over another fresh color favors the mix.

CONTROL THE PAINT BRUSHLOAD.
Do not overload the brush so that the paint does not clog up or the colors contaminate each other.

COLORS FROM THE SAME RANGE.
When mixing directly on the painting, it is important to take advantage of colors from the same range.

Exercises

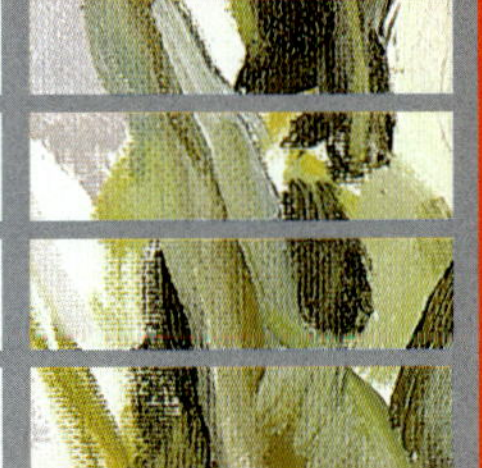

FLOWERS PAINTED DIRECTLY ON
THE PICTURE

Direct painting can tackle subjects which are very rewarding for the plastic results they give. However, as we have seen throughout this chapter, certain rules must be followed to ensure that the colors do not make each other impure or form too thick impastos. In the step by step exercise we will now do, the majority of the mixing is done directly on the picture.

Necessary material

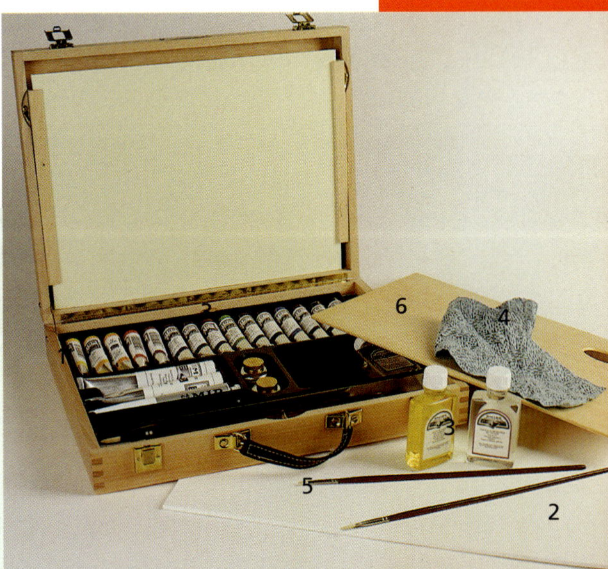

Box of oil colors (1), card (2), linseed oil and turpentine oil (3), a cloth (4), brushes (5), and a palette (6).

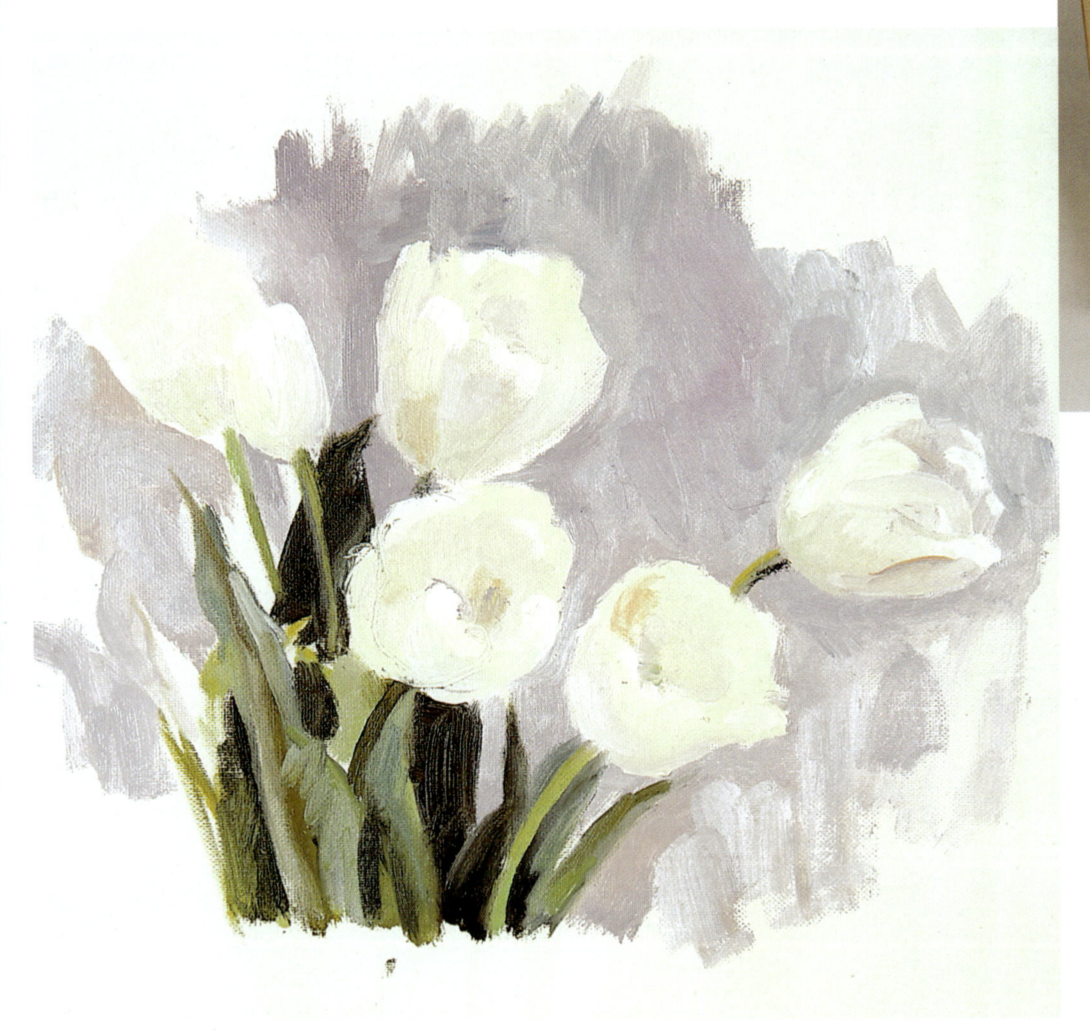

Exercises

1·Without needing to do a sketch beforehand, you can start work on the unique zone that will outline the whites of the flowers. Paint in a violet tone to define the background, against which the flowers will be perfectly cut out. Inside the flowers paint in an almost white tone made from Naples yellow mixed with white.

2·The background zone can be considered almost finished, although later on we will add a few more strokes. From now on the work will be focused on the flower forms and painting directly on the picture to bring out the luminous interior tones. Without cleaning the brush, load some white on the brush and start painting the zones which must be halftones. As the brush is not perfectly clean, on the picture a whitish violet mixture will be created. The stroke direction is very important because it defines each one of the flower planes. In the zones of the most luminous highlights, the whites remain untouched and pure, contrasting against the off-white.

3·On top of the luminous flower tones, on the ridges of the petals, paint in different tones, directly in yellow where the light acts directly, allowing the drag of the brush to mix with the lower tones. In the zones which require more contrast, paint carefully in violet.

4·In this close up you can appreciate how the yellow stroke creates a fusion with the white below, and how this tone, although very luminous, contrasts with the adjacent violet, rendering the whites even more brilliant.

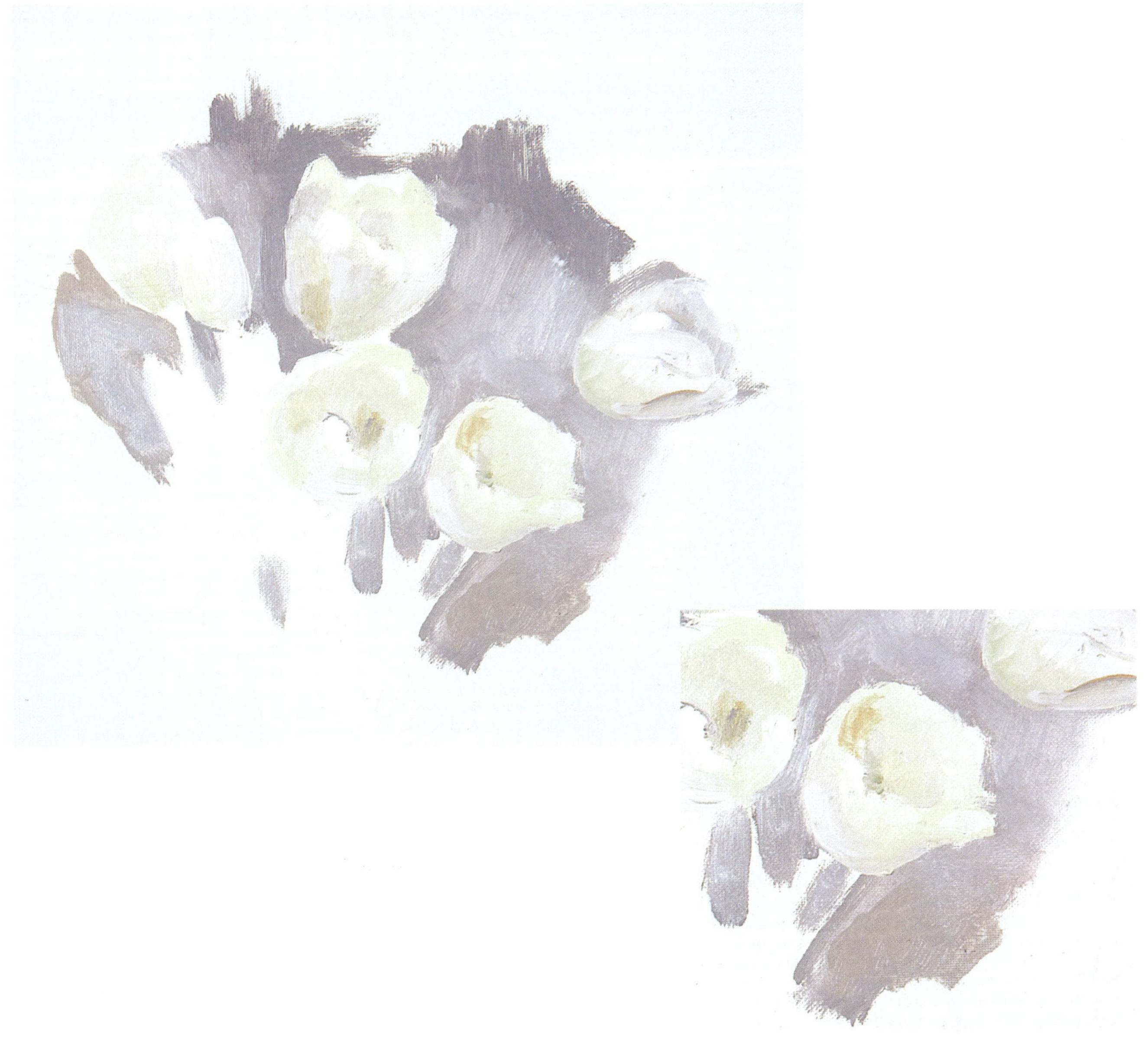

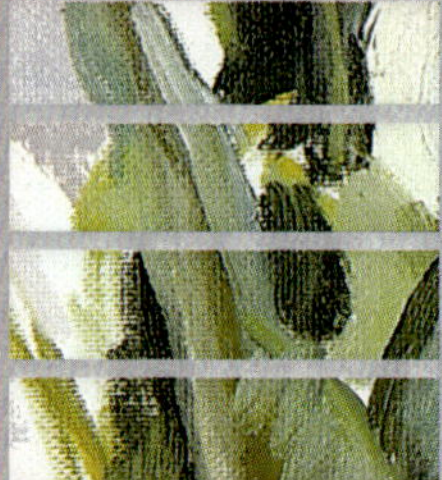

Exercises

5·Equilibrium has been achieved in the flowers, so do not insist too much on them. This is an important question when mixing directly on the painting. If you do not learn when to stop, you will probably end up spoiling the zones which were valid. Following the rules of painting directly on the picture, paint the color of the most luminous zones on the stems. On top of the green do a few dashes of yellow.

6·Now the strokes are centered on the flower stems, superimposing the contrasts and taking care not to smudge the brightest areas. The process must always follow the same rules. Firstly the lightest colors are painted and on top of these the darker ones and the stains that define the stems. The leaves are painted in halftones and finally the dark greens are put in.

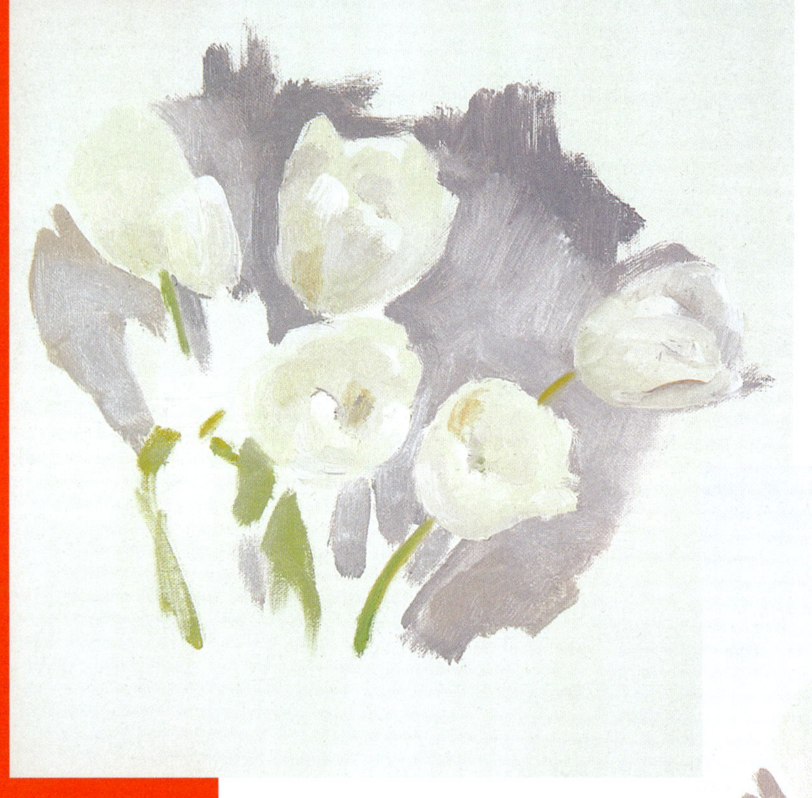

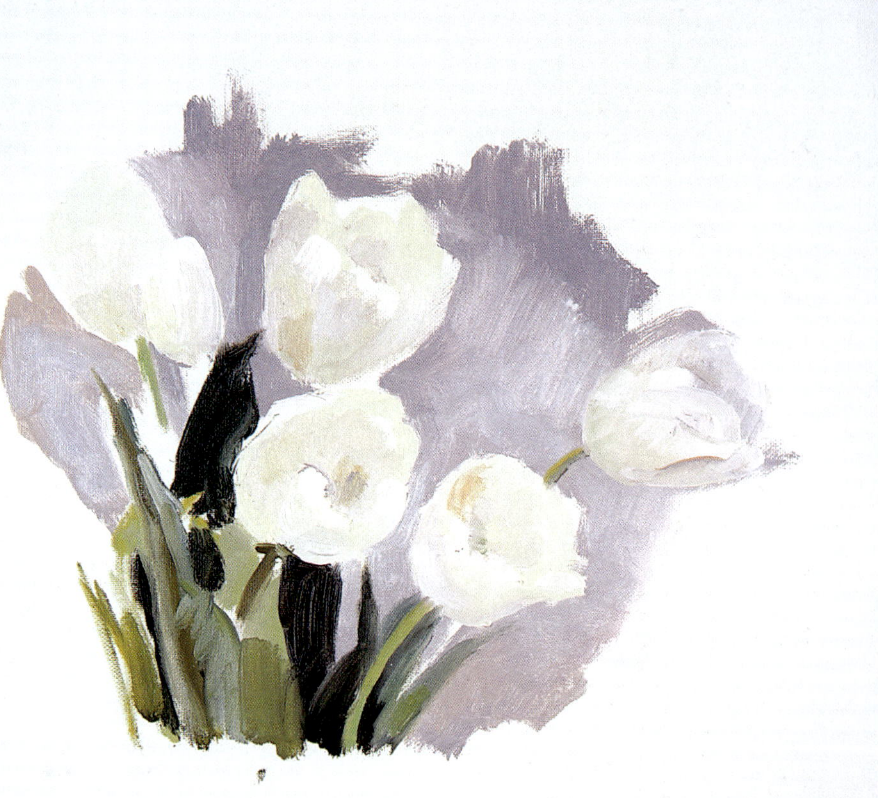

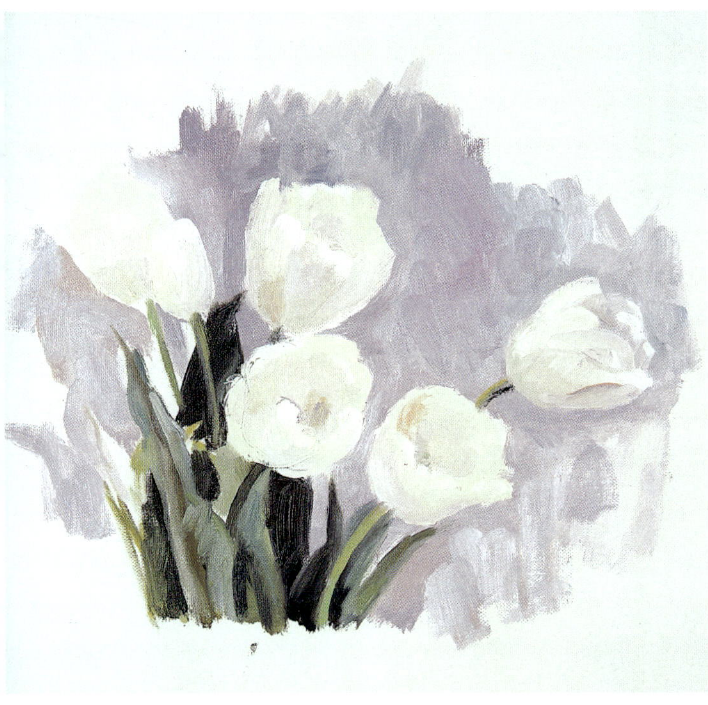

7·Dark green is used to finish the outline of the stems and leaves. In some zones you can appreciate how the direct mixing has been done on top of the lightest tones, giving them a halftone feel. Finally, to finish this rapid piece, paint the background again in the same violet color used at the beginning of this exercise. The final detail is to do some carmine strokes in the background and then to blend them.

Summary

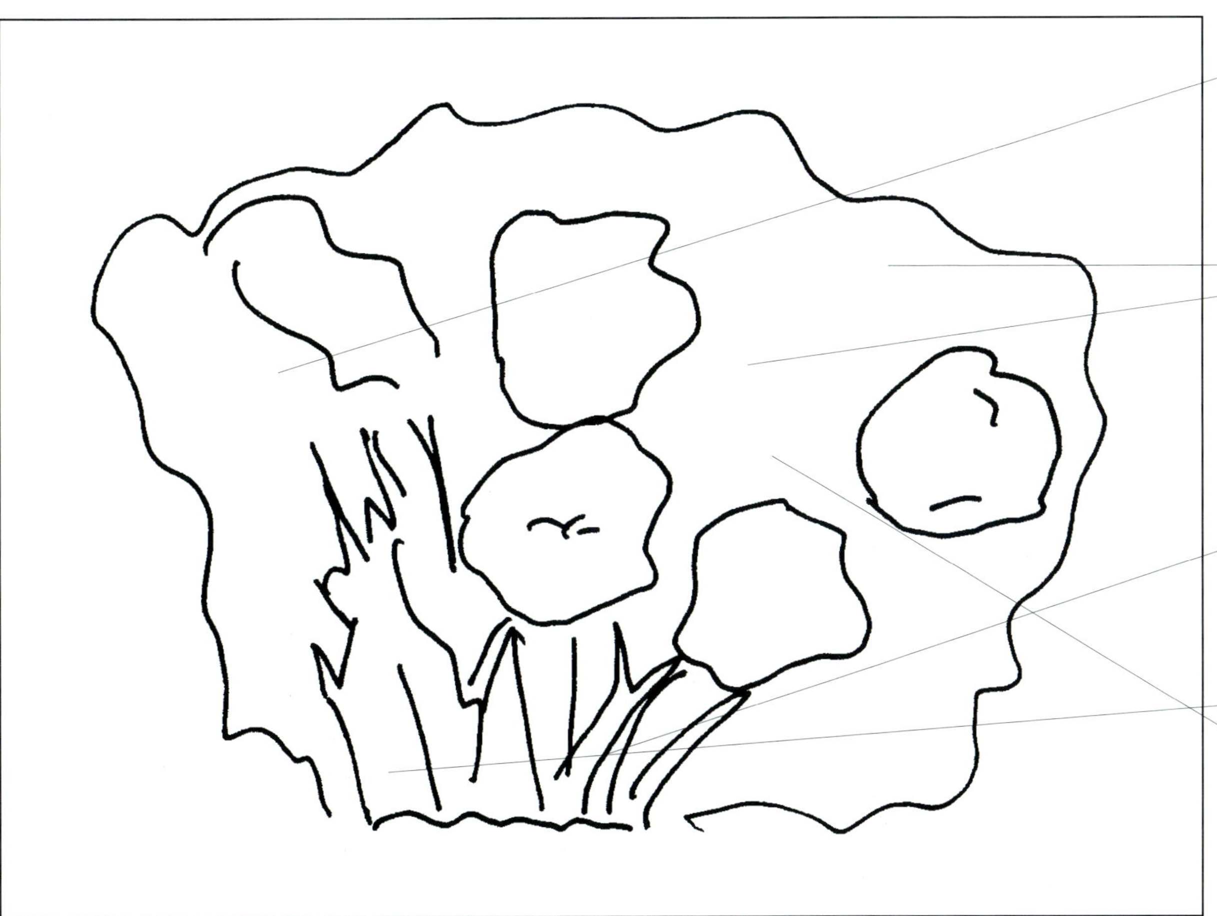

The background is painted directly, marking out the flower forms.

The initial strokes are free and spontaneous. As you advance they caress and blend the color into the background.

The first greens on the stems are whitish and on top of these stain directly with yellow.

The flower stems are painted firstly in very luminous greens and then, afterwards, denser, darker tones are added.

Carmine is painted in the background at the end. The tone is blended in by passing the brush over repeatedly.

Chapter 12

Color values

Color valuation in oil colors is one of the most classic processes in this type of painting. The oiliness of the paint permits highly soft transitions from one gradation to another.

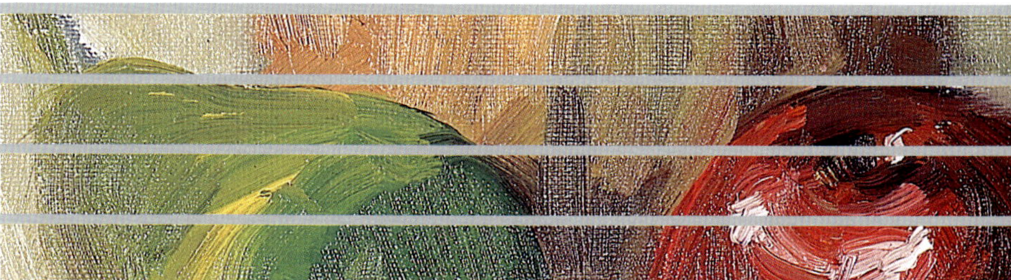

The bristles of the brush must be top quality if you do not want to leave a mark on the painting. The range of brushes shown on the right are manufactured with very soft bristles.

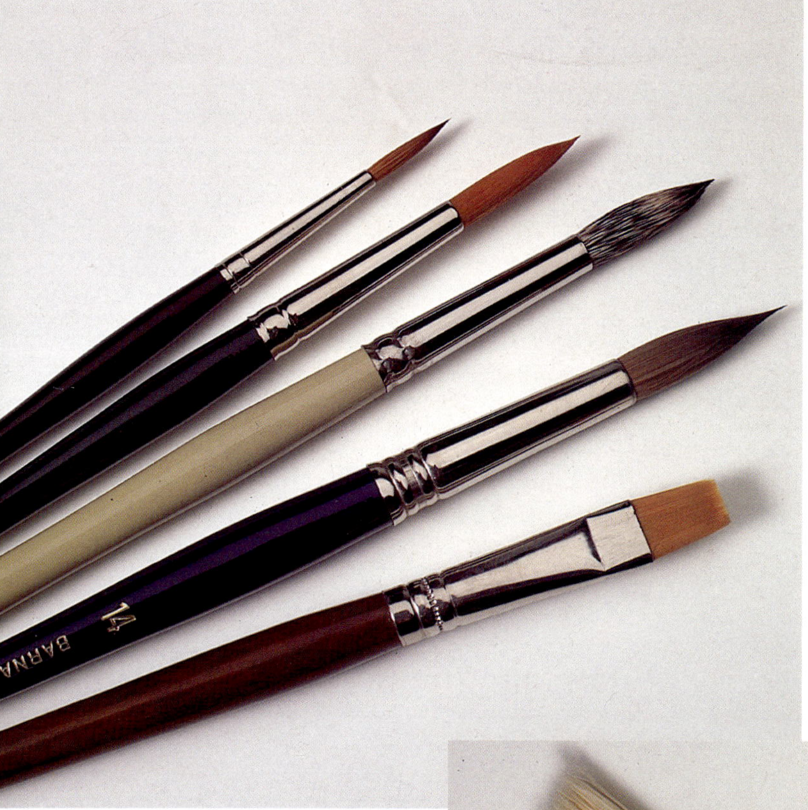

Although in previous Chapters we have studied valuation starting from the tones, in this Chapter we are going to deal more thoroughly with form modeling. It is a process that requires dedication and patience, so we will not be mechanically plowing through exercises. Instead we have chosen ones which will enable us to put into practice the explanations offered in this Chapter. Spherical forms are the most complicated to do and therefore we have chosen forms made up of flatish curves: a female anatomy and the close up of a white vase. The first impression may be that the human body will be more complicated than a simple form like the vase. In fact the opposite is true: symmetrical shapes are more difficult than organic forms. Color value work is an arduous process that requires a great deal of tact and feeling when softening the contours with the brush. It is possible that when doing these exercises, the learner loses their patience when they see how a dark tone, almost perfectly integrated with the background, becomes sullied by light tones. This is why it is important to pay attention to the stroke direction: it will be the solution to the majority of problems cropping up, or, indeed they can be anticipated before they occur.

The choice of brushes used is important because otherwise you will not be able to get a perfect fusion of the tones. Hard hog bristles will not give a good result. This fan shaped brush allows you to softly blend the edges of the tones.

A few notes on the materials

For valuation and modeling work it is important to remember the vital role played by the materials and equipment. The mark left by a hard hog bristle brush should be avoided at all costs and this can be achieved with a wide brush as shown in the image below. Very practical for doing blendings between tones and color value work, it is not just any old brush: it must have soft, top quality highly springy hairs.

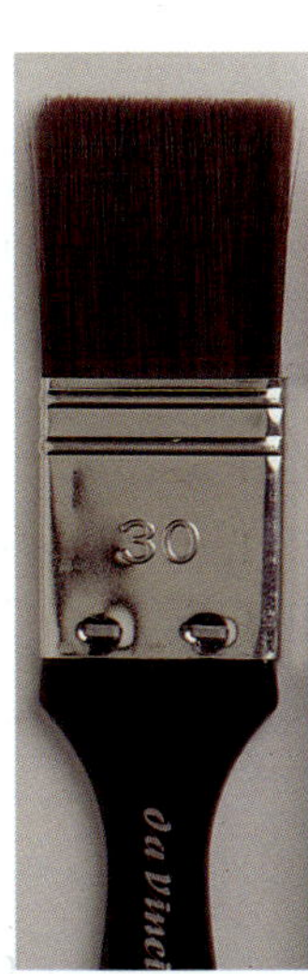

One of the best wide brushes uses synthetic hairs.

Trying out the brush

Before starting to do these complex exercises it is a good idea to try out a few brushes to see that it is possible to do blendings without leaving any brush mark whatsoever.
There are many ways of trying out the brushes. Have a go at this one: paint a spherical form with thick, slightly pasty lines. Afterwards use a soft brush, better if it has sable or synthetic hairs, to go over the paint repeatedly, adding a little of a second color. The fusion between the two colors should be perfect without there being any brushmark. If there were, you would have to use a softer haired one.

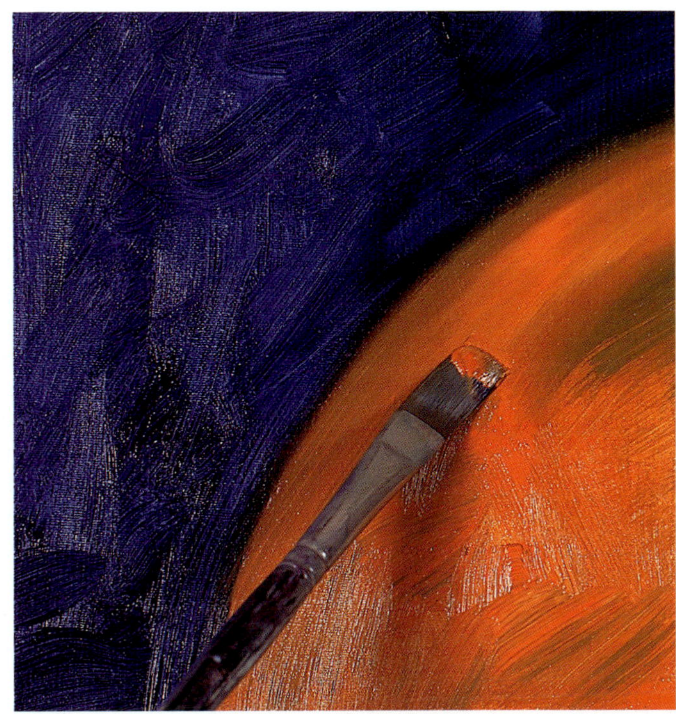

This simple exercise enables you to determine the quality of the brush bristles. If they leave a mark you will have to choose a softer one.

The tone scale: the beginning of valuation

The valuation establishes a tone for each shadow zone. It will not be a waste of time practicing obtaining tones from colors of the same chromatic range. In this image we have started with sienna darkened with umber. As the tone is gradated, the amount of umber is reduced and yellowish ochre is added. When the tone is the same as the yellowish ochre, white is added.

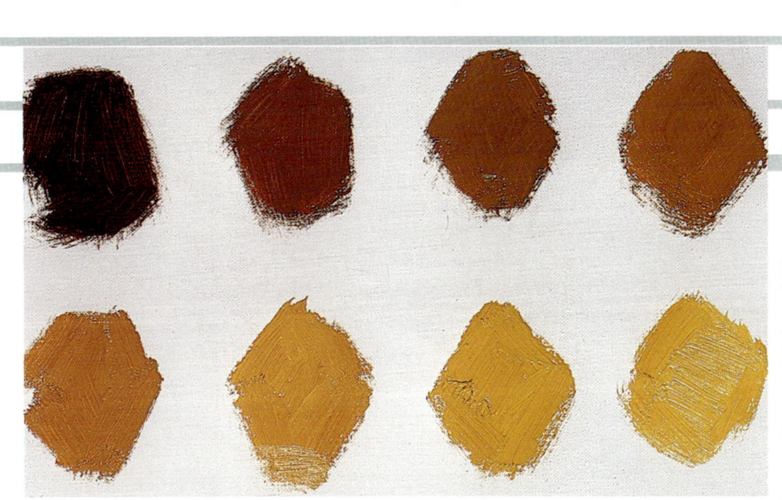

From chiaroscuro to intense color values

Chiaroscuro is the technique in which medium tones are practically eliminated and replaced with radical contrasts of light and allows us to understand the beginning of valuation. In the small details it distinguishes the light and shadow zones of the object. Although this Chapter is not principally about chiaroscuro, we must start out from this concept when locating the most important zones. The following exercise, which appears easy, will now make this clear, but do not over-relax because, as we said before, geometric forms are the most complicated shapes to do, above all when we are dealing with smooth, very luminous textures. In this first exercise we will depict a ceramic vase. During its elaboration we will explain the principal questions related to color values and modeling in oil painting.

The light zone and the shadow zone

For any valuation work the light and shadow zones must be precisely defined from the very beginning, on top of the first drawing made. The scheme can be drawn with a line that separates the light parts from the shadowy parts, or as is the case here, the first touches of dark colors can define the zones. In this exercise it is better to use the second method as it is a complex form and the brush strokes can model the vase once the principal colors are down. The background is painted completely: it will not be worked on again until the end when the curved forms can be readjusted.

The line is very important in this first stage because the mark indicates the direction of the plane that is going to be painted. For the time being, blending is not necessary and can be left until later.

Blending two tones in the same direction as the plane

When the dark parts of the object have been defined and the color values decided, you can then go ahead and paint the light parts. Be careful with this process. If you do not want to stain the brightest color you will have to paint in the middle of the vase first. These strokes are not definitive: do horizontal lines without worrying too much about the construction of the spherical plane.

Once the central zone is completed, continue to work on giving form and volume to the shadow zones painted at the beginning. To do this, the line is made in the same direction as the form you are modeling. The stroke must be soft and progressively drag part of the dark color, blending it at the same time with the light color. The fusion is realized in the same direction as the plane, using soft, long, unbroken and insistent strokes. Every stroke must go over all the zone you wish to blend so there is no possibility of unexpected stains showing up.

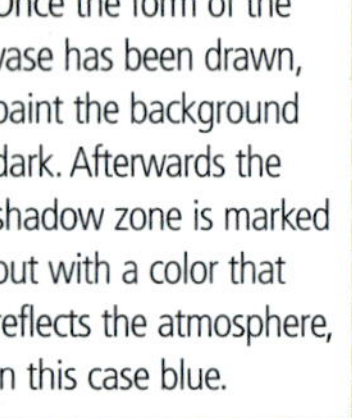

Once the form of the vase has been drawn, paint the background dark. Afterwards the shadow zone is marked out with a color that reflects the atmosphere, in this case blue.

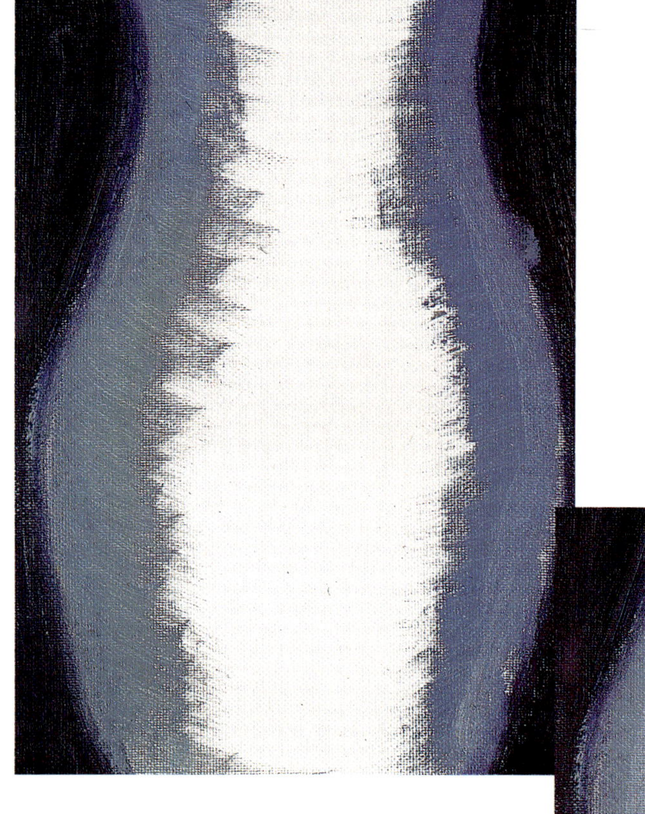

The brushstroke in the central zone is, in principle, horizontal. Afterwards blend it with the shadow zone until you get a perfect gradation.

Stroking the color until it is blended

With the aid of the wide, soft brush, the colors are softly blended on the picture. All you have to do is make repeated movements with the brush until the tone fusion is complete. However, it is an especially delicate phase of the modeling because when part of the light color is dragged it can be dirtied by the dark color. Soften this effect by going over the paint insistently with the brush. It is probable that when this part of the modeling process seems to be complete, a new application of the wide brush can change the look of the dark zone. It does not matter: continue with the soft strokes until the colors are totally blended.

Adding other tones

When the main part of the modeling has been done, new form and color enriching tones can be added. All color additions must be soft. Always bear in mind the illumination effect you are pursuing in the picture. In this exercise a red stroke is applied, in one long movement, along all the left side of the painting, although it may drag part of the lower color.

The final blending

To finish off this modeling exercise the strokes applied to the vase will have to be completely blended. Start by softening the tones on the right and at the same time add a little blue. Gently drag the brush around the edges of the form, repeating this as many times as is necessary until the colors are blended and the brush traces are invisible. Finally, paint the bright parts and the highlights without blending them.

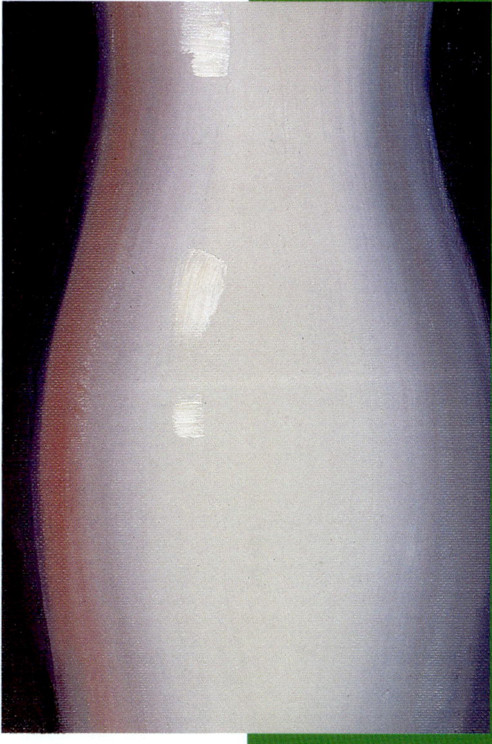

Make a long red stroke all along the left side. You have to do this in one continuous movement even though you may drag part of the lower color.

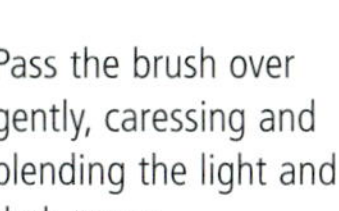

Pass the brush over gently, caressing and blending the light and dark tones.

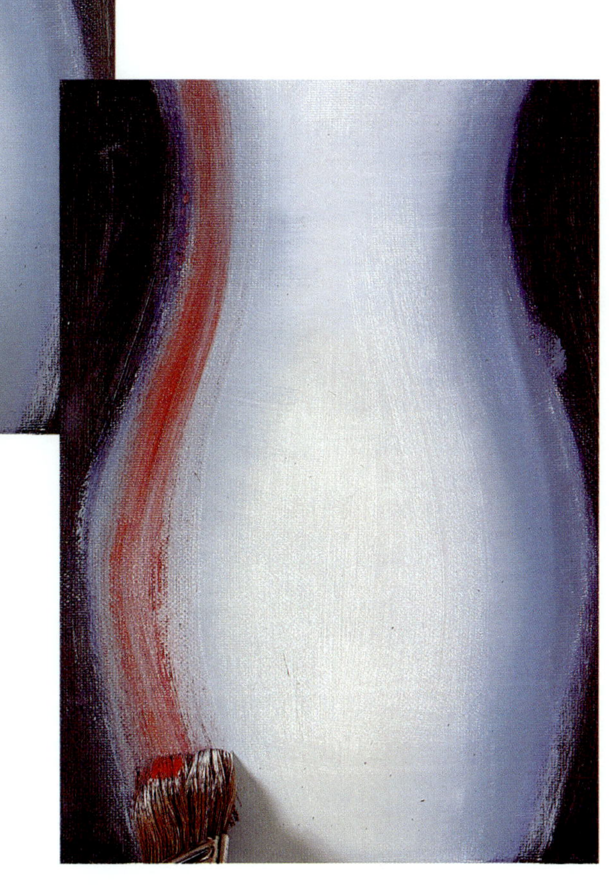

The final blending finishes off the integration of the tones added over the background. The final step is to outline the form against the dark background color.

From chiaroscuro to the modeling

In this masterpiece you can appreciate how the great painter Caravaggio used the infinite variety of the effects of light on the subjects in the modeling process. The shadows, although radical, softly gradate into the brightest zones until they become luminous and the colors contrast intensely. In the same way, the flesh parts include a series of light and dark tones so skillfully blended in that it is impossible to distinguish the trace of the brush.

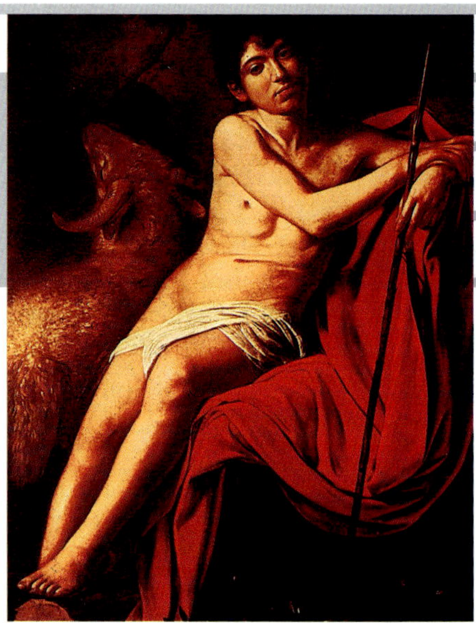

Caravaggio (1571-1610). Saint John the Baptist, oil on canvas in the Borghese Gallery, Rome.

Brightness and tones in the color values of the figure

In the last exercise we studied color value and modeling on a white ceramic object. There is no doubt that it was a challenge to achieve the required sensitivity in the line and the drag of the brush. The next exercise is to do the back of a woman using traditional value work. If you have understood what the last exercise was trying to get over, it will be much easier to do this one. The most difficult part of the modeling and the value work is to construct the figure and distribute the light. Once this has been done, tone fusion completes the modeling of the forms.

Dark priming and the drawing

The classic application of color values and modeling are normally done on top of a dark background because this enables you to play with the flesh contrasts and to work with the background color as if it were another paint. The priming can be done in several ways: the background can be painted with thinned oil color and doing an artisanal priming with gesso and pigment. Alternatively, acrylic colors can be used, as is the case here. Acrylic colors allow the painting to be done rapidly and dry in a few minutes. Once all the background has been painted in acrylic, wash the brush in water. Once the background is dry, go round the figure form in white using a quite unpasty stroke. Remember that the first layers of color must be thinned in linseed or turpentine oil. When the figure has been outlined, draw the shadow limits.

Flesh and color values

Firstly the dark parts are painted in earth colored tones on the side and bluish tones on the buttocks and the back. Next to these intense darks, paint the most luminous flesh tones using an orange cadmium, ochre, yellow, carmine, sienna, white and a little green. These colors are painted next to the dark parts. When all the principal tones have been painted completely, go over the edges between the zones with successive lines with the wide brush, modeling the forms by gently dragging.

On top of the background primed in blue, outline the figure in white.

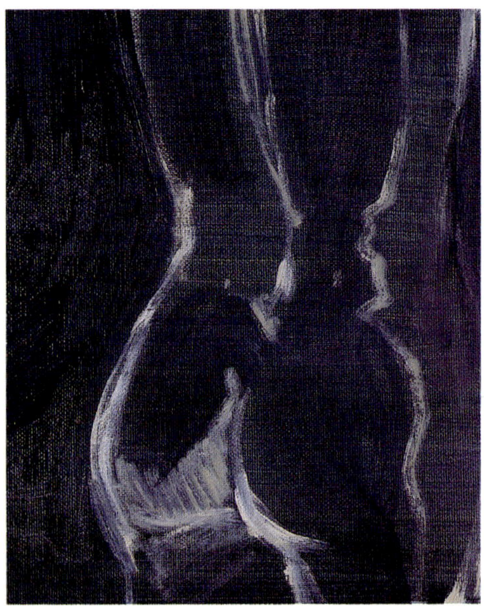

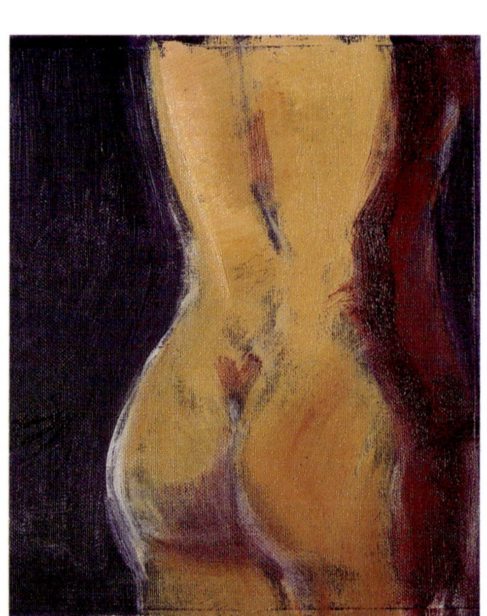

After painting all the principal tones, use soft strokes to blend the shadow zones.

Blend the dark areas into the background at the same time as you paint them. This will give you the half tones and simultaneously model the forms. The strokes must be soft and long, following the body forms. As you can see, not all the colors take on the same hue. When a soft dark is painted onto a zone which previously had luminous colors, a semi modeling effect is created.

Softening the finish

The painting of the body is finished by adding little tone dashes to enrich the forms. The most luminous colors are painted last of all. In this case, pink tones are blended with the wide brush. Later on a soft finish will be applied with the fingertip.

Once the last tones have been blended, paint the most luminous points, the highlights: they are what culminate the sensation of volume. In this last step the tones are somewhat more direct than the blendings realized before. They are left as free, pasty zones.

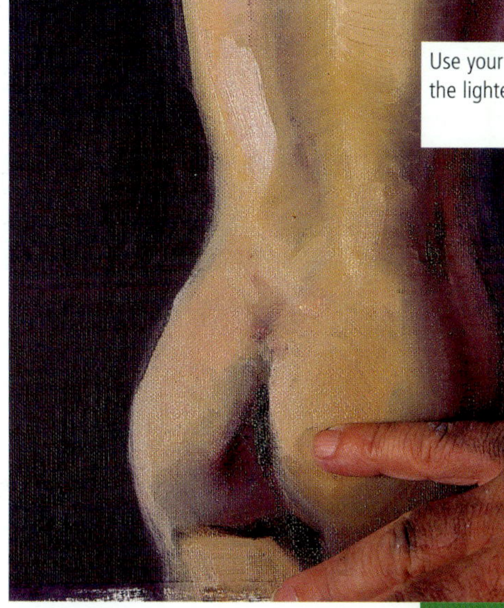

Use your finger to blend the lightest tones.

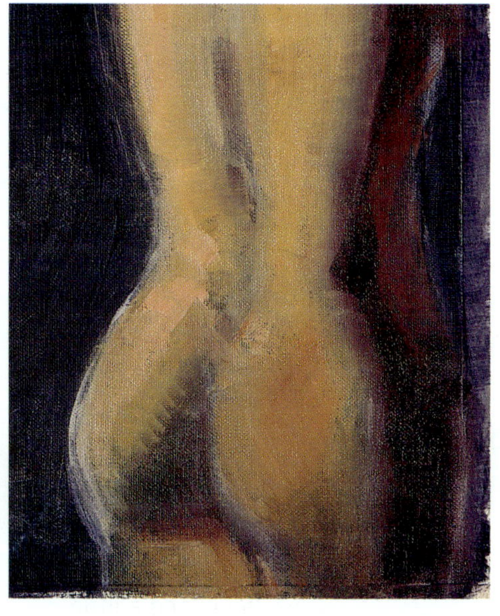

The colors are added in small quantities and are blended in by successive, long brush strokes.

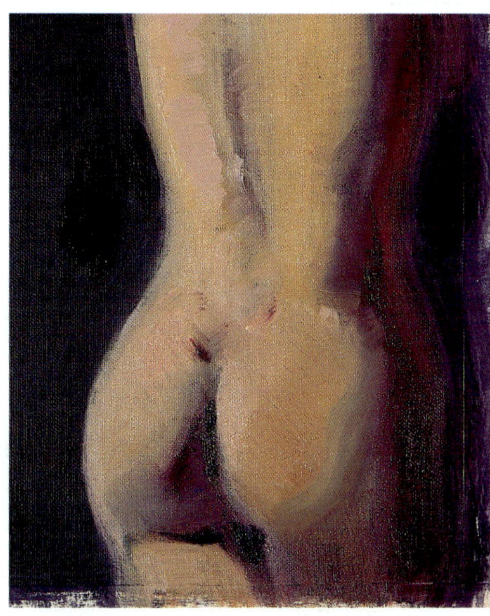

The most luminous tones are applied last of all. Blend them in with the wide brush.

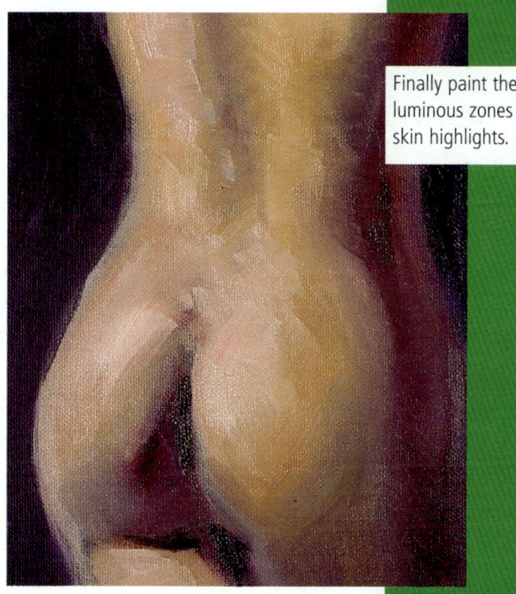

Finally paint the most luminous zones in the skin highlights.

Summary

MODELING THE WHITES
The modeling of the white objects reflects the color of the atmosphere in the shadows.

SOFTENING THE CONTRASTS
The wide brush is the best for softening the transition between the tones.

STARTING FROM A COLOR GROUND
When a dark color provides the ground, the form modeling has a good base for the contrasts.

THE HIGHLIGHTS LAST
The most luminous tones are painted last. They are softly blended over the background.

Exercises

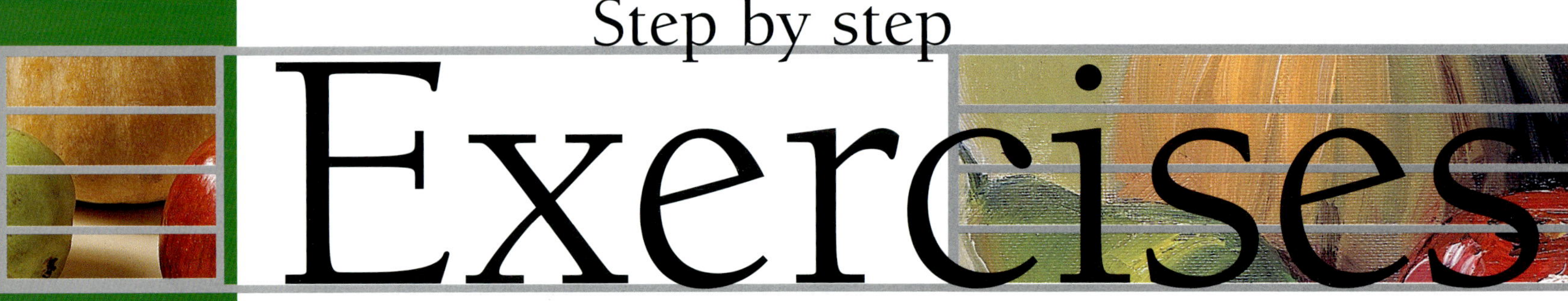

COLOR VALUES ON TWO PIECES OF FRUIT

As we have studied throughout this chapter, color values give a remarkably realistic sensation of volume when the dark and light tones are correctly situated. The valuation process is culminated in the modeling and the dark tones are obtained by more contrasted variations of the original colors. It is important to bear in mind the line direction once the principal colors have been situated because the line models the object and gives it form. In this exercise we will do a still life to practice modeling and color values. The colors are varied and the forms present different types of shadows.

Necessary material

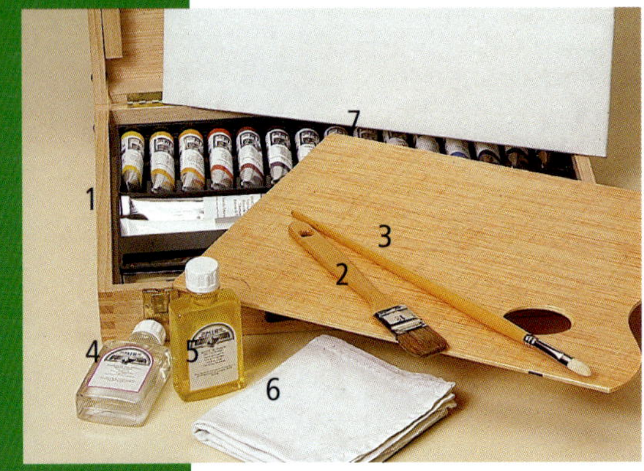

Oil colors (1), brushes (2), a palette (3), linseed oil (4), turpentine oil (5), a cloth (6) and primed card (7).

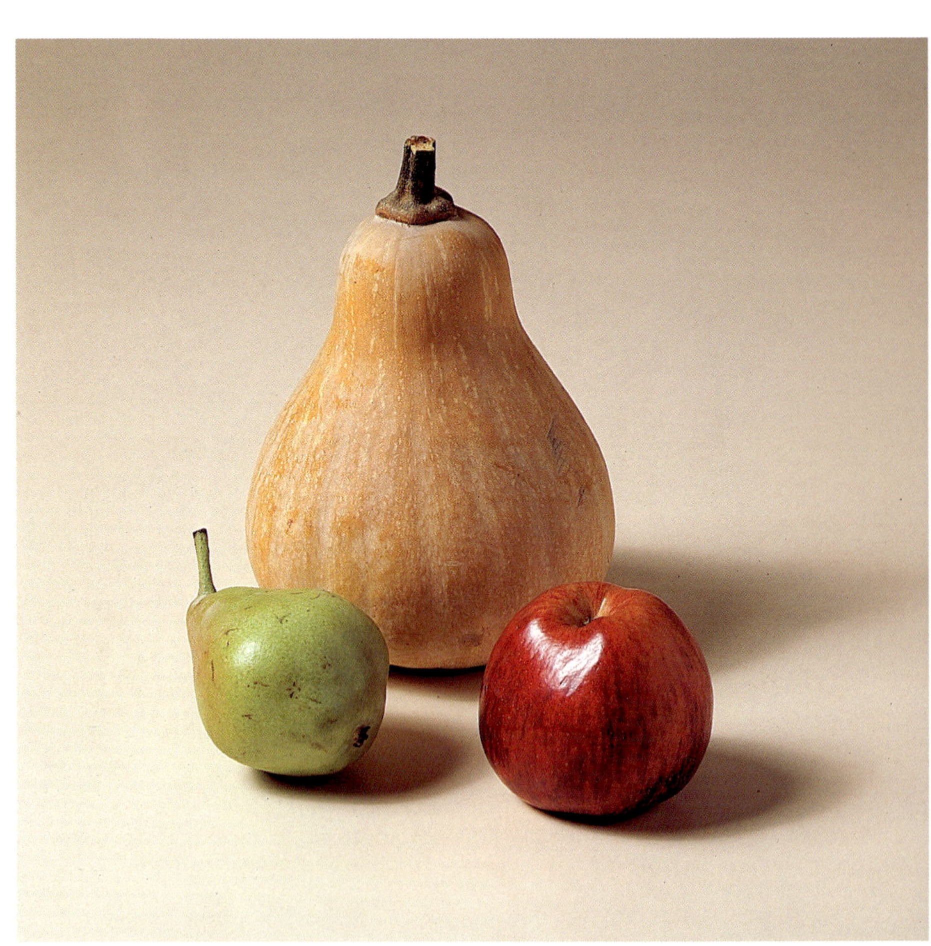

1. The initial outline is done directly in dark, thinned oil colors. In this type of work in which the color values are obtained by stretching the color out with soft strokes, we must avoid thick colors. The finer the layer is, the more the color can be stretched out with the brush. Moreover, when tones are being superimposed, it is much easier if the first layer is well diluted.

2. Start by painting the background in a broken color obtained by mixing luminous green, orange, blue and white. This color is used to surround the fruit and the pumpkin. The most luminous zone of the latter is painted in orange cadmium mixed with yellow. The shadow part is painted in luminous green. When this zone is painted part of the orange on the pumpkin is dragged.

3. Paint the darkest shadow part of the pumpkin in burnt sienna. By now you have established three tones on the same object. The pear is painted in two tones of green, the modeling on the shadow being painted with brushstrokes in the same direction as the form.
The apple is painted red around the highlight zone. Dark carmine is used for the half tone of the shadows and burnt sienna for the darkest shadows. The table base is painted in an off-color similar to the background, but a little more luminous.

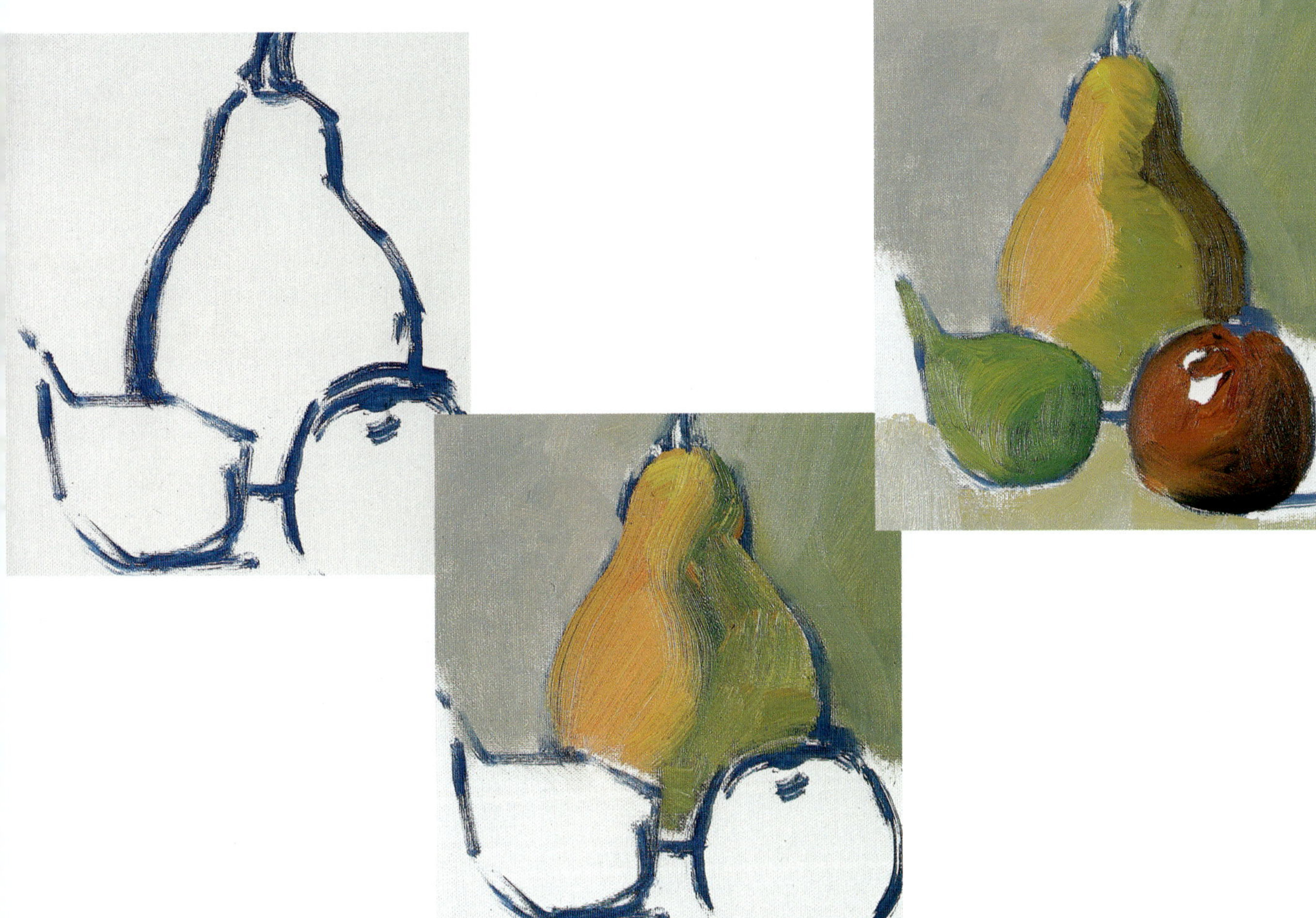

4. Blend the pumpkin colors. Once the tones have dried, add the contrasts that give form to the texture. These tones are burnt umber for the shadow zone and green for the light part. Soften the tones in the background and the foreground, where you add a little Naples yellow. Begin to depict the shape of the pear using very luminous strokes.

The wide brush is used very softly, dragging part of one color over the other. When the operation is repeated, the colors delicately blend together.

5. Paint the darkest tones on the apple using a little burnt umber mixed with carmine. The stroke progressively becomes softer, making circular strokes that outline the surface form. The central part of the apple is now much more luminous. Paint in bright yellow a highly lit area on the pear. Start to soften the tones, being careful not to dirty the finished zones.

The modeling shadows are done in tones which incorporate the luminous colors of the object being modeled and also the dark colors from the same color range. As far as is possible avoid using black.

6. In this close up you can see how the apple is realized. After modeling the apple forms, the final contests are applied to darken the right side. This time the stroke is much softer and it situates the luminous tones on the left. To finish off the apple, paint a highlight on the most luminous part using a direct white accent.

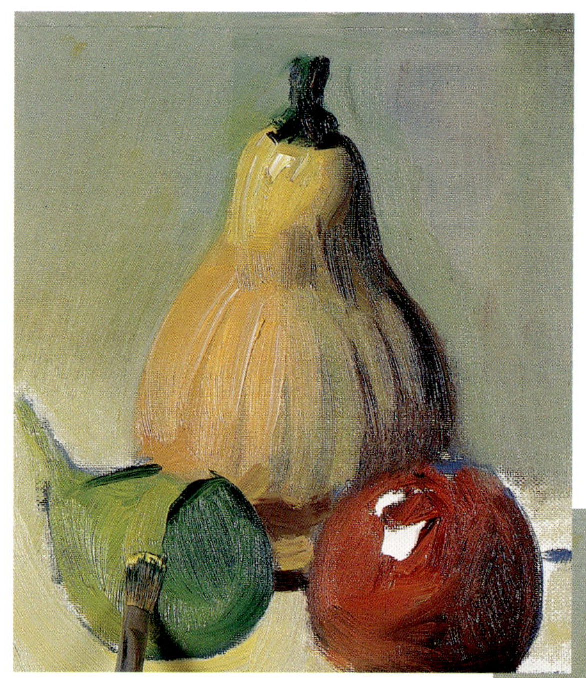

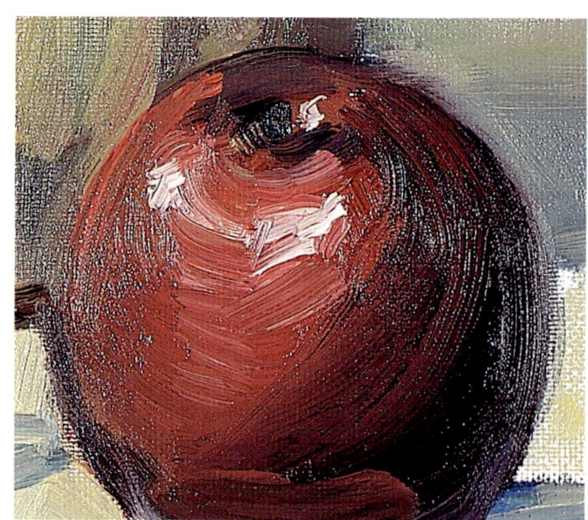

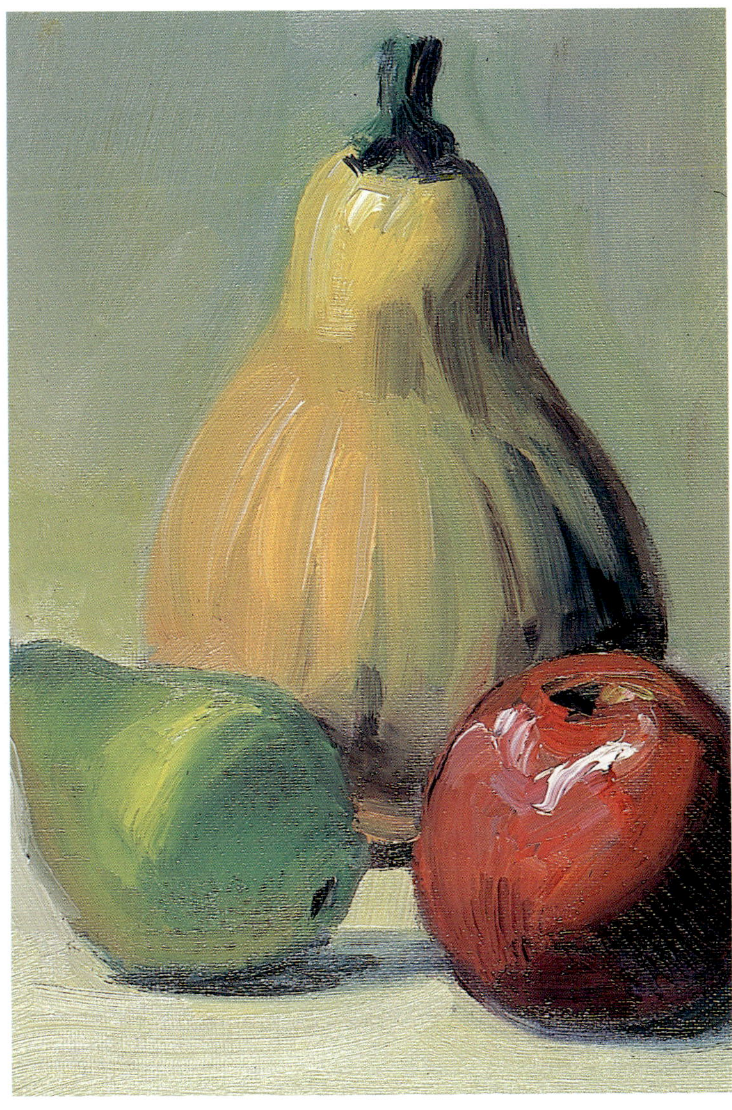

7. All that remains to be done is outline the forms. Use the wide brush to blend away the hard edges on the fruit. Lightly intensify the fruit shadows with a little blue which contrasts with the previous color mass. The final touch is to apply some new highlights that give relief to the apple. This will have concluded this piece centered on color values and modeling.

Summary

The shadow colors on the pumpkin incorporate tones from the light zones.

The initial outline is made in thinned oil color, with a straight, clean stroke.

The impact of the light on the apple is realized with a direct accent.

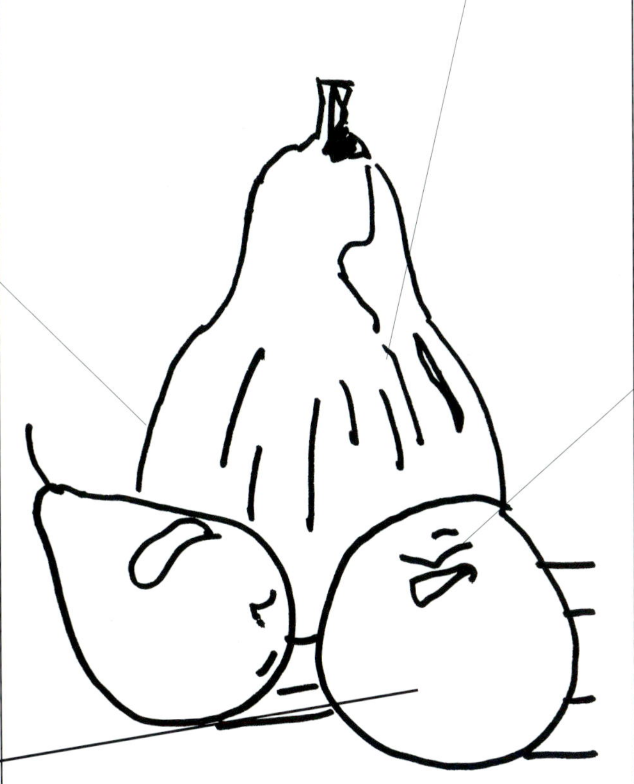

The form of the apple is softly modeled with successive brushstrokes.

Chapter 13

Oil colors: light on the objects

Light changes according to the atmospheric conditions. The variations in luminosity throughout the day alter the chromatic characteristics of the picture.

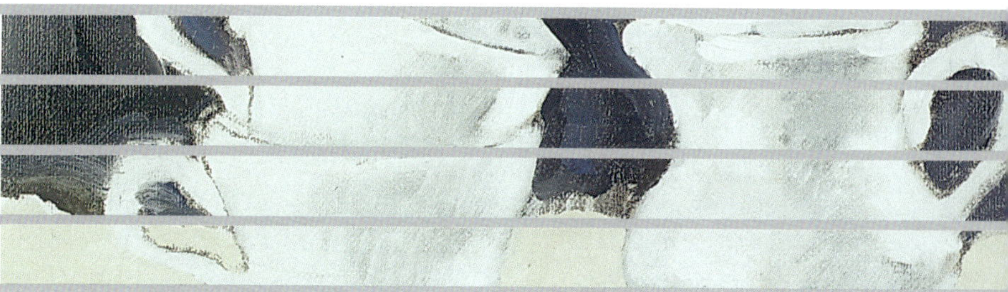

Artificial light also modifies the colors depending on the type and color of the light source. Artificial light can be divided into warm and cool sources; the degree of warmness affects the colors painted.

A lateral light source throws sloping shadows that make the color on the objects less saturated and they appear less intense.

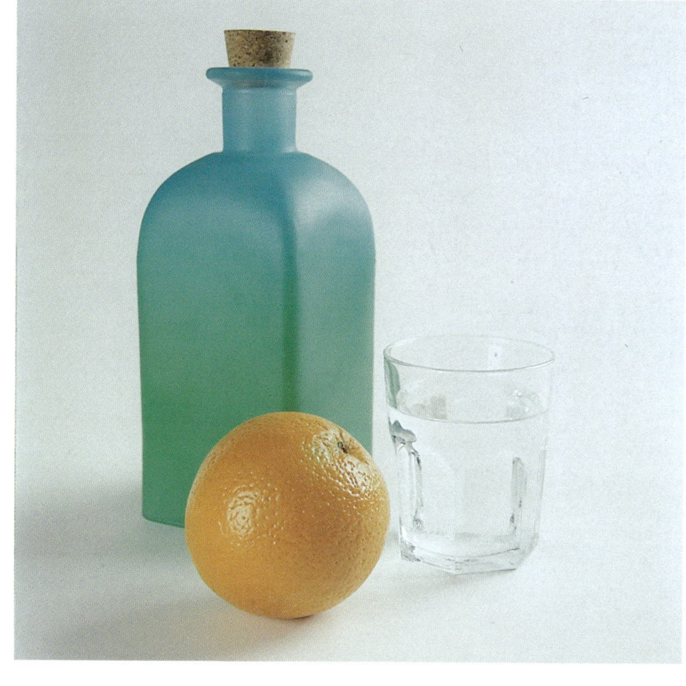

How the colors change with the light

The perception we have of an object depends on its form, which may be undulated, spherical, but, it goes without saying, never entirely one dimensional. This influences the way the light intensity is distributed and creates tone values, luminosity and saturation of the color, contrasts between lights and darks and the consequent plastic effects. Another factor which can change the object form and color is the point of view of the observer.

The position of the object and the light direction

The perception of the color depends on the position of the object and the direction of the light. Moving the light source -whether it be from the front, lateral, from below, direct or indirect, near or far off- varies the intensity of the light beams and consequently provokes color saturation. Sometimes a change on the surface of an object with respect to the light source modifies the response of the picture, both the illumination and the surface color.

The distance between the object and the light source

The source, be it a lamp or daylight through the window, and the distance between the object and the observer influence directly on the color perception. The object progressively loses tonality, turning grayer, as the distance from the source grows. The objects around us, like the trees, houses or hills, seen in daylight are perceived in function to their proximity. The greenness of the trees seen close up tends to be warm, while this melts into cooler tones, with a blue tint, as the distance increases. The difficulty in having a constant perception of the colors when the objects are beyond a certain distance exists due to the effect of the air, regardless of the humidity. However, the latter does make an impact but it is not the only cause. Visibility increases in dry air.

The atmosphere affects the colors

The colors of the surroundings influence the color of the objects being painted because they will reflect the chromatic tones and luminosity around them. Color does not exist in a vacuum: it is interrelated with other colors, each tone throwing off its chromatic response into the surrounding space. Some colors and objects have diverse, changing characteristics. The sky constantly shifts through blue, gray, red, yellow and orange, constituting one of the best examples of this tendency to mutate.

Three essential aspects of color and its variations depending on sunlight and artificial light

The three essential aspects of color are its tonality, clarity (or luminosity) and the saturation. The tonality is the color itself, i.e. what makes a yellow different from an orange or a green. Therefore a color is defined by the uniform surface and the influences that act on it, the light source itself and the low-key reflections of other objects, always depending on the time of day and on whether the light source is artificial or natural. Clarity is the degree to which it

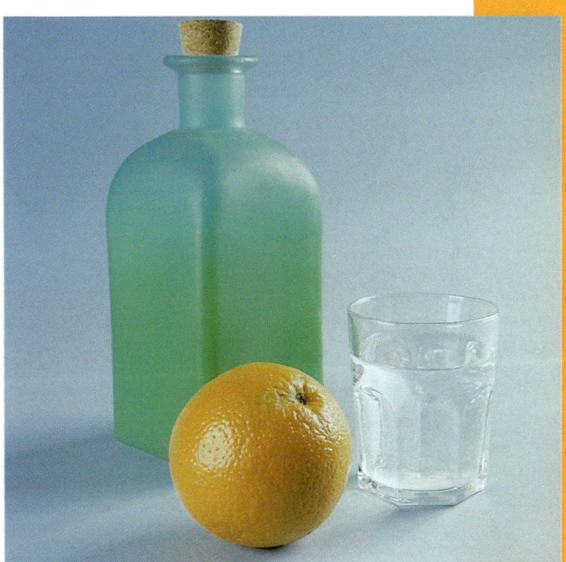

The distance between the object and the light source makes the colors more or less intense.

reflects or radiates light (darkness or brightness) and defines the color value. The saturation is the sensation given by a color according to its shininess and intensity. It is the degree of chroma or purity.

Brightness and color saturation

Striking highlights

The chromatic key of a painting refers to the brightness and the saturation of the colors. Paintings with a low key are characterized for using not saturated colors but nuanced ones. Low key paintings are duller but can have the quality of being more delicate and subtle. High key paintings are renowned for their use of brilliant saturated, primary or secondary colors

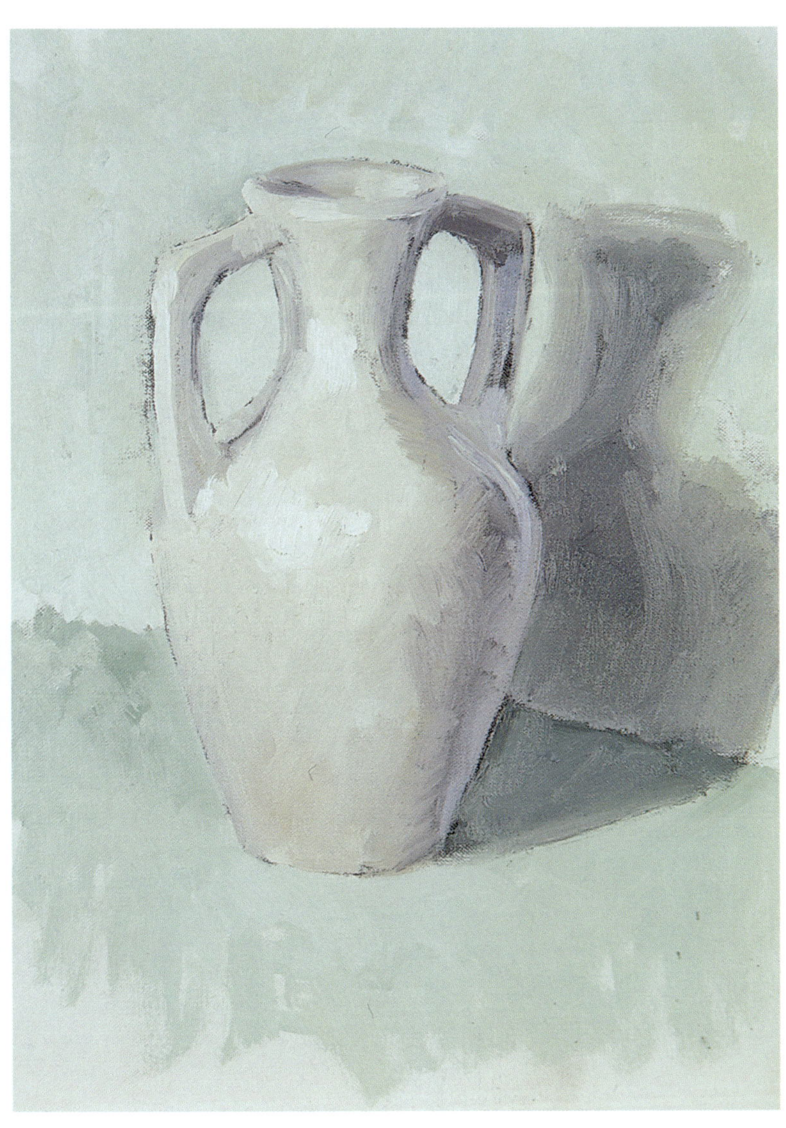

Low key: these paintings use nuances of gray to obtain subtle, delicate effects.

which are applied as pure tones without mixing and produce a brilliant, luminous and fresh appearance. These effects can be provoked by the juxtaposition of complementary colors. Since the middle of the nineteenth century artists began to assimilate the theory of complementary colors and to capture these contrasts conscientiously in their paintings. You only have to see the work of Van Gogh. These effects are especially suitable for oil painting because of its crispness, great depth of color and subtle tonal transitions.

When high key colors are used, the most striking highlights will be obtained. Technically this is a very sure way of painting as all the paint in one zone is applied in a unique session, or at least while the surface to be painted is wet. This means there is no problem with the amounts of oil or resin, nor with the drying processes of the different layers (in reality there is only one). This method was a great success among the impressionists, who so as to be able to paint wet onto wet as long as possible used slow drying oil colors. Today the technical facilities have improved and it is possible to paint with any of the standard oil paints. In many ways high key painting is the most difficult method to use because every stroke must be correct, not only in what it expresses but also with respect to color and tone, and the relationship with surrounding hues. It is feasible to lightly scratch or rub a painting while it is still fresh to correct the marks. Many painters do so until they manage to give it a spontaneous and flowing feel. It is an acceptable approach provided that it is done well. The ability to observe an image and to transfer it directly on to the canvas is the fruit of long practice and, almost always, of using resuming pictorial methods. Practice helps the artist to create a personal language in the use of paint, becoming fluent in which also implies having sufficient intuition to be able to calculate and prepare the adequate hues and tones for each zone, and to apply them with the right brush and method. Paintings realized without a preliminary sketch possess an intimacy and a freshness to which the observer responds spontaneously.

Blended brightness

The soft, buttery consistency of oil colors and their slow drying time allow the artist to go over a zone repeatedly so that the colors blend imperceptibly. Depending on the subject, and on the style, blendings can be obtained by stroking a color along the edge with the next one until fusion occurs. The down side of this technique is that the

Striking highlights or highkey. The most saturated colors give the most intense, vivid tones.

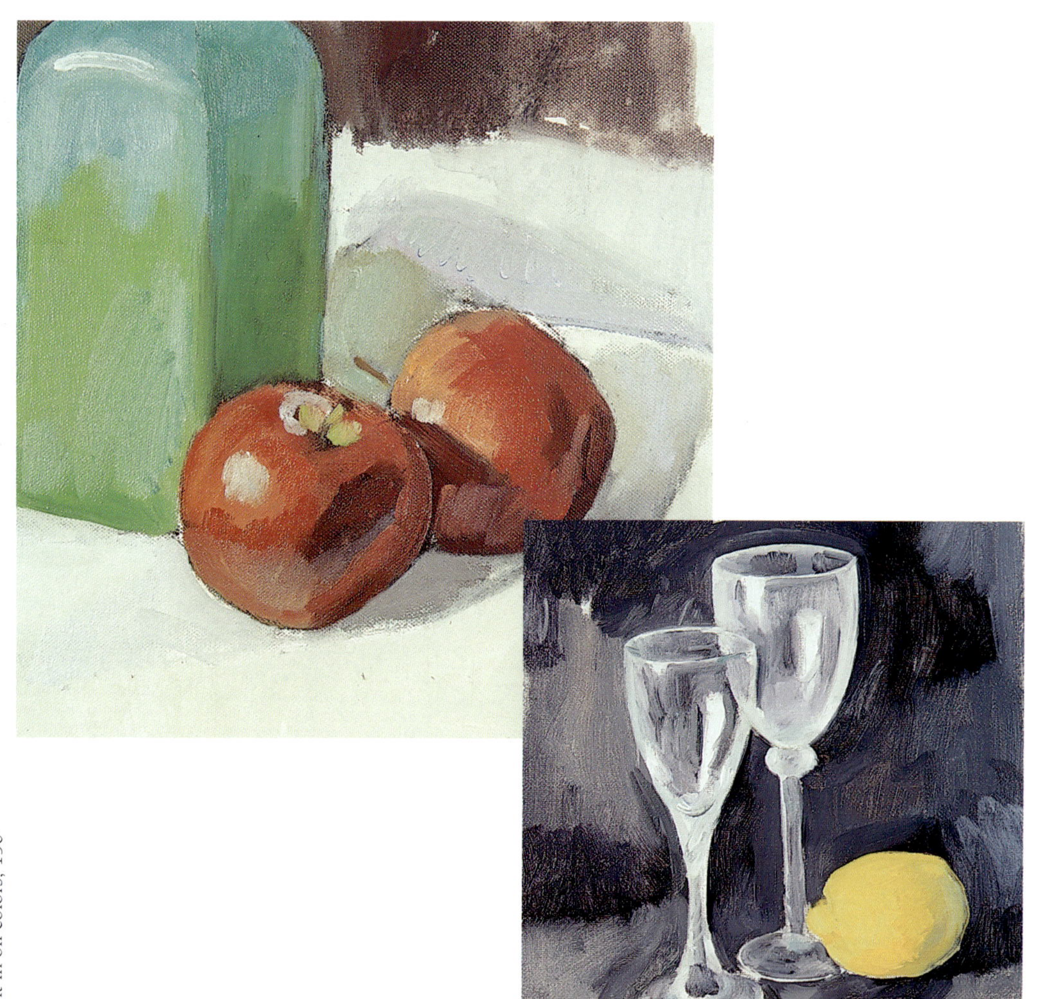

When colors are saturated we can appreciate the bright blending and the striking highlight. On top of this dark background we can see a luminous lemon. It is important to make the contrast between the background (bright and blended) and the foreground (striking highlight).

brush marks are visible. Another option is to mix the strokes methodically with a soft-haired brush, or fan brush, to create a subtle union and the imperceptibility of the brush marks.

Although oil colors are ideal for dense, thick layered marks, they are also capable of giving subtle textures and softly blended strokes, revealing a gradual transition from light to shadow, or from one color to another.

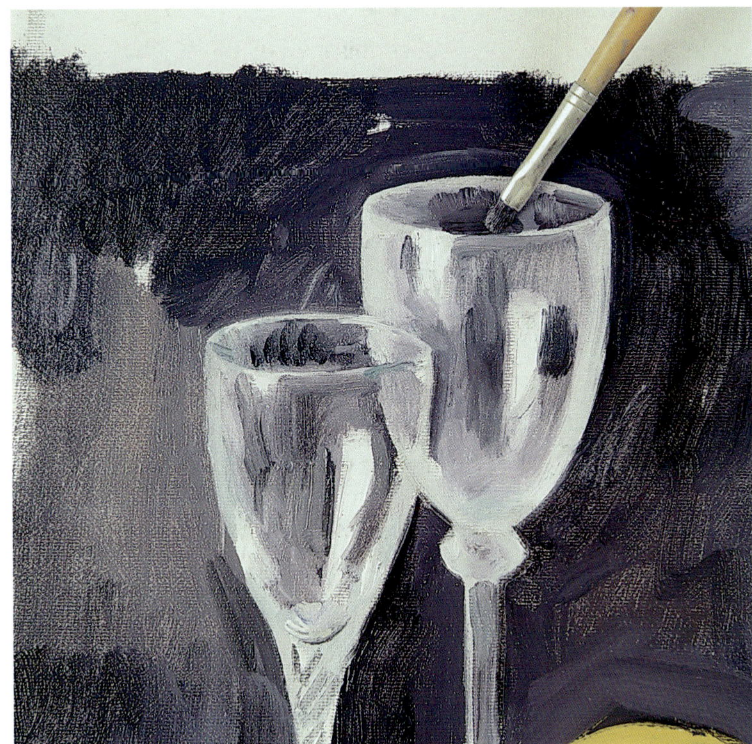

Example of a highlight blended in the background gradation. The stroke on the white of the crystal between the two cups gives a striking bright area.

Brightness in a zone of penumbra

Diego Velazquez (Sevilla, 1599) perfected the art of painting. In his early years Velázquez managed to master with extraordinary skill his representation of real life scenes using successive layers of glazes and economical but informative brush strokes. He was prepared to exploit creative tricks, novel techniques, thin, transparent darks, shadows, and strong light sources focused so as to accentuate volumes. He bestowed an unprecedented dignity on common everyday objects placing them in the foreground of the light.

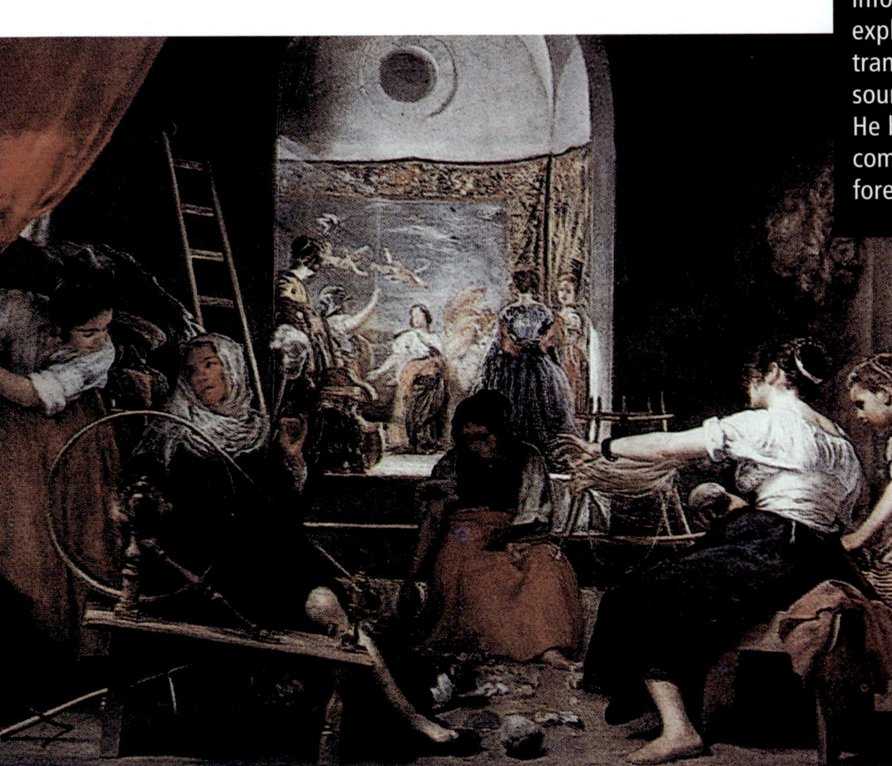

Master painting.
Velázquez.

Accelerating the drying

The drying times of oil colors do not vary much, although a siccative, a drying agent, can be added to the paint to reduce the wait. The molecules of the liquid drier solidify to form a film, the impact of which is not only on the drying time but also on the aging process of the paint. If a lot of siccative is used, the paint will age more rapidly and will therefore be susceptible to cracking and flaking. Therefore we should use as little siccative as possible.

Cobalt siccative

- This product accelerates the drying of oil colors when used correctly in the right proportions. Overused it can provoke wrinkles and cracks. It works rapidly and with great energy. You can dilute it with white spirit. The proportions in which it can be used go from 0,5 to 5%.

Glazes

Realizing a glaze

Glazes are one of the techniques traditionally associated with oil colors. The renaissance painters used them for doing mixes, although instead of actually mixing the colors on the palette what they did was apply them separately in successive glazes of fine, transparent paint, similar to the particles of a stained glass window, each one of which modified the lower color. The result was crisp, rich and luminous tones.

Oil colors are therefore an excellent medium for applying thin layers of paint, or glazes. They can be on top of other layers already painted (zones of opaque colors) and the effect is totally different to that obtained from mixing two colors. The light goes through the transparent layer and is reflected in the opaque color underneath to produce singular depth and luminosity. This is best achieved when the paint is suitably diluted in a liquid painting medium, preferably one containing beeswax. Linseed oil should be avoided with glazes because it tends it tends

A sample of cobalt siccative.

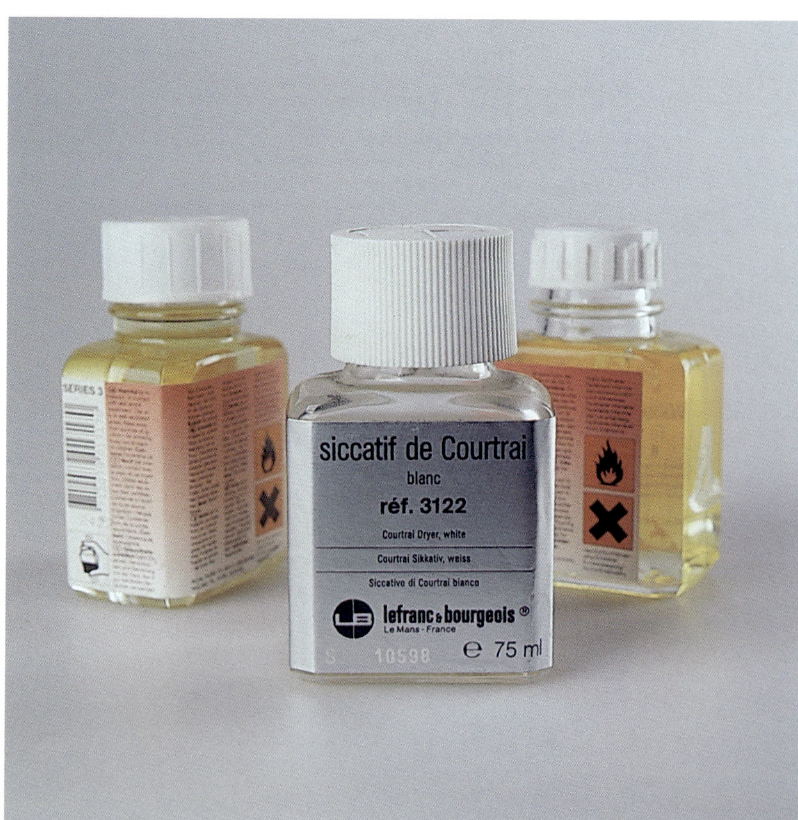

shift once it has been put down. Each successive glaze acts on the lower color but it does not completely darken it. This incomplete fusion combines with the effect of light reflection and is what confers the idiosyncratic luminosity on the glaze.

Applying glazes

The best results are obtained with transparent colors when the glaze is applied on a background touch dry. Mix the paint with a glaze medium until it acquires a buttery consistency. Apply the glaze and let it settle for a few minutes. If it turns out too intense, take a clean fan-brush (or simply a shaving brush) and do a few short strokes over the glaze, holding the brush vertically. When the paint sticks to the hairs, hit them with a cloth to keep them clean and dry.

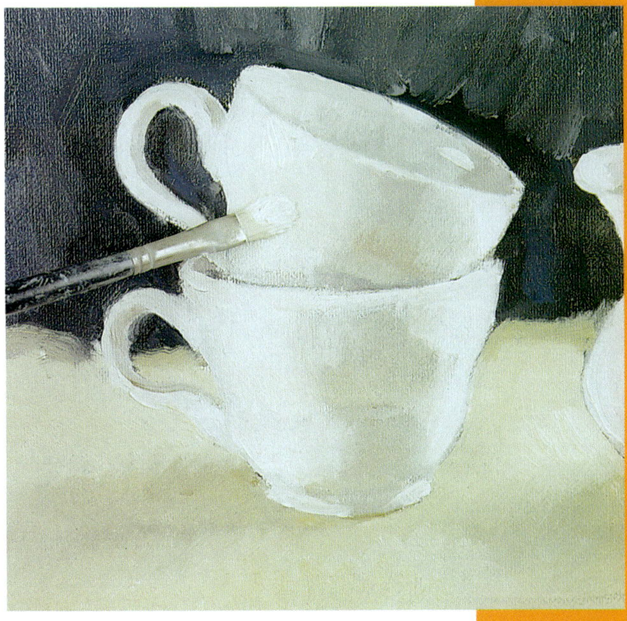

With a slow drying medium like oil colors, glazes are a laborious process because each layer has to be completely dry before the next one is applied, otherwise they will merely blend giving rise to a blurred color. In this close up, however, the glaze has permitted an intensity in the colors impossible from mixing them physically on the palette.

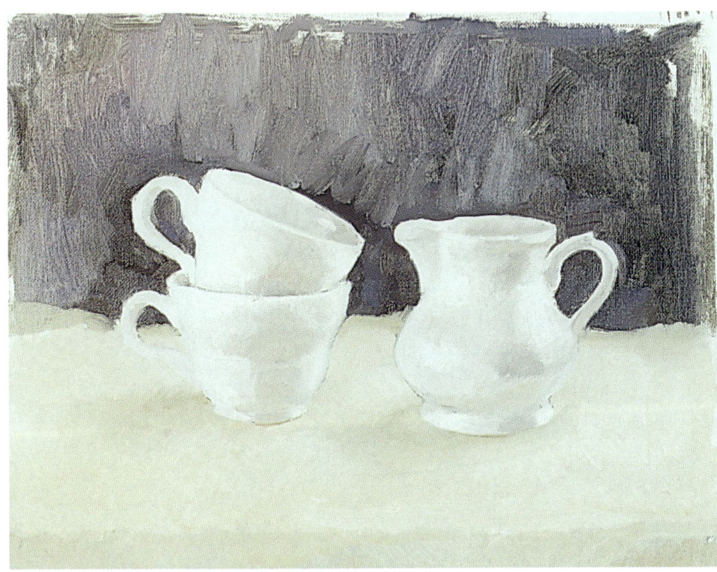

In each composition a soft and brilliant film, through which the background is visible, has been created. The glaze allows just the right amount of paint to be taken off to form this thin, shiny film.

Summary

HOW THE COLORS VARY ACCORDING TO THE DIFFERENT LIGHT CONDITIONS.
Changing the position of the light provokes the saturation of the colors.
The object progressively loses tonality, becoming grayer, as it is moved away from the light source.

SHININESS AND COLOR SATURATION.
There are two ranges with which we can work: high key, striking bright colors, and low key. To get shiny blendings we must stroke the color along its edge with the next color so that they are merged together.

THE DRYING PROCESS.
Siccatives are added to the paint to shorten the drying time. However, this technique can provoke premature aging of the paint.
Cobalt siccative must be applied in a proportion of between 0.5% and 5%.

GLAZES.
Oil colors are an excellent medium for applying thin layers of transparent paint, or glazes.
The best results are obtained with transparent colors when the glaze is applied on a background touch dry.

Exercises

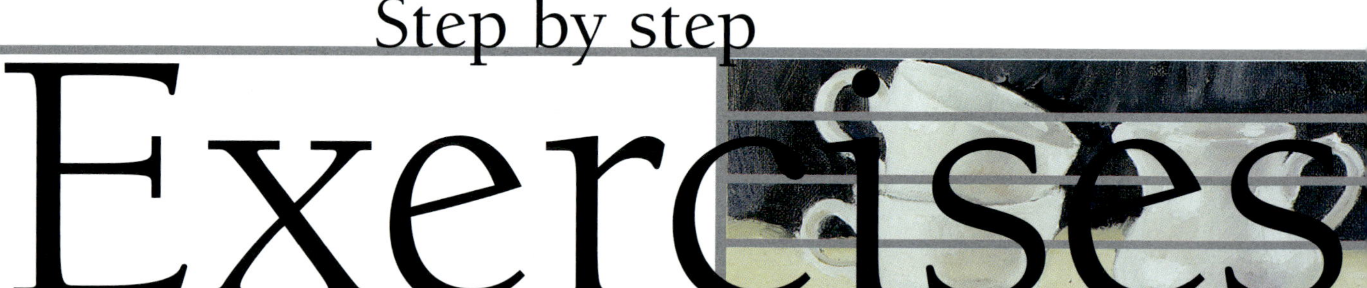

A PORCELAIN CUP.
A STUDY OF DIFFERENT SHINY AREAS.

Necessary material

We will continue working with the effects of light on the objects. In this exercise you will be able to observe different and intense shiny areas on white porcelain. They are created by the light direction and the influence of the surrounding ochre tones.

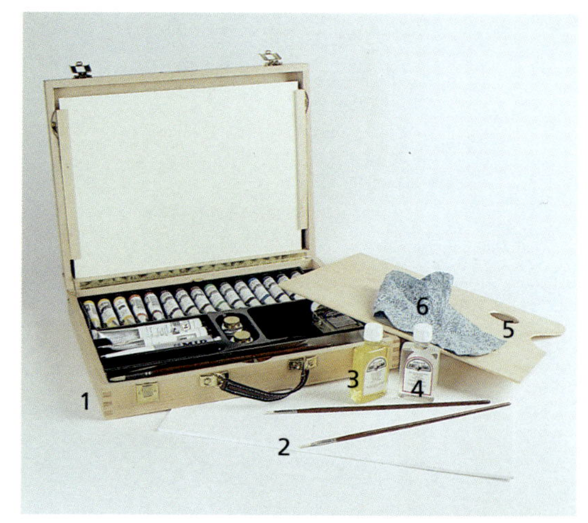

Box of oil colors (1), brushes (2), turpentine oil (3), linseed oil (4), a palette (5), and a cloth (6).

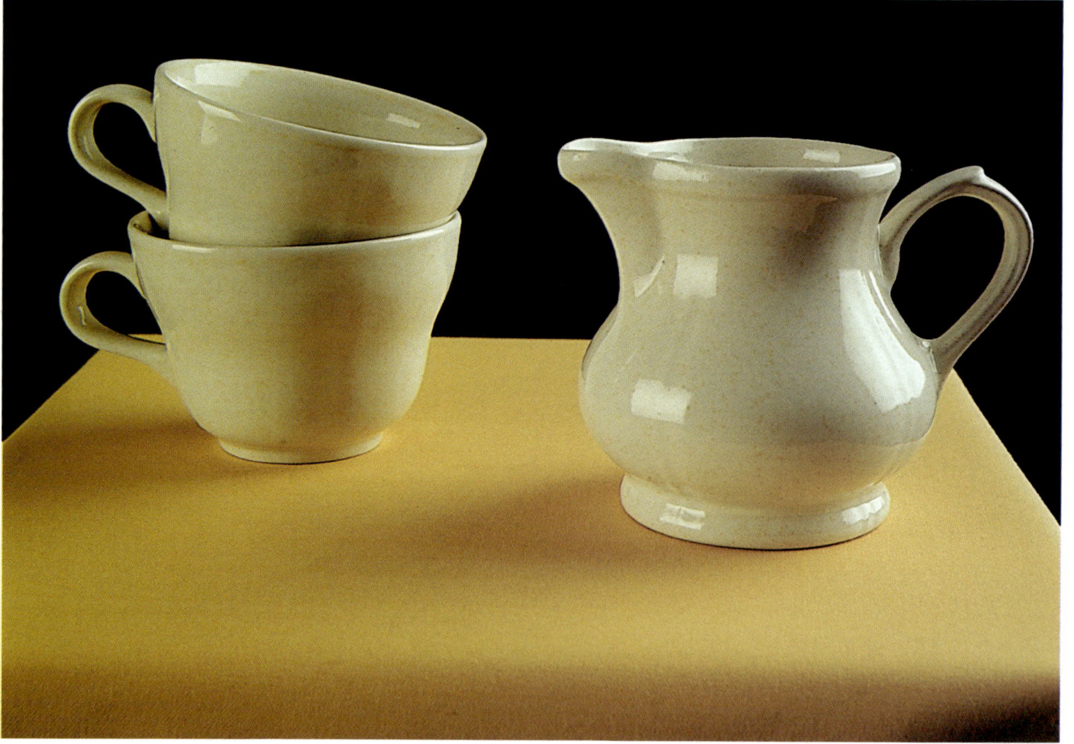

1·The first step is to draw the composition in charcoal and to define where the light and dark zones will be before the first color masses are put down. Work with the shadows to explain the volume and the light direction. This preliminary drawing enables us to identify the chiaroscuro contrast before starting to work with the different tones.

2·Using the chiaroscuro range, start to paint applying the first highlights to show the volume of the two objects and the influence on them of the intense light. It is important in this step to determine the stroke direction as it will help us to depict volume in this still life.

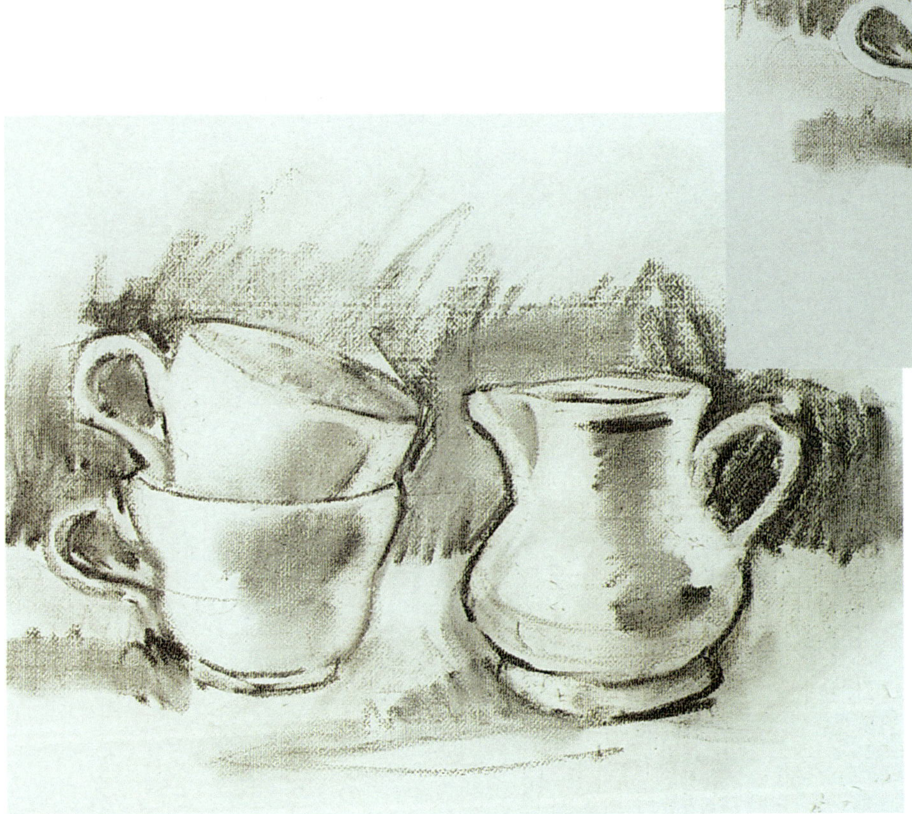

Exercises

3·Start to paint the background aiming for the maximum contrast in the black. In this step the general color masses, the direction of the light, and the construction of the volumes are already decided on. We only have to apply the first ochre tone to the base.

4·We are working on the tones in the background as well as some form details, paying special attention to the darkening of the shadows on the cups and on the porcelain jug. In this step, make the background more intense so as to provoke a greater contrast with the highlights, or shiny areas. The same thing happens with the table surface. All this makes the still life much more contrasted against the dark background and captures the subtlety of the chromatic range of the blended colors, as well as the intense, shiny areas which reflect so much light.

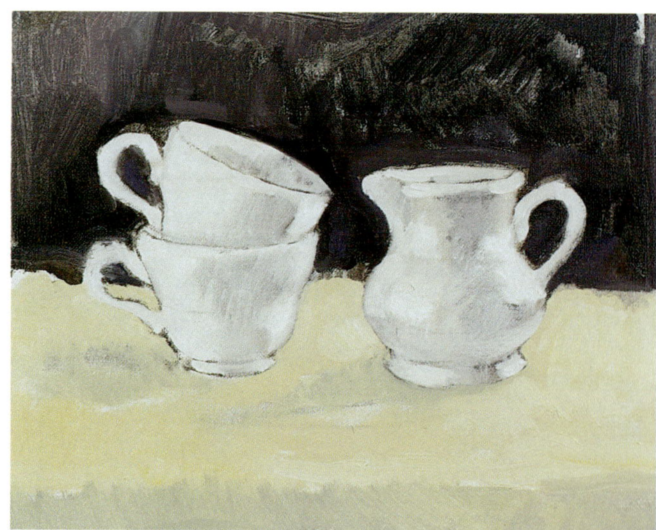

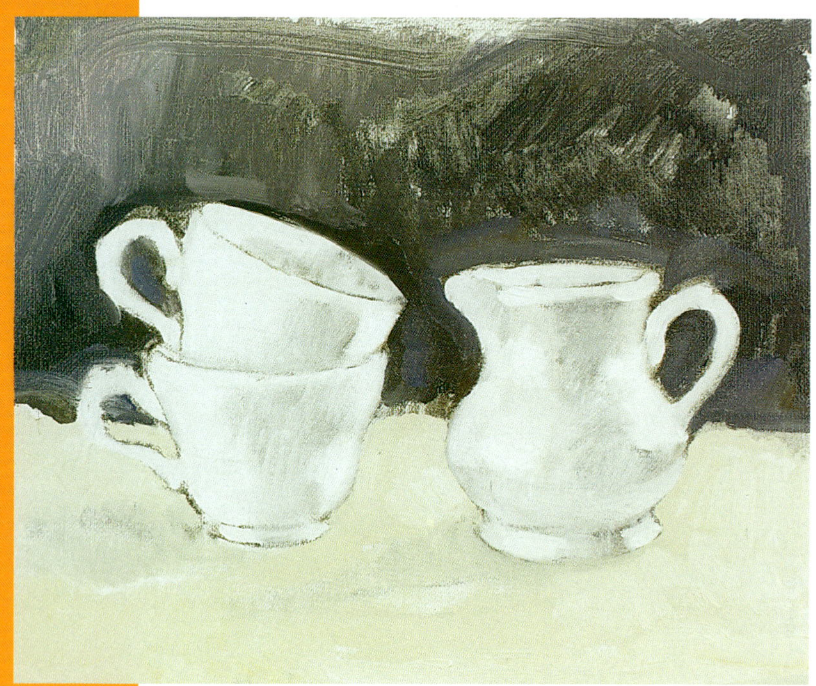

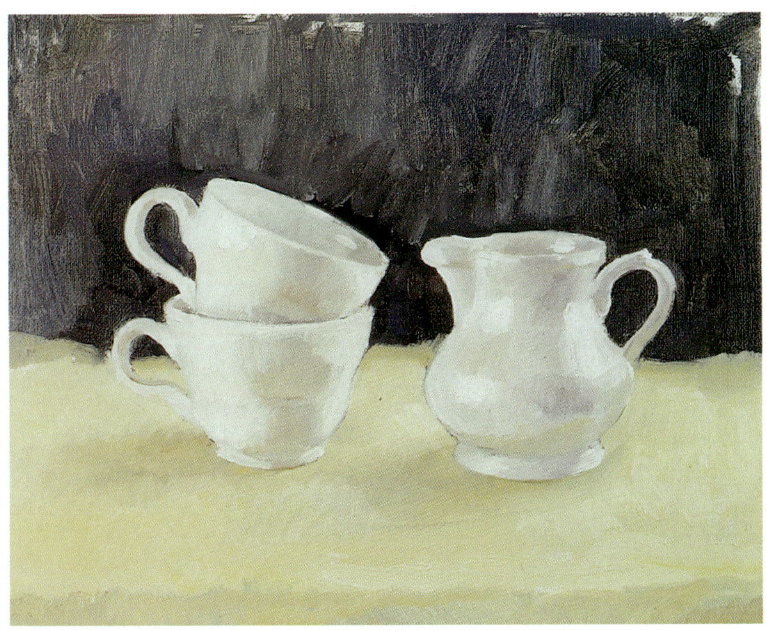

5·To finish this exercise we must contrast the background colors even more. Intensify the shiny areas on the table using the shiny blended areas described in this chapter. Introduce some warmth into the shadows. They must be reflected in the shininess on the white objects.
-The shadows are reflected in the range going from warm to cool, emphasizing the impact of the light focus through more intense strokes.
-The result of the exercise shows a warm still life representation through the use of blended bright colors and emphasizing the light with striking bright areas.

Summary

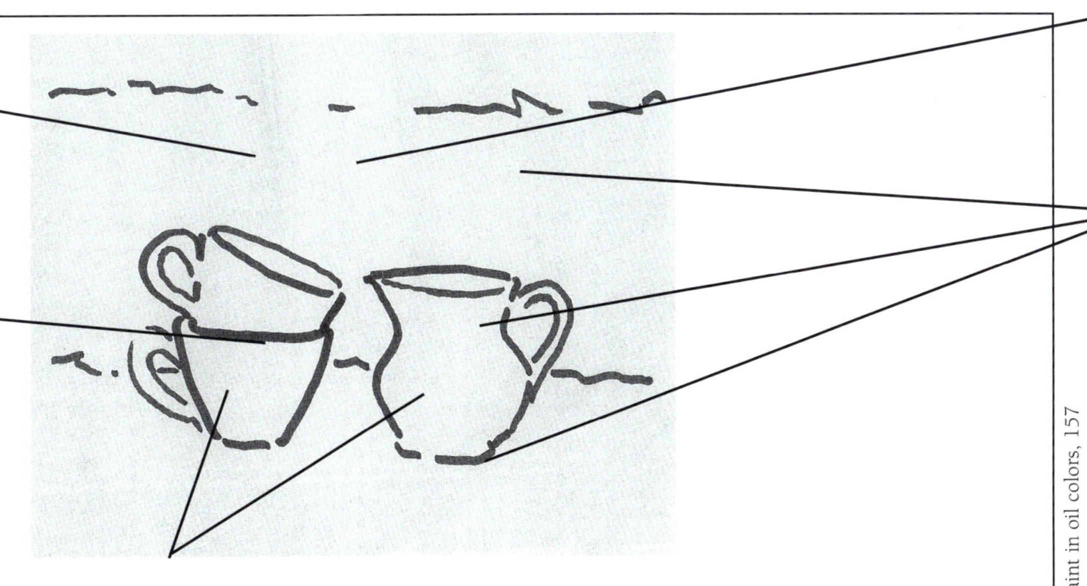

Start to paint the background aiming at the maximum contrast in black.

It is important to determine the stroke direction which will help us to depict the volumes in the still life.

To finish the exercise, contrast the background colors even more.

Start to draw the composition in charcoal and lay out the light and dark areas.

Pay special attention to the darkening of the shadows on the cups and on the porcelain jug.

Chapter 14

Glazes

Oil painting permits fine, transparent layers, which modify the tones and colors below, to be realized. These transparent films are called glazes.

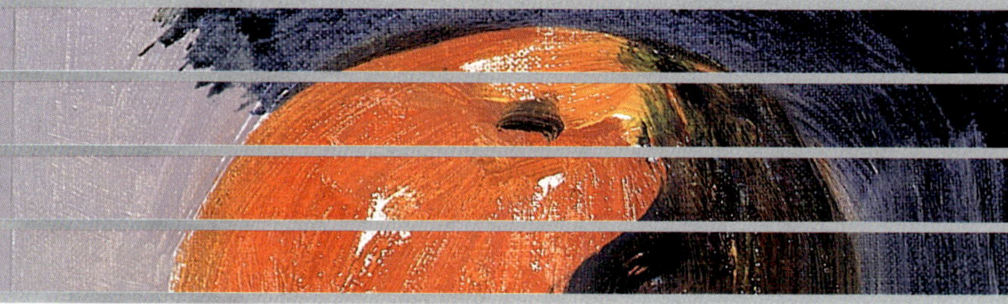

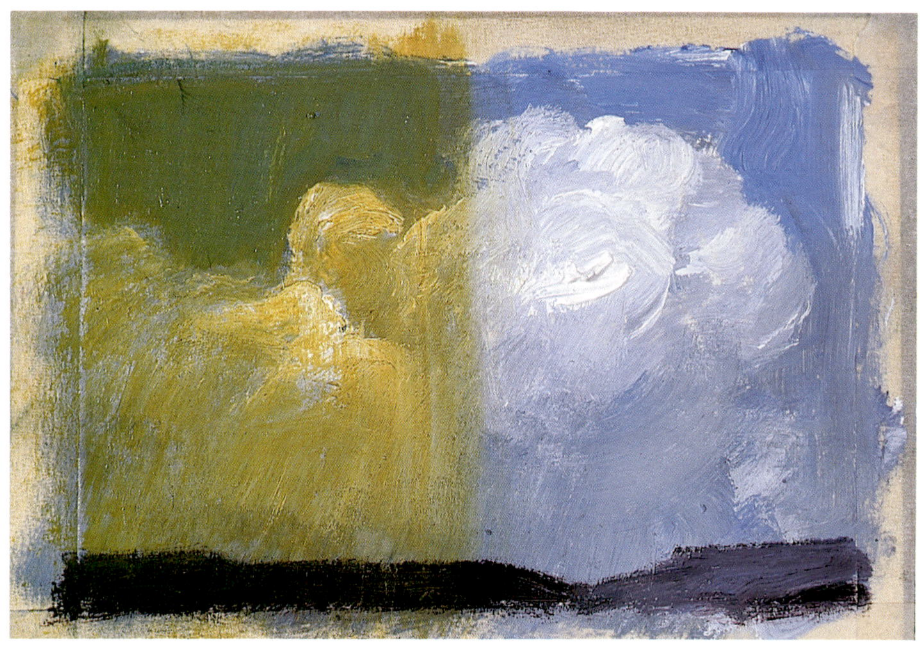

The principal function of a glaze is to change the color below by placing a transparent film over it. This means that the lower colors have to be 100% dry.

In this Chapter we are study the technique of glazes, one of the slowest that can be practiced with oil colors. The drying itself is very slow. To be done properly, glazes require that the layers underneath are dry, so the colors do not drag, before the next ones are put downr.

The classic procedure

To do glazes it is important to be clear about the amount of time one layer needs to dry before it can be correctly stained by another more liquid layer without the colors mixing. You must know when the colors mix, or blend, and when a glazing is created. A mix means that the colors, or tones, blend together and the particles of the medium and pigment come into contact. Glazing does not let the colors come into contact. What happens is the superimposition of one transparent layer over another, like a film. The glaze does not hide away the form of the line below. It merely changes its intensity, luminosity and chromatic impact.

Why glazes are used

Glazes are used as a pictorial recourse which allow colors to be superimposed without mixing with the tones underneath. This characteristic means that it is possible to create atmospheric effects, unify zones or simply do transparent layers.

What is necessary to paint with glazes?

Painting with glazes is a complex process even in the demanding context of oil colors. A glaze, which can be executed in diverse ways, is a very liquid layer of paint. Basically it is oil color diluted and therefore rendered more transparent. However, it must meet the following conditions:
-It must be completely fluid so that it can be handled on the brush, neither being too sticky or too oily.
-It must be manufactured with materials that stand the test of time.
-It must have a relatively quick drying time.

-It must not dissolve the colors on top of which it is applied.
-It must be resistant to the action of the finishing varnish.
-It must not run on the picture surface.
The most appropriate material is oil paint itself, but treated in a special way. To do a general glaze the following ingredients could be used, all of them available in Fine Arts shops:

Polymerized oil 28.4 cc.
Damar's varnish 28.4 cc
Turpentine oil 142 cc
Cobalt siccative 10 drops
Transparent pigment of the glaze color.

These products should be properly mixed so that the resulting oil color is sufficiently flowing to produce artisanal glazes. However, the safest bet is to used already manufactured oil colors and therefore you will save yourself the majority of complications that making your own glazes can entail.
This second option for doing glazes requires the following materials:

Good quality oil color in a tube (it will already include the necessary quantity of siccative)
Damar's varnish
Linseed oil

Turpentine oil
In any case, whichever method is used, a recipient will be necessary to do the mix.

Oil color, Damar's varnish, turpentine oil and a recipient for doing the mix.

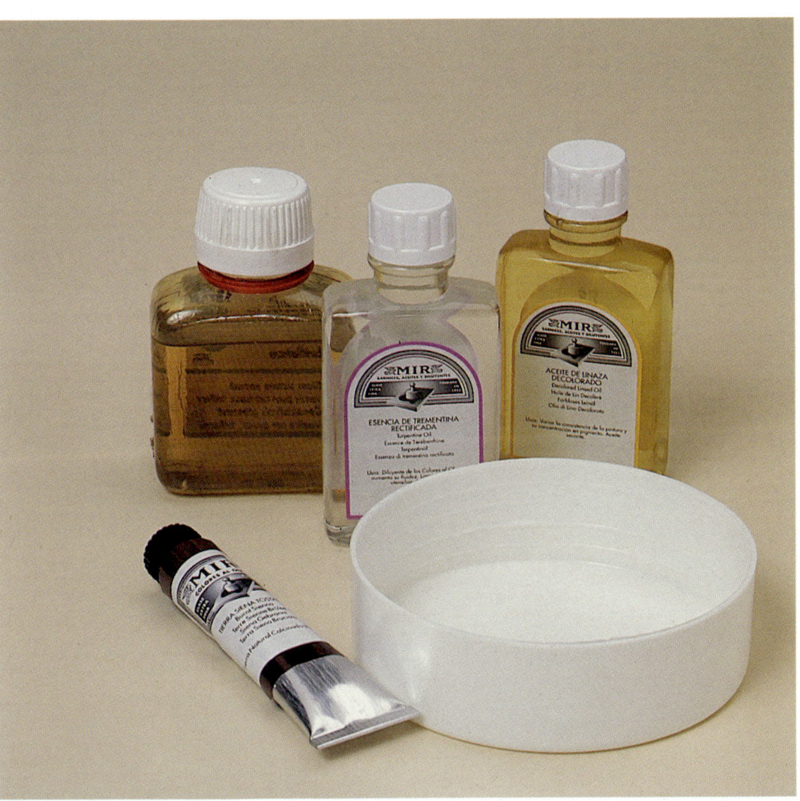

Oil color, Damar's varnish, turpentine oil and a recipient for doing the mixing.

The importance of letting the paint dry

The glazes should be realized when the layer below is completely dry. To avoid the formation of wrinkles on the surface of the oil painting, it is always necessary that the layers applied on top be thicker than those below. This means that every time a new glaze is painted it must contain a little more oil color. The process is thus in line with the premise "always thick on top of thin". Never should a thinned layer be painted on top of a thicker one. If the lower level were still wet, a blending would take place, not what we are after, a superimposition.

Glazes by dragging

Glazing by dragging means creating a glaze by dragging the brush successively over the paint. It is one of the most common ways of doing glazes and implies a wrist action.
The glaze must be made in a white recipient so that you can see the color you are going to apply. We will now do different exercises in which you will be able to observe the distinct types of glazes. Firstly we will work on an apple, then we will modify the white on a luminous glaze, changing the color of the light that surrounds its.
When the first strokes are put down, the colors must be thinned. They need not be intense because the darks will be painted later. First the colors of the earth are painted in whitish tones of green.

The initial color

As with all oil color techniques the first colors must be applied thinned. Every time a new layer is applied it must contain a little more oil color than the previous one. When doing glazes this has to be one of the guiding rules and always born in mind.

Dark transparencies

Glazes can be luminous and transparent or dark when they are intended to strongly modify the color underneath, but never covering it completely. A not very transparent glaze is in fact a rather translucent oil color. Once the first colors have been painted, you can start to apply the glazes. Remember that before starting to paint the glazes the initial color must be totally dry, otherwise the colors would mix instead of superimposing and the whole point would be lost. Firstly, cover the background in cobalt blue, a dark but not completely opaque color. The same color is used to start to glaze the dark part of the apple. This glaze will only cover the shadow zone and must be applied dragging the brush load so as to create a uniform layer.

Applying a half-tone glaze

Dark glazes can be used to define the dark areas and shadows of the objects, but it is also possible to paint light glazes to correct a tone or to add new effects. It has to be said that a completely transparent color painted over another darker one will not go as far as tinting it. Therefore, if you want to glaze a dark color with a more luminous one, the latter must have a certain degree of opacity. In this case, use a reddish glaze to correct the shadow zones on the right and to obtain a half tone.

When the first strokes are painted, the colors have to be thinned. They need not have intense values for the dark colors will be put down later. Firstly, the colors of the earth are painted in whitish tones with a little green.

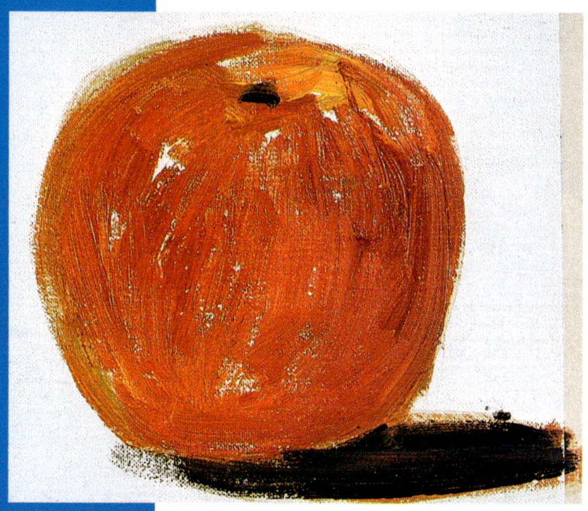

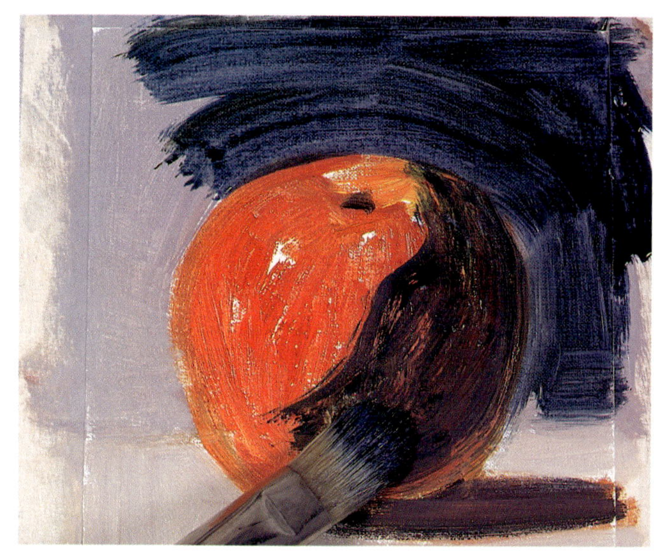

Use a dark blue glaze to paint part of the background and the shadow zone of the apple. As you can appreciate, the glaze is transparent and varies according to the color over which it is painted. The colors in the foreground are darker and more contrasted than further back.

Use a reddish, semi opaque glaze to cover part of the shadow on the right.

The background is painted in a violet color. In the background, a light tone helps to increase the depth effect.

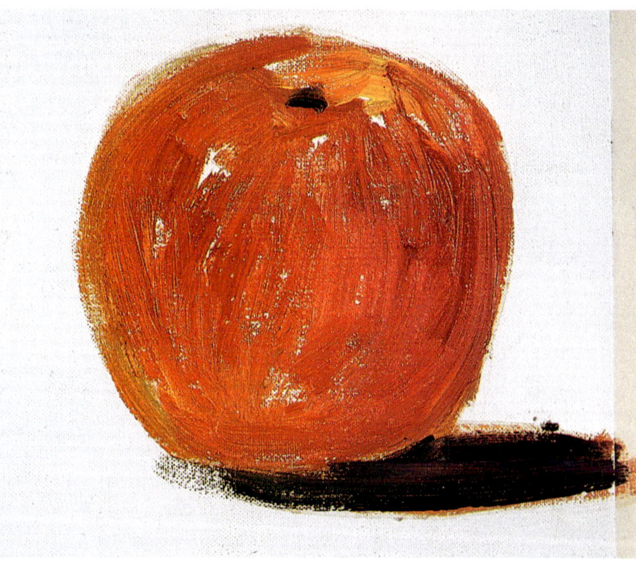

A sensation of volume

The volume effect is obtained by modeling the color values of the distinct tones. It is therefore important to establish the most luminous parts and the dark areas you are modeling. On the upper part of the apple the highlights are realized with direct accents in white and greenish yellow. When these zones are dry, it is possible to apply a new glaze which corrects the atmosphere lighting. The very transparent blue will modify the brightness of the white. The dark zones are reglazed. The background acquires a denser sense of depth, much more attractive than if it were painted in a completely opaque color. The shadow of the apple is also given a glaze of the same color.

Isolating the brightest zones with glazes

In this example we are going to paint a white flower. As you can see in the image, the process is not at all hard to comprehend. No glaze is painted until the complete flower is realized. This is the final stage and it adds the necessary atmosphere and luminosity to the already finished picture.
You have to wait for the picture to dry completely before doing the transparent glaze. Firstly, on the right of the flower, paint a very luminous ochre glaze. Afterwards, paint a very transparent blue glaze for the darkest part of the flower and part of the background. Observe how the transparency impacts in distinct ways on the light and dark colors.

So far no glaze has been painted.

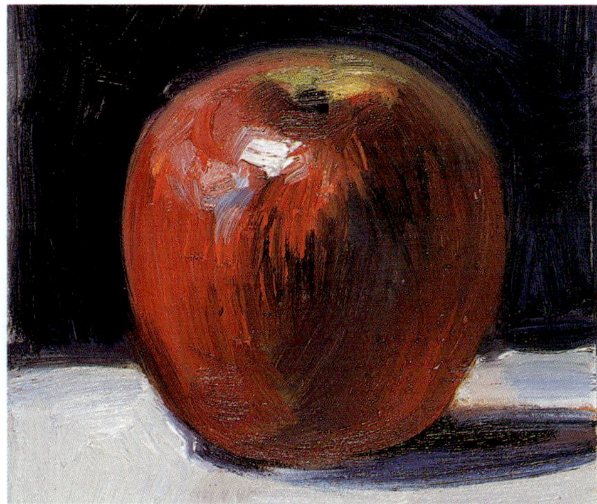

A glaze allows the apple highlight to be softly tinted and the darkness in the background to be enriched.

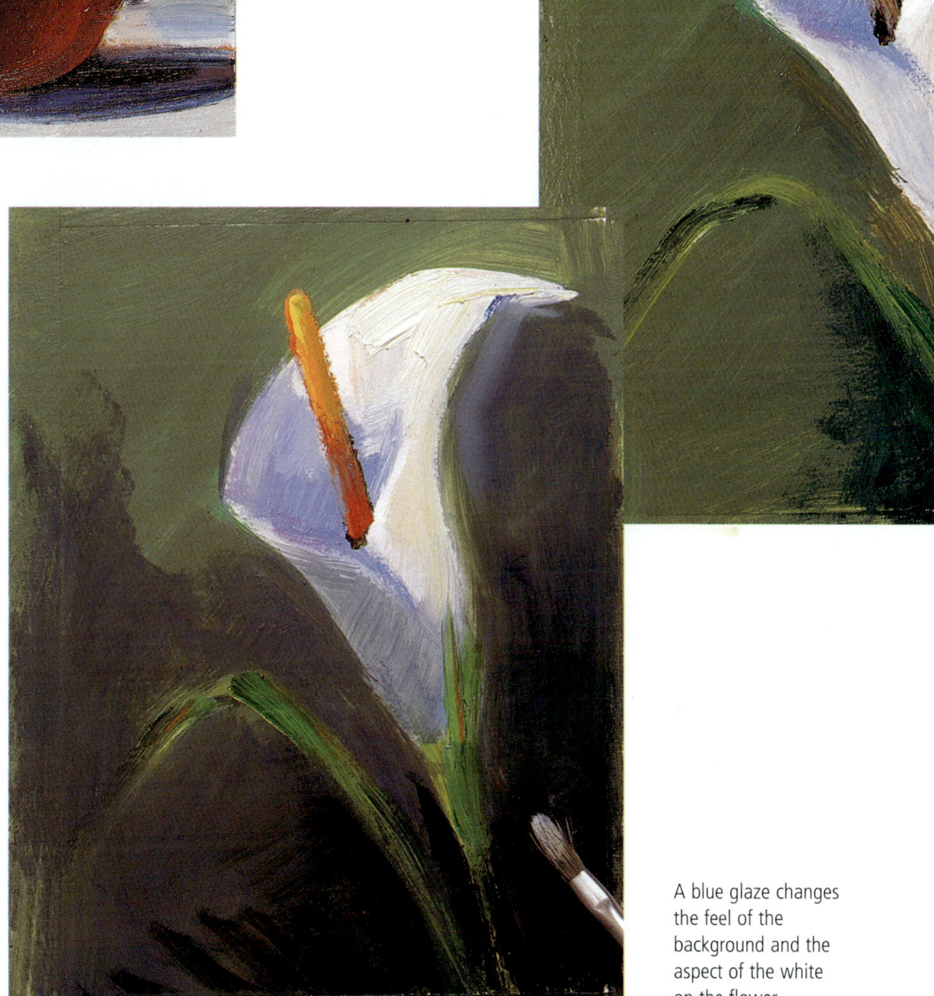

A blue glaze changes the feel of the background and the aspect of the white on the flower.

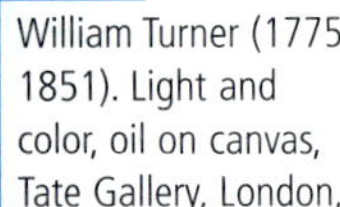

Glazed contrasts

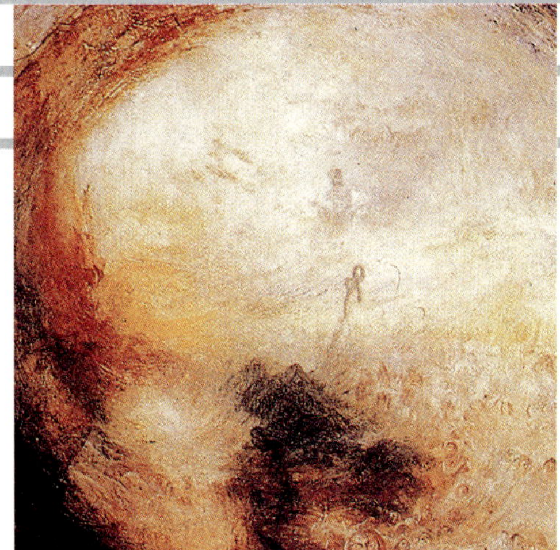

In this outstanding picture Turner revealed himself to be ahead of his times tackling questions which were to fascinate the impressionists at the end of the nineteenth century. The almost magical light of the painting is achieved by superimposing very transparent glazes to embellish the background. The ochre glazes softly nuance the whites and provide the atmospheric effect the artist desired.

William Turner (1775-1851). Light and color, oil on canvas, Tate Gallery, London,

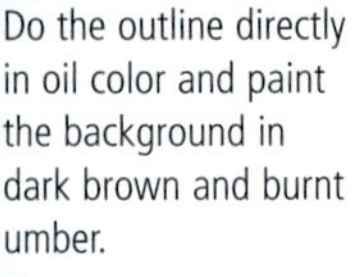

Do the outline directly in oil color and paint the background in dark brown and burnt umber.

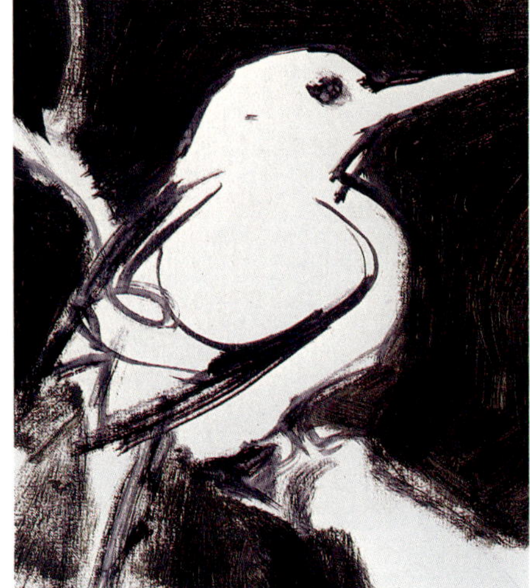

Once the head of the kingfisher is dry, paint a blue glaze. It will turn into a purplish tone.

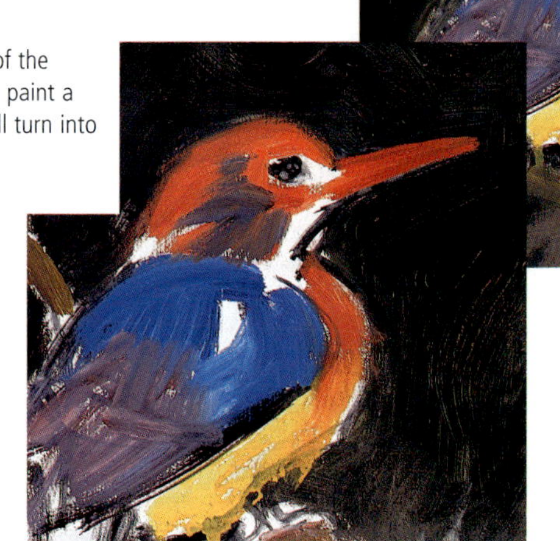

The background is nuanced with a greenish, ochre glaze. After doing a few brown touches in the background, go over the tone on the branch.

Glazing and color

Glazes offer a wide range of possibilities, from creating atmospheric effects through to getting the exact hue. In this section we are going to do a simple exercise consisting of painting a kingfisher. Its bright, vivid colors are so rich that all types of glazes are possible. Pay special attention to the dark zones in the background. Here, the colors are not only dark, they are also dense but this does not mean that tone-modifying glazes are ruled out: they remain valid..

Painting dark zones to mark out light areas

Do the outline of the bird directly in oil color, correcting any errors with a cloth dampened in turpentine oil. As the drawing gradually becomes defined, you can begin to put down the first colors sure of what you are doing. When the drawing is finished, paint the background clearly, outlining the kingfisher and the branch on which it is perched.

Color as the ground for the glaze

The colors on top of which you are going to paint the glaze must be as pure as possible, without too much value work, because any glazes are bound to darken them. Paint the head in bright colors (cadmium red) and gradate towards a yellow in the breast area. The wing is painted in very thinned blue and violet. Once the kingfisher's head is dry, paint a blue glaze which due to the transparency will turn violet.

Glazes which nuance the background

The dark areas in the background are nuanced by a green and ochre transparency. These tones do not completely cover the hues below but they do modify the dark ground. The dark colors in the background are now completely dry, but even so it is important not to rub too hard with the brush as this could soften the paint. Gently apply the glaze with successive strokes. If, for any reason, you dragged part of the undercolor, it would be better to let it dry out thoroughly.

Alternating glazes and opacity

Once the principal colors have been laid out in the picture, you can start to paint the opaque zones that finish off the form definition, for example in the illuminated part below the beak, the dark parts of the visible wing and the vegetation in the background. At the same time, as the previous colors are now dry, you can start to work on the glazes that will add the luminous nuances to the colors of the feathers. Paint the front of the head in a very transparent yellow; make it somewhat more opaque further back. On the wing, paint a dark blue glaze that almost completely covers the light background blue. However, this glaze will allow some zones to give luminosity to the feathers. Work on the highlight of the beak with almost transparent white strokes.

Unifying the glazes

Once the main glazes, and the opaque colors which culminate the picture, have been put down, you can unify the zones between the colors by softly going over them with the brush. In this stage it is important not to drag the fresh opaque colors towards the glazed zones: the final work should be very controlled. The fusion between two glazes, or between a glaze and an opaque zone, must only be done exactly where they come into contact, without dragging.

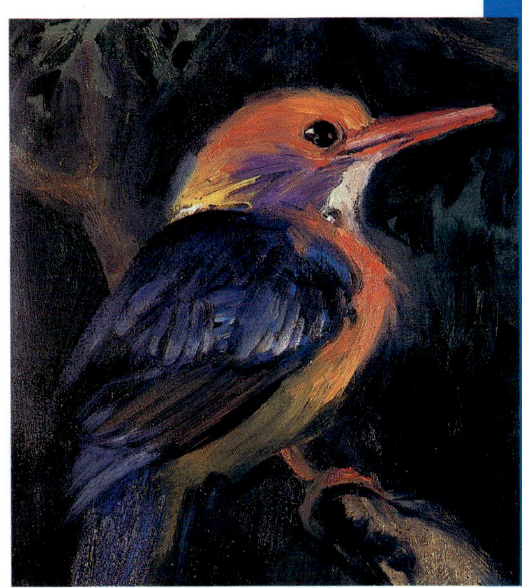

This is what the finished picture will look like.

In this stage the glazes are combined with opaque paint.

Softly blend where the different tones come into contact: Darken the lower part of the bird with a brown glaze.

Summary

GLAZES
A glaze is a transparent film aimed at changing the fully dried tone or color underneath.

GLAZES ON TOP OF DARK COLORS
On top of dark colors, glazes which modify the tone can be painted.

GLAZES OVER LUMINOUS COLORS
Any colored transparency on top of a light color influences its luminosity.

ALTERNATING TRANSPARENCY AND OPACITY
Transparent colors can be alternated on top of fresh, opaque colors provided that they do not mix with each other.

Exercises

A STILL LIFE

Working with glazes can be heavy going because it requires a great deal of elaboration. The drying times must always be respected, to ensure the colors do not mix and that the glazes are transparent modifiers of the colors below. However, it is working with glazes which enables us to exploit the immense possibilities of oil colors and their transparent properties. To practice the concepts explained throughout this chapter we are going to do a still life with a straightforward composition. This will focus our attention on the right way to use the colors.

Necessary material

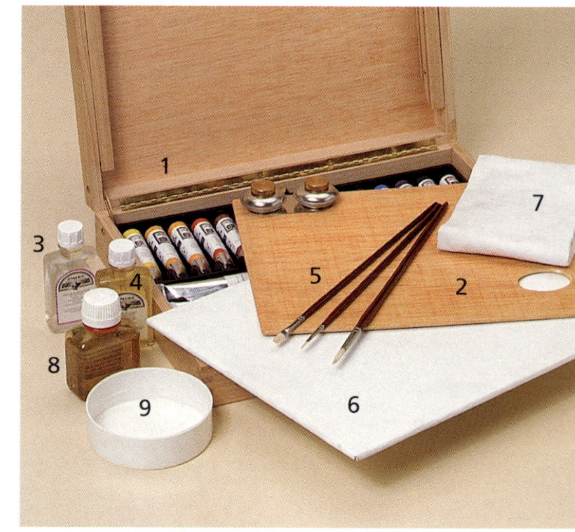

Oil colors (1), a palette (2), linseed oil with siccative incorporated (3), turpentine oil (4), oil color brushes (5), primed card (6), a cloth (7), Damar's varnish (8) and a recipient for doing the glazes (9).

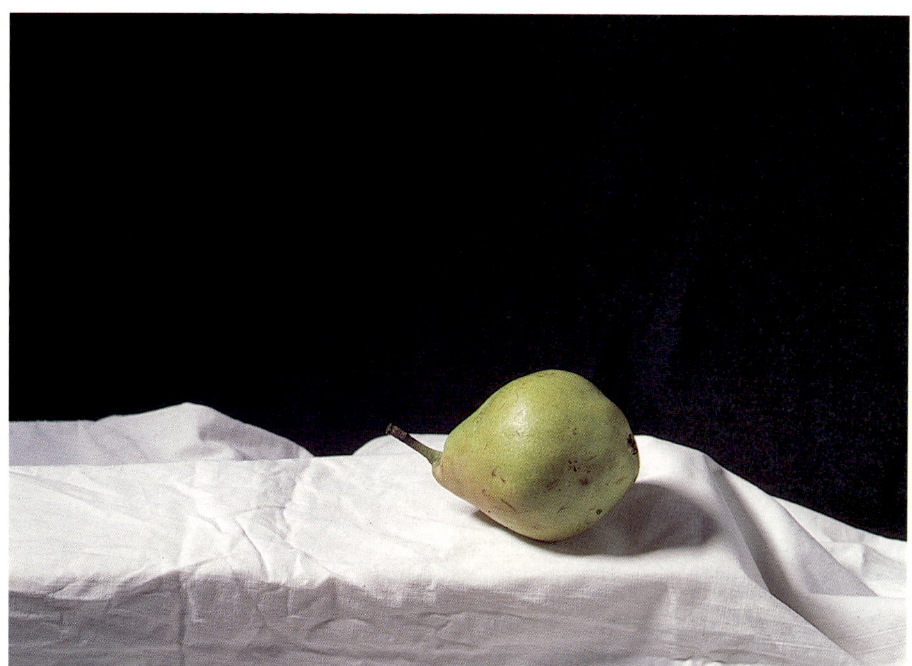

1·LThe first colors painted are the dark ones which cover the background and outline the most luminous forms of the still life, the pear and the table covered by the cloth. The dark color is painted flowing, slightly diluted not totally runny. The tone used is obtained from dark brown, a bit of black, English red and blue cobalt. The light parts of the tablecloth are left untouched while the dark parts are painted in light blue and transparent violet. This is where the first glaze is done. First do an almost transparent cerulean blue, and once it is dry (after a few hours), on top, do a violet glaze.

2·When the background is completely dry, start to paint the left-hand side in an orangy glaze. It will clearly modify the dark tone and indicate where the light source comes from. In the last step, green had been used to paint the shadow zone of the pear. This color serves as the reference for other green and yellowish tones which model the form of the fruit. On top of the completely dry, dark part of the tablecloth, do a new sienna glaze to contrast with the luminosity of the fold on the right.

3·Continue the value work on the pear dragging the green towards the illuminated zone. Paint the stem of the fruit. The principal part of the glaze work is being done on the tablecloth. Use a very luminous blue to paint this zone, modifying the colors previously put down, but do not make them disappear. On the right of the crease, paint the entire zone more opaquely.

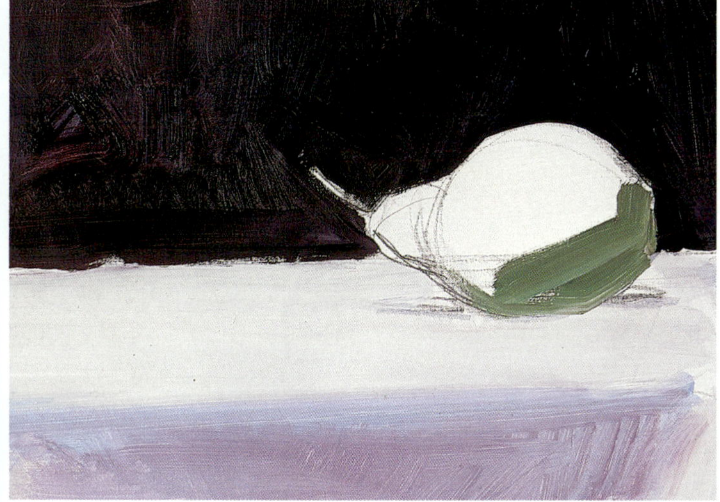

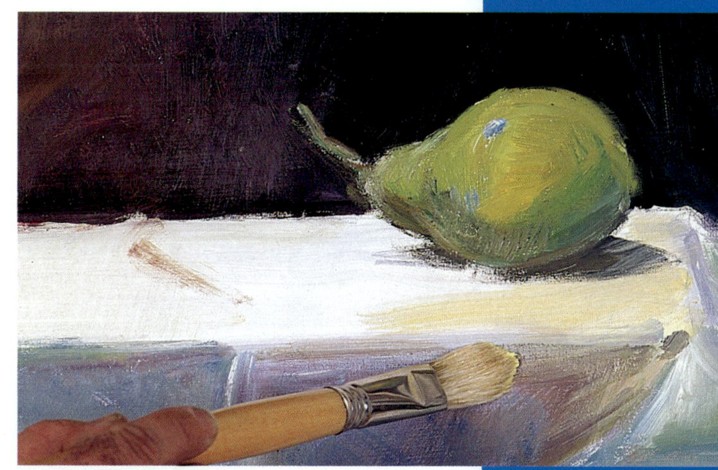

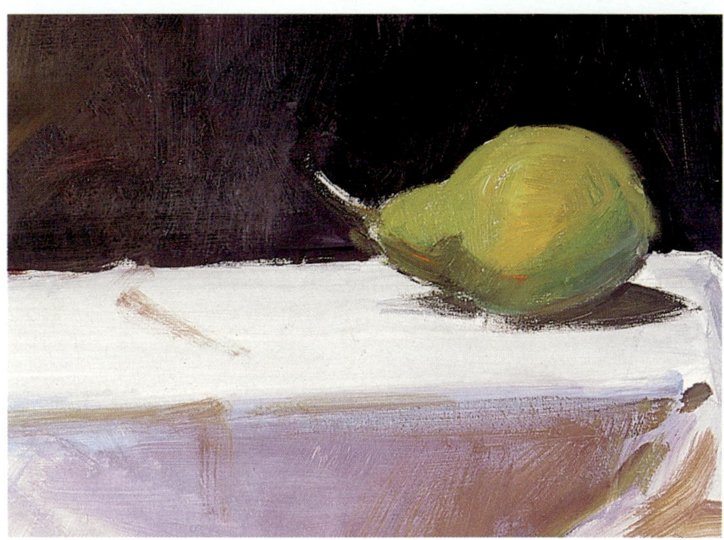

Exercises

4·Observe how a transparent, luminous glaze which must modify the tablecloth tone is painted. The only way that this glaze acts as such on the lower colors is if the colors are completely dry. The cream colored glaze gives its color to the white area, while, over the darker colors, the ochre transparent glaze shifts the initial tone.

Getting the most out of glazes requires patience and quite a lot of time. Between layer and layer sufficient time has to go by so that each new addition does not drag the color below. One sound tip so you do not lose your patience is to have two pictures on the go at the same time. Work on one while the other is drying.

5·Paint all the lit zone of the tablecloth in white, yellow and ochre. Make the stokes long and horizontal. By now the background is once again dry and is ready to receive a reddish glaze which will alter the original black tone. This color will give the atmosphere a warm illumination.

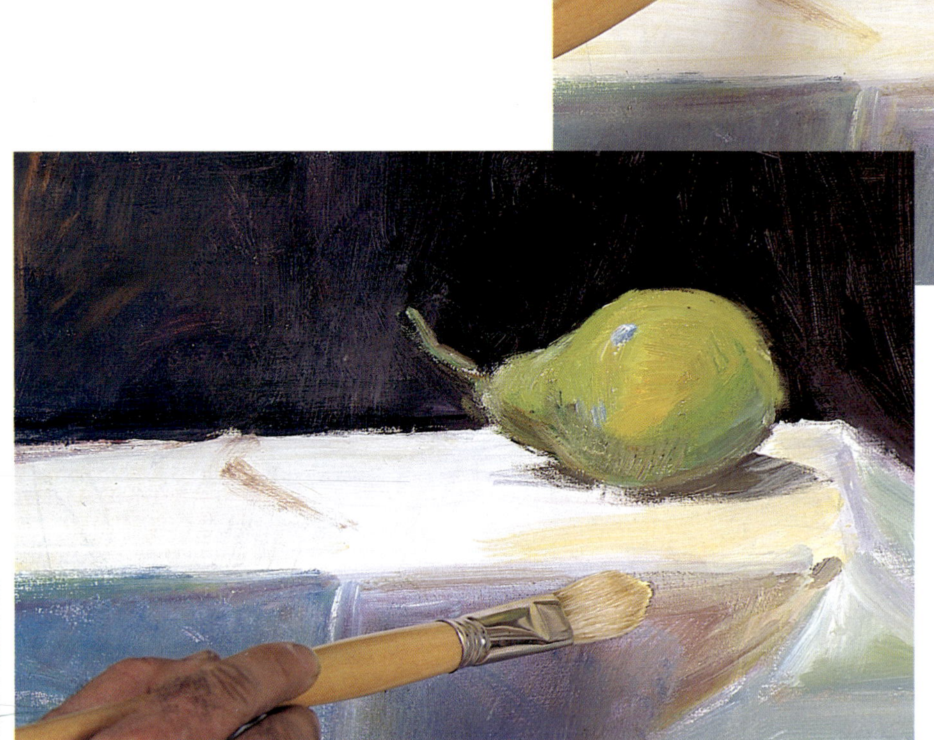

6·Once all the colors are dry, you can start to repaint the picture without fear of dragging the lower colors. Now, on top of the pear, paint the dark parts of the shadows with a blue glaze on the right and cadmium red on the left. On the tablecloth the work is much more detailed. Several glazes are combined with opaque, lighter colored paints in the shadow areas. The top of the table is painted in luminous white on the right. On the left, it is toned down with Naples yellow.

7·Use light, almost white tones to give the final touches to the folds in the cloth on the left. This final detail finishes off this piece which has focused on glazes. It has taken quite a long time, although the end result has made the effort and patience worthwhile.

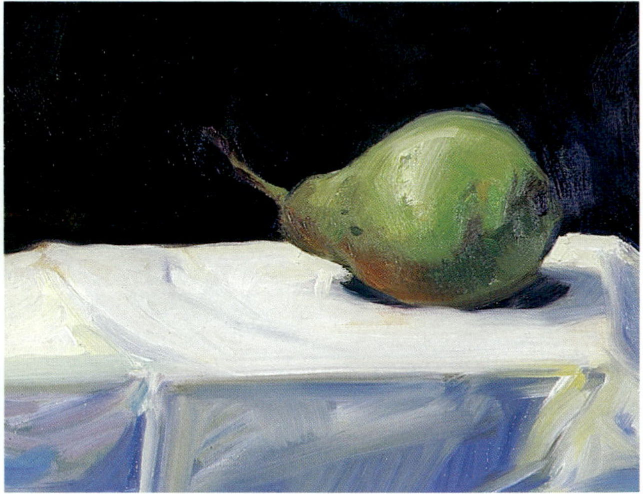

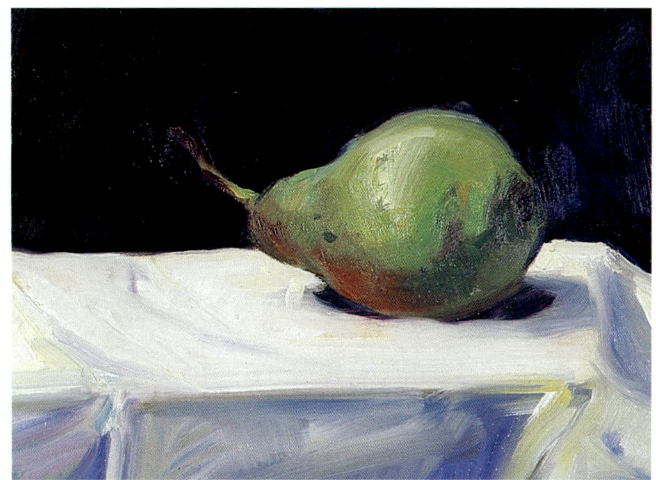

Summary 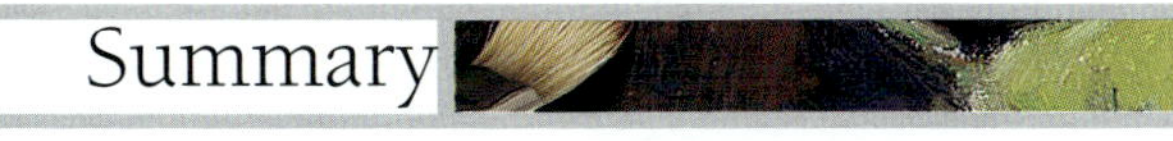

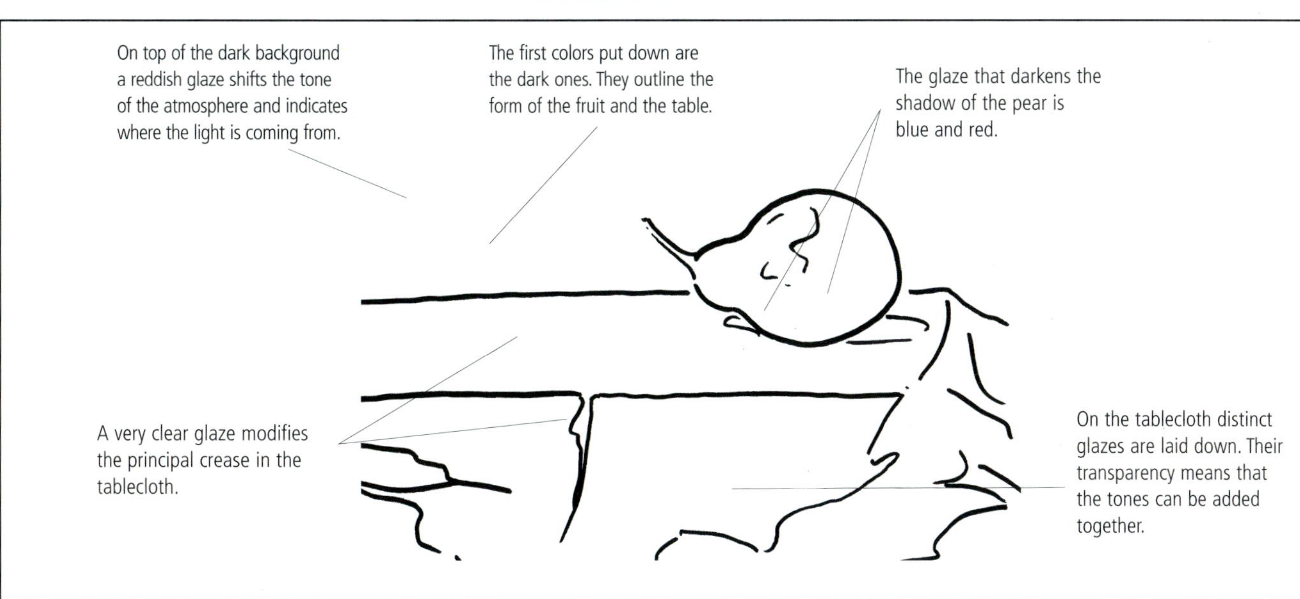